INDIA
HIGHER
EDUCATION
REPORT 2016

Thank you for choosing a SAGE product!
If you have any comment, observation or feedback,
I would like to personally hear from you.

Please write to me at **contactceo@sagepub.in**

Vivek Mehra, Managing Director and CEO, SAGE India.

Bulk Sales

SAGE India offers special discounts
for purchase of books in bulk.
We also make available special imprints
and excerpts from our books on demand.

For orders and enquiries, write to us at

Marketing Department
SAGE Publications India Pvt Ltd
B1/I-1, Mohan Cooperative Industrial Area
Mathura Road, Post Bag 7
New Delhi 110044, India

E-mail us at **marketing@sagepub.in**

Get to know more about SAGE

Be invited to SAGE events, get on our mailing list.
Write today to **marketing@sagepub.in**

This book is also available as an e-book.

INDIA
HIGHER
EDUCATION
REPORT 2016
EQUITY

Edited by

N.V. Varghese
Nidhi S. Sabharwal
C.M. Malish

Los Angeles | London | New Delhi
Singapore | Washington DC | Melbourne

First published in 2018 by

SAGE Publications India Pvt Ltd
B1/I-1 Mohan Cooperative Industrial Area
Mathura Road, New Delhi 110 044, India
www.sagepub.in

SAGE Publications Inc
2455 Teller Road
Thousand Oaks, California 91320, USA

SAGE Publications Ltd
1 Oliver's Yard, 55 City Road
London EC1Y 1SP, United Kingdom

SAGE Publications Asia-Pacific Pte Ltd
3 Church Street
#10-04 Samsung Hub
Singapore 049483

National University of Educational Planning and Administration (NUEPA)
17-B, Sri Aurobindo Marg
Opposite Adchini
New Delhi – 110016

Published by Vivek Mehra for SAGE Publications India Pvt Ltd, typeset in 9.5/12 pt Trebuchet MS by Fidus Design Pvt. Ltd., Chandigarh and printed at Chaman Enterprises, New Delhi.

Library of Congress Cataloging-in-Publication Data
Names: Varghese, N.V., editor. | Sabharwal, Nidhi Sadana, editor. | Malish, C.M., editor.
Title: India higher education report 2016: equity/edited by N.V. Varghese, Nidhi S. Sabharwal and C.M. Malish.
Description: New Delhi, India; Thousand Oaks, California: Sage, 2017. | Includes bibliographical references and index.
Identifiers: LCCN 2017042113| ISBN 9789386602244 (print (hb): alk. paper) | ISBN 9789386602268 (e pub 2.0) | ISBN 9789386602251 (e book)
Subjects: LCSH: Education, Higher—Social aspects—India. | Educational equalization—India.
Classification: LCC LA1153 .I468 2017 | DDC 378.54—dc23
LC record available at https://lccn.loc.gov/2017042113

ISBN: 978-93-866-0224-4 (HB)

SAGE Team: Rajesh Dey, Guneet Kaur, Kumar Indra Mishra and Ritu Chopra

Contents

Part III:
Equity in Outcomes

Part IV:
Diversity and Discrimination

List of Tables

List of Figures

List of Abbreviations

ADB	Asian Development Bank
AICTE	All India Council for Technical Education
AISHE	All India Survey on Higher Education
AP	Andhra Pradesh
BFSI	Banking, Financial Services and Insurance
BPO	Business Process Outsourcing
CABE	Central Advisory Board of Education
CBSE	Central Board of Secondary Education
CCE	Continuous and Comprehensive Evaluation
CEC	Consumer Expenditure Classes
CGPA	Combined Grade Point Average
CSS	Compulsory Social Service
CSSEIP	Centre for Studies of Social Exclusion and Inclusive Policies
DEC	Distance Education Council
DG	Diversity Gap
DGE&T	Director General of Employment and Training
DI	Diversity Index
DU	Delhi University
EEO	Equal Educational Opportunities
EIOP	Eligible for Improvement of Performance
EMEA	Europe, the Middle East and Africa
EMIS	Educational Management Information System
EOC	Equal Opportunity Cell
EXIM	Export Import
FICCI	Federation of Indian Chambers of Commerce and Industry
FYP	Five-Year Plan
GATE	Graduate Aptitude Test in Engineering
GATS	General Agreement on Trade in Services
GDP	Gross Domestic Product
GER	Gross Enrolment Ratio
GoI	Government of India
GPI	Gender Parity Index
GSDP	Gross State Domestic Product
GSP	Gross Science Product
GTAR	Gross Tertiary Attendance Rate
GTP	Gross Technology Product
HCU	Hyderabad Central University

HDI	Human Development Index
HE	Higher Education
HEA	Higher Education Attendance
HEI	Higher Educational Institutions
HEPSN	Higher Education for Persons with Special Needs
HRD	Human Resource Development
HS	Higher Secondary
IAS	Indian Administrative Services
IATA	International Air Transport Association
ICSSR	Indian Council of Social Science Research
ICT	Information and Communication Technology
IDS	Institute of Development Studies
IHE	Institutes of Higher Education
IIMB	Indian Institute of Management Bangalore
IISc	Indian Institute of Science
IIT	Indian Institute of Technology
ILO	International Labour Organization
IPR	Intellectual Property Rights
IRAHE	Independent Regulatory Authority for Higher Education
ISST	Institute of Social Studies Trust
IT	Information Technology
ITES	Information Technology Enabled Services
ITI	Industrial Training Institute
JEE	Joint Entrance Examination
JNU	Jawaharlal Nehru University
JNV	Jawahar Navodaya Vidyalayas
JNVST	Jawahar Navodaya Vidyalaya Selection Test
KC	Kothari Commission
KBC	Knowledge-based Capital
KPO	Knowledge Process Outsourcing
KV	Kendriya Vidyalaya
LFPR	Labour Force Participation Rate
MANUU	Maulana Azad National Urdu University
MBA	Master of Business Administration
MPhil	Master of Philosophy
MCD	Municipal Corporation of Delhi
MCI	Medical Council of India
MDG	Millennium Development Goals
MHRD	Ministry of Human Resource and Development
MOBC	Muslim Other Backward Classes
MoI	Medium of Instruction
MP	Madhya Pradesh

MPCE	Monthly Per Capita Expenditure
MUC	Muslim upper classes
NAACP	National Association for Advancement of Coloured People
NCC	National Cadet Corps
NCERT	National Council of Educational Research and Training
NCHER	National Commission for Higher Education and Research.
NCTE	National Council for Teacher Education
ND	Non-Disabled
NFLMW	National Floor Level Minimum Wage
NGO	Non-Governmental Organisation
NILERD	National Institute of Labour Economics Research and Development
NMOBC	Non-Muslim Other Backward Classes
NMUC	Non-Muslim Upper Classes
NPE	National Policy on Education
NRCVEE	National Resource Centre for Valued Education in Engineering
NSDC	National Skill Development Corporation
NSS	National Sample Survey
NSSE	National Survey of Student Engagement
NSSO	National Sample Survey Organisation
NUEPA	National University of Educational Planning and Administration
NVS	Navodaya Vidyalaya Samiti
OBC	Other Backward Classes
OCD	Obsessive Compulsive Disorder
OECD	Organisation for Economic Co-operation and Development
OM	Other Minorities
PG	Postgraduate
PHEI	Private Higher Education Institutions
PoA	Programme of Action
PWD	Persons with Disabilities
RPL	Recognition Prior Learning
RSA	Royal Society for the Arts, Manufactures and Commerce
RUSA	Rashtriya Uchchatar Shiksha Abhiyan
RWS	Regular Wage Salaried
SAM	Sensitisation, Awareness and Motivation
SC	Scheduled Castes
SSA	Sarva Shiksha Abhiyan

ST	Scheduled Tribes
TEPSE	Teacher Preparation in Special Education
UCH	Upper-Class Hindus
UG	Undergraduate
UGC	University Grants Commission
JRF	Junior Research Fellowship
SRF	Senior Research Fellowship
UK	United Kingdom
UNCRPD	United Nations Convention on the Rights of Persons with Disabilities
UNDP	United Nations Development Programme
UNESCAP	United Nations Economic and Social Commission for Asia and the Pacific
UP	Uttar Pradesh
UPSS	Usual Principal and Subsidiary Status
USA	United States of America
UT	Union Territory
VMC	Vidyalaya Management Committee
WFPR	Workforce Participation Rate
WSC	Women's Study Centre
WTO	World Trade Organisation

Preface

It is being widely recognised that higher education plays an important role in promoting economic growth, social progress, human development and political stability, and various other facets of development—in short, in the overall development of the nations. Economists have also shown, with robust research, that higher education, by facilitating smooth transition of graduates from educational institutions to labour market, enhances individual earnings and plays a major deterministic role in augmenting wealth of the nations. While higher education is an important source of economic growth, it can also be a source of inequalities in income and wealth, if opportunities for higher education are not equally distributed.

The recent decades experienced an unprecedented expansion of higher education, both globally and in India. The emergence of knowledge economy has enhanced skill requirements and qualification levels for job entry to a minimum of post-secondary levels. Similarly, the anti-poverty initiatives and Education for All (EFA) programmes have contributed to the massive expansion of education at the school level, leading to increased social demand for higher education. These two factors necessitate the formulation of meaningful and sound approaches and policies towards massification of higher education in most of the countries.

India experienced the highest rate of growth in higher education from the turn of this century. With more than 700 universities, 40,000 colleges and 33 million students, India has the second largest higher education system in the world. It can be expected that the expansion will continue given the favourable demographic dividend reflected in growing social demand for higher education. It is expected that India will have the largest youth population in the 2020s.

While expansion of the higher system is to be celebrated, it is equally important to analyse and identify the winners and losers in the process of expansion. Did expansion of the system lead to the widening of access to higher education among previously under-represented groups and regions? Needless to add that a higher rate of growth in the enrolment of under-represented groups than that of the general population is a necessary condition to level off social inequalities in access to higher education. In other words, an expanding system with higher rates of growth of the deprived groups is a necessary condition to promote equity in access to higher education. Promotion of such a pattern of expansion requires progressive state policies centred on the idea of inclusive growth and allocation of resources—financial and non-financial—in favour of the disadvantaged groups.

Strong and successful democratic societies have low tolerance to socio-economic inequalities; they pursue effective measures towards redistribution of resources, favouring the weaker sections. However, many democratic regimes in the present century have embraced market-friendly economic reforms in both the manufacturing and service sectors, including social sectors. However, unlike states, markets are less reliable agents for promoting social justice and ensuring redistribution of resources. Therefore, from an egalitarian perspective, expansion of higher education based on market mechanisms raises serious questions.

The present *India Higher Education Report*, second in the series, initiated by the Centre for Policy Research in Higher Education (CPRHE) of the National University of Educational Planning and Administration (NUEPA), raises some of these issues in the context of higher education development in India. The series is envisaged to provide an in-depth analysis of some of the critical dimensions of higher education in India, with contributions from eminent scholars, engaged in research, policy and planning in the area of higher education. The first report, IHER 2015, provided a comprehensive account of the situation of higher education in the country, focusing on various challenging issues that the higher education sector in India is facing.

The present IHER 2016 is devoted to the theme of equity in higher education. The aspects covered in the volume include issues related to expansion of education, economic inequalities, discrimination, diversity and the changing roles of the state, market and private sectors. Scholars, who have contributed in the volume, also examine regional disparities, gender and inequalities by social groups, castes, religions and so on. Inequalities in outcomes are also examined, considering learning outcomes, employment and employability of graduates.

We are grateful to the authors of various chapters for their valuable contributions and continued support. I take this opportunity to place on record my deep appreciation for the efforts made by my colleagues at CPRHE, NUEPA, Professor N.V. Varghese, Director, and faculty members Dr Nidhi S. Sabharwal and Dr C.M. Malish in bringing out this important volume.

Jandhyala B.G. Tilak
Vice Chancellor, NUEPA
25 May 2016
New Delhi

Acknowledgements

CPRHE published the first issue in the *India Higher Education Report* (*IHER 2015*) series. We are happy to present the second volume *IHER 2016* titled *Higher Education in India: Equity*. *IHER 2016* discusses various aspects of equity concerns in higher education in India, focusing on regional, social and gender inequalities and issues related to disability rights. This volume, as the previous one, is the outcome of support received from various intellectuals and institutions and the efforts put in by CPRHE.

IHER 2015 was a comprehensive volume covering various issues and challenges that higher education in the country is facing. It was felt that the subsequent issues should focus on specific themes. The theme considered for the current *IHER* is Equity. This proposal was discussed and approved in the Executive Committee meeting of CPRHE in 2015. We would like to express our sincere thanks to members of the Executive Committee of CPRHE.

We remain grateful to our Vice Chancellor, Professor J.B.G. Tilak, for his guidance and support at every stage in the progress and preparation of the report.

The volume includes chapters by some of the leading academics and policymakers in higher education. They not only contributed the chapters but also contributed substantially to shape the current volume through their extensive comments on chapters by others. We gratefully acknowledge the valuable contribution of all the authors.

We are grateful to the Registrar, NUEPA, Shri Basavaraj Swamy, and his team for their support in facilitating the publication process and procedures. We also thank Dr Pramod Rawat, Mr Amit Singhal and other members in NUEPA publication department for their help at different stages.

We thank the SAGE team which has been interacting with us at every stage in the processing of the manuscript for publication.

We are also grateful to all colleagues at CPRHE, Professor Mona Khare, Dr Garima Malik, Dr Anupam Pachauri, Dr Jinusha Panigrahi and Dr Sayantan Mandal, for their continuous support and several rounds of comments. We also thank Dr Gautam for helping us to follow up and put together final versions of the papers.

Ms Anjali Arora, Mayank Rajput and Monica Joshi extended all logistics support to organise peer review meetings and contacting the authors. We gratefully acknowledge their support and efforts to prepare this volume.

N.V. Varghese
Nidhi S. Sabharwal
C.M. Malish

1

Higher Education and Equity: Introduction to IHER 2016

N.V. Varghese, Nidhi S. Sabharwal and C.M. Malish

HIGHER EDUCATION AND INCOME INEQUALITIES

This century experienced positive economic growth in almost all the countries until the onset of the economic crisis in 2008. Education plays an important role in augmenting and distribution of national income. The human capital theory postulates and empirically validates the positive effects of education on augmenting labour productivity and promoting economic growth (Becker 1964; Schultz 1961). In fact, the empirical evidence shows that one of the most important factors contributing to economic growth in the recent decades is human capital (Engelbrecht 2003). In all societies, earnings from professions, as a share of national income, have increased. The high economic growth in many countries was propelled, very often, by higher rates of growth experienced by the knowledge segments of the economies. Higher education played an important role in promoting growth of the knowledge sectors of the economy.

The rates of growth of the economies among countries varied, contributing to the widening of income inequalities among them. The experience in the recent past has shown that inequalities are widening in many of the developed countries. A study (OECD 2008) showed that the gap between rich and poor in most countries of the Organisation for Economic Co-operation and Development (OECD) has widened over the past two decades. An analysis of human development in the past 25 years shows that impressive human progress has been achieved in reducing poverty and expanding access to education. But these advances have been uneven. Deepening globalisation and rapid technological change while providing new opportunities have also contributed to the risk of exclusion (Jahan 2016). This implies that, in the absence of positive discriminatory policies, inequalities may widen in the market-led globalising context of development.

The higher growth, in most instances, is also accompanied by widening income inequalities between regions within a country. The earning advantages associated with higher education degree holders encouraged higher rate of growth in earnings among them, and widening of individual earning differentials between them and the less educated. In other words, an unequal distribution of higher education opportunities may be an important source of inequalities in income distribution. It seems that higher education plays a role in the widening of inequalities in the absence of equal opportunities to pursue higher education.

Higher education system in developing countries has relatively limited access, and it can be a source of low growth and wide inequalities. In general, countries with limited access to higher education tend to have low levels of income and high levels of inequalities. Countries where higher education is universalised tend to have higher per capita income at times and lower levels of income inequalities (Varghese 2001). It can be argued that it is important to equalise opportunities for the provision of higher education to promote economic growth and social equity.

While the expansion of higher education is driven by economic agenda, the equity concerns are driven by social agendas concerning democracy and social justice. Since education is intimately related to income and wages, fostering equality in education is a powerful tool to decrease income inequality and, in this sense, equity in education supports social equity (OECD 2007). The question is not only of expansion of higher education but also of widening access to higher education to previously under-represented groups.

A faster progress of under-represented groups is necessary to level off inequalities in access to higher education among social groups. In quantitative terms, this may imply that a reduction in inequalities in an expanding system is the ideal situation since it reflects a faster growth in enrolment among the under-represented groups than among the privileged groups. State policies will play an influencing role in the distribution of higher education opportunities in a country.

STATE, MARKETS AND EQUITY

Education is an important factor influencing job entry and salaries of those recruited. In other words, education plays an important role in promoting growth in national income and an equally important role in the sharing (distribution) of national income through employment and earnings. When educational opportunities and attainment are unequally distributed, they become an important source of inequalities, and it requires corrective public policies.

State policies play a significant role in promoting equity in access to higher education. State policies under democratic political regimes follow an egalitarian approach to development and fairness in the distribution of resources and benefits of growth. Thus, progressive state policies under democracy will not tolerate unequal distribution of opportunities, income and wealth. More importantly, democracy may imply redistribution of resources if the existing distribution is not fair. This redistributive dimension of democracy stems from the belief that equality in the political arena will be followed by equality in the economic and social domains (Sirowy and Inkeles 1990), and this idea keeps the democratic aspirations high among the poor.

The public good nature of higher education demands an increased role of the state and greater public investment in the sector. In the absence of public intervention, higher education will not only be in short supply but also that the facilities to pursue higher education may be distributed unequally. Further, the global public good nature of knowledge and its production provide a strong rationale for global/international collective action (Stiglitz 1999) in the higher education sector. The public good nature of higher education may be one of the reasons for continued state support to massify, and even universalise, higher education in the developed market economies. It is interesting to note that universalisation of higher education in the matured market economies was facilitated not through markets or private institutions but largely through public higher education institutions.

While the public good nature of higher education remains a strong argument for public support, the market intervention in higher education follows from the sector's role in production. When higher education is seen as a factor of production, investments in education may also come from the private sector or from the individuals who seek higher education. Firms like to appropriate the returns on their investment in knowledge and skills. If they cannot appropriate the returns from their investment, they will have limited incentives to invest in knowledge production or transmission. Many economies may not be in a position to ensure appropriation of returns by the firms investing in education. Consequently, market-mediated expansion of higher education may be in undersupply.

The private providers of higher education, very often, offer limited number of study programmes. They offer market-friendly and employment-oriented courses. These courses help them expand enrolment, enhance student fees and improve financial status and profit margin of the private institutions. From a macro perspective, the emphasis of the private institutions in selected number of courses can lead to disciplinary distortions, as has been happening in India.

The market intervention in education can be seen also as direct investments in the sector to make profit. In this case, the market in higher education will respond to the demand for higher education by the households and supply of higher education by the private providers. The recent developments in higher education indicate that there is an insatiate household demand for higher education and that the public institutions have not succeeded in responding favourably to the growing demand for higher education. This provides a favourable condition for PHEIs to grow and expand their influence.

The nature of state regulations will decide the operation of private institutions and their outcome in higher education. For example, a right-based approach to education is an important step to promote an egalitarian distribution of educational opportunities at lower levels and may lead to large number of secondary school graduates from diverse social conditions that are eligible for admission in higher education institutions. Such a broad base accompanied by equity policies such as quota system may be an important measure to minimise inequalities in access to higher education.

Higher education in most of the countries was traditionally offered through public institutions, which offer courses in a wide range of areas, follow equity-oriented admission policies aligned to the state policies, levy low or no fees, etc. The deteriorating fiscal capacity of the state and the changing ideological orientation, especially from the mid-1980s, did not support an expansion of public universities to accommodate the increasing demand for higher education. This led to two phenomena: the privatisation of public institutions and the promotion of private institutions (Varghese 2006).

While privatisation implied public institutions operating, based on the market principles with dominance of cost recovery measures, private institutions implied ownership, management and financing by non-state operators. There are two types of private higher education institutions (PHEIs): for-profit and not-for-profit institutions. For-profit PHEIs levy high fees, offer market-friendly courses, create a surplus and are profit-seeking institutions. Not-for-profit institutions, too, offer market-friendly courses, but they levy moderate fees. Some of them, especially in Africa, are affiliated to religious institutions of Christian or Islamic faith. Very often than not, the equity principles are traded off in favour of profit motivations in private institutions, especially belonging to the for-profit category. Not-for-profit private institutions maintain low levels of fees and attract students from all social backgrounds; admissions criteria are flexible and may contribute more to equity than other category (for-profit) of private institutions.

The policy dilemma may be that when the higher education system had limited access, thus catering to the elite, it was subsidised and received full state support in many countries. When the system started expanding and admitting students from diverse non-elite backgrounds, state funding declined and the students' households were expected to pay, whether they were studying in private or public institutions. This directly conflicts with the state's prescribed policies on equity and may result in widening of inequalities in access to higher education.

It seems that state is in a better position to ensure equity. Therefore, the ideal situation would have been relying entirely on state funding to expand higher education. However, the fiscal capacity of the state to support the growing demand for higher education seems to be limited. Consequently, private providers have entered the higher education sector. The market for higher education is an attractive avenue for investment. The market operations in higher education have a potential to widen inequalities in access; hence, there is a need to strengthen the regulatory role of the state to protect the interests of the less-privileged groups and equity considerations.

ACCESS POLICIES IN HIGHER EDUCATION: MERITOCRACY, EQUAL RIGHTS AND EQUALITY OF OPPORTUNITY

The access policy in higher education was dominated by three principles, namely, inherited merit, equality of rights and equality of opportunity (Clancy and Goastellec 2007). The concept of 'inherited merit' relates access to higher education to the circumstances of birth (being born to prosperous parents), and access to higher education becomes the preserve of favoured social groups (Roemer 1998). Under this framework, the higher education sector remained small with limited access to the non-privileged groups.

In the second half of the 20th century, due to ideological and political pressures, this approach to access to higher education was challenged and changed. The idea of inherited merit was replaced by the notion of equality of rights (Goastellec 2006) which helped the expansion of higher education access to students, regardless of their social origin. This approach, in a sense, reflects a friendly attitude towards national diversity, extension of democratic principles and legitimacy of actions by democratically elected governments. This policy helped in minimising the effect of formal barriers to entry to higher education of women, ethnic/racial and social groups and minorities.

The next phase in policy change is denoted by the notion of equality of opportunity that looks more closely into the variations in the opportunity structure. Talents are randomly distributed and the policy of equal opportunities places a responsibility on higher education institutions to widen their net to select talents from all social groups. The merit-based admission needs to be augmented by some form of affirmative action to ensure that national elite is drawn from all social classes. Most of the countries follow this policy of equality of opportunity in their student admissions to institutions of higher education.

Equity is an inclusive notion, and inclusion implies provision of a basic minimum standard of education for all (Santiago et al. 2008). Equal inputs need not always lead to equal outcomes in education. In fact, unequal inputs may be needed to achieve equity in outcomes in education. Students coming from different socio-economic backgrounds may vary in their ability to compete. Those from privileged backgrounds may have an advantage over those from less-privileged backgrounds. The idea of providing additional resources to students from deprived groups is to equalise the conditions for competing and succeeding in the system. In other words, inequalities in inputs (in favour of deprived groups) are tolerated, since they produce advantages for the less-privileged groups and may help improve overall equity in education and eventually in all domains of human activity.

Inequalities in higher education are influenced by inequalities in the preceding levels of education. In a country where basic and secondary education facilities are not equally distributed, it is very difficult to attain equality of opportunity in higher education. Higher education will be offered to those who completed secondary level, and the existing inequalities in secondary education may be reflected in the higher education sector too. On the other hand, countries where secondary education is universal, as is the case in most of the developed countries, equity in access to higher education may be more easily achieved.

The evidence on inter-generational mobility has highlighted the strong and persistent link between parents and children in their educational attainment (Black and Devereux 2010). It reveals that the opportunities are not evenly distributed and that life chances of individuals very often reflect factors for which they are not responsible. Therefore, fairness and inclusion in access are suggested to improve equity in higher education (OECD 2007). Fairness implies that personal and social circumstances, such as gender, socio-economic status, ethnicity and region of residence, should not be an obstacle to educational access and success. Inclusion implies a minimum standard of education provided for all and has to do with whether overall levels of provision are sufficient and effective.

It can be argued that system expansion has been accompanied by an overall decline in inequality of access to higher education. However, it does not seem to have significantly reduced social ine-qualities in access. Empirical studies (Arum, Gamoran and Shavit 2007) have shown that expansion does not reduce class inequalities until the advantaged groups reach a point of saturation. Expansion will contribute to reduction in inequalities beyond the point of saturation since privileged groups cannot increase attendance rates any further (beyond 100%). However, expansion with targeted state interventions in favour of deprived groups can improve equity even before the privileged groups reach a point of saturation in terms of their enrolment.

When inequality indices in access are growing in an expanding system, the benefits from expansion benefit the rich; when it is sta-ble, expansion benefits the poor as well as the rich (Shavit et al. 2007). Moreover, when it is declining, it is inclusive and allows access to higher education to a larger proportion of students from lower social strata. Even when opportunities to access higher education are provided to the less privileged, they have to have completed secondary education at a satisfactory level to take advantage of it. Therefore, in the absence of available graduates from the secondary level, equal access might be of less help for the less privileged.

The irony of state policies in higher education is that when the system was publicly funded, the higher education sector was small with limited access and the privileged took advantage of the system. When the system expanded and the less privileged started getting access to higher education, many governments started reducing subsidies in higher education and introduced cost recovery measures, resulting in widening of inequalities. It can be noticed that while massification of higher education in many instances in the developed world is publicly funded, it is funded through cost recovery measures and limited state financing in the developing world.

Empirical evidence shows that one group that benefits, often more than other groups, from higher education expansion, with or without any affirmative action, is women. For example, the gender parity index (GPI) in higher education in 2010 exceeded 1.0 globally and in most regions, except South and Southwest Asia and sub-Saharan Africa (UIS 2010). What is more interesting is the speed at which female enrolment in higher education has increased.

STRATEGIES TO IMPROVE EQUITY

The student admission and retention policies in higher education show that many countries have in place some type of affirmative action favouring the less advantaged groups. Some of them aim at attracting disadvantaged students to higher education while others favour institutions to admit and retain students belonging to less advantaged groups. The quota-based admission policies are examples of affirmative policies to promote equity.

Many of the strategies are common across countries. The strategies, in general, include strong affirmative action or a quota system, supporting institutions to enrol students from disadvantaged groups and, thus, creating an environment conducive for them to continue their studies, and establishing specialised institutions. In Brazil and India, for example, affirmative action measures have been implemented in the form of 'quota' system (which set a fixed share of slots that can only be held by members of the target group). In the United States and South Africa, affirmative action takes the shape of 'preferential boosts', which gives such candidates additional points to boost their scores to help compete for positions. Furthermore, among the strategies, one of the most common is targeted interventions such as relaxing admissions criteria and extending financial support to students and schools to allow them to continue in the system. For example, in the United Kingdom, the 'Ethnic Minorities Achievement Programme' is specifically targeted to tackle achievement disparities and raise the achievement of children from minority ethnic group. Schools are provided with additional financial and staff resources in order to mainstream ethnic minorities achievement into development plans and implement the project (Bent et al. 2012). Such proactive measures have worked well in many countries. Some countries follow a policy of establishing special institutions to admit and train students from disadvantaged groups. For example, Australia, Mexico and New Zealand set up specialised institutions for selected disadvantaged groups. India follows a similar policy for students belonging to tribal groups at the school level. The policy of establishing special institutions of higher education for the disadvantaged groups may have limitation, at least, on two counts. First, disadvantaged groups may be diverse and dispersed in their settlement pattern, and it is not easy to set up institutions specifically focusing on students from disadvantaged groups. Second, in such institutions, students from disadvantaged groups socialise among themselves, which is not very good for their integration with students from the regular stream.

HIGHER EDUCATION AND EQUITY IN INDIA

The expansion of the higher education sector in India is phenomenal. With more than 700 universities, nearly 40,000 colleges, 1.4 million teachers and 33 million students, India has the second largest higher education system in the world. India, during the post-independence period, followed a public sector-led strategy of development in all sectors of activity including education. The state funding and expansion of the sector through public institutions characterised the design of development during this period.

In the 1960s, all new institutions opened were in the public sector and also that many private institutions became public institutions. Access to higher education was limited and the enrolment ratio in higher education remained below 5% even after two decades of independence (Varghese 2015). The 1970s experienced establishment and a fast growth of the aided colleges in India. Institutions in the aided sector were very similar to those in the public sector in many respects. Institutions in the aided sector followed the same study programmes, offered the same courses and students appeared for the same examinations conducted by the public universities and obtained the same degrees as students admitted in public institutions and affiliated to the same university.

It was during the 1970s that the private sector started entering the higher education sphere. From the mid-1970s, the private individuals and trusts established self-financing colleges in professional and technical subject areas. This phenomenon of private self-financing institutions started in Karnataka and soon spread to Andhra Pradesh, Tamil Nadu and Maharashtra. Another important development during this period, especially in the 1980s, was the diversification of the sources of funding by the public higher education institutions through cost recovery measures.

Cost recovery measures adopted by the public institutions marked the beginnings of privatisation of public institutions in India (Varghese 2013). As part of the privatisation measures, some of the state governments established self-financing courses in public institutions and later started establishing self-financing public institutions. This stage reflected a situation of continued influence of the government in the governance and management of institutions of higher education, even when there was a move towards reduced reliance on state funding for expansion of the sector. In other words, reliance on public institutions and public funding for expansion of the higher education sector started declining.

The period 1970–90 was a period of a relative decline in public funding and privatisation of public institutions, which marked the beginning of private unaided higher education institutions in India. Even though there was multiplication of providers, their effect on growth in enrolment was not substantial. The increase in GER during this period was marginal, from 4.2 to 5.9%. In fact, the average annual growth rate in enrolment declined from 5.6% during 1950–70 to 4.0% during the 1970–90 (Varghese 2015).

The higher education sector expanded at a fast rate during this millennium. The number of institutions proliferated, and there was an explosion in student numbers. For example, while India created more than 200 universities between 1950 and 2000, the country created the same number of universities during the first decade of this millennium. The difference, of course, is that most of the universities established in the previous century were public institutions, while those established in this millennium are private institutions.

The enrolment ratios in higher education improved steadily and quickly during this century. The GER increased from 8.9 in 2000 to 23.6 in 2014. The country entered a stage of massification of higher education (Varghese 2015) by the turn of this decade. A major share of the expansion was accounted for by private institutions. In other words, the revival and expansion of the higher education sector in this century was relied on private institutions and household funding.

The expansion of higher education in India is accompanied by persisting disparities—regional disparities, group disparities and disparities between sexes. Variations in GER are good indicators of existing disparities in higher education development among the states. During the period between 2002–03 and 2011–12, GER increased in all states. There was three times increase in GER in states such as Andhra Pradesh and Tamil Nadu, two times increase in many of the other major states and a relatively meagre increase in states such as West Bengal. The variation in rates of growth is widening of inter-state disparities in enrolment. For example, in 2002–03, the GER varied between 5.0% in Jammu and Kashmir and 28.7% in Chandigarh. The variation in GER in 2012 was between 4.4% in Daman and Diu and 51.0% in Chandigarh. This shows that the variations in GER increased from 23.7 percentage points in 2002–03 to 46.6 percentage points in 2012–13.

The disparities in enrolment among social groups continue to be high in India. In 2012–13, scheduled castes (SC) accounted for 12.2% of the total enrolment in higher education in India. And, the corresponding share of the scheduled tribes (ST) was 4.5%. The GER varies between 8.3% for rural females and 30.5% for urban female and between 7.7% for the ST population and around 45% for the Christian population.

Women account for 44.4% of the total higher education enrolments in India in 2011–12. Kerala has the highest share (58.5%) of women in colleges followed by Meghalaya (56.8%). There has been progress towards gender equality in enrolment. However, the GPI remains at 0.78. In some of the states, where GER is relatively high, the number of girls enrolled is larger than that of the boys, resulting in a GPI of greater than unity. For example, the GPI in Kerala is 1.16 and is 1.1 in Jammu and Kashmir.

India has followed reservation policies since the early 20th century to promote equity in all spheres, including education. The quota system in admissions and job recruitment is a constitutional provision in India. It helps increasing the representation of disadvantaged groups in economic, social and educational spheres. The quota system initially covered students belonging to SCs and STs only. The share of students covered under the reservation quota has been increasing in India and, over a period of time, it included several groups who were not included in the initial stages but were identified as disadvantaged groups in later decades. The Supreme Court ruling increased the share of students to be admitted from disadvantaged groups to 49.5% in all central universities and private and professional institutions, except minority institutions. The Supreme Court ruled that the reservations should not exceed 50% of the total enrolment, although in some of the states, such as Tamil Nadu, the share of disadvantaged in admissions exceeds 50%. Thus, since independence, the union and states have had a concerted and a continuous focus on the representation of the disadvantaged groups to promote inter-group equality in higher learning institutions.

IHER 2016: EQUITY IN HIGHER EDUCATION

The recent five-year plans emphasised on the role of education in promoting equity and considered equity in education as crucial for achieving inclusive growth. Equity initiatives at the federal and state levels have helped providing greater opportunities for access to quality education at all levels. The idea of achieving excellence with equity necessitates closing the achievement gaps among different social groups. Understanding equity in higher education requires deep engagement with the issues that reflect present status and future targets to be achieved. It also requires in-depth engagement with theoretical discourse and empirical evidences on equity, participation, procedural and distributive justice.

With this objective, the Centre for Policy Research in Higher Education (CPRHE), has initiated multiple projects to develop deeper insights into equity concerns in higher education. These research projects attempt to understand the growing diversity in the student body and varying experiences of the disadvantaged groups in higher education institutions and their performance and academic success. Today, students belonging to different religions and lower castes, from poor families and rural areas, and speaking minority languages coexist with students from high caste, urban and rich parents. The widening diversity of the student body is reflected through varying ideological orientation, values and differing styles of social interactions in the campuses. In collaboration with Indian Council of Social Science Research (ICSSR), this research probes into diversity dynamics in higher education institutions located in different regions of the country. The Centre is also engaged in another research to study the effects of schemes initiated by the University Grants Commission (UGC) to foster higher education success, career and occupational mobility of disadvantaged. The schemes under study are remedial coaching for SC/ST/other backward classes (OBC) and minorities, coaching for NET/SET for SC/ST/OBC and minorities, and coaching classes for entry into services for SC/ST/OBC and minorities. More than simply an educational initiative, they aim to address various dimensions of social inclusion, inclusive development and equity.

One of the important activities of the Centre is bringing out an annual publication on higher education in India. The Centre invites articles from renowned academics and experienced decision-makers. The process involved peer review meetings of these authors to arrive at a common framework and understanding on the Report, while individual authors differ in their analysis and arguments. The first issue, *IHER 2015*, was a comprehensive one, which covered various issues within higher education. The second issue, *IHER 2016*, focuses on the theme of equity in higher education. The present report, titled *India Higher Education Report 2016: Equity*, contains important and interesting contributions from several renowned authors and policy specialists in the area of equity and inclusion in higher education.

The report is organised into four major themes. They are (a) equity and development, (b) regional and social inequalities, (c) equity in outcome and (d) diversity and discrimination. The first theme of equity and development consists of four chapters, dealing with issues such as state, markets and equity, equity and excellence in higher education, educational and economic inequalities, and equity and private higher education.

The theme of regional and social inequalities consists of five chapters, focussing on empirical evidences on regional inequalities in access to higher education, inequalities among social groups including religious minorities and between sexes. While the chapters in this section deal with social groups such as SC, ST, OBC and general categories, they also discuss disparities in participation of women, Muslim minority and person with disabilities.

The third theme of equity in outcome consists of three chapters dealing with examples of achieving equity and excellence in school education and transition from secondary to higher education, on one hand, and from higher education to labour market on the other.

The fourth theme of diversity and discrimination consists of three chapters. Chapters in this section include discussion on diversity in student composition, post-admission phase of student life in higher education campuses with a special reference to socially disadvantaged groups and how growing student diversity can be better channelled for civic learning.

REFERENCES

Arum, R., A. Gamoran, and Y. Shavit. 2007. 2008. 'More Inclusion than Diversion: Expansion, Differentiation, and Market Structure in Higher Education'. In *Expansion, Differentiation and Inequality of Access to Higher Education: A Comparative Study*, edited by Y. Shavit, R. Arum, and A. Gamoran. Stanford, CA: Stanford University Press.

Becker, G.S. 1964. *Human Capital: A Theoretical and Empirical Analysis, with Special Reference to Education*. New York: National Bureau of Economic Research.

Bent E., J. Hill, J. Rose, and L. Tikly. 2012. *Making the Difference: Ethnicity and Achievement in Bristol Schools*. Bristol: University of Bristol.

Black, S.E., and P.J. Devereux. 2010. *Recent Developments in Intergenerational Mobility*. NBER Working Papers, No 15889. National Bureau of Economic Research, Washington DC.

Clancy, Patrick, and Gaele Goastellec. 2007. 'Exploring Access and Equity in Higher Education: Policy and Performance in a Comparative Perspective'. *Higher Education Quarterly* 61 (2): 136–54.

Engelbrecht, Hans-Jurgen. 2003. 'Human Capital and Economic Growth: Cross-section Evidence for OECD Countries'. *Economic Record* 79 (Special Issue): S40–S51.

Goastellec, G. 2006. 'Accès et Admission à l'Enseignement Supérieur: Contraintes Globales, Réponses Locales? (Access and Admissions to Higher Education: Global Constraints and Local Responses) *Cahiers de la Recherche sur l'*, *Education et les Savoirs*, 5 (5): 15–36.

Jahan, Selim. April 2016. 'Announcing the Theme of the 2016 Report'. *Human Development Today* (UNDP Newsletter).

OECD. 2007. *No More Failures: Ten Steps to Equity in Education*. Paris: OECD.

———. 2008. *Growing Unequal? Income Distribution and Poverty in OECD Countries*. Paris: OECD.

Roemer, J.E. 1998. *Equality of Opportunity*. Cambridge, MA: Harvard University Press.

Santiago, P., K. Tremblya, E. Basri, and E. Arnal. 2008. *Tertiary education for the knowledge society*, Vol. 2. Paris: OECD.

Schultz, T.W. 1961. 'Investment in Human Capital'. *The American Economic Review* 1 (2): 1–17.

Shavit, Y., R. Arum, and A. Gamoran. 2007. *Stratification in Higher Education: A Comparative Study*. Stanford: Stanford University Press.

Sirowy, Larry, and Alex Inkeles. 1990. 'The Effects of Democracy on Economic Growth and Inequality: A Review'. *Comparative International Development* 25 (1): 126–57.

Stiglitz, J. 1999. 'Knowledge as a Public Good'. In *Global Public Goods: International Co-operation in the 21st Century*, edited by I. Kaul, I. Grumburg, and M. Steve, 308–25. New York: Oxford University Press.

UIS. 2010. *Global Education Digest 2009: Comparing Education Statistics across the World.* Montreal: UIS.

Varghese, N.V. 2001. 'Higher Education and Distributional Equity'. *Perspectives in Education* 17: 95–109.

———. 2006. *Growth and Expansion of Private Higher Education in Africa.* Paris: IIEP/UNESCO.

———. 2013. 'Private Higher Education: The Global Surge and Indian Concerns'. In *India Infrastructure Report 2012: Private Sector in Education*, 145–56. London and New Delhi: Routledge Taylor and Francis Group (IDFC).

———. 2015. *Challenges of Massification of Higher Education in India.* CPRHE Research Papers No. 1, CPRHE/NUEPA, New Delhi.

PART I

EQUITY AND DEVELOPMENT

2

The State, Markets, Equity and Quality in Higher Education

Rajan Gurukkal

INTRODUCTION

The state's assurance of equity in education is a hope so entrenched that we almost hesitate to question it. Promotion of markets in the higher education sector has been part of the national development strategy from the 1980s. The signing of the World Trade Organization's (WTO) General Agreements on Trade in Services (GATS) in 2005 further deepened the process of marketisation in higher education. Globalisation of the higher education sector, especially during the last two plan periods, influenced decisions regarding the governance structure of the sector, programmes of study offered and competencies to be postulated as outcomes. This chapter attempts to explore how the state and markets have been influencing higher education decisions and their effects on equity and quality.

What is attempted is a reflexive exercise based on the critical political economy of higher education in the country, which necessitates a brief statement of the theoretical preliminaries of the study at the outset. The central theoretical framework of comprehension here is critical political economy of capitalism (Marx 1867) as supplemented by allied explanatory constructs that characterise in detail the present phase of global economy (Feenberg 1991; Perelman 2004; Suarez-Villa 2009, 2012). What constitutes fundamental to the framework is the primacy of the economy's role in determining the nature of the content, context and conduct of the higher education sector. A few social theories supplement this mode of understanding by unveiling the niceties and nuances about how the correlation between the economy and education works. They are the conceptual formulations such as the *discourse* (Foucault 1972), as power–knowledge combined, transforming the mind and body of the individual to be the subject; the *habitus* (Bourdieu 1990), as the milieu that structures the behaviour of individuals to suit the social structure; and the *autopoiesis* (Luhmann 1990), as the social systemic reproductive process involving conversion of everything, including antithetical elements into self-referential components. An explanatory exercise such as this has to situate itself by drawing the broad contours of the demographic and socio-economic scenario of the country.

In Foucault's terms, the discourse is regulated by the rules of exclusion, internal systems of control and delineation, and conditions under which discourses can be employed. It is a process that combines knowledge and power, wherein education plays a strategic role. Each discourse turns the individual into its subject and in that sense, each individual is a complex of multiple subjectivities. The theory is helpful in explaining how education facilitates the process of objectification or dissemination of knowledge with which subjectivities are created in the society.

Pierre Bourdieu's *habitus* refers to structuring principles of social practices which are not formally imposed rules but underlying principles of practices in a given social system wherein the people rather lives them than obeying. *Habitus* is inherent and, hence, not the effect of conscious obedience to rules. It ensures individuals' social practices to be instrumental to the reproduction and perpetuation of the social structure, as the social structurally created rhythm of individual behaviour required by the social order. This 'socialised subjectivity' of individuals is what binds them into a system. In the process, the *habitus* also undergoes the dynamics of continuity and change. There are various forms of *habitus*, which reproduce, justify and maintain the system of domination. It makes the dominated feel solidarity and fellowship to the dominant, by enabling the former to see the forms of domination imposed upon them, natural and compliance normal. In the present study, the theory is used to explain how education serves the purpose of strengthening the mindset of conformity.

Similarly, Niklas Luhmann's *autopoiesis*, a term borrowed from the biological context of self-reproduction, but adapted to a transdisciplinary perspective, refers to the processes and mechanisms of the systemic reproduction of the society. It theorises the institutional and ideational ways through which the social system reproduces and perpetuates itself. In social science, it helps us perceive the manifestations and functioning of the power to reproduce and maintain a system by transforming and containing all that impedes the process. It is a process of incorporation and absorption of the antithetical elements for ensuring systemic sustenance. In the capitalistic social system, the *autopoietic* power is so enormous that it can convert even the most antagonistic elements into elements of systemic reproduction. How critical thoughts generated through quality education are contained by the capitalistic system is explained by using the theory.

DEMOGRAPHIC SITUATION

India is distinguished and has a demographic advantage, and the country will have the largest youth population in the world in the 2020s. It is extremely important for the nation to design judiciously effective strategies for equipping the youth to be at their best with competencies of the 21st century to reap the benefits of this demographic dividend. The International Labour Organization (ILO) anticipates that in India, there would be the availability of 116 million youth in the age group of 20–24 by 2020, a strength that exceeds the Chinese youth population by 22 million (ILO 2011). With more than 60% of the aggregate population of the country in the age group of 15–59 and the average national age becoming 29 years, by then, as distinguished from those of developed countries such as America (40 years), Japan (46 years) and Europe (47 years), the national dependency ratio shall be remarkably beneficial. About 140 million youth in India would be in the age group requiring to access higher education, and one out of five graduates in the world is expected to be from the country (ILO 2011).

It is understood that the state cannot afford to finance the expansion of higher education in the public sector. Since Eleventh Plan onwards, the policy has been incrementally that of privatisation and commercialisation under the excuse of the state's financial inability amidst its unavoidably huge revenue expenditure for national defence, industrial development and urban infrastructural expansion. It is strange that the distinctly advantageous demographic conditions excite no seriousness in the minds of national planners about the urgency of treating higher education as a very crucial sector of investment, which they have been disregarding as a field of heavy expenditure.

Before being optimistic about the demographic advantage, one should extrapolate the reality about what percentage of people would get the opportunity to take the dividend. What would be the economic plight of this huge population when viewed against the current trend of growth under crony capitalism with no concern for equity? Is the nation really serious about equipping the youth with socially useful and sustainable knowledge base and competencies? Outside the rhetoric, which committee of higher education reforms has examined the problems of access disparity, absence of social preparation strategies for improving the number of the eligible youth among the poor families for enhancing the national GER, socially contingent learning difficulties, poverty, child labour and gender discrimination? It is significant to raise basic questions such as this and seriously rethink the criteria of rationalisation followed in plan allocation for higher education.

SOCIO-ECONOMIC SCENARIO

The current socio-economic situation of India is that of a nation of unevenly developed peoples of different ethnic, caste, religious and regional identities and of glaring economic inequalities with a lion share of the population lying below the poverty line. It is one of competitive coexistence of diverse groups, mainly of the middle class with a relatively low percentage of higher income groups placed above and a number of the tribal people, scheduled castes and other backward people placed below. These groups are increasingly resorting to the politics of caste as well as religious and ethnic identities cutting across class contradictions for gaining power and resource control. The structure, composition, organisational set-up and the scenario of competitive interaction of the various caste/ communal and other groups in the country help us hold the reasonable presumption that the Indian people represent a complex of manifold contestations of the caste and religious groups, expressed through the politics or organised bargaining.

The upper-middle-class people with upper-caste domination have greater access and control of economic resources, advanced agricultural and marketing expertise, superior technical capabilities based on higher education and training, wide exposure to sophisticated information and party politics. With the result, they involve in a variety of economic enterprises, hold positions of political power, high salaried white-collar jobs in government, quasi-government and private sectors, and control the exchange of goods and services. They are the main actors in government that belongs to the middle class in both theory and practice. On the whole, the upper-middle-class people are more security conscious and status sensitive than their lower counterparts. Many of them have a long tradition of higher social status and ranking, based on the economy as well as caste. Obsessively, non-dependent and nuclear family centred, they yearn to maintain a closure of self-contained life of the neighbours' envy. Highly pretentious and characteristically opaque, they never share problems with others. Naturally, these people constitute the most anxious and tense stratum of the contemporary society.

Estimates based on the data generated by the 71st and 70th Rounds of National Sample Survey show that socio-economic inequalities have been substantially increasing in both the urban and rural areas of the country. The economically well off groups are able to incrementally access quality higher education, acquire expertise for higher remuneration jobs or develop entrepreneurial capabilities and thrive, while the lower income groups run into debt traps by accessing expensive higher education. At both the state and national levels, the rich are becoming richer and the poor, poorer by struggling to access the benefit of healthcare and higher education. A major reason for this has been the gradual withdrawal of the state from, and the steady growth of privatisation and commercialisation of, these vital sectors. It has been clearly shown how glaring has been the inter-state inequalities in the sectors of healthcare and higher education (Thorat 2006).

LOW ENROLMENT RATIO

In the beginning of the Eleventh Plan, the GER was 12.1% and the plan target as advised by UNESCO was a 3% increase. Nevertheless, estimates in the national survey reports of higher education show about 9% increase in the GER, which is 5% above the human resource development (HRD) target. According to the All India Survey of Higher Education (AISHE), the GER in 2012–13 was 21.1%, with a break-up of 22.3% as the GER of males, 19.8% as the GER of females, 15.1% as the GER of the scheduled castes and 11.0% as the GER of the scheduled tribes (MHRD 2014). The total student population in higher education is around 29.6 million with 16.3 million males and 13.3 million females. However, the GER in India is lagging behind the world average.

The widely and repeatedly aired cause of low GER is the insufficiency of the number of higher educational institutions. Academic backwardness is generally assigned to low standard and poor quality of education, ignoring the explicit issue of the convergence of economic backwardness and academic low quality. The main cause that the ministry of human resource development (MHRD) has approved is the shortage in the number of higher educational institutions of standard and quality, and various national educational reforms underway are postulated avowedly to address the issue. It is part of the rhetoric of tricks of the trade for the institutions that are engaged in competitive commercialisation of knowledge with little or no resources for quality assurance. They have good infrastructure in most cases, but lack academic resources for quality assurance.

Not many social scientists in the country believe that the nation's poor GER is due to shortage of institutions and, therefore, proliferation of unaided colleges and private universities is the solution (Gurukkal 2012; Gurukkal and Varghese 2012). Nevertheless, our education reformers do believe it, and their recommendations have led to the rise of a large number of private colleges and universities claiming 'world-class quality and excellence' as their distinct institutional attribute. The ministry's decision to open up as many new colleges and universities as possible was a direct response to the alleged shortage in the number of higher educational institutions. It is true that there exists a gross mismatch between eligibility rates and enrolment rates. But, this is not an indication of the mismatch between the institutional intake capacity and eligibility enrolment ratio. It is significant to note that many of the eligible candidates do not get enrolled hardly due to the dearth of institutions in their region but due to their economic and social backwardness. It is essential to devise a set of effective measures of socio-economic preparation for enhancing the number of youth capable of accessing higher education.

It is extremely important to analyse the socio-economic factors contributing to low GER as well as the poor quality with a view to expose the political economy of the legislative remedy in general. The main cause of low GER is not the insufficiency of the number of institutions and their low quality as often made out, although they are the problems. The central cause of low GER and poor quality of higher education is socio-economic. What it requires is a set of legislative measures to combine economic growth with equity. Unfortunately, the legislative cure administered by the MHRD in the form of a few reform bills has nothing to do with this social development objective. None of the proposed bills addresses itself of basic socio-economic issues relating to educational development. Opening of more colleges and universities, indigenous or foreign, will not necessarily help enhance the GER of disadvantaged for it can only intensify the socio-economic barriers that account for access disparity leading to national deficit of youth with academic capabilities. There is nothing accidental about these changes for the decisive force behind them has been the dominant economy.

A document of the World Bank (Dahlman and Utz 2001) says that India has many of the key ingredients ideal to play an effective role in the knowledge economy. Foremost among them is the availability of an impressive mass of skilled, English-speaking knowledge-workers, especially in sciences. Other ideal ingredients are a well-functioning democracy, a huge national domestic market that is one of the largest in the world, and a large and impressive Diaspora, creating valuable knowledge linkages and networks. The list goes on by adding other features such as macroeconomic stability, a dynamic private sector, institutions of a free market economy, a well-developed financial sector and a broad and diversified science and technology infrastructure, a developed ICT sector, prospering IT, status of a global provider of software services, etc. World Bank informs that building on these strengths, India can harness the benefits of the knowledge revolution to improve its economic performance and boost the welfare of its people. All this is about certain misleading surface features with which the neoliberal economic policy fabricates its rhetoric. But truth below the surface is extremely alarming. Higher Education Committee Reports in India engendered the state under neoliberal reforms and repeat the exhortations in the World Bank documents. They invariably hush up the alarming truth about the life and people in the country and illuminate middle-class dreams about development real, for it helps subsidising the global economy.

India, a multilingual country with English as the official medium of instruction at the tertiary level, has a relatively poor GER of 21%, with about 70% of the rural undergraduate students unable to understand English, about 40% of the postgraduate students unable to use English for higher cognition, and about 60% of the youth between 22 and 35 with innovative faculty and creativity belonging to the villages where education is imparted in the Indian language (Dutz 2007). Knowledge base of the Indian languages with respect to advanced sciences and areas of emerging importance is abysmally poor. About 80% of the total population do not have any participation in the production of Knowledge because of historically and culturally contingent limitations such as class, gender and caste discrimination (Balatchandirane 2007).

THE DOMINANT ECONOMY AND MARKETS

Ever since the signing of GATS agreement by the nations, education has become legally a profiteering private enterprise. According to the provisions provided for in the agreement, an educational institution charging a fee, even if it is a meagre sum, shall be treated under the category of trade. As a result, knowledge is regarded as a commercial item licensed for exchange across the present day world. Education has ceased to be a public good of socio-cultural use-value, once knowledge began to be produced and transmitted as an object of exchange for accumulating profit. Commercialisation of education is a worldwide phenomenon today. In developing countries, its consequences are more intense. It has created serious access disparity with respect to opportunities of knowledge acquisition in India.

Due to the heavy dependence of the economy on technological innovation, this phase of capitalism is called techno-capitalism (Feenberg 1991). Techno-capitalism is fast rising as the dominant economy in India as well. In this phase of capitalism, new knowledge is both commodity and capital. Needless to mention that the role of research in the economy that counts gross domestic product (GDP) in terms of gross technology product (GTP) and gross science product (GSP) is decisive. It has opened up an era of intellectual assets, often called intangible assets, relating primarily to technology. Intangible or intellectual assets constitute both commodity and capital in the economy. The techno-capitalism is spawning new forms of corporate power and organisation of major implications for the 21st-century higher education (Suarez-villa 2000). Corporate houses have erected universally the system of intellectual property rights (IPR) for confiscating creativity with profound impacts on the economy, science, technology and culture (Perelman 2004; Suarez-villa 2009).

Knowledge economy turns knowledge into a commodity that acquires multiple forms, each of which is differently priced based on its market demand. Let the beneficiary pay for acquiring knowledge is the neoliberal approach to education. Knowledge, as the philosophic means to a better life, is contrasted with knowledge as a commodity under capitalism. Commoditisation of knowledge is a process of transformation of knowledge into an explicit, standardised, codified and priced object of exchange value. Commoditisation is conversion of results of human labour into commodities to be transacted by the market.

Techno-capitalist industrial enterprises the world over are being run by corporate establishments, depending extensively on research and intellectual appropriation. They have given rise to new experimentalist organisations deeply grounded in technological research, as opposed to manufacturing and services production of the past system. All developed countries have corporate establishments investing heavily in the sector of knowledge production. They are rich in knowledge-based capital (KBC) or intangible assets turned capital. Investment and growth in Organisation for Economic Cooperation and Development (OECD) economies is increasingly driven by KBC or intangible capital. In many OECD countries, firms now invest as much or more in KBC as they do in physical capital such as machinery, equipment and buildings. This shift reflects a variety of long-term implications of economic and institutional transformations in OECD economies as well as in the third world.

Under techno-capitalism, 'new knowledge' and 'creativity' become the most valuable resources, as much as what raw materials and factory labour used to be under industrial capitalism. This accounts for the global recognition of patents and IPR under International Laws (Perelman 2004). It has been argued that the emergence of techno-capitalism in the process of globalisation and the growth of techno-capitalist corporations have been identified as a new version of capitalism that generates new forms of organisation, designed to exploit 'intangibles' such as 'new knowledge' and 'creativity' (Suarez-Villa 2009, 2012). These new organisations, are referred to as experimentalist organisations which are deeply grounded in technological research, as opposed to manufacturing and services production of the phase of industrial capitalism. They are heavily dependent on the corporate appropriation of research outcomes as intellectual property.

Techno-capitalism is a very advanced phase of commodity fetishism, which is rooted in technological innovation and corporate power. Intangibles, most of all, knowledge and creativity, are the core of techno-capitalism, equal to what tangible raw materials, factory labour and capital were to industrial capitalism. Intangibles already account for as much as four-fifths of the value of most of the products and services in existence. Conversely, the most valuable tangible resources for industrial capitalism are losing value relative to those intangibles in every product or service. Technological creativity is turned into both commodity and capital under new techno-capitalist corporate regimes that are primarily oriented toward research and intellectual appropriation.

Progress of commoditisation of knowledge, detaching it from the (user) person and making it an independent economic entity, has given rise to the phenomenon called capital fetishism, from which arose the practice of owning and controlling knowledge as intellectual property. Easily distributed via global communication networks, knowledge with authorial ownership began to become an important source of personalised profit, necessitating special legal protection. It has been shown how corporations have erected a system of IPR to confiscate creativity, with profound impacts on the economy, science, technology and culture. Corporate houses compete with one another to buy patents and IPR, which increase their market power, to be first to come up with new products and services. Perelman says that this competition is leading to substantial theft of patented knowledge and infringement of IPR. Corporate establishments resort to various clever ways and means for the appropriation of research outcomes through new relations of power. Often, it becomes a reckless confiscation of the intangibles—'new knowledge', 'creativity' and 'innovativeness' of the researchers. Naturally, one of the outcomes of this is increase in the litigations relating to IPR theft and infringement.

Just to cite one example, the huge experimentalist establishment of DuPont consists of over 10,000 scientists and engineers addressing human needs projected to 2050. It is said that in 2013, the DuPont establishment introduced nearly 1,800 new products that secured about 1,050 new US patents. Another lot of products have 1,800 US patents in the pipeline. The DuPont innovation delivery system has already generated $10 billion out of these new products. Looking ahead the value, DuPont establishment seeks to fund the pursuit of new discoveries in this line. In corporate research, highly specialised employees from all over the world work in multiple capital-intensive projects on technological breakthroughs such as software development, robotics, engine management, etc. Thousands of young scientists of instrumentation culture often qualified as the innovators of tomorrow are working like robots in corporate research establishments at various locations around the world.

It has been shown that the emergence of corporatocracy, based on the vast and growing power of corporations over public governance around the world, is fundamental to techno-capitalist globalisation (Suarez-Villa 2012). It is a new type of governance that enmeshes and destroys democracy in order to virtually surrender the state power at the feet of corporations. A group of transnational elites tied to corporate power constitute the principal actors in the system. They penetrate into the democratic system and reconstitute it as the government of, for and by corporations, rather than of, for and by the people. In actual practice, it quells democracy from within and substitutes it with a new form of imperialism, based on the global corporate power, imbued with an array of highly sophisticated and intrusive technologies. Corporate houses have globally established a powerful techno-military complex of electronic sophistication and juridical devices for confiscating the intangible assets and gaining monopolistic control over them through the purchase of patents and IPR. It has naturally reflected on the nation's state structure and bureaucracy.

This is a set-up of neo-imperialism that would certainly lead to a series of major social, economic and political consequences in the country because it enables corporatism to be ever more intrusive and rapacious through its militant control over technology and innovation. Politicians and bureaucrats in India think higher education a sector of expenditure rather than investment. The nation is investing 0.89% of GDP for higher education. At the same time, several actors in the Government go recklessly extravagant and there is no financial discipline in the working of the Government. Naturally, production of new knowledge, which is highly sophisticated and enormously expensive, is extremely rare in any of the fields of modern sciences. Even traditional Indian knowledge systems are new meadows only for foreigners who take patents in them. Indians, uninitiated in traditional knowledge language of their country, draw blank about its scientific dimensions. Corporate houses are seeking to enhance monopolistic control through patents and IPR over the country's traditional knowledge as a major source of production of new knowledge. Recommendations of the Planning Commission of India 2012, under a beautiful title 'Fostering Social Responsibility in Higher Education in India', match this global process pretty well. What they mean by 'Strengthening Community Engagement in Higher Education in India' is exactly the opposite of the concept of people-centred and empowerment-oriented initiatives for enhancing social participation in higher education.

India is long way off from the emerging sciences and technologies of the 21st century. Advanced software and molecular processors in computing and communications are among various new technologies that are going to be symbolic of the 21st century, in much the same way as aviation and mass production were of the 20th century. Suarez-Villa points out that nanotechnology, biotechnology and its various related fields, such as synthetic bioengineering, bioinformatics, biopharmacology, biomedicine, genetic engineering, agrobiotechnology and branches of biomimetics such as robotics, are emerging areas of importance (Suarez-Villa 2012). The country, far behind in the discovery and invention sciences concerned, can only subsidise techno-capitalism through the purchase of high-tech electronic goods, hard and soft, rather than gaining profit by selling new knowledge, creativity and innovativeness. Now, transnational exploitation of intellectual assets under techno-capitalism is far more extensive than what it had been about raw materials under industrial capitalism. The state is tending to be a mere agency for diverting national revenue for supporting the aggressive expansion of techno-capitalism under the guise of development. The ultimate political consequence shall be the reappearance of an imperial state.

STATE AND EQUITY

There has been a steady intensification of privatisation of public assets and commercialisation of education. This process has been pushing the country into solvency crisis, where public sector disinvestment forged ahead under the pretext of an economic policy reform, transferring national resources into the hands of the capitalist minority. Integrated to the process of decentralisation, most of the local public assets are being privatised in alignment with this new national economic policy. In the wake of this, several neoliberal practices, such as 'out-sourcing', 'down-sizing the public sector', 'multiple stakeholders approach', 'non-governmental organisations', 'voluntary agencies', etc., have become part of the functioning of the state and its bureaucracy. Thanks to the most misleading term, 'development', the nation has reached a stage of accepting any undemocratic scheme natural to democracy. Hence, it has become unnecessary for the state to hide its instrumental role in the conversion of people's common property into private assets of a capitalist minority. Today, the state is openly an agency determined to subsidise capitalism and by all means, facilitate its expansion at the cost of the nation's economic sovereignty. A major social consequence is the threat to poor people's livelihoods (Gurukkal 2012).

In the process, the state power itself has been getting privatised in the form of sale of public credits or bidding of the job of recovering government loans or the task of crime investigation with the consequences such as mafia rule, drug abuse and terrorism. Major excuses for the state measures for the privatisation of its functions are the lack of concern of the beneficiary public, irresponsibility of the public servants, incapability of the public sector institutions, bureaucratic inefficiency in government, bribery and other forms of corruption. All this allows the capitalist minority to loot the public revenue under the connivance of the state under the pretext of one development reform or the other. This phase is called crony capitalism, for which there are many instances in India. In a crony capitalist state, the government is recklessly diverting national revenue for the aggressive expansion of techno-capitalism under the veil of development.

As regards to the higher education sector, the state has become determined to streamline all institutions and practices with a view to quickening the process of expansion of education as an industry with more and more private players. Ever since signing of the WTO's GATS, the state openly made its withdrawal from most of the sectors of people's welfare, especially health and education. Hence, there have been legislative efforts in that direction as a part of the ongoing process of structural adjustments ever since the 1990s, but all the more emphatically, after the nation signed GATS on 1 January 2005. GATS required legislative reforms, apparently, to gain from trade in services (in effect to benefit developed countries). In fact, its groundwork was over way back in 1985 itself by changing the name of the ministry of education to that of human resource development. Accordingly, several reform bills, generally known as neo-liberal initiatives for 'improving' the country's higher education sector, have been proposed, and the Private University's Act of 1995 was the first to be legislated among the lot. Foreign Education Institutions (Regulation of Entry and Operations) Bill 2010, Prevention of Malpractices Bill and the Education Tribunal Bill 2010, National Accreditation Regulatory Authority Bill 2010, and Higher Education and Research Bill 2011 (HE&R) are some of the examples. Shrouded in controversies even over their constitutional validity, all of them are pending legislations. Being sure about the withdrawal of HE&R Bill 2011, the government had constituted the University Grants Commission (UGC) review committee on 30 July 2014 itself to re-examine the Commission's regulatory function. This has necessitated liberalising of the statutory restrictions administered through the UGC and its councils. It has been a matter of consensus among the neoliberal higher education reformers that there should be a single regulator at the national level to serve the purpose of liberalisation, saving time and money.

It was the National Knowledge Commission (2005) that recommended the replacement of the UGC along with other regulatory national councils in the higher education sector by a single regulator has been a long standing plan under neoliberal reforms in the country, for the first time by an Independent Regulatory Authority for Higher Education (IRAHE) through an Act of Parliament in order to set standards and determine eligibility criteria for new institutions. Yashpal Committee Report on Higher Education in India (2009) reiterated the recommendation for the single regulator. Soon it acquired concrete form in the National Commission for Higher Education and Research (NCHER) 2011 that was to subsume all regulatory bodies in higher education such as the UGC, All India Council for Technical Education (AICTE), National Council for Teacher Education (NCTE) and Distance Education Council (DEC). In spite of the fact that this Bill, summarily withdrawn on 24 September 2014 after nationwide debate and sustained opposition for over three years, is back again as National Higher Education Authority (NHEA) Bill, 2015. Who are these rare ones, wiser and more learned than any of the specialist academics in the country to constitute the infallible 'authority' of higher education? The first direct recommendation of the corporatisation of higher education came in the N.R. Narayana Murthy Committee Report (Government of India 2012).

One has to see the move towards placing the entire higher education sector under a single regulator as a part of the corporate disciplining system, the urgency of which is explicit in the context of techno-capitalism. It is knowledge economy that is exerting a tremendous pressure on universities and research institutions for being of world-class quality in teaching and research. Tertiary education is obsessed with the term 'innovativeness', the latest version of 'commodity fetishism' that obscures the true economic character of the relation between the innovator and the corporate exploiter. It is an urgent need of the corporate houses to bring universities and research institutes under a militaristic discipline for exploitation of intangible assets, but put up as a national agenda of making gains through the production and exchange of new knowledge.

India's emergence as a major player in the global knowledge economy is one of the reasons stated for replacing the UGC, too outmoded an institution to cater to such complex needs that include world-class quality assurance, international credit transfer system, mobility across streams of general higher education, professional skills programmes and teacher training. Other major issues in the higher education sector, which the UGC and other regulatory bodies could not resolve, are the unwieldy affiliating system, inflexible academic structure, uneven capacity across various subjects and eroding autonomy of academic institutions. The implicit presumption is that the 'authority' can do all that the UGC and other regulatory bodies have failed to fulfil. But how? The illogical presumption that a handful of 'experts' can do what multiple bodies of specialists could not, clearly indicates the mode of execution to be inevitably arbitrary and authoritarian. This is the corporate style, pure and simple.

Their real objectives purposely hushed up, the stated ones were altogether bogus and the remedial prescriptions remained unfounded and self-contradictory. NHEA's priority being the ministry's terms of reference, what wonder can it make with regard to quality assurance. Neoliberal reformers are not happy about any of the 14 regulatory bodies in professional knowledge fields, such as AICTE and MCI besides advisory boards such as CABE, in the higher education sector because their regulatory functions disturb the 'autonomy' and insist upon the 'quality' of the institutions concerned for determining the grants (CABE on Autonomy of Higher Education Institutions 2005). NHEA is to subsume all these bodies, including the UGC, and overcome their regulatory stipulations impeding the flow of funds. The state has already gone ahead with measures in this direction, although the Bills are pending legislations. Already, the UGC's disbursing function that is based on expert appraisal of academic performance, the foremost among its primary responsibilities, has been bypassed in a big way through the introduction of Rashtriya Uchchatar Shiksha Abhiyan (RUSA) in 2013. This shift from the system of expertise-based academic assessment to an alternative system of liberal guideline-based administrative decision, as the necessary prerequisite for the allocation of grants, is justified (often sensibly) under the alleged distributive imbalance and delay in the disbursal of UGC grants.

Most of the allegations are ironical and self-contradictory as exemplified by the one accusing the UGC for not regulating 'private, not-for-profit entities in higher education and for not suggesting any measures to curb commercialisation'. Truly, what irritates the neoliberal reformers in the Committee is the UGC's regulatory intervention in the privatisation and commercialisation of higher education. UGC is an institution of nuisance for them and, hence, its de facto removal is their main target. There is no compatibility between the nature of problems identified and the functional capability of the institutional solutions proposed. A sheer lack of analytical comprehension and fundamental causation of the problems in the light of specialised scholarship is explicit here. Most of the causal connections observed by the Committee are commonsensical and musty. One may not expect its members to be inclined to draw insights from critical political economy of techno-capitalism and be wary of the negative impact of the corporate trade in knowledge. However, everybody expects them to be using the extant science of effective teaching and learning as well as social scientific explanations for the poor quality and standard in the higher education sector. Quality assurance is largely projected as a question of managerial efficiency by most of the committees and, therefore, most of their recommendations invariably emphasise measures of privatisation and commercialisation, which guarantee standard through competition. This approach has always precluded the possibility of analysing what quality means and how it develops. There is no dependence on specialised knowledge in the related fields such as the science of pedagogy, cognitive science and neurology of learning for diagnosing the problems and resolving them. Hence, the reports of such committees are managerial implementation packages with little academic insights into the problem, although they jointly represent two decades of accelerated national education reform.

It has been an oft-repeated excuse of these committees and commissions that the government cannot afford founding and maintaining too many higher educational institutions all by itself (thanks to the constraint of school education being its 'primary effort area') and, hence, enhanced participation of the private sector has to be promoted. We owe the number of unaided institutions, which has been steadily rising since the beginning of the 1990s to the liberal policy, promoting enhanced private sector participation. During the last five years, their mushrooming has been phenomenal. According the latest available official estimates, higher education institutions falling into three broad categories come to 665 universities, 35,829 colleges and 11,443 stand-alone institutions (MHRD 2014). Uttar Pradesh (UP), Andhra Pradesh, Maharashtra, Karnataka, Rajasthan, Tamil Nadu and Madhya Pradesh (MP) are the states with the highest number of colleges in India. Puducherry ranks foremost in college density with a total of 61 institutions, while Bihar and Daman and Diu are at the bottom with only six each, respectively.

A substantial number of higher education institutions in the country, that is, 32% universities and 73% colleges, are privately owned and controlled. Andhra Pradesh is the state with the highest number of private institutions, and of the total number of private-unaided colleges in the state's share comes to a little above 80%. Although this apparently reflects a higher rate of availability of the youth in the age group of 18–23 with eligibility in the state but in reality, there is no match between the total institutional intake capacity and the number of the eligible candidates there. This is true of all the states of high institutional density in the country. Obviously, candidates, mostly of bare minimum eligibility, drawn from other states sustain the excess intake capacity. This has caused a steady decline in the standard of education due to the non-compliance of the national criteria of quality assurance. State patronage of commercialisation and privatisation has made meaningful functioning of statutory regulatory bodies extremely difficult. Market competition has not led to quality enhancement in the country's education sector because of the national shortage of the eligible clientele.

Can the state and markets combined ensure a wider access and equity in the higher education sector is a question that the theory precludes. The present day clamour for equity in higher education is natural in the context of commercialisation and privatisation of higher education, which has brought the professional and job-oriented streams to the fore. Medicine and engineering rank the foremost among the professional streams of highest market demand due to their significantly vocational, well paid and eminently regarded competencies. They are the most commercialised of all streams, and hence are the most expensive too. Naturally, the streams preclude equity. Those of management studies and law position the next in market demand, based on their potential economic benefits, social status and ranking. They are being privatised and made expensive too, making equity difficult. The paramedical programmes, especially of the nursing science, having the potential of foreign employment, have been extensively privatised all over the country, but with equity rendered plausible to a certain extent due to its demand being largely confined to the lower-middle class. Teacher education colleges constitute the last of the commercialised streams. Streams of basic sciences are the least privatised and commercialised, which accounts for their greater equity. Among the streams of general education in arts and social sciences, the only commercialised one is that of commerce education. A few among the poor are eligible to access these streams of demand despite the facility of caste/communal reservations, merit-cum-means scholarships and loans.

Technology education is the worst hit stream through privatisation of higher education. As of 2014 estimate, the country has about 6,375 engineering colleges and about 3.96 million seats of which Andhra Pradesh (340,007), Tamil Nadu (236,417), Maharashtra

(146,116), UP (136,417), MP (96,536) and Karnataka (92,376) have huge shares of intake (AICTE 2015). As a natural consequence of the reckless inflation of seats under profit motive, there has been a steady decline in the academic standard and quality. Most of the engineering colleges in the country have an abysmally poor pass percentage; the national average has dropped from 33% to 22% in two decades. This has resulted in the production of worthless engineering graduates in spite of AICTE quality control. Growth of intake capacity should not be mistaken for the improvement of equity, for in the case of socio-economically and academically backward students with bare minimum eligibility, the inflation of seats has proved to be an inescapable trap—failing to complete the programme, the get trapped and lose their academic career. Most of them would have made them employable by graduating in the general stream. This terrible social as well as academic injustice, consequent on the supply-driven trade in the stream of engineering education, should be a revelation for neoliberalists who propagate access, equity and quality through commercialisation.

Often, the streams of market demand are identified as useful and hence symbolic of quality higher education, which the state has been allegedly failing to expand, causing shortage of institutions and denial of equity. Much of the hue and cry about the country's poor quality higher education and access disparity has been mere rhetoric to prepare an appropriate environment and legitimacy for commercialisation of higher education, by devaluing the public higher education sector and spreading the hope that the competitive private sector will render wider access, equity and quality plausible in the higher education sector. Recommendations of higher education committees and commissions repeat privatisation of higher education as the means to achieve better access, equity and quality.

QUALITY QUESTION

Theoretically speaking, it is the dominant economy that decides what is to be learnt or what competencies are to be acquired through higher education. Accordingly, quality education is the one that satisfies the needs of the dominant economy. Techno-capitalism, the dominant economy of our times, would recognise the one that imparts competencies essential for the effective participation in the economy, as quality higher education. Those who develop through higher education the faculty to produce new knowledge become eligible for a privileged participation in techno-capitalism, for creativity or innovativeness is the economy's central resource. Nevertheless, its present number can certainly be enhanced considerably through suitable pedagogic strategies supplemented by measures of economic security, social links and politico-cultural exposures. Pedagogic strategies include learner-centric course and curriculum design with stated learning outcomes, use of appropriate learning experiences, learning-specific assignments, scholarly instructional support, concurrent evaluation and sustained institutional demand for self-learning or learning by doing. Measures of economic security are usually in the form of various scholarships and soft loans, but they should be more of hands-on type enabling to earn by learning.

Quality higher education for a country such as India should be the one that engenders critical insights essential to understand the implications of the commercialisation of knowledge and its denial of equity unleashed by techno-capitalist globalisation. Critical faculty helps students understand that the growing global importance of intangibles, such as new knowledge and technological innovativeness, is widening the inequalities between nations and aggravating brain drain. It makes clear to them that the techno-military-corporate complex is growing, dominant and becoming ever more intrusive and rapacious through its control over technology and innovation (Suarez-villa 2012). Techno-capitalism requires an apathetic, unaffected, regimented and uncritical contingent of experts of micro-specialisation, precluding holistic perspective. What the dominant economy needs is a well-disciplined, workaholic and apolitical youth trained in various skills. Whatever education that produces this robotic youth is quality education or innovative education to it. Innovative education is only a rhetoric and not real. Techno-capitalists know that innovators need not be produced everywhere, for they can be procured from wherever they are available. For this, quality education is the one that would check as far as possible the production of ethical, political subjects of critical consciousness. This is the most ponderous pedagogical paradox in the education today. As a result, critical consciousness is almost alien to our pedagogy at all levels. One is supposed to be acquiring critical consciousness in the process of higher education, but it hardly happens today. Even the critical attitude of a liberal pragmatic kind, which spontaneously comes up in any educated citizen of democratic values, passions and ethical postulates, is uncommon today.

Committees inspired by neoliberal schemes fail to realise that these are the principal actors in the dominant economic system, who decide what new knowledge is and how we should acquire it. In techno-capitalist economy, science and technology constitute the knowledge of critical function, forming the foundation of capitalist forces of production and the principal source of accumulation (Aronowitz 1988). Capitalism recognises science and technology as its knowledge base, for it is amenable to profitable application. Other forms of knowledge are being co-opted, incorporated, subordinated, subjected, marginalised or destroyed, depending upon their levels of amenability to profitable application. It is natural that no committee bothers to understand the primacy of critical consciousness in higher education and the significance of promoting people-centred and empowerment-oriented higher education, which is going to decide the strength of the nation in the era of its demographic advantage. Committees and commissions talk about electronic sophistication of learning through ICT or multimedia for quality education. Unless the content is carefully and profoundly designed, media will act as the messenger and serve as the ideological veil effectively masking the truth. What then gets promoted in the name of quality learning is an altogether mechanical and alienating process that divests learning of its real quality—the critical consciousness. In short, quality education is of two mutually antagonistic types: one that addresses the needs of the dominant economy and the other that engenders critical consciousness about the economy.

Of all, the most influential impediment in the path of quality and equity in higher education is the dominant economy. Democratisation of quality and equity is not its interest, which is not only unnecessary for its enterprises, but also unfavourable, for the former is realistic, deep and hence critical while the latter is ethical. Higher education is being divested of its critical quality by historically contingent social structural devices, which thinkers have theorised differently. Marx viewed it as ideology (false consciousness), Michel Foucault (1972) as discourse (power and knowledge combined), Pierre Bourdieu (1990) as *habitus* (behavioural structuring power), Niklas Luhmann (1990) as *autopoiesis* (social reproductive power), etc. These devices constitute the societal everyday life with routines, conventions, normative ideas, practices, institutions, concepts and meanings. They govern social common sense. Higher education has to wrench itself away from these shackles to be a self-consciously realist and critical process of cognitive encounter.

It is easier said than done, for capitalism, as a global system, has its built-in power to reproduce and perpetuate itself by turning even its most formidable enemies into self-referential constituents. In social theory, this power is technically called *autopoiesis* (Livingston 2006; Luhmann 1990). It operates in myriads of ways through the entire people, relations, institutions, practices, ideas and spaces. Knowledge is a very crucial object of *autopoietic* control and, hence, its production as well as transmission would not escape the influence of *autopoiesis*. Naturally, education, one of the most powerful social institutions, is inevitably a major channel of operation for *autopoietic* power. Its main function is containment of antithetical elements in the capitalist socio-economic system involving dehumanising processes and relations, which could otherwise cause upsurges. *Autopoietic* strategies of containment would act as a safety valve averting systemic overturns.

In the capitalist world, the critical dimension of knowledge is not easily available to all because of its being incessantly diffused and strategically distracted. Knowledge production is an alienated and highly encumbered activity. It is inevitably under the systemic control of capitalism. Knowledge production is so designed as to be incapable for any researcher to be disseminating the politics of it. There is a strong and built-in system for depoliticising the students through the process of acquisition of knowledge. Spread of the myth that knowledge is invariably neutral is the basic strategy. Delinking of knowledge with social reality is another strategy. Yet another strategy is the conversion of knowledge itself as a part of the rhetoric and ideology of capitalism. They draw blank about the social use or consequences of it. They become neutral, self-centred, apolitical and least perturbed by social consequences, if any. This predicament demands organised intellectual efforts towards re-politicisation of knowledge.

Knowledge production and transmission under the control of capitalism would be ideologically modulated processes, blunting their critical dimension and enabling the promotion of conformity through *autopoiesis*, which in various ways distract the learners from social reality. This process of depoliticisation leaves us not only bereft of critical consciousness but also unconcerned about the dehumanising activities around us. Movements demanding restoration of knowledge as a public good, and assurance of access-parity and equity, have been there all over the world, but mostly getting contained by the economy's *autopoietic* power, letting commoditisation of knowledge advance unhindered.

CONCLUSION

A policy recommendation of top priority is social preparation, primarily through the economic empowerment of the poor for improving the number of youth eligible to higher education and ensuring their enrolment. Measures of economic empowerment under the state initiative should involve, other than various scholarships and soft loans, hands-on type support, enabling the economically backward to earn by learning, which can guarantee a steady acquisition of competencies. There should be efforts to enhance the standard and quality of education both as construed by the dominant economy and as its critique—the former to ensure job security and the latter to guarantee a good citizenry capable of critical participation in public policy debates. Since the present academic standard can be remarkably improved through suitable pedagogic strategies and institutional quality-assurance, it is crucial to revitalise the regulatory institutions and bodies such as the UGC and other statutory councils. They should be urged to provide comprehensive guidelines for quality assurance and insist upon the higher education institutions' adherence to them for being sure that the latter have well-updated learner-centric courses and curricula with stated learning outcomes, the habit of using appropriate learning experiences, giving learning specific assignments, providing scholarly instructional support and practising the system of concurrent evaluation. All regulatory measures should be strictly enforced to ensure academic quality through sustained institutional demand for practical self-learning.

It is important that the state turns serious about checking the unbridled promotion of commercialisation and privatisation of higher education, which further intensifies access disparity and accelerates quality impairment. The state has to distinguish well-studied recommendations from those of the empirically and theoretically impoverished vision documents and reports propagating privatisation as the path towards academic excellence through access, equity and quality. Keeping in view of the demographic phenomenon of the youth becoming dominant, the state should be able to allocate at least 6% of the GDP for what it calls human resource development, suitable to the 21st-century global requirement, with the distinct understanding that it is an eminent investment rather than expenditure. Let the democratic councils, bodies and institutions with academic specialisation in emerging areas of importance debate and decide upon which courses should be taught, where, how and for what competencies.

REFERENCES

AICTE. 2015. *All India Council of Technical Education: Approval Process Handbook, 2015–16*. AICTE: New Delhi.

Aronowitz, S. 1988. *Science as Power: Discourse and Ideology in Modern Society*. Minneapolis: University of Minnesota Press.

Balatchandirane, G. 2007. *Gender Discrimination in Education and Economy*. VRF Series No. 426. Tokyo: Institute of Development Economics Publications.

Bourdieu, P. ed. 1990. 'Structures, *Habitus*, Practices'. In *The Logic of Practice*. Stanford, CA: Stanford University Press.

Dahlman, C., and A. Utz. 2001. *India and the Knowledge Economy: Leveraging Strengths and Opportunities*. Washington DC: World Bank Institute.

Dutz, M.A. ed. 2007. *Unleashing India's Innovation*. Washington: World Bank Publications.

Feenberg, A. 1991. *Critical Theory of Technology*. New York: Oxford University Press.

Foucault, M. 1972. *Archaeology of Knowledge*. Translated by A. Sheridan. New York: Balmes and Noble.

Government of India. 2012. *N.R. Narayana Murthy Committee Report*. New Delhi: Planning Commission.

Gurukkal, R. 2012. *Resistance and Hope: Freedom Struggles in India Today*. Kappen Memorial Lecture. Bangalore: Visthar Publications.

Gurukkal, R., and R. Varghese. 2012. *Encounters: A University on Trial*. Kottayam: SPCS Publication.

ILO. 2011. *Estimates and Projections of the Economically Active Population 1990–2020*, 6th edition. Geneva: International Labour Organization.

Livingston, I. 2006. *Between Science and Literature: An Introduction to Autopoetics*. Champaign: University of Illinois Press.

Luhmann, N. 1990. *Essays on Self-reference*. New York: Columbia University Press.

Marx, K. 1867. *Capital: Critique of Political Economy*, Vol. 1. London: Penguin.

———. 2014. *All India Survey of Higher Education 2012–13*. New Delhi: Department of Higher Education.

Perelman, M. 2004. *Steal this Idea: Intellectual Property Rights and the Corporate Confiscation of Creativity*. London: Palgrave Macmillan Publishers.

Suarez-Villa, L. 2000. *Invention and the Rise of Techno Capitalism*. Lanham, Maryland, New York and Oxford: Rowman & Littlefield.

———. 2009. *Globalization and Techno-capitalism: The Political Economy of Corporate Power and Technological Domination*. Burlington VT: Ashgate Publishers.

Suarez-Villa, L. 2012. *Techno-capitalism: A Critical Perspective on Technological Innovation and Corporatism*. Philadelphia: Temple University Press.

Thorat, S. 2006. 'Higher Education in India: Emerging Issues Related to Access, Inclusiveness and Quality'. Nehru Memorial Lecture, University of Mumbai, Mumbai.

3

The Redefinition of Equality and Excellence and Declining Goals of Democratic Egalitarianism in Higher Education

Padma Velaskar

INTRODUCTION

The past two decades have witnessed a dramatic departure from the post-independence model of education and social transformation. This transformation is spearheaded by the forces of globalisation. There is a considerable global pressure to redefine egalitarian national ideals and national goals. With its own brand of neoliberalism as a governing ideology, supported by soft or hard versions of neoconservative cultural majoritarian ideology having made a significant impact on the political scenario, the Indian state's development strategy grounded in welfare capitalism is well on the decline. The national education system reflects this ideological shift with marked changes in its goals, policies, structures and content. The national education system reflects this ideological shift with marked change in its goals, policies, content and structures. The education system is now tied closely to the market, seriously eroding the state's role as prime educational provider and redefining its control. The 'right turn' in Indian education, to use Michael Apple's apt label (2001), has set alarm bells ringing among the nation's egalitarians, already deeply concerned about the dwindling capacities of the education system to redress mounting educational inequalities. The growth of the private sector in education is feared to further widen inequalities in social access to education. The protagonists of the market, however, assure that the entry of private capital into what is increasingly termed as the educational 'sector' would not only stimulate expansion but breathe life into a moribund state system, advancing access, quality and excellence in ways that can only fetch rich dividends to the nation in a globally competitive world.

In a deeply stratified and divided society, it is important in the context of such massive changes to address questions of what happens to basic national goals and the agenda of attaining equality and justice, based on constitutional values. Given that education was assigned a central role in establishing a democratic egalitarian nation state, what promise do the new economic adjustments, political and ideological, and policy shifts hold out for those subordinated by multiple bases of structural oppression—gender, caste, class, religion and tribal community—out of which derives their conditions of educational exclusion, discrimination and disadvantage? Taking a historical–sociological perspective, the chapter examines the shifting definitions of equality and excellence as they relate to each other and principles underlying them in higher education in India. We further examine the implications of these shifts for fulfilling the hitherto unfulfilled agendas of attaining greater equality as well as higher and equitable levels of excellence. The chapter argues for a more structural and historical understanding of the relationship between social inequality, national educational agendas and their implications for the attainment of national goals.

Traditional concern with educational equality and excellence has largely revolved around the issues of access and attainments on the one hand and on issues of standards and meritocracy on the other. Key dimensions of educational environments that impinge on equality and excellence such as cultural, political and social processes, social relations and the shaping of educational experiences while being increasingly problematized in research do not enter the dominant discourse on educational equality. Also, quite ignored are curricular content and process which also shape access, experiences and outcomes. Theoretical debates on the close links between knowledge and power and perspectives on knowledge as power have fostered wide-ranging critiques of epistemologies of knowledge from southern, feminist and multiple subaltern perspectives. The issues of how societal links between knowledge culture, ideology and power get represented in knowledge selection and transmission in higher education curriculum should be of central significance to concerns of equality and excellence.

We argue, from the outset, that both ideology and practice of equality and excellence fell far short of societal needs and demands and that they were narrowly construed and indifferently implemented. Further, there was a gap between policy rhetoric and policy implementation which resulted in a post-colonial educational development that was marked by deep inequalities—regional, social, cultural. We argue that higher education was more committed to 'national' concerns of economic development and consolidation of social power than to social transformation. With respect to the latter, both discourse and policy fell short in social cultural and economic terms and in the realms of both structures and contents designed. This, in turn, gave higher education an elitist character and as with school education, expansionism served largely as a masquerade for equality (Velaskar 2010). Not only did it fetch concrete gains in terms of access, attainment and mobility but also provide the space and the wherewithal to enable ongoing cultural challenges and structural shifts in the context of economic change and democratic politics. Concurring with the critical view that dominant notions of meritocracy and the performative conceptions of excellence that they overwhelmingly demanded, served as a facade, a smokescreen for the maintenance of privilege, we argue that such standardised notions of excellence which, in the context of the Indian education system, took extremely narrow forms, do not resonate with multiple educational goals and ideals of public good and democratic citizenship. We suggest the need for broader, deeper, consensual and relevant notions of excellence.

Neoliberalism marked a systemic change: from a principally state institution, education made the transition to a largely private one, to be organised along quasi market principles wherein considerations of investment–profit trade-offs and of economies of scale would not be viewed as illegitimate and be in tune with the demands of national and international markets. India reflects global trends of massification, privatisation, diversification and internationalisation of higher education even as the official notion of equality gets further diluted. The spiralling demand and burgeoning enrolments in private institutions notwithstanding, we argue that though the new policies appear to have both positive and negative effects, they are predominantly negative. The claimed positive egalitarian and excellence effects are illusory, and prospects for enhancing them stand reduced. We argue that even as access to higher education has grown multifold, 'real' educational gain in terms of equitable quantitative and qualitative attainment is completely unassured. Behind the chimera of rising educational and job opportunity created by global movements of labour and business and rapid urbanisation, there is a quiet consolidation of old and new emergent patterns of stratification. In this context, the policy of reservations has gathered new strength and is seen as panacea by an increasing number of groups and communities who perceive themselves to be disadvantaged. At the same time, resentment of beneficiaries continues to be a ground for more hostility and discrimination. The climate for the pursuit of democratic egalitarianism is further vitiated by the rise of neoconservative ideology, which casting a shadow on constitutional ideological principles, attempts to use the education system to reconfigure them along their exclusionary and discriminatory cultural majoritarian beliefs.

The chapter is organised as follows: The first section presents a brief backdrop of nationalist ideology of equality and social justice and also reflects on the principles applied and strategies formulated to address constitutional directives with a focus on state designated social categories requiring special attention. The next section critically reviews the notions of equality and excellence as expressed in national higher education policy and practice. Finally, moving on to the Indian experience of globalised neoliberalism, we attempt to capture and evaluate the shifting paradigm of equality and excellence in the context of ideological change, political dynamics and structural shifts in the higher education system. The chapter ends with a brief concluding section that considers prospects for the future.

NATIONALIST IDEOLOGY OF EQUALITY AND SOCIAL JUSTICE

The ideology of equality and social justice took shape over a century and half of popular upsurge against unjust excesses of colonial rule as well as revolts against oppressive dimensions and ideologies of indigenous society and culture and in the modernist context of the nationalist aspirations articulated by the freedom movement. Its official embedding in the constitution of the post-colonial state was a political compromise between different contending groups. The ideology was bitterly contested as discourses from all sides attempted to change the terms of discourse with differing formulations of state, nation, community and citizenship. For a society that had lived by principles of hierarchy, heredity and fatalism, the granting of formal equality, which made all castes, religious groups, races, the genders equal in the eyes of law, was truly revolutionary. The constitution itself was 'by its existence a social revolutionary statement' (Austin 2000), giving expression to a new national conception of the good society. It guaranteed equality of citizenship, equal protection in the eyes of the law to all, irrespective of ascriptive status and substantive equality in terms of access to public space and public political participation (Kaviraj 2000). It rested on solemn resolution, on behalf of the people, to secure for all citizens justice—social, economic, political—and equality of status and opportunity along with the other two core ideals of liberty and fraternity.

In the context of a consociational democracy, equality measures proceeded cautiously on consensual lines. In a contextual democracy which essentially sought a modern transformation of a traditional society, liberal constitutional principles of individual liberties and rights were combined those of group/community rights, adapting to ground realities of group identities and cultural pluralisms (Frankel 2000). Untouchability was abolished and caste, gender, religious and any other form of invidious discrimination was prohibited. The constitution promised both individual and group rights and converted constitutional arrangement for a majority–minority framework that would provide the basis for real political equality (Kaviraj 2000). In this context, egalitarian ideology essentially constituted a synthesis of two divergent principles, the meritarian and the compensatory (Beteille 1983). Even as legal equality guaranteed non-discrimination on ascriptive criteria and promised equal opportunity to each individual, in apparent contradiction to this first principle, was upheld a second principle. The latter is based on the conviction that socially disadvantaged groups whose 'backwardness' stems from a history of oppression need special support. It hence rejects passive non-discrimination. Grounded in the histories of oppression, indignities and disabilities, the principle is underscored by notions of justice, fairness, restitution and reparation that would offset systemic and cumulative deprivation (Galanter 1984).

Positive discrimination was bitterly debated and opposed in the constituent assembly debates. The violation of the first principle of equality, namely, equal treatment of all, was recognised by the constitution makers, including Nehru and Ambedkar, the main architects of India's democratic–egalitarian project. Ambedkar himself recognised it as a violation of the first principle of equal treatment, but supported the compensatory principle as an essential temporary measure to overcome historical inequalities, injustices and deprivations and participation on more equal terms with the rest of society. This broader vision attempted to dissolve the perceived contradiction between individual rights and group rights that is inherent in the synthesis. A legal framework was already in place since colonial times. Expanding the framework, there are now varied articles of the Constitution under which the state is empowered to make special provisions for identified groups. To begin with, four social categories, namely, the scheduled castes (SCs), scheduled tribes (STs) and other backward classes (henceforth, OBC) and women, were identified as potential beneficiaries. While the policy was accepted for the SCs and STs, the formulation of national policy along similar lines for the OBC became a controversial affair. The First Backward Classes Commission was shelved by the Centre following a pragmatic decision to let the states decide the matter. The issue of whether economic class or caste should be the ground of backwardness was settled in the favour of caste which in effect came to mean marginalised backward (predominantly Shudra) castes other than formerly so called untouchable castes. The issue of positive discrimination for the OBCs was revived at the national level in 1990, when the Janata Dal-led National Front government revived the Second Backward Classes Commission (also known as Mandal Commission) which was appointed in 1978.

As against the castes, equality issues concerning the STs, conceptualised as groups 'outside state and civilisation', proved a more complex category to respond. They are singled out for special protection and compensation due to their inaccessibility, spatial and cultural isolation, dialects, animism, primitive religion occupation and language (Galanter 1984). For Tribals, arose distinctive ethical moral problems of defining their place in the new nation state. Tribal 'equality' posed dilemmas in the context of complex variations in the social location and historical presence of the concerned communities. They demand a sensitive approach which would take into account complex histories and peculiarities arising out of distinctive heterogeneous cultural characteristics and heritages. The basic dilemma was whether to assimilate or insulate the tribes and what should be the nature of state policy in tribal development. While sharing Constitutional provisions for social, political, occupational and educational empowerment through positive discrimination with the SCs, there is an extensive set of safeguards towards preserving their territorial and cultural integrity and autonomy in the course of their 'development'. Living in remote niches in hills, forests and plains, their location, numbers and characteristics all underscore their marginality and vulnerability. Equality and justice concerns the preservation of their ways of life with equal respect; justice and dignity give them the autonomy to define their life course. However, constitutional promises have been betrayed again and again.

Equality legislation towards gender equality was deeply affected as was towards caste by dominance of the conservative element in the decision-making processes. Male supremacist forces in national and constitutional leadership were in no mood to accord anything more than formal equality to women as reflected in the turbulent Constituent Assembly debates on women's right to property (Som 2008). Moreover, the long history of struggles waged by moderate and radical social reformers, women's dynamic participation in the freedom struggle, their hard fought educational and political achievements and the trail-blazing launch of an autonomous women's movement could not assure women's uncontested acceptance as equal and enlightened citizenry. After the Independence, the Constitution went little beyond formal equality to enable this 'weaker' section to gather strength. It is in the aftermath of 'Towards Equality', the central government's report brought out in 1975, which showed a shocking decline in women's status and participation during what was assumed to be an era of post-colonial progress, that the state took notice of widening gender inequality. However, it was left to the second more militant, radical and grassroots phase of women's movement to lock horns with the state on women's rights and issues and provide substance to the state commitment to gender equality. To the movement, goes full credit for firmly ensconcing women's issues on the national political agenda, getting new empowering legislations passed and widening the terms of the gender discourse in the country.

Two kinds of minorities were recognised by the Indian constitution—religious and language based. Colonial debates about political representation and safeguards to the minorities were set aside; the minorities were firmly placed in the domain of culture in post-colonial and post-partition contexts (Hasan 2009; Mahajan 2011). Religious groups were constructed as cultural communities and accorded religious freedom, freedom to conserve language script and culture. Both religious and linguistic minorities were accorded equal access to state supported institutions as well as rights to establish their own. They were also protected from state discrimination (Hasan 2009; Robinson 2012). Minority issues were not considered within the purview of social justice, but cultural justice through the granting of cultural rights and their politico- economic concerns were reduced to sphere of preserving culture. Stiff opposition precluded the extension of reservations to minorities so much so that Dalits of Christian and Muslim origin were excluded from this benefit. Paradoxically, no such discrimination exists with respect to Christians of tribal origin, to whom the category of STs applies (Robinson 2012). Specific problems, especially concerning the Muslim minority in the context of communalisation of polity, have been intermittently addressed through setting up institutional and policy frameworks without incorporating them into constitutional framework.

How does the basic egalitarian structure and concerns related to equality and integration of the various disadvantaged groups get reflected in educational discourse and, more specifically, how were equality and excellence conceptualised in higher educational policy within a long-term developmental perspective? The next section addresses these issues.

HIGHER EDUCATION: EQUALITY AND EXCELLENCE IN POLICY DISCOURSE AND PRACTICE

In the context of the Nehruvian state's commitment to a modernised development of agrarian and industrial economy and to the formation of a democratic egalitarian society, a great faith was placed in education as a master instrument of development. However, despite the call for its revolutionisation, the monumental task of preparing a blueprint for an education system as a whole was neglected until the appointment of the Kothari Commission (KC) in the mid-1960s. Higher education was prioritised early with the appointment of the University Education Commission in 1948. The reports of both the Commissions provide a good understanding of the educational thought of the political and intellectual elite of the times. The University Education Commission, chaired by S. Radhakrishnan, took a broad view of educational purpose assigning lofty goals to higher education in the creation of a new India. It held a balanced, holistic view of education, emphasising on social sciences and humanities, agricultural and rural higher education and the need to preserve the country's composite culture. However, in its conceptions of democracy, equality and social justice, it was peculiarly ambivalent, articulating an individual-oriented approach in a society of massive injustices and inequalities and a wistful longing for village community. The KC, operating within a cultural frame of liberal–democratic, technological modernity, portrayed the university as a modern liberal institution oriented to the public good. In its view, the objective of university education was to serve as the conscience of nation. The critical assessment of society, objectively and unafraid, was a crucial function of universities in the absence of enlightened public opinion. An emphasis on the importance of individual thinking and dissent within a climate of tolerance was to be accompanied by the preservation of intellectual integrity with the responsibility to improve the society. University was seen as a forum for critical assessment, dissent, tolerance and autonomy (Government of India 1966). The KC championed lofty goals of humanism, deepening understanding, the developing moral leadership and the promotion of equality and justice. However, it did not engage deeply with nationalist educational discourse that emerged in the course of the freedom struggle or with educational discourses of anti-caste, women's or tribal movement or subaltern knowledge critiques and alternatives.

The KC expressed a strong commitment to the constitutional ideology of equality of opportunity. The ideal was to be mainly pursued through structural reform of the school system. A common school system, it ambitiously believed, would lay a strong foundation for 'just meritocracy' by tapping the entire 'national pool of ability' and taking responsibility to cultivate all available talent, and ensure progressive equality of opportunity to all sections of the population (Government of India 1966). This 'equality of opportunity and of quality' was no doubt a radical policy directive in a historically exclusionary context that cried out to the need of attending to those historically excluded. At the higher education level, however, the Commission posed the issues of equality and excellence oppositionally. It advocated a policy of restricted expansion of and selective admissions in higher education, drawing attention to the worrisome fact of an overproduction of general graduates. The KC, thus, recommended the special nurture of talent and special opportunities for 'the meritorious' and asserted that the goal of higher education was to train and select the most talented people for important technical jobs. It did not seem to be concerned with equality of opportunity at this level. For all its modernist views, the KC also propounded a highly conservative view on women's higher education, defining its main purpose in terms of entry into nurturing occupation along with domesticity. It, thus, undermined the constitutional vision of women as equal and autonomous citizens. It is significant that there was a studied silence on equality for the SCs, STs and minorities.

Excellence, a nebulous and arbitrary concept, was constructed by the KC in a broad sense. It lay in the achievement of the basic educational purpose, namely, the cultural production of ideal democratic citizens. However, also of considerable policy concern was the issue of 'standards' of institutional and individual excellence. They were defined in the more conventional terms of quality of facilities, teaching–learning processes and outcomes. The KC also came up with an elitist solution of creating major universities that would be models of excellence in certain core areas that were pertinent to industrial economy. While the model was exclusivist, in all fairness to the KC, it must be acknowledged that there was also a commitment to building a tradition of academic life in India that would be comparable to the finest in the world.

A discussion of what constitutes valid knowledge did not enter policy discourse of either equality or excellence in education. Policy was unequivocal in prioritising desired fields of colonial knowledge (in particular, science and technology) and in establishing hierarchical rankings of knowledge in institutions. Setting aside nationalist critique of Eurocentric knowledge and indigenous philosophies of nationalist education, an elite consensus on higher education policy attributed cognitive authority to dominating knowledge of the Western sciences (Bhattacharya 1998). Higher education was charged with developing the frontiers of this knowledge, promoting a new culture of technological modernity and producing qualified personnel to fulfil manpower needs. Even the vision for agricultural development rested on an application of science and technological knowledge to achieve higher production levels (Kumar 1996), where even Gandhi's ideas of basic education were confined to the margins, neither the rich corpus of indigenous knowledge systems (philosophical, productive, humanistic) nor the critical social and emancipatory knowledge of the subalterns would find a space (Marglin and Marglin 1990; Nandy 1988; Rodrigues 2006). In hindsight, it is clear that the KC's perspective was not grounded in historical sociocultural and political realities of the common people but it represented rather the worldview of the English educated elite of the times. It lacked a critical perspective on society and a theory and philosophy of social transformation, which would envisage a society based on social justice and equality rather than on social integration.

The first national educational policy that was enunciated in 1968 was an incredibly weak reflection of the KC's vision. The policy rejected the KC's recommendation of restricted access to higher education and brought into force a policy of expansionism, ostensibly on the grounds of equality. Equality of educational opportunity was translated as expansionism at all levels of education (Velaskar 2010). Indeed, expansionism was well in force even prior to framing of the policy. So was the pursuit of the dream to build world-class national institutions of science and technology and other prestigious fields.

However, there were many glaring gaps between policy—especially what was most valuable and worthy in it—and its implementation.

THE POLITICS OF INEQUALITY AND HIGHER EDUCATIONAL EXPANSION

Post-colonial higher education grew dramatically but unequally and unevenly between the 1950s and 1970s. Education being a concurrent subject (until 1976), national policy took divergent forms and trajectories, shaped by the economic health, structural inequality and the political commitment to educational development of individual states and union territories. Although accepted in principle, the common school ideal, on which was hinged the KC's project of equal educational opportunities (EEO), was never pursued. Some states did build robust public education systems but failed to achieve universalisation of elementary education.

Secondary education and higher education were both restricted. The enrolments were modest and the GER remained low, and the expansion was in advanced states and among the urban elite and middle classes with limited access to the rural groups. There was an uncontrolled expansion of higher education in contexts, where democratic polity exerted considerable influence on public policy of higher education (Rudolph and Rudolph 1972), and nobler goals envisaged by the KC fell by the wayside. The elites cornered grants to set up aided institutions that minimally followed norms of excellence or egalitarian directives. Colleges used political influence to pursue goals and protect stakes (Rudolph and Rudolph 1972). Thus, even though a public good in theory, in practice higher education was a private good whereby benefits are accrued to elite and privileged. Moreover, the agenda of universal egalitarian expansion of higher education became sectarian and parochial. A statement by Kaviraj (1997) that public institutions failed to remain public was eminently applicable to education.

The close interaction between politics and education displaced educational goals. Standards of institutional and individual excellence were sacrificed at the altar of credentialism. A deep concern with quality and of standards was frequently voiced and the (mal)functioning of the university system in terms of internal structural issues, funds, politics and corruption was critically analysed (Bharadwaj 1987; Rath 1992; Sethi 1983; Singh 1983, 1985). The challenge of maintaining excellence and the high traditions of a public institution could be met by very few. Moreover, a dichotomous policy ensures that a part of the system operates at a high level of quality (Altbach 2004). The former serves the need of a high-tech economy and interacts with international knowledge systems. The rest of the system, comprising state and mofussil universities, caters to the spiralling demand without having basic infrastructure or adequate funds. Caught between elitism and politicisation, the higher education system as a whole failed to deliver either equality or excellence. In fact, equality and excellence were seen as opposing ideas. It needs to be emphasised that the opposition was created through policy and practice and need not be assumed. It may also be pointed that institutions certified as 'excellent' may be academically so but may hold rather poor records on equality. A case in point is that of the IITs, which long resisted the implementation of positive discrimination policies.

In this bleak scenario, equality goals stood largely aborted. The progress made is mixed and unequal for women, still leaving them disadvantaged in terms of ideological constraints and institutional barriers that constrain choices. The policy of positive discrimination played a major role in equalising access for the socially disadvantaged groups, the Dalits and the Tribals. Some progress was made but the latter have lagged behind the former. While it has been a protracted struggle by the subordinated groups against the apathetic, if not hostile state implementation machinery, the policy has been successful in redistributing educational opportunity. In particular, the mobility levels and political consciousness attained by the Dalits have vindicated Ambedkar's expectations of the role that higher education would play in Dalit liberation. Inspired by emancipatory ideologies, Dalits and Tribal groups fought societal and institutional resistance and discrimination to engage in self-motivated struggles to utilize state policies (Velaskar 1998). In the meanwhile, the logic of private interest in higher education witnessed further extension through the establishment of capitation fee for colleges in advanced capitalist regions in the period prior to the invasion of global capitalism.

CHANGING CONCEPTIONS OF EQUALITY AND EXCELLENCE UNDER GLOBAL CAPITALISM AND NEOCONSERVATISM

It was on this predominantly unequal terrain of higher education that global neoliberal agenda was foisted in the late 1980s. Global

capitalism exerted pressure on India to structurally adjust and liber-
alise its economy. Information and innovation, knowledge, goods and
services are fundamental to global processes. Transnationalism of
education policy and provision followed and the national systems
of knowledge and higher education were inexorably geared to new
knowledge and skill requirements of globalising economies (Brown
et al. 1997; Burbules and Torres 2000; Carnoy 2000). There is a huge
empire of knowledge creation and self-validation (Apple 2000 and
2001). Under the tutelage of bilateral and multilateral funding
organisations, higher education policy in India involved a drastic shift
from state-funded to private sector provision of education, and the
transformation of education from a public, merit good to a private,
non-merit one. The structure and content of higher education is
linked to changing economy, and is also internationally defined. New
relationships were forged between the state and the market, with
the state circumscribing its role as policymaker and provider and
turning into a facilitator of commercial enterprise in education (Tilak
2005). Recommendations of strongly anti-egalitarian corporate interests are privileged, while those of eminent scholars and educators
(e.g., Yashpal Committee Report) languish. Most fundamentally,
given the powerful impact of global economy and job markets on
knowledge, the very purposes and meanings of education have
undergone a drastic change. Education became almost exclusively
economistic in its goals, a means of fulfilling individual career dreams
and eventually a market commodity like any other.

The resultant processes have been well charted: growing privatisation with remarkable increases in private universities and self-
financing colleges; privatised massification of education reflected in
soaring enrolments; a massification of the post-higher secondary
system, including of the non-university 'higher' education at the
post-secondary stage; diversification and vocationalisation of institutions and curricula, oriented largely to employability in the new
service, knowledge and entrepreneurial economies; decline in
social sciences, basic research components of university education
(Altbach 2004 and 2009; Das 2007; Jayaram 2004; Tilak 2004, 2014;
Varghese 2015). The persistent neglect of standards and the negative implications of commercial elements and neoliberal knowledge
in recasting democratic goals have been powerfully highlighted
(Hargopal 2010; Patnaik 2010; Shah 2005).

What happens to the state's equity and excellence agenda? In
accordance with the new global ideology of equity, the Indian state
too has 'downsized' its egalitarian commitment from equality of

opportunity to equity. This is tantamount to a shift away from con-stitutional principles. Equity as an ideological construct/ideal rests on notions of needs and justice and makes value judgements about fair distributions/apportionment of resources and equal representa-tion of social groups. In recasting the constitutional ideological syn-thesis, the education policy 1986 articulated a curious merger of EEO and equity: 'The new policy will lay special emphasis on the removal of disparities and to equalize educational opportunity by attending to the specific needs of those who have been denied equality so far' (Government of India 1986, as cited in Velaskar 2010). At the turn of the new century, a more restricted notion of equity—that of sta-tistical representation—is now deployed in a context where univer-salisation of even elementary education was yet a distant dream. This approach is accompanied by a selective strategy that seeks to address issues of under-provision and underrepresentation through locating and targeting disadvantaged areas and groups. The educa-tion policy of 1986 instituted a host of support measures at school level for those severely educationally disadvantaged groups such as Dalits, Adivasis, girls and minorities (especially, Muslims). Reservations for the differentially abled in higher education were introduced. In an economic context of polarising economic inequality and persis-tent poverty and the dominant logic of the market, which is inher-ently anti equality, and complex dynamics in the politics of caste and backwardness, it is politically essential for governments to sustain inequality at manageable levels. Most of the policy and program-matic interventions, however, are limited in scope, economically frugal and aimed at addressing distress (Congress-led UPA's Common Minimum Programme). At the higher education level, public funding is geared for the maintenance of central universities and institutions and to fill up backlog of institutional provision in several hitherto neglected states and regions, for example, the Northeast India.

The institution of 27% OBC reservations in 2006 via Mandal II could also be viewed as a bid to assuage discontent and anxiety among the non-privileged on the educational front in the context of growing privatisation by redistributing scarce goods. As rightly stated, 'The grammar of entitlements has become the new language of politics' (Hasan 2009). The move raised complex issues about criteria of social backwardness and the continued expansion and extension of the reservation policy in public debate. It also had negative effects in terms of escalating social tensions and caste–class hostilities at a time when expansion of the public system was being perceptibly curtailed and any new equity measure brought on the wrath of

non-beneficiaries across the spectrum. A worsening communal scenario led to responses to minority communities, for example, the
appointment of the Sachar Committee to look into the developmental issues of the Muslims. The present dispensation, however, known
for its antagonism to reservations has failed to fulfil its obligations
even to Dalit students, evoking student anger and protest. In a recent
event, this cold apathy caused the tragic suicide of a Dalit student.

What are the prospects for attaining the conception of equity
effects? In a structurally transformed higher educational structure,
the differentiation of various sectors, colleges and fields of study is
also accompanied by stratification in terms of global worth of the
knowledge field, academic standards, social prestige and economic
cost. The ability to pay and academic scores are the two main criteria
of admission. It is a money-cum-merit system in which merit continues to be measured in terms of scores in qualifying exams. The
examination system has been discredited in many parts of the country
for serious malpractices apart from the fact that it gives unfair advantages to those with capital. The system today is more finely stratified
and crystallised than before; it ranges from elite private institutions
catering to the rich at the top to the ill-equipped teaching shops that
serve the poor at the bottom. In terms of social composition, the different components of the higher education system reflect the hierarchical and divided character of society. In a system dominated by
private sector, state efforts to regulate access policies of the different types of higher education institutions in the favour of those without money, power and/or with social disadvantage/disability are
weak and ineffective. So also does the state fail to regulate normative
practices of institutions, whether in terms of the structure of paid and
merit seats or their infrastructural and academic standards. The system favours those with superior economic, social and cultural capital
the most. The 'best' institutions are both exclusive and exclusionary.
In context of internationalisation of education, there are new kinds of
goal posts that are set by privileged. Those at the bottom end of the
class–caste hierarchy are still excluded at elementary or secondary
school levels itself. Others are tracked into inferior streams of this
expanding private system and are increasingly expected to bear the
cost of this inferior education. State support in terms of public institutions and positive discrimination falls woefully short of demand.
Consequently, the system perpetuates old inequalities and generates
multiple new ones based on wealth, prestige and power.

Further, in a global environment in which national goals are set
in terms on enhancing competitiveness in global knowledge, the

privatised, hierarchised system produces new parameters and hierarchies of excellence and levels of authoritarianism that do not augur well for the creation of democratic institutions. Moreover, in a society wherein market values are now prized societal values, notions of higher educational excellence have also become narrow market specific, judged in terms of market value of the professional knowledge that one gains. Excellence is redefined and is increasingly emphasised in relation to parameters set by global economy that have little to do with public good in the country. The devaluation of social sciences, humanities and arts as being foundational to a good education is aimed at destroying critical social thinking. Notwithstanding token initiatives to include women's, Dalit or Tribal studies in the higher education system and the beneficial impacts that they have had, the focus of state policy is on mainstreaming people into dominant ideologies and cultures and eclipsing 'minor' languages and cultures. As with individuals, excellence of institutions and degrees and performances as products are media packaged, promoted and sold. Whatever the privileges and material goods it fetches, these characteristics do a disservice to not only society but also to youth, the supposed beneficiaries who are shaped by them. We are making lives of even rich kids poor by narrow constrictive educational experiences overlaid by anxieties and insecurities of achievement expectations, aggressive competition and failure. Gender, caste, class, religion and tribe, and regional chauvinism still endemic in society also overtly or covertly mark higher educational institutions leading to growing levels of caste, gender, tribe and minority harassment and violence. Values of humane individualism and collectivism, egalitarianism and fraternity are vanishing. Today, their place is taken by vocational skilling, which is equated with education. Universities are not seats of learning and character formation, education in wider sense, but institutes with brand values. By allying with global markets, higher education is also made complicit in spreading knowledge streams associated with destructive development that has brought ruin to the masses and to the environment. Notions of merit developed by those who have given shape to these realities can only be false.

CONCLUSION

The chapter has argued that the shifting paradigm in the context of the transition from colonial to post-colonial to global society has meant a weakening of the constitutional principles, reflected in the decline of both equality and excellence goals of higher education. Failing to draw upon historical legacies of subaltern resistance and its own home-grown radical ideologies of equality, humanity and dignity, and put into place a more authentic social transformation project that was relevant to the common people, elite consensus on equality and excellence was essentially elitist, restrictive and minimalist from the outset. The education system was not true to the overall structure of constitutional egalitarianism. Mainly the nation state's neglect of primary and secondary education has cost the nation heavy in terms of fulfilling its democratic egalitarian goals. Building equity in access and excellence on a foundation of established inequalities and inequities with neoliberalism and neoconservatism, as governing ideologies today, is impossible. What may be best expected in under the new system in a market economy is minimalist, segregated, unequal inclusion based on intersections of gender, caste, tribe, religion, region, disability, etc. Also, may be expected is a deeper entrenchment of class inequalities in opportunities for 'excellence' in terms of existing global definitions, as barriers posed by the 'merit-cum-money' system are impossible to cross for the socially subordinated and the poor. Substantive equality of outcomes and achievement cannot be serious considerations in the present context, as the neoliberal minimalist equity and diversity strategies do in fact show. Massification is more of a strategy of political containment and social representation than of social justice or equality.

There are no half ways to equality, democracy and excellence. Even as one may be compelled to contend with dominating forces, the contemporary economic and cultural ideology that governs education and its educational purpose, including the growingly authoritarian and undemocratic threats from within and outside the higher education system, must be challenged. There is an attack on egalitarian norms and values and threat to egalitarian ideals. The new minimalist diluted ideology of neoliberal equity and inclusion conceals the deeper entrenchment of class inequalities, which albeit shaped by caste, gender, tribe, religion and multiple ethnicities, have come to dominate the education system at the national and local levels. As the 'violence of imperialist categories' and knowledge systems that were once considered of public interest knowledge are revealed, there is a need to engage with the rising questioning of hegemonic, ethnocentric and oppressive forms of new and old dominating knowledge systems, whether western or indigenous. It is time to strengthen alternative viewpoints, and universities must strengthen themselves to provide the space for critical and authentic structural and cultural expressions in the interests of equality, social justice and 'true' excellence.

REFERENCES

Altbach, P.G. 2004. 'The Past and Future of Asian Universities: Twenty-first Century Challenges'. In *Asian Universities: Historical Perspectives and Contemporary Challenges*, edited by P.G. Altbach and T. Umakoshi, 13–32, Baltimore: The John Hopkins University Press.

———. 2009. 'The Giants Awake: Higher Education Systems in China and India'. *Economic and Political Weekly* 44 (23): 39–51.

Apple, Michael. 2000. *Official Knowledge Democratic Education in a Conservative Age*. London: Routledge.

———. 2001. 'Comparing Neo-liberal Projects and Inequality in Education'. *Comparative Education* 37 (4): 409–23.

Austin, G. 2000. *The Indian Constitution: Cornerstone of a Nation*. New Delhi: Oxford University Press.

Beteille, A. 1983. *The Idea of Natural Inequality and Other Essays*. USA: Oxford University Press.

Bharadwaj, K. 1987. 'Unrest in Higher Education: The Broader Issues'. *Economic and Political Weekly* 22 (42/43): 1801–04.

Bhattacharya, S. 1998. *Contested Terrain: Perspectives on Education in India*. New Delhi: Orient Blackswan.

Burbules, N.C., and C.A. Torres. eds. 2000. *Globalization and Education*. New York: Routledge.

Carnoy, Martin. 2000. 'Globalisation and Educational Reform'. In *Globalisation and Education Integration and Contestation Cultures*, edited by Nellie Stromquist and Karen Monkman. London: Rowman and Littlefield publishers.

Das, S. 2007. 'The Higher Education in India and the Challenge of Globalisation'. *Social Scientist* 35 (3/4): 47–67.

Frankel, Francine. 2000. 'Introduction Contextual Democracy: Intersections of Society, Culture and Politics in India'. In *Transforming India: Social and Political Dynamics of Democracy*, edited by Francine R. Frankel, Zoya Hasan, Rajeev Bhargava, and Balveer Arora, pp. 1–25. New York: Oxford University Press.

Galanter, M. 1984. *Competing Equalities: Law and the Backward Classes in India*. New Delhi: Oxford University Press.

Government of India. 1966. *Education and National Development: Report of the Education Commission 1964–66*. New Delhi: Ministry of Education.

Halsey, A.H., Lauder, Hugh, Brown, Phillip, and Amy Stuart Wells. 1997. 'The Transformation of Education and Society: An Introduction'. In *Education Culture, Economy, Society*, edited by Halsey A.H. et al., 7–44. Oxford: Oxford University Press.

Hargopal, G. 2010. 'Right to Higher Education: An Overview'. In *Neo-liberal Assault on Higher Education: An Agenda for Putting India on Sale*, edited by Anil Sadgopal, 11–26. Hyderabad: All Indian Forum for Right to Education.

Hasan, Z. 2009. *Politics of Inclusion: Castes, Minorities and Affirmative Action*. New Delhi: Oxford University Press.

Jayaram, N. 2004. 'Higher Education in India: Massification and Change'. In *Asian Universities: Historical Perspectives and Contemporary Challenges*, edited by P.G. Altbach and T. Umakoshi, 85–107. Baltimore: The John Hopkins University Press.

Kaviraj, Sudipta. 1997. 'The Modern State in India'. In *Dynamics of State Formation*, edited by Doornbos and S. Kaviraj, 225–50. New Delhi: SAGE.

———. 2000. 'Democracy and Social Inequality'. In *Transforming India: Social and Political Dynamics of Democracy*, edited by F.R. Frankel, 89–105. New York: Oxford University Press.

Kumar, Krishna. 1996. 'Agricultural Modernisation and Education Contours of a Point of Departure'. *Economic and Political Weekly* 31 (35/37): 2367–73.

Mahajan, Gurpreet. ed. 2011. *Accommodating Diversity: Ideas and Institutional Practices*, 1–50. New Delhi: Oxford University Press.

Marglin, F.A., and S.A. Marglin. 1990. *Dominating Knowledge: Development, Culture and Resistance*. Oxford: Clarendon Press.

Nandy, Ashish. ed. 1988. *Science, Hegemony and Violence A requiem for Modernity*. New Delhi: Oxford University Press.

Patnaik, Prabhat. 2010. 'Alternative Perspectives on Higher Education in the Context of Globalization'. In *Neo-Liberal Assault on Higher Education: An Agenda for putting India on Sale*, edited by Anil Sadgopal, 27–39. Hyderabad: All Indian Forum for Right to Education.

Rath, Nilkanth. 1992. 'Higher Education: A Plea for Reorganisation'. In *Economic and Political Weekly* 27 (10/11): 535–39.

Robinson, Rowena. ed. 2012. 'Introduction'. In *Minority Studies*, 1–48. New Delhi: Oxford University Press.

Rodrigues, Valerian. 2006. 'Dalit Bahujan Discourse in India'. In *Political Ideas in Modern India: Thematic Explorations*, edited by V.R. Mehta and T. Panthan, 46–72. New Delhi: SAGE.

Rudolph, S.H., and L.I., Rudolph. 1972. *Education and Politics in India: Studies in Organization, Society and Policy*. Delhi: Oxford University Press.

Sethi, J.D. 1983. *Crisis and Collapse of Higher Education in India*. New Delhi: Vikas Publications.

Shah, A.M. 2005. 'Higher Education and Research: Roots of Mediocrity'. *Economic and Political Weekly* 40 (22/23): 2234–42.

Singh, Amrik. 1985. *Redeeming the University Essays in Educational Policy*. New Delhi: Ajanta Publications.

Singh, N. 1983. *Education Under Siege: A Sociological Study and Private Colleges*. New Delhi: Concept Publications.

Som, R. 2008. 'Jawaharlal Nehru and the Hindu Code: A Victory of Symbol Over Substance?' In *Women and Social Reform in Modern India: A Reader*, edited by Sumit Sarkar and Tania Sarkar. Bloomington: Indiana University Press.

Tilak, J.B.G. 2004. 'Public Subsidies in Education in India'. *Economic and Political Weekly* 39 (4): 343–59.

———. 2005. 'Higher Education in Trishanku: Hanging Between State and Market'. *Economic and Political Weekly* 40 (37): 4029–37.

———. 2014. 'Private Higher Education in India'. *Economic and Political Weekly* 49 (40): 32–38.

Varghese, N.V. 2015. *Challenges of Massification of Higher Education in India*. CPRHE Research Paper No.1. New Delhi: National University of Educational Planning and Administration.

Velaskar, Padma. 1998. 'Ideology, Education and the Political Struggle for Liberation: Change and Challenge among the Dalits of Maharashtra'. In *Education, Development and Underdevelopment*, edited by S. Shukla and R. Kaul, 210–40. New Delhi: SAGE.

———. 2010. 'Quality and Inequality in Indian Education: Some Critical Policy Concerns'. *Contemporary Education Dialogue* 7 (1): 58–93.

4

Economic and Educational Inequalities in India: Access and Outcome Indicators for Different Socio-religious Groups

Amitabh Kundu

INTRODUCTION

The development performance of India is viewed optimistically both in the current scenario and in terms of its sustainability in the coming three to four decades. The deceleration of growth in the early years of the second decade, after recording over 8% growth performance during a large part of the first decade of the present century has been viewed as a temporary phenomenon. Asian Development Bank has predicted that the 21st century would belong to Asia, including South Asia. Understandably, the contribution of India, which accounts for 33% of Asian and 73% of the South Asian population, is viewed as extremely important in this transformation. There is, however, a shared concern that a developing country such as India would fail in achieving the goal of economic development if it is unable to realise the potential of demographic dividend by making adequate investment in capacity building among the youth and by addressing the problem of inequality in the access to middle, high and professional education. It would, therefore, be extremely important to analyse the inequality in different dimensions of human development, focusing sharply on education which would have significant impact on other dimensions in the medium and long run, particularly in the Indian context.

The plan of the chapter is as follows: the next section presents an overview of development scenario at global level. It groups the countries into three categories in terms of their levels of human development and proceeds to analyse the pattern in their loss of human development due to inequality. The loss has been computed as the difference between the original and inequality adjusted indices in three dimensions—income, education and health—as proposed by UNDP (2010). The third section makes a similar analysis by taking all the states of India as units of analysis. In the fourth section, the outcome indicators such as enrolment, attendance, dropouts from schools, literacy rate, percentage of persons with higher levels of education, etc. have been analysed across social groups to assess the magnitude of developmental deficits in the country in the field of education. The fourth section also analyses the variation in attendance rate in educational institutions across socio-religious groups for boys and girls in 5–24 age group. An attempt has been made to build up an explanatory framework for enrolment, retention and dropout of children in the next section, in terms of the factors identified by the households as important. The proposition that livelihood and affordability issues are still very important for a household in sending children to schools has been analysed here. The sixth section presents the percentage of persons active in labour market in the age group of 5–24, both in rural and urban areas, to understand how need for employment and labour market conditions could impact on withdrawal or retention of boys and girls in schools. The distribution of boys and girls who are neither in educational institutions not in labour market is the subject of discussion in the seventh section. The final section gives a summary of findings and provides a perspective for educational development in the context of inequities in the socio-economic system.

INEQUALITIES IN THREE DIMENSIONS OF HUMAN DEVELOPMENT AND THEIR IMPLICATIONS

A major concern in the context of the targets set through Millennium Development Goals (MDGs) for 2015 is that there are significant deficits in the achievements and that these are high in the developing countries, including the emerging economies. The deficits are particularly high in terms of educational indicators that can be attributed to the inequalities in availability, access and utilisation of educational facilities across regions, particularly between rural and urban areas, and most importantly, across social and religious groups.

A large number of less developed countries in Asia, Africa and Latin America are noted as having high deficits in human development, and their rankings in human development index (HDI) turn out to be below that of per capita income at *purchasing power parity*. The deficits in HDI are largely due to poor performance in educational indicators. There are serious disparities in the levels of and access to the facilities across regions, socio-religious groups and households in different income categories within the counties.

UNDP, since 2010, is bringing out *inequality adjusted index* of human development besides the *original HDI*. Furthermore, it computes the loss in the value in the three dimensions of human development—income, education and health—based on the gap between the two indices, taken as a percentage of the original index. The figures for the loss for all the countries for the year 2012, taken from UNDP (2013), have been analysed in this section. The countries have been placed in three categories of human development. Figure 4.1 depicts the loss in the dimensions of income, health and education due to inequality, taking into consideration 94 countries in 'very high' and 'high' development category, arranged in a descending order. A few countries in each category, unfortunately, report no information, and consequently there are discontinuities in the graph. It may be noted that the loss in income index, due to intra-country inequality,

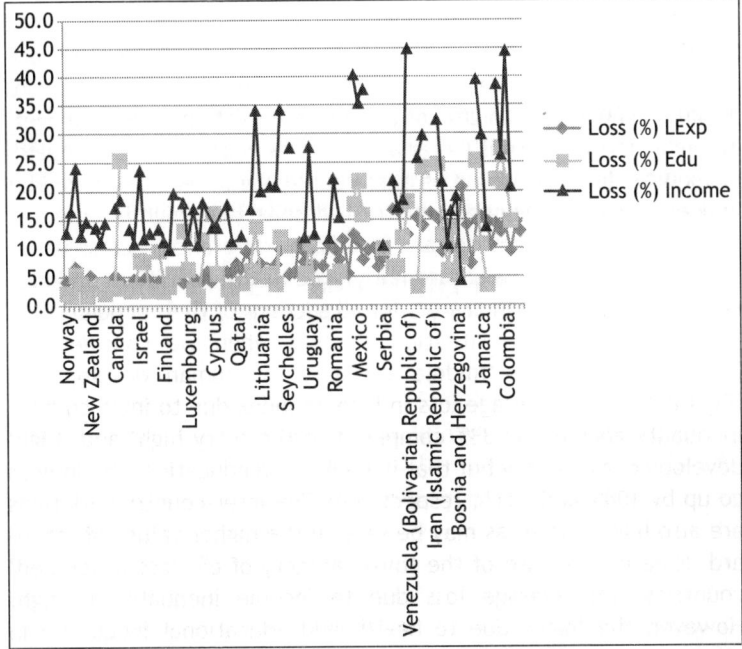

Figure 4.1

Loss in the Inequality Adjusted Indices of Human Development for the Countries in Very High and High Development Category, in Descending Order of Overall HDI, (HDR 2013)

Source: UNDP (2013).

Table 4.1

Percentage Loss in Three Indices of Human Development due to Inequality Adjustment (HDR 2013)

Category of Countries	Life Expectancy	Education	Income
Average			
Developed (High and Very High)	8.1	9.1	20.1
Medium Developed	16.5	21.1	26.8
Least Developed	32.9	34.6	28.8
India	33.20	41.22	13.96
Standard Deviation			
Developed (High and Very High)	4.1	7.2	9.5
Medium Developed	5.4	11.6	8.7
Least Developed	10.2	10.5	11.3
India	7.99	5.43	2.56

Source: Compiled from UNDP (2013) and Suryanarayana, Agrawal and Prabhu (2011).

is very high compared to the loss in other two indices, as assessed from the high average value of the loss. This is true also for the variation in the loss across the countries, measured through standard deviation (Table 4.1). In case of the loss in education index, the average value is low and so is its variation. Furthermore, the loss in health index is the least and so is the inter-country variation in the loss. This implies that the developed countries, despite their high income inequality within the countries and significant differences across them, are able, in general, to ensure fairly good health conditions and high educational outcome indicators for all sections of their population.

Unfortunately, the situation changes when we consider the 27 countries in the 'middle category' of human development (Figure 4.2). The average loss in income index due to intra-country inequality goes up by 33% compared to the 'very high' and 'high' development category but that in health and education, the indices go up by 104% and 131%, respectively. The inter-country variations are also higher here, as may be seen in the higher values of standard deviation. In case of the third category of 65 'less developed' countries, the average loss due to income inequality is high. However, the losses due to health and educational inequality in absolute and relative terms are extremely high, much above that of other two categories of countries (Figure 4.3).

The pattern, emerging from the inequality adjusted indices for the three human development dimensions in India at the state level (Suryanarayana et al. 2011) for 2010–11 (Figure 4.4), confirms this

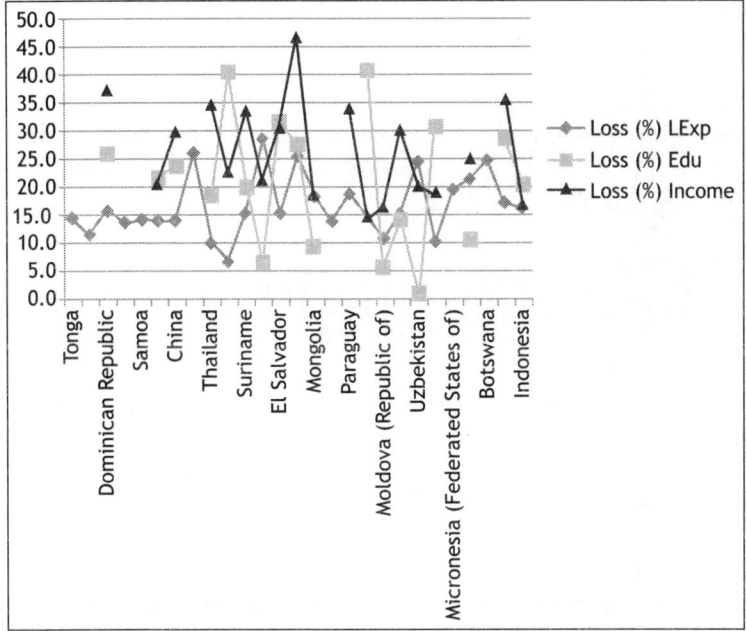

Figure 4.2

Loss in the Inequality Adjusted Indices of Human Development for the Countries in Medium Development Category, in Descending Order of Overall HDI (HDR 2013)

Source: World Development Indicators (2010).

pattern. Clearly, the loss in income due to inequality is 14% only, significantly below than that of health and educational index which works out as 33% and 41% respectively (Table 4.1). The loss in income/consumption index in India would have been higher if the measure of inequality was worked out by using household level data, instead of state level data. Importantly, the inter-state inequality is very high for educational index, more than twice that of income index. The correlation between the inequality index for income and that in education based on state level data works out as negative (−0.19) but statistically insignificant. The correlation between income and health index is also negative but statistically significant (−0.47). More importantly, the inequality indices for education and health relate positively (0.77).

One can argue that inequality in health outcome to an extent is determined by the inequality in income but that in education is not significantly affected by the latter. Besides economic affordability,

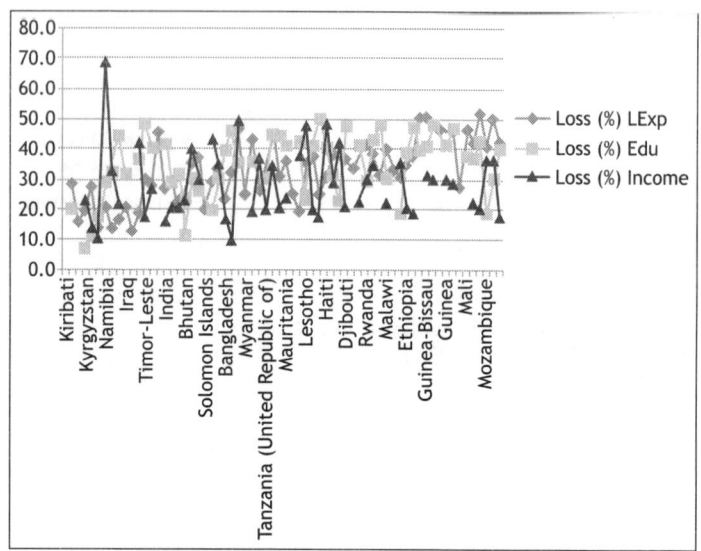

Figure 4.3
Loss in the Inequality Adjusted Indices of Human Development for the Countries in Low Development Category, in Descending Order of Overall HDI (HDR 2013)

Source: World Development Indicators (2013).

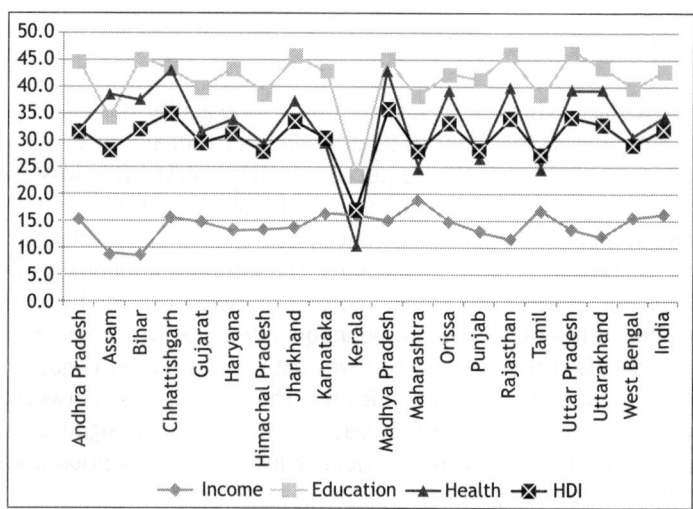

Figure 4.4
Percentage Loss in the Three Inequality Adjusted Indices of Human Development for the Indian States 2011

Source: Suryanarayana et al. (2011).

factors such as nature and organisation of employment, location in rural areas/small towns/large cities, gender, socio-religious group, etc. exacerbate the problem of access to quality education. Consequently, educational inequality works out to be much higher than income inequality. Furthermore, educational and health inequalities showing negative relationship with per capita income across the states reveals that the poorer state tend to have higher inequality. The strong positive relation between health and educational inequalities has serious policy implications. One can, for example, argue that the health outcome, such as infant mortality in vulnerable communities, can be reduced by reducing inequality in education.

DIFFERENTIAL EDUCATIONAL ATTAINMENTS FOR DIFFERENT SOCIO-RELIGIOUS GROUPS: AN OVERVIEW BASED ON INTERVENTION AND OUTCOME INDICATORS

Education is a key factor for societal change and equitable economic development in any country. Its outreach to marginalised socio-religious groups is important for India, if larger proportions among the youthful population have to be productively employed and the demographic dividends are to be translated into incremental rates of economic growth. Using a general equilibrium model, Asian Development Bank has predicted a growth rate between 6 and 7% in the country for the next four decades. This projection, however, is critically dependent on capacity building for the youth and realisation of the potential of demographic dividend. Given this perspective, an analysis of the disparities across these groups in terms of attendance in schools, dropout rates, children never attending any school and differential levels of educational attainment would be extremely important in identifying the bottlenecks and areas of future policy intervention.

An analysis of the patterns and trends for a select set of educational indicators pertaining to higher education, built from the unit level data of National Sample Survey (NSS) from its 60th and 66th Rounds have been used here in the diagnostic assessment. The percentage of persons of 16 years or more with higher secondary or higher levels of education exhibits higher degree of variation across the groups (Table 4.2) than that for primary education, discussed above, both in 2004–05 and 2011–12. Despite a few exceptions, Muslims are noted having lower figures compared to SC, ST and OBC

Table 4.2

Percentage of Persons Above 16 Years of Age with Higher Secondary or Higher Level of Education 2004–05 and 2011–12, and the Differences in Percentages

Socio-religious Group	2004–05					2011–12					% Difference (2004–05 to 2011–12)				
	Rural	Million Plus Cities	Other Urban	Urban Total	Total	Rural	Million Plus Cities	Other Urban	Urban Total	Total	Rural	Million Plus Cities	Other Urban	Urban Total	Total
Hindu ST	3.2	15.8	18.5	17.9	4.5	6.0	36.4	23.3	26.8	8.2	2.7	20.6	4.8	8.9	3.7
Hindu SC	4.7	12.1	12.6	12.5	6.3	7.6	24.4	19.8	21.3	10.8	2.9	12.3	7.2	8.8	4.5
Hindu OBC	7.2	25.1	20.5	21.4	10.4	11.7	40.4	29.4	32.3	17.1	4.5	15.3	8.8	10.8	6.7
Hindu Others	14.4	45.8	41.4	43.0	26.3	21.4	53.3	47.2	49.5	33.9	6.9	7.6	5.8	6.5	7.6
All Hindu	7.8	34.3	27.5	29.5	13.5	12.2	43.9	34.3	37.3	19.5	4.3	9.5	6.8	7.8	6.0
Muslim OBC	4.6	9.3	9.1	9.2	6.2	6.9	17.3	15.0	15.6	10.2	2.3	8.0	5.9	6.4	4.1
Muslim Others	4.1	21.4	14.0	16.6	8.5	7.7	23.0	17.8	19.8	12.2	3.6	1.6	3.8	3.2	3.7
All Muslim	4.3	19.4	11.8	13.8	7.6	7.3	20.8	16.3	17.6	11.2	3.0	1.4	4.5	3.8	3.6
Other Religion	10.9	41.7	36.0	37.8	19.1	16.3	49.6	41.7	43.9	26.0	5.4	7.9	5.6	6.1	6.9
Total	7.6	32.9	25.6	27.7	13.2	11.8	40.7	31.9	34.6	18.8	4.2	7.8	6.3	6.9	5.6

Source: Computed from National Sample Survey Organisation (NSSO) unit level employment and unemployment data.

Hindus in all settlement types at both the time points. The pattern of improvements in the values of different socio-religious groups worsens the inequality in rural areas. The improvements in the values for the ST/SC and Muslims are less than the average. The improvements in metro and non-metro cities are larger for SC and ST population compared to the average. The improvements for the Muslims are very low, particularly in urban areas, placing them in a position of great relative disadvantage.

The percentage of graduates among population aged 16 and above in rural areas is the lowest among the ST, with the figures for Muslims and SC being slightly higher than that in 2004–05 (Table 4.3). OBC Hindus have the next highest figure but the upper-caste Hindus (UCH) are at the top, reporting a huge gap with all other groups. The pattern, however, is different in urban areas. Here, the STs in general are above the SC and Muslim population due to the programmes of affirmative action. Interestingly, the figure for the Muslims is higher than both SC and ST, due to historical reasons, in Million plus cities where the Moghul Empire had thrived. In smaller urban centres, Muslims report a lower figure than SC, ST and OBC population, as in the case of rural areas. The improvement over time for Muslims has in general been less than that of other groups in all spatial categories. Muslims in rural areas and small towns, thus, remain extremely underprivileged, reporting figures below that of SC population, being at a relatively more disadvantageous position in 2011–12. For the SC and ST population, the improvements in the figures are significantly higher, for both metro and non-metro cities, during the period under consideration.

The percentage of young boys and girls attending educational institutions among Muslims in the age group of 15–19 years is similar to that of the SC/ST population (Table 4.4). The same is noted in the case of the youths in 20–25 age group as well. One can argue that despite Muslims seeking employment mostly outside agriculture, wherein the educational requirements tend to be higher, they are much more deprived than the general population in terms of intermediate and higher education. The improvements over the period under consideration for them are much lower than that of the general population; these are less than or equal to that of the SC and ST population in the country. However, these are much less for UCH and other minorities (OM), comprising Sikhs, Christians, etc.

It is a matter of serious concern that the levels of technical education for the Muslim population aged 15 years and above are lower than that of general and OBC population at the three different

Table 4.3

Percentage of Persons Above 16 Years of Age with Graduation or Higher Level of Education in 2004–05 and 2011–12, and the Percentage Differences

Socio-religious Group	2004–05					2011–12					% Difference (2004–05 to 2011–12)				
	Rural	Million Plus Cities	Other Urban	Urban Total	Total	Rural	Million Plus Cities	Other Urban	Urban Total	Total	Rural	Million Plus Cities	Other Urban	Urban Total	Total
Hindu ST	0.9	5.4	7.5	7.0	1.5	1.6	20.1	10.1	12.8	2.8	0.6	14.8	2.5	5.7	1.3
Hindu SC	1.5	4.9	5.0	5.0	2.2	2.2	11.6	8.7	9.6	3.9	0.7	6.8	3.7	4.6	1.7
Hindu OBC	2.3	13.3	8.5	9.5	3.9	3.6	21.5	13.6	15.7	6.8	1.3	8.3	5.1	6.2	2.9
Hindu Others	5.8	28.3	22.8	24.8	13.7	8.3	33.3	28.3	30.1	18.1	2.6	5.0	5.5	5.3	4.4
All Hindu	2.8	20.1	13.6	15.5	6.1	4.0	25.5	18.2	20.5	8.8	1.3	5.4	4.6	5.0	2.7
Muslim OBC	1.2	4.2	3.1	3.2	1.9	1.7	7.3	5.4	5.8	3.3	0.6	3.1	2.3	2.6	1.4
Muslim Others	1.5	11.0	6.1	7.8	3.7	2.7	12.1	7.5	9.2	5.1	1.2	1.1	1.4	1.4	1.4
All Muslim	1.4	9.8	4.7	6.1	3.0	2.2	10.2	6.3	7.5	4.2	0.8	0.4	1.6	1.4	1.2
Other Religion	2.9	25.1	17.5	19.9	8.1	5.1	29.9	20.2	22.9	11.4	2.2	4.8	2.7	3.1	3.3
Total	2.6	19.1	12.5	14.4	5.9	3.9	23.4	16.4	18.6	8.4	1.3	4.3	3.9	4.2	2.5

Source: Computed from NSSO unit level employment and unemployment data.

Table 4.4

Percentage of Persons Attending Educational Institutions in 2004–05 and 2011–12 in Two Age Cohorts and the Differences in Percentages

Socio-religious Communities	15–19 Years			20–25 Years		
	2004–05	2011–12	% Point Difference	2004–05	2011–12	% Point Difference
Hindu SC/ST	36.2	55	19	7.0	11.2	4
Hindu OBC	44.6	68	23	8.7	17.3	9
Hindu Other	63.9	78	14	16.8	27.6	11
All Hindus	46.9	66	19	10.3	18.0	8
Muslim OBC	34.9	49	14	6.5	9.7	3
Muslim Others	36.9	52	15	8.0	12.8	5
All Hindus	36.1	50	14	7.5	11.3	4
Other Minorities	57.5	72	14	14.5	22.9	8
Total	46.0	63.9	18	10.2	17.3	7

Source: NSSO (2004, 2011).

levels considered here, namely, technical graduate, under graduation and graduation in 2004–05 (Table 4.5). The change over time has been similar across the socio-religious categories, resulting in the position of the Muslims remaining at par with that of the SC/ST but significantly below than OBC and UCH in 2011–12 (Table 4.6). This requires immediate policy intervention since a

Table 4.5

Percentage of Persons Having Technical Education Among Persons Aged 15 Years and Above (2004–05)

Socio-religious Communities	No Technical Education	Technical Graduate	Undergraduate Diploma/ Certificate	Graduate Diploma/ Certificate	Total
Hindu SC/ST	99.1	0.1	0.7	0.2	100.0
Hindu OBC	98.0	0.2	1.4	0.4	100.0
Hindu Others	95.8	0.7	2.1	1.4	100.0
All Hindu	97.7	0.3	1.4	0.6	100.0
Muslim OBC	98.8	0.1	1.0	0.2	100.0
Muslim Others	98.8	0.2	0.6	0.4	100.0
All Muslim	98.8	0.1	0.7	0.3	100.0
OM	95.6	0.4	3.0	1.0	100.0
Total	97.7	0.3	1.4	0.6	100.0

Source: Computed based on unit level data of NSSO (2004).

Table 4.6

*Percentage of Persons Having Technical Education Among Persons
Aged 15 Years and Above (2011–12)*

Socio-religious Communities	No Technical Education	Technical Graduate	Undergraduate Diploma/ Certificate	Graduate Diploma/ Certificate	Total
Hindu SC/ST	99.3	0.1	0.5	0.1	100.0
Hindu OBC	98.3	0.2	1.1	0.4	100.0
Hindu Others	96.9	0.5	1.6	1.0	100.0
All Hindu	98.2	0.3	1.1	0.5	100.0
Muslim OBC	99.3	0.1	0.5	0.2	100.0
Muslim Others	99.1	0.2	0.4	0.2	100.0
All Muslim	99.2	0.1	0.5	0.2	100.0
Other Minorities	96.7	0.3	2.2	0.8	100.0
Total	98.2	0.2	1.0	0.4	100.0

Source: Computed based on unit level data of NSSO (2011).

large section of the Muslim youth get into professions that require technical knowledge and professional training, much more than in other groups.

The overview reveals that SCs, STs and Muslims are the most vulnerable population groups in the country, both in rural and urban areas. Developments between 2004–05 and 2011–12, unfortunately, have not reduced the relative deprivation of the communities. In fact, these have widened the gaps. Muslims initially had an edge over the SC/ST population, particularly in rural areas but that have disappeared over time. In the urban context, Muslims emerge as the most educationally backward community among all the population groups, considered in the analysis.

SINGLE AGE-WISE REPORTING OF SCHOOL ATTENDANCE ACROSS SOCIO-RELIGIOUS GROUPS AND CHANGES THEREIN

The percentages of male children attending educational institutions in rural and urban areas across different socio-religious groups in 2004–05 are presented in Figure 4.5, for ages from 5 years to 24 years. As the information is based on single year age reporting by the head of the household, there could be bias in the information

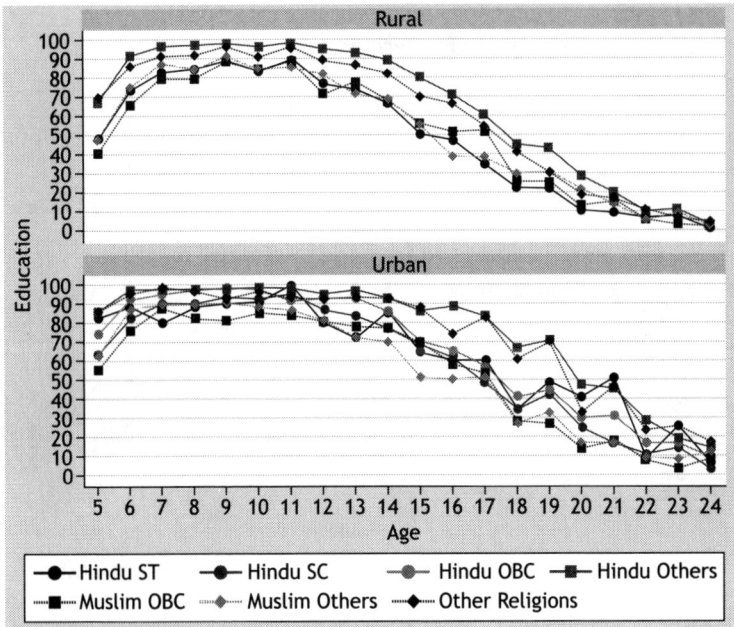

Figure 4.5
Percentage of Male Children (5–24 Age Group) Attending Educational Institutions (61st Round 2004–05)

Source: NSSO (2004).

due to digital preference which is unavoidable. Despite the limitation, the basic contours of school attendance and dropout rates at different ages emerge clearly.

It is impressive that the attendance figure ranges between 80% and 98% in ages between 7 and 11 years in 2004–05. The drop starts in the 12th year of the children in rural areas while in urban areas, it starts one year later. The curves showing attendance for STs, SCs and Muslims appear on the lower side of the band and remains so in all age groups. UCH and OM are on the higher side, both in rural and urban areas. Understandably, the dropout rates are higher for the vulnerable groups, both in rural and urban areas. The attendance rate drops to below 50% at the age of 16 years for all groups in rural areas. This happens in urban areas too, except for UCH and OM.

The pattern happily has changed for better in 2011–12 (Figure 4.6). It is noted that 80–98% of the boys are staying in schools until the age of 14 in rural areas and until 16 years in urban areas. The location of

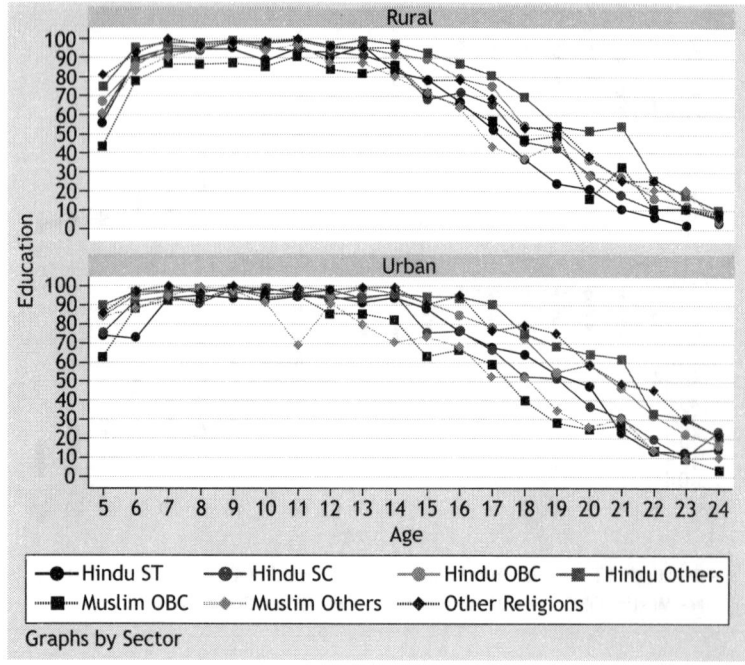

Figure 4.6
Percentage of Male Children (5–24 Age Group) Attending Educational Institutions (68th Round 2011–12)
Source: NSSO (2004).

different socio-religious groups within the band, however, remains unchanged. The curves for UCH and OM crisscross at the upper side while that of Muslims and ST do that at the lower end of the band. These are not happy patterns in the context of skill development for the youth and encashment of demographic dividend. The fact that the slopes of the curves have become flatter (as there has been decline in the sharpness of the slope) is a matter of some satisfaction. This suggests that the years of schooling have gone up for all the communities, both in rural and urban areas. Muslims and STs, however, remain the most educationally deprived groups.

The pattern of attendance for the girls and women in rural and urban areas should be subjects of more serious concern. The figures are lower than the corresponding figures for males and the maximum attendance in the 7–11 years is 95%, less than that of males, in 2004–05 (Figure 4.7). The dropout rates are also higher and yet

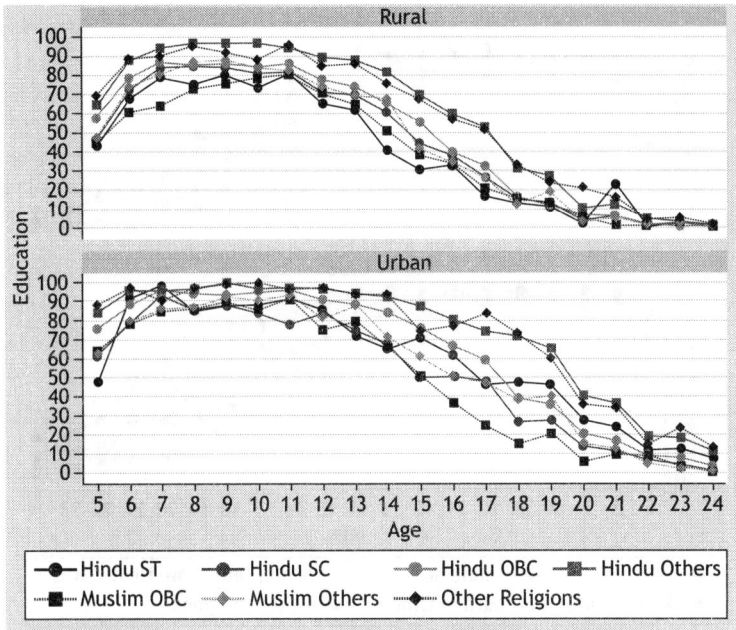

Figure 4.7
Percentage of Female Children (5–24 Age Group) Attending Educational Institutions (61st Round 2004–05)
Source: NSSO (2004).

there is not much of gender inequality till 12 years of age, in both rural and urban areas. The placements of the curves for different socio-religious groups remain mostly unaltered within the band, as noted in case of the males.

The patterns of attendance for the girls and women have changed but this is similar to what was noted in case of boys and men (Figure 4.8), as discussed above. The curves in 2011–12 are a lot flatter, suggesting higher retention in educational institutions, and this is noted both for rural and urban areas. Importantly, although Muslim girls report lower retention figures beyond the age of 14 years, this matches with the corresponding figures for boys, suggesting less gender disparity within the community. Both, nonetheless, decline faster than the UCH males. The developments during the period under consideration, however, have not changed the placement of the curves for different socio-religious groups within the band.

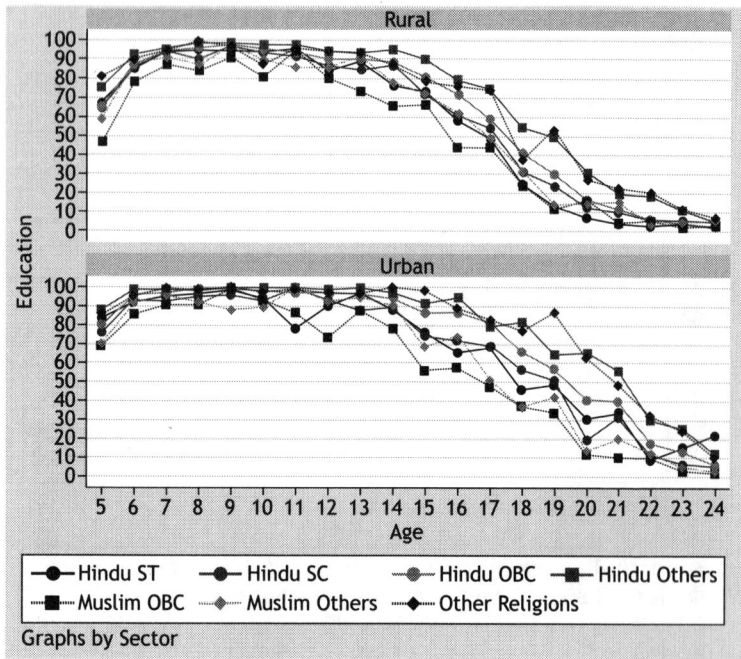

Figure 4.8
*Percentage of Female Children (5–24 Age Group) Attending
Educational Institutions (68th Round 2011–12)*
Source: NSSO (2004).

EXPLANATION OF VARIATION IN ENROLMENT, RETENTION AND DROPOUT RATES ACROSS SOCIO-RELIGIOUS CATEGORIES BASED ON HOUSEHOLD RESPONSE

It would be useful to build an explanatory framework for differential educational outcomes for the children and adults in different socio-religious groups in terms of their affordability and economic status. Information on the reasons for not going to educational institutions or dropping out were collected for the year 2007–08 in the 64th Round of the NSS across various religious groups. Here, affordability emerges as the major explanatory factor. The percentage distribution of the students, belonging to the two age groups, that is, 5–14 years and 15–24 years, by the stipulated reasons is presented in Table 4.7. Three major reasons accounting for much of the non-enrolment and drop out are (a) parents not interested,

Table 4.7
Distribution of Those Not Enrolled/Dropped Out/Discontinued by Reasons by Religion, 5–14 Years (%)

Age Group	Religion							
5–14 years	Hinduism	Islam	Christian	Sikh	Jain	Buddhist	Zoroastrian	Total
Parent not interested in studies	26.5	23.8	10.2	32.3	16.2	7.8	–	25.5
Inadequate number of teachers	0.2	0.1	–	–	–	–	–	0.1
School is far off	2.1	1.6	3.3	0.6	2.3	5.1	–	2.0
To work for wage/salary	0.8	0.5	–	–	–	–	–	0.7
For participating in other economic activities	1.5	1.2	0.7	3.7	0.1	0.8	–	1.4
To look after younger siblings	1.2	0.7	–	–	0.7	–	–	1.0
To attend other domestic chores	2.1	1.7	1.2	0.5	0.7	4.4	–	2.0
Financial constraints	19.4	29.4	23.5	11.1	26.8	9.5	–	21.8
Timings of educational institution not suitable	0.1	–	–	–	0.2	0.4	–	0.1
For helping in household enterprises	0.8	1.0	–	–	1.4	0.2	–	0.8
Language/medium of instruction used unfamiliar	0.1	0.4	–	–	0.1	–	–	0.2
No tradition in the community	2.4	3.2	4.9	4.8	0.4	4.6	–	2.7
Education not considered necessary	12.6	11.3	9.6	17.7	9.0	10.7	100	12.3
Child not interested in studies	11.1	10.0	27.1	5.7	10.1	42.3	–	11.1
Unable to cope up or failure in studies	2.1	1.3	4.8	3.2	6.7	0.9	–	2.0
Unfriendly atmosphere at school	0.1	0.1	1.0	–	–	–	–	0.1
Completed desired level/class	0.5	0.5	–	0.2	0.8	–	–	0.5
Non-availability of lady teacher	–	0.1	–	–	–	–	–	–
Non-availability of ladies toilet	–	–	–	–	–	–	–	–
Others	16.4	13.0	13.7	20.3	24.3	13.2	–	15.6
Total	100	100	100	100	100	100	100	100

Source: NSSO 64th Round (2007–08).

(b) education considered not necessary and (c) financial difficulties. These reasons account for over 60% of the cases in the younger group and over 50% in the older group.

It is important to note that in the 5–14 years age group, 25% are not in school for the reason that their parents are not interested in studies. The reluctance on the part of Muslim parents, however, is not stronger than that of other groups since the percentage figure is marginally below that of the general population. Surprisingly, the figure for the Sikhs is much higher, over 32%.

The unwillingness on part of the children to go to school being responsible for higher non-attendance for the Muslims can be dismissed since the relevant percentage figure is the same as that for all other religious groups. Interestingly, this factor emerges once again, as an important one for the Sikh children, as their figure is more than three times that of the general population. The most important factor responsible for the low enrolment of the Muslim children is the financial factor, as high as 30% respondents mentioning this, compared to 20% among Hindus and the general population. For Sikhs, the figure is one-third that of the Muslims.

For young men and women in the 15–24 years age group, Muslim parents can possibly be held responsible for their withdrawal from education. The percentage of persons opting out of education as a result of this factor, however, is only marginally higher than the general population. The Muslim youth not finding interest in higher education can also be dismissed as a factor, as the corresponding figure falls below that of Hindu and Christian population. Poor financial condition emerges as a critical factor yet again since as high as 28% of the households have given that as the reason for their youth not attending educational institutions. The only group which reports a higher dropout rate due to this factor is the Buddhist, which is understandable since it comprises of a large segment of SC population.

ENGAGEMENT IN ECONOMIC ACTIVITIES FOR PERSONS IN THE AGE GROUP OF 5–24 ACROSS SOCIO-RELIGIOUS GROUPS

The workforce participation rate (WPR) in the age of 5–24 years is largely determined by enrolment and attendance in educational institutions. A higher level of attendance in schools and colleges can reduce the WPR, both for boys and girls, in this age group. NSS provides information on activity pattern of persons based on single year age reporting, made by the head of the household (Table 4.8).

Table 4.8

Distribution of Those Not Enrolled/Dropped Out/Discontinued by Reasons by Religion, 15–24 Years (%)

Age Group 15–24 years	Religion							
	Hinduism	Islam	Christian	Sikh	Jain	Buddhist	Zoroastrian	Total
Parent not interested in studies	13.3	15.5	8.4	12.7	7.6	8.4	6.1	13.4
Inadequate number of teachers	–	–	–	–	–	–	–	–
School is far off	2.8	1.4	1.9	2.4	0.6	3.8	–	2.5
To work for wage/salary	4.7	4.0	3.0	5.5	9.1	3.2	1.7	4.6
For participating in other economic activities	5.1	5.4	5.9	12.7	4.8	8.3	10.4	5.2
To look after younger siblings	0.8	0.8	0.4	1.3	2.4	0.6	1.7	0.8
To attend other domestic chores	5.0	4.0	5.6	8.1	3.5	3.1	3.9	4.8
Financial constraints	21.1	26.8	23.7	11.4	22.8	28.6	5.6	22.1
Timings of educational institution not suitable	0.1	0.1	–	–	0.1	–	–	0.1
For helping in household enterprises	2.7	2.7	2.1	6.7	1.4	1.1	8.7	2.7
Language/medium of instruction used unfamiliar	0.1	0.2	0.1	–	–	–	–	0.1
No tradition in the community	1.0	2.1	1.0	0.1	0.2	–	–	1.2
Education not considered necessary	4.8	5.4	4.6	10.0	2.4	2.0	3.1	4.8
Child not interested in studies	16.5	14.1	20.4	11.5	16.9	15.4	16.5	16.2
Unable to cope up or failure in studies	9.0	6.8	7.1	8.0	13.9	15.6	11.7	8.8
Unfriendly atmosphere at school	0.2	0.2	0.2	–	0.3	–	0.5	0.2
Completed desired level/class	7.5	5.2	11.2	5.3	8.1	6.1	22.1	7.2
Non-availability of lady teacher	–	0.1	0.1	–	–	–	–	–
Non-availability of ladies toilet	–	–	0.1	–	–	–	–	–
Others	5.2	5.2	4.3	4.1	6.0	3.8	8.0	5.2
Total	100	100	100	100	100	100	100	100

Source: NSSO 64th Round (2007–08).

This can be used for understanding the behaviour of different socio-religious communities in the context of withdrawing their children from education system and sending them to labour market. Charting of activity profiles by age can help in assessing the barriers in school attendance across social groups and the impact of age on this. Identification of the proximate causes keeping them away from education and skill development would be extremely important for developing programmes of skill development in the country.

The percentages of males in 5–24 years age group reporting work as the major activity during the major part of the survey reference year 2004–05, as per the NSS data, have been presented in Figure 4.9. The NSS has a moving reference year and, therefore, the estimates discussed here can be considered to be reflecting the average situation. One can observe that the economically vulnerable social groups, such as ST and SC population, report high WPR

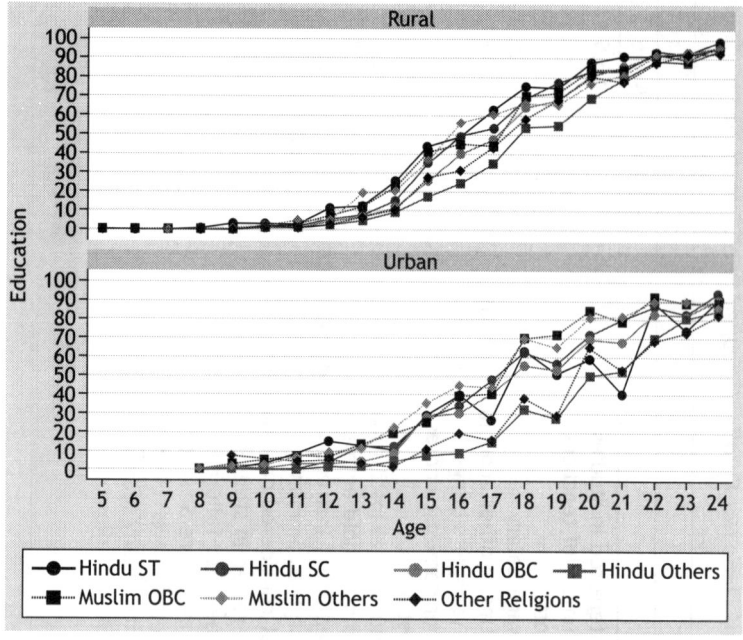

Figure 4.9
Percentage of Males Aged 5–24 Years, Reporting Work as the Main Activity (61st Round 2004–05)

Source: NSSO (2004).

in the ages between 10 and 20 years, both in rural and urban areas. This pattern is further confirmed by the data for the year 2011–12 (Figure 4.10). However, Muslim boys report even higher percentage figures in most of the ages, both in rural and urban areas in 2011–12.

For the female population, the pattern is somewhat different. Understandably, the tribal girls in the rural areas report significantly higher work participation, compared to other socio-religious groups, both in 2004–05 and 2011–12 (Figures 4.11 and 4.12). In fact, the width of the band of the curves becomes very large because of the higher work participation rate among the tribal girls/women, and that for the Muslim women being way below of the total population. This can easily be attributed to socio-cultural factors. In urban areas, too, the ST population reports the highest percentage of workers in the 5–24 age group, although the difference is not as

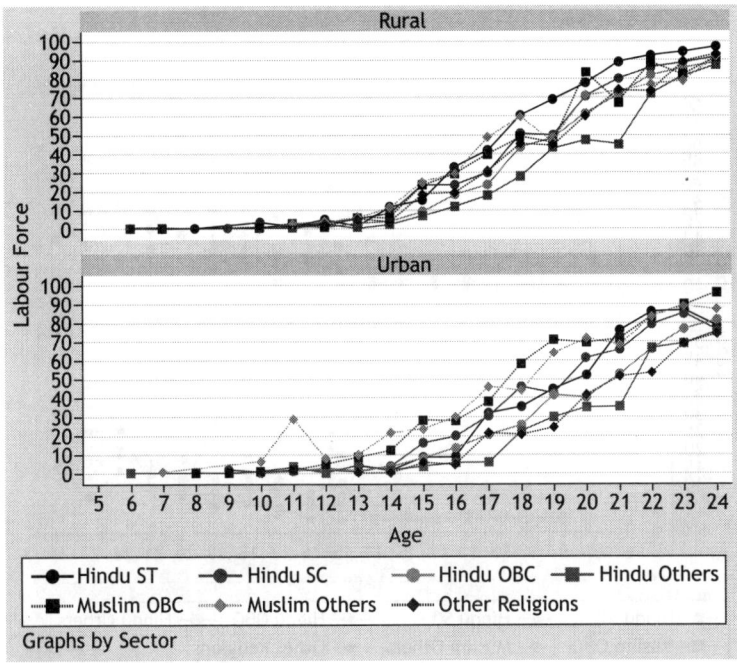

Figure 4.10
Percentage of Males Aged 5–24 Years, Reporting Work as the Main Activity (68th Round 2011–12)

Source: NSSO (2011).

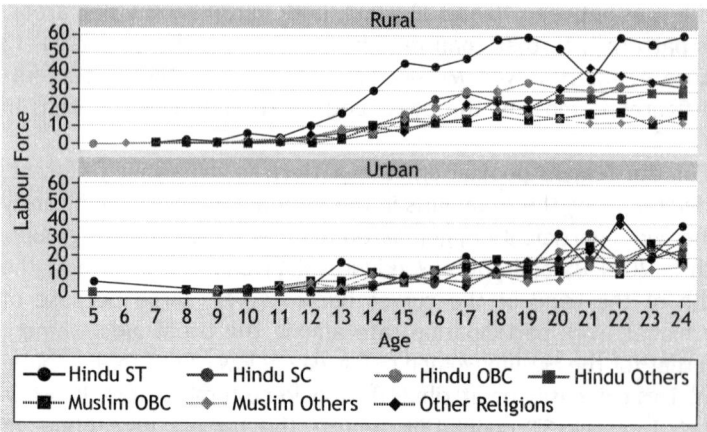

Figure 4.11
Percentage of Females Aged 5–24 Years Reporting Work as the Main Activity (61st Round 2004–05)

Source: NSSO (2004).

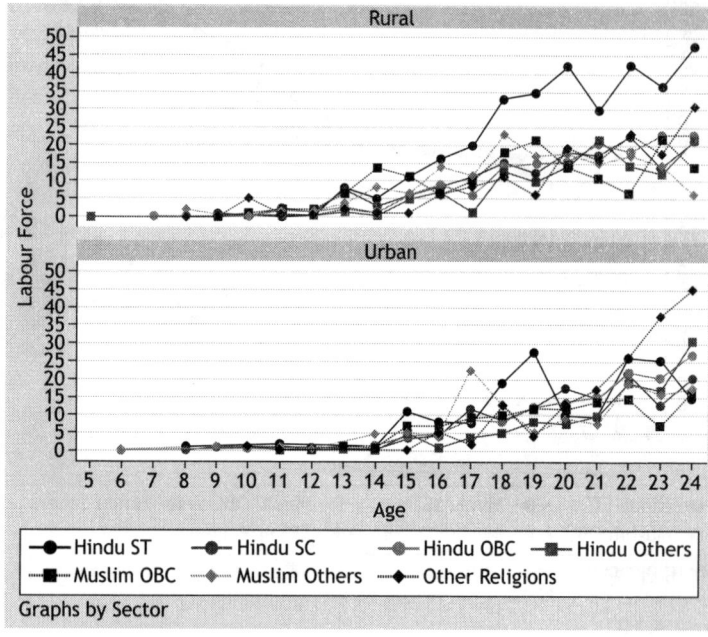

Figure 4.12
Percentage of Females Aged 5–24 Years, Reporting Work as the Main Activity (68th Round 2011–12)

Source: NSSO (2011).

significant as that noted for rural areas. The pattern has not changed much over time and consequently the curves for the year 2011–12 look very similar to that of 2004–05.

PERSONS OUTSIDE EDUCATION SYSTEM BUT NOT IN LABOUR MARKET: IMPLICATIONS OF LARGE NOWHERE CHILDREN IN INDIA

The boys and girls, who neither attend the educational institutions nor are a part of labour force, have been euphemistically described as 'nowhere children', their percentages in different ages in between 5 and 24 are presented in Figures 4.13, 4.14, 4.15 and 4.16. Figures are very high for the Muslim, ST and SC boys in rural areas in that order, particularly in the younger age groups of 5–24 year in 2004–05 (Figure 4.13). At higher ages in this range, figures go down as the boys in the vulnerable groups enter the labour market. A similar pattern can be noted in urban areas as well, boys in these population groups recording very high percentage of 'nowhere children'.

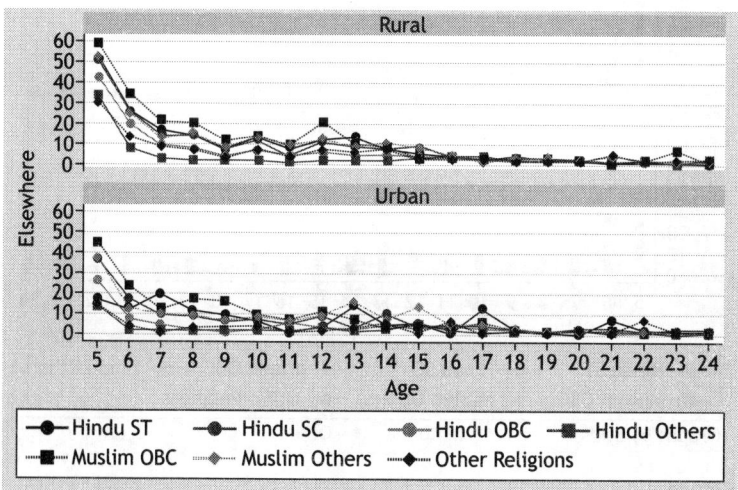

Figure 4.13
Percentage of Males Aged 5–24 Years, Neither in Labour Force Nor Educational Institutions (61st Round 2004–05)
Source: NSSO (2004).

The pattern, however, has somewhat changed over time as the tribal boys record higher figures compared to the Muslims for many of the age groups. However, the significant 'edge' that Muslims had in terms of their high WPR over other communities have not gone down much over the years (Figures 4.13 and 4.14). Particularly, the fact that the percentage of OBC Muslim boys outside the schooling system in rural areas is between 12% and 18% in the age group of 8–14 years must be a matter of concern from the perspective of socio-political stability in the country, besides the issue of human rights.

The problem of dropout from schools seems to be much more serious in the case of girls (Figure 4.15) and consequently the per-centage of nowhere children works out to be much larger than the boys. The band of the graphs is much larger since the socio-cultural factors bring in significant variation in the rates across population groups. Muslim girls report high figures as they leave the schooling system earlier than the girls in other communities and do not seek employment due to traditional factors. They record very low WPR, both in rural and urban areas. ST/SC girls report low percentages of nowhere children as they join the labour market after leaving the schools early.

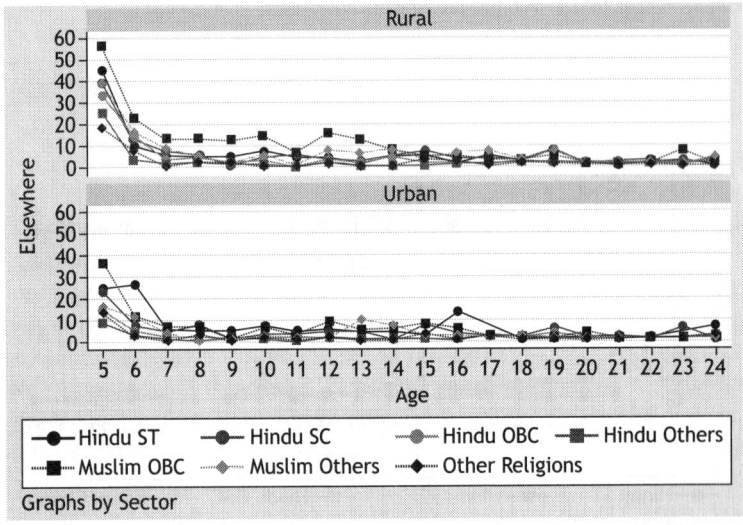

Figure 4.14
Percentage of Males Aged 5–24 Years, Neither in Labour Force Nor Educational Institutions (68th Round 2011–12)

Source: NSSO (2011).

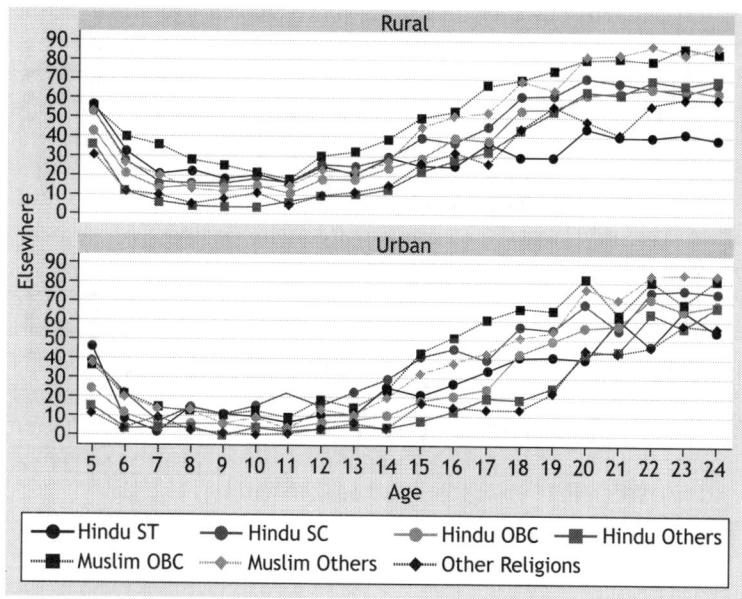

Figure 4.15
Percentage of Females Aged 5–24 Years, Neither in Labour Force Nor Educational Institutions (61st Round 2004–05)
Source: NSSO (2004).

A comparison of the Figures 4.15 and 4.16 reveals that the pattern has also not changed over time. Predictions of high income growth of India in the coming decades is critically dependent on the assumption that WPR would go up significantly, particularly for women, leading to realisation of demographic dividend. The fact that different socio-religious groups would be able to increase their WPR (particularly for women) with different time lag would imply that the process of realisation of demographic dividend would be slow but a prolonged affair. Currently, a very large percentage of Muslim women are neither in labour force nor in educational institutions in 14–20 age group. The figures are very high for SC, ST and OBC women as well. These must be considered as a matter of serious concern by the policymakers in the context of gender empowerment, livelihood generation and poverty alleviation.

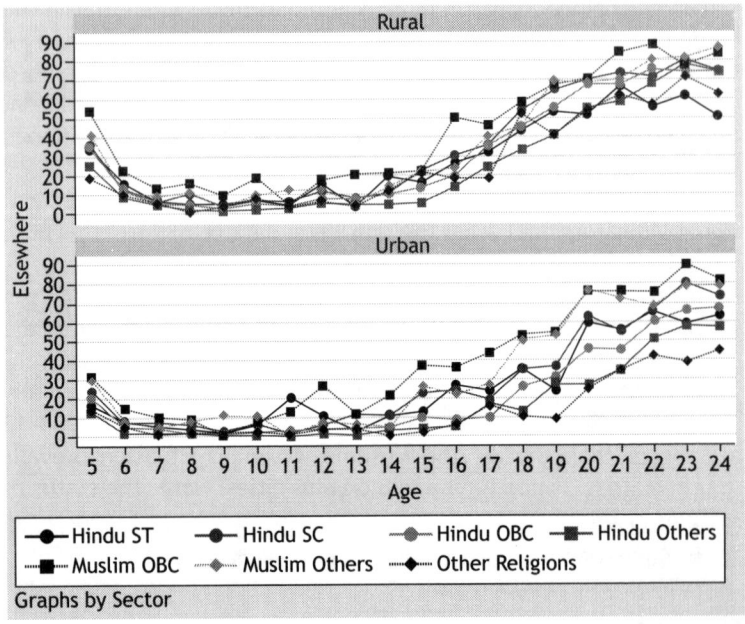

Figure 4.16

Percentage of Female in 5–24 Age Group, Neither in Labour Force Nor Educational Institutions (68th Round 2011–12)

Source: NSSO (2004).

CONCLUSION AND A PERSPECTIVE FOR POLICY

Inequalities in different dimensions of human development in countries across the globe vary significantly with their levels of development. The countries at 'very high' and 'high' levels of human development tend to have high inequality in the income dimension but record low values in health and educational dimensions. The inequality in the latter two dimensions, however, tends to increase as we move from countries of 'very high' to 'middle' and 'low' levels of human development. The income-based global rankings of the less developed countries are often higher than those in other two dimensions. What is more significant is that their inequality in educational development is much higher than that of other groups of countries. Educational inequality can be posited as central to the inequalities in all other dimensions of human development.

Educational inequality in India is noted as higher than that in the other two dimensions. It is noted to be much higher than most of the less developed countries. More importantly, the less developed states in India, such as Odisha, Madhya Pradesh, Bihar, Uttar Pradesh, etc., record higher educational inequality, compared to the developed states.

An analysis of the trends and patterns for a select set of educational indicators built from the unit level data of NSS from its 60th and 66th Rounds help in taking stock of the inequality across socio-religious groups and their changing profiles. It is noted that the school attendance rate for Muslim (particularly OBC) children in the 6–14 years age group in rural areas is the lowest across socio-religious groups. ST and SC children are the other two groups, equally vulnerable. However, their rates of improvement during 2004–12 are higher than that of the Muslims. A similar situation prevails in urban areas, including the million plus cities. Here, the status of Muslims is relatively worse off, compared to SC and ST, in terms of their level of attendance as also improvement in that, overtime.

Muslims and STs emerge as the most vulnerable population groups in terms of other educational outcome indicators as well, both in rural and urban areas. Shockingly, in metro cities, the relative deprivation of Muslims is extremely high by several indicators considered in the study. Importantly, improvements in the educational status of the SCs and STs are far sharper than that of Muslims in all settlement categories during 2005–12. This is largely owing to the policy of reservation, which excludes the Muslims. The general conclusion emerging from the multi-variate analysis would be that the Muslims remain underprivileged group in India, particularly in urban areas, where they belonged to the ruling elite class a couple of centuries back.

Importantly, the percentage of literates among persons of 7 years of age are higher for Muslims in rural areas, small towns and metro cities, compared to SC and ST population. This pattern contrasts with the present pattern of attendance, dropout, etc. This is because the Muslims in earlier decades had better access to education. This pushes up their literacy rates in the higher age groups and consequently, their aggregate literacy status works out as better than that of the SC/ST population. On the whole, the relative literacy situation has deteriorated for this underprivileged minority community in the recent years due to differential access to the facilities.

The percentage of persons of 16 years having higher secondary or higher levels of education exhibits a higher degree of variation across the socio-religious groups than that for primary education. Barring a few exceptions, Muslims are noted as having lower figures, compared to the SC, ST and OBC Hindus in all settlement types, at both the time points under consideration. The pattern of improvements has further worsened the inequality. The improvements in the values for the ST/SC and Muslims are less than the national average. The improvements for the Muslims are generally less than that for even ST and SC, particularly in urban areas, placing them in a position of great relative disadvantage. It is also unfortunate that despite most of the Muslims seeking employment outside the agriculture sector, their share in technical education is much less, even when compared to the national average or other vulnerable groups of population.

The SC, ST and Muslim boys get out of the education system quite early in their life. The work participation rates for the first two groups work out as very high in rural areas, which can be attributed to their relatively higher level of economic deprivation and desperation in accepting any available job, besides inability to continue with their education. Muslim boys record the highest work participation rate in urban areas for identical reasons. It is unfortunate that ST, SC and Muslim boys enter the labour market without a reasonable level of skill and consequently, many ends up with earnings below the poverty line. The high dropout of young men and women from the formal education system and their not being absorbed in technical or professional education would come in the way of realising the demographic potential in the country. Furthermore, the low rate of absorption of persons in 10–18 age group in economic activities results in the problem of nowhere children, particularly among the Muslims, which can convert demographic dividend into a demographic disaster.

As far as women are concerned, their dropout rates are higher than that of men. Unfortunately, many of them do not seek absorption in labour market due to socio-cultural factors and, thus, swell the number of 'nowhere children'. Furthermore, many among those who seek employment fail due to difficult labour market conditions and gender discrimination. Programmes to increase their retention rate in education system, provisioning of formal technical and professional training as also informal programmes for skill development would help their skill development. These could be effective means for reducing educational inequality which would, in turn, contribute to reducing income inequality. This must be an integral part of inclusive development in the country for maximising the demographic dividend and enabling India emerge as a major economic power by the third decade of the present century.

REFERENCES

National Sample Survey Organisation (NSSO). 2004. India-*Employment and Unemployment 2004–05, 61st Round*. Ministry of Statistics and Programme Implementation, Government of India, New Delhi.

———. 2011. *India: Employment and Unemployment 2011–12, 68th Round*. Ministry of Statistics and Programme Implementation, Government of India, New Delhi.

Suryanarayana, M.H., A. Agrawal, and K.S. Prabhu. 2011. *Inequality-adjusted Human Development Index for India's States, 2011*. New Delhi: United Nations Development Programme.

UNDP. 2010. *The Real Wealth of Nations: Pathways to Human Development*. Human Development Report 2010, United Nations Development Programme, New York.

———. 2013. *The Rise of the South: Human Progress in a Diverse World*. Human Development Report 2013, United Nations Development Programme, New York.

5

Private Sector and Equity in Higher Education: Challenges of Growing Unequal Access

Sukhadeo Thorat and Khalid Khan

INTRODUCTION

The goal of providing equal opportunity in higher education to all has been emphasised from the very beginning of policy initiative on higher education in India. The Radhakrishnan Commission of 1948–49 on higher education and Kothari Commission of 1964–66 emphasised this goal. The first policy statement on education of 1968 also emphasised on equity in access to higher education. The clear focus on equity in education, however, was brought by 1986 National Policy on Education and Programme of Action (PoA) of 1992. Although more initiatives have been taken through five-year plans, the 1986 Policy on Education and PoA of 1992 remained the last official policy statement, which guided the actions of the central government as well as the state governments since its adoption.

The PoA 1992 recognised the intra-group and inter-group disparities in enrolment. In the former, it highlights the inequalities in enrolment between poor and non-poor within the same social group and in the latter, it pointed to disparities between male and female, minorities and majority, tribal and non-tribal, and between lower caste and higher caste, particularly between scheduled caste (SC), other backward classes (OBC) and higher caste. Thus, gender, caste, ethnic and religious disparities were clearly recognised by the PoA of 1992, with a focus on the poor from each of these social groups.

Although it is difficult to know the dimension of policy for equal access, particularly at state level, due to lack of information, the initiative at central level and state level can be summarised to include (a) the public institutions, (universities and colleges/institutions) and private aided colleges, with affordable tuition fees, and (b) other measures that include affordable hostel for girls and boys, scholarship, lower fees and exemption from fee for poor students, supply of books at lower prices, special assistance for girls, etc., and (c) the reservation in admission to SC/ST/OBC, and similar informal policy for girls including special universities and colleges for girls.

The threefold policy initiatives of affordable fees structure through public education institutions and philanthropic private aided institutions, subsidised support in various forms, and formal reservation for SC/ST/OBC and informal measures for girls have provided an access to the groups and the poor who lag behind the others in attainment of higher education. These three initiatives have been the cornerstones of our policy for an improved access to the poor and educationally lagging social groups since 1950.

However, since the early 1980s, there has been a change in these pro-poor policy initiatives, due to reversal in some of these measures. The changes that have reduced the access of poor to higher education mainly include stagnation in the percentage share of public universities and colleges, and decline in private aided colleges, with a corresponding increase in self-financing private universities and colleges. There has been a rapid privatisation of higher education of commercial variety since the early 1990s with high fee structure, particularly in professional courses that have put the access of poor beyond their reach. In 2014, there were about 90 private deemed universities, 176 private state universities, which account for about 35% of the total of 757 universities. Further, about 76% of 38,056 colleges are private (MHRD 2015, 1–2). The share of students in private unaided self-financing institutions, universities and colleges has increased from 7.1% in 1995 to 63% in 2014 (MHRD 2015, 3).

At the same time, the policy of financial assistance and subsidised hostel and other support has become narrower and narrower. There has been a gradual shift away from assistance in the form of scholarship, fee waiver, hostels and loans as a source of financing higher education studies. Both the unaffordable self-financing private higher education and the decline in assistance to students have reduced the access of relatively poor students, which they enjoyed in government and private aided institutions in early policy regime. The SC/ST/OBC, however, experienced a double blow. Like any other group, an unaffordable private education with reduced financial support has affected them, but more importantly, their entry-level access through reservation has been significantly reduced due to the absence of reservation in private sector education institutions. The recent figures bring out quite clearly the low share of poor and SC, ST, OBC and Muslim students in self-financing private higher education institutions, compared with economically better off and high caste, non-tribal and non-Muslim groups. It appears that we are heading towards crises of inequality in higher education. But at the same time, we do not see much concern about this crisis, which is going to blow up sooner or later.

In this context, this chapter discusses the issue of growing inequality in higher education. To place the issue in perspective, the discussion is organised into three parts. First, we discuss the debate over education as public and private good, a theoretical issue which is at the centre of argument for privatisation of higher education. Second, we examine the theoretical debates around privatisation of higher education in India. Third, we highlight the present status of inequalities in access to higher education using 2014 data. And in the last section, we reflect on the possible solution to address the problems of growing unequal access to higher education.

HIGHER EDUCATION PUBLIC OR PRIVATE GOOD: THE DEBATE CONTINUES

Treating higher education as public or private good has policy implication for its supply by government at affordable cost or by private sector at a cost incurred by the supplier, irrespective of the affordability of the consumers, namely the students. It is argued that, if the higher education is a public good, then it is the responsibility of the government to supply it at a cost which is affordable for all. On the other hand, if it falls in the category of private good, then like any other commodity, it will be supplied at given cost to the consumers by the private supplier, whether it is affordable to the poor or not. What then is the private good? The neoclassical economists classify a good into private and public, based on the technical characteristics intrinsic to other good itself. Following the Samuelson (1954) approach, two important characteristics of a public good are non-excludable and non-rivalrous.

The former implies that individuals cannot be excluded from consuming a public good and the latter implies that consumption by one individual will not reduce availability of the same good to others. Private goods, on the other hand, are excludable in the sense that those who afford can have its ownership and can prevent others from consuming it unless they pay for it. This is based on the justification that private goods cost and, therefore, the beneficiaries should pay for it. By implication, it also means that in the case of private goods, those who do not pay can be excluded from its use. Since public goods can be consumed by those who do not pay, its free use is possible. The 'for-profit provision' of public good is difficult because it is impossible to recognise the spread of benefits and beneficiaries. The positive externalities attached to public good, however, demand public provision, as private suppliers would not come forward to supply public goods.

In the case of higher education, there are views opposite to each other, while some assume middle ground. The strict application of neoclassical framework renders higher education as a private good. This view holds that there are possibilities to make consumption of higher education excludable. The view that treats education as a private good is advocated by scholars who treat education as an investment in human capital, yielding high private return to individual on higher education (Becker 1964; Mincer 1958; Schultz 1960). Since expenditure on education is treated as investment that brings improvement in productivity and earning of beneficiaries, charging for the cost incurred is justified.

The alternative view argues that, in the case of higher education, there are major obstacles in identifying the beneficiaries and benefits of higher education (to individual and society) and the principle of exclusion does not work fully, due to presence of externalities. Therefore, it ceases to be a pure private good due to the presence of externalities. The presence of externalities implies that persons should be able to access education without paying the cost. The externalities also take the benefit of education beyond the individual beneficiary to the society in various ways. While the benefits to the beneficiaries of education in term of higher productivity and earning can be captured, the benefits to others in society are difficult to capture. Thus, while cost of education to the supplier could be factored in, it is difficult to estimate the ultimate beneficiaries and benefits to the society, economy and polity. Higher education contributes to the society through knowledge development. It is difficult to prevent knowledge dissemination to people who do not pay in the first instance. There are pieces of knowledge which are non-excludable in nature. Education brings increased awareness, increased participation in democratic process and enhanced civic capital, all of which are of great significance for the country.

The externalities also take the form of improvement in health, income distribution, strengthening democracy, rapid adoption of new technologies, etc. The only benefit that economists tried to measure is private benefit in terms of earning. But the enormous externalities associated turns higher education into a different kind of private good. Given the massive positive benefits of higher education to society, some prefer to treat it as a quasi-public good, (Tilak 2005), while others considered it as a private good with externalities (Musgrave and Musgrave 1989). Stiglitz (1999) describes education as publically supplied private good, exclusion made possible due to limit on the number of seats, but at the same time, knowledge assuming a character of global public good, due to free cross-country dissemination of knowledge.

There is, however, a third view which propagates a 'rights based or entitlement approach'. This view holds that like other basic needs, education is something that everybody needs irrespective of its character as public good or private good. Everybody is entitled to education and needs an opportunity to expand capabilities (Dreze and Sen 1998; Saito 2003) and overcoming worst aspect of human deprivation (Haq 1995). Therefore, it has to be made affordable whether supplied by public or by private players.

DEBATE IN INDIAN CONTEXT

The story of privatisation in India is as old as the beginning of modern education in the early 19th century. It is also complex in character. Therefore, we first examine the nature of private sector's presence in higher education sector. Higher education (university and college/institution) is supplied by both government and private sectors. In the case of government, both central and state are involved in education. The central government set up central universities (including central and deemed universities), colleges and other degree-awarding institutions. This also includes distance education or open learning. Similarly, the states have state universities, colleges and other degree-awarding institutions, including open universities. The private sector's presence is in all the three spheres, namely, deemed universities, universities, colleges and other degree-awarding institutions, which also include open learning and distance education. Besides, there are self-financing courses or degrees offered in public universities and colleges, particularly in the state universities and colleges. Thus, if one were to define the size of private sector, it would comprise the private deemed universities, private state universities, private colleges and similar degree-awarding institutions, private open learning and distance education institutions, and self-financing courses/degrees in government institutions. It must be mentioned that these exclude a very large private sector in higher education that offers diplomas of various duration.

In the case of private colleges, we have to draw distinction between private aided (by government) colleges and self-financing or unaided colleges/institutions. In the case of private aided institutions, they receive substantial aid from government and follow same curriculum, teaching, examinations. The fee structure is also regulated by the government. The private unaided or self-financing colleges/institutions have freedom to levy higher fees than the aided sector and offer programmes of study that may not be available in the public or aided institutions. It is this segment of the private sector that has serious implication for inequalities in higher education.

The justification for self-financing private sector originated with the constraints on public financing of higher education, and later in the commercial potential of self-financing programmes of study in public universities and private state universities. While the Seventh Plan (1985–90) emphasised the need to make higher education system self-supporting (Planning Commission 1985), the Eighth Plan placed emphasis on cost-effectiveness (Planning Commission 1992). The National Education Policy 1986 and PoA 1992 (MHRD 1992) also encouraged the institutions to generate their own fund, which encouraged a move towards, self-financing courses in higher education institutions. The Ninth Plan was more forthright and direct in observing that 'since budget resources are limited and such available resources need to be allocated to expanding primary education, it is important to recognise that universities must take greater efforts to supplement resources from the government' (Planning Commission 2002, 10).

The Eleventh Plan came out strongly in favour of increased role of private unaided institution for higher education. In fact, it targeted half of the increased enrolment in private institutions during the Eleventh Five Year Plan (2007–12). It recommended financial autonomy for institution to mobilise resources from user fees, review of fee structure and consultancy services. It argued that the operating cost of providing technical and medical education is much higher than the general education and, therefore, fees in these institutions should be higher. For students, it recommended loans to support their education. Thus, Eleventh Plan document brought shift towards privatisation of technical education. The Twelfth Five Year Plan took it further by recommending for-profit institutions in selected areas where shortages are high (Planning Commission 2013).

The shift toward privatisation was advocated by various commit-tees and commission. Soon after the New Economic Policy of 1991, the Private Universities Bill was introduced in Rajya Sabha in 1995. This remained unimplemented ever since. Soon after the introduction of Private Universities Bill in 1997, the government classified higher education in non-merit good in the Central Government Subsidies in India (Tilak 2004). The controversial Birla–Ambani Committee regarded higher education as a profitable investment opportunity (Prime Ministers' Council on Trade and Industry Government of India 2000). Another step towards privatisation of higher education came through the UGC (Establishment of and Maintenance of Standards in Private Universities) Regulations 2003. In 2003, the UGC (Establishment of and Maintenance of Standards in Private Universities) Regulations were issued to communicate the neces-sary standards of private universities set up through state acts (University Grants Commission 2003).

The Government of India, in its Report on Subsidies of 2004, treated higher education as merit-II good and primary education as merit-I good (Ministry of Finance 2004). The Report to the Nation 2006–09 of the National Knowledge Commission also regarded higher education as a private good (National Knowledge Commission 2009). Several states have passed private universities bill in their assemblies. This has led to the proliferation of private universities in these states.

Judiciary also played an important role in defining the power of the private education institutions in admission and fees structure and their regulation by the government. The successive judgments of the courts lent a helping hand in giving power in admission and fixation of fees by self-financing unaided education institutions in the country and also putting up a limit to their power with regard to admission and fees. The issue of capitation fees figured promi-nently in various verdicts. The verdict in 'Mohini Jain v. Karnataka State 1992' put a restraint on capitation fee in private educat-ional institutions (Supreme Court of India 1992). It recognised that capitation fee involves commercialisation of education and puts education beyond the reach of the poor. It argued that charging capitation fee in educational institutions is arbitrary and violates the constitutional right of the student (Article 14). The judgment in the case of 'State of AP v. J/B Education Society' (1998) justified regulation of technical institutions by the state. The ruling held that permission from the state government, approval from the council and affiliation from the concerned university are necessary for establishing technical institutions.

From time to time, the private sector institutions have challenged the restriction on freedom with respect to admission and charging of fees. The judiciary generally facilitated more freedom to the private sector. This shift was clear in the ruling of 'Unni Krishnan v. Andhra Pradesh', 1993, case. It favoured the freedom of private educational institutions in charging fees higher than the government institutions subject to the ceiling. It also held that state had no monopoly in establishing educational institution. The judgment by Supreme Court (1999) provided certain autonomy to deemed universities in the state. Citing the Priti Srivastava case, the Supreme Court ruled that the state governments had no control over deemed universities in the state, as they are set under the Section 3 of the UGC Act. The verdict delivered by the Supreme Court in 'Islamic Academy of Education v. State of Karnataka' and others in August 2003 also reiterated the position and ruled that institutions should have the freedom to fix their own fee structure and to generate surplus for the betterment and growth of that educational institution. The judgment in 'P.A. Inamadar and Ors v. States of Maharashtra and Ors' (August 2005) case also covered important aspects of private unaided institutions. It ruled that private colleges are not required to meet reservation quotas and they have full autonomy in their admissions of students, subject to fair, transparent and non-exploitative procedure (Supreme Court of India 2005). The judgment also allowed full freedom of the institutions in devising their own fee structure, subject to the limitation that there can be no profiteering and no capitation fee charged directly or indirectly, or in any form. Thus, the ruling in the case of Islamic Academy and Inamadar granted autonomy in various aspects ranging from determining fees to admission policy. This was a clear shift in the favour of recognising the privatisation of higher education with power and freedom with respect to admission and fess, with some limits.

EXPANDING SIZE OF PRIVATE SECTOR

The policy of privatisation of higher education described above has brought a significant shift from government educational institutions (universities/colleges/other degree-awarding institutions), and private aided institutions to self-financing (or student financing) higher education institutions. As mentioned above, the size of private sector comprises the private state universities, private deemed universities, private colleges and similar degree-awarding institutions, private distance education institutions and self-financing courses/degrees in government institutions. It must be mentioned that these exclude a very sizable component of private sector of higher education which offers diplomas of various duration. The size of the private sector is measured by taking both, the education institutions and the students in these institutions.

As regards the institutions, in 2014, there were about 90 private deemed universities, 223 private state universities, and together these 313 private central and state universities accounted for about 39% of the total universities and institutions of national importance. If we take the ratio of private universities (313) to total universities (729), then the proportion of private universities increased to about 43% in the country. Further, about 76% of 38,056 colleges were private MHRD 2015, 1–2).

With respect to students in 1995, of the total students in higher education institutes, the government institutions accounted for 57.5%, private aided 35.5% and private unaided 7.1%. The private aided and unaided together accounted for about 42.6%. Between 1995 and 2014, the share of private unaided has increased from 7.1% to 33%, at the per annum rate of 10.2%. The increase in private unaided institutions was accompanied by simultaneous decline in the share of private aided from 35.5% in 1995 to 25.3%, and in the share of government institutes from 57.5% to 41.4%. The share declined at per annum rate of about 1.8% for private aided and government institutions. Together, private aided and unaided educational institutions accounted for about 59% in 2015, up from 42.5% in 1995. Thus, as Tables 5.1, 5.2 and 5.3 showed, the private sector had replaced the government sector as the predominant sector in higher education.

Table 5.1
Number of Educational Institutions by Types

Institution	Number	Percentage
Central University	44	5.81
State Public	321	42.40
State Private	176	23.25
Deemed: Government	37	4.89
Deemed: Private	90	11.89
Deemed total	127	16.78
State Open Universities	14	1.85
Institute of NI	69	9.11
Others	6	0.79
Total	757	100
College	38,056 (approx)	–

Source: MHRD (2015), Provisional, T-1.

Table 5.2
Enrolment by Type of Institutions in Higher Education

Year/Institution	Government	Private Aided	Private Unaided
1995	57.5	35.5	7.1
2007	46.9	29.1	22.6
2014	41.4	25.3	32.7
Growth during 1995–2007	–1.7	–1.6	10.2
Growth during 2007–14	–1.8	–2.0	5.4
Growth during 1995–2014	–1.7	–1.8	8.4

Source: National Sample Survey on Participation and Expenditure in Education
and Survey of Social Consumption: Education.
Note: Horizontal sum for share is 100.

Table 5.3
GER by Social and Income Groups

Social Group	1995	2007	2014	Growth 1995–2007	2007–14	1995–2014
Gender						
Male	10.78	18.76	32.14	4.72	7.99	5.92
Female	6.76	14.72	27.73	6.69	9.47	7.71
Caste and Tribal Groups						
ST	3.43	7.22	17.19	6.39	13.2	8.85
SC	4.84	11.35	22.31	7.37	10.13	8.38
OBC	NA	14.57	29.36	NA	10.53	NA
Others	NA	26.22	41.65	NA	6.83	NA
Others + OBC	10.53	19.44	34.13	5.25	8.37	6.39
Religious Groups						
Hindu	NA	17.85	31.97		8.68	
Muslim	NA	9.35	16.54		8.49	
ORM*	NA	22.12	42.02		9.6	
Quintile Consumption Expenditure Class						
0–20	1.06	3.99	9.89	11.64	13.86	12.45
20–40	2.39	6.97	18.31	9.33	14.8	11.31
40–60	4.73	10.03	26.64	6.46	14.97	9.52
60–80	9.39	18.53	41.55	5.83	12.22	8.14
80–100	29.91	47.56	73.79	3.94	6.48	4.87
Total	8.82	16.83	30.06	5.54	8.64	6.67

Source: NSS on Participation and Expenditure in Education & Survey of Social
Consumption: Education.
Note: *ORM stands for Other Religious Minorities.

ACCESS TO HIGHER EDUCATION: CHANGE AND CURRENT STATUS OF GROSS ENROLMENT RATIO

We now discuss the current status on access to higher education by using the indicator of gross enrolment ratio (GER). Since the data on university and college enrolment by income, gender, caste, ethnic and religious groups is available from the National Sample Survey (NSS) on education, 1995, 2007 and 2014, we use the same source. From first Round in 1995 to latest Round in 2014, it covers a period of 20 years. The period between 1995 and 2014 gives an idea of changes for about 20 years. We examine the changes and level in interpersonal inequalities and group inequalities. The interpersonal inequalities are captured by taking monthly per capita expenditure (MPCE) in term of quintile, and social group inequality for caste, ethnic and religious groups.

In 2014, at all-India level, the GER was about 30%. However, it varied across the MPCE. Table 5.3 shows that in 2014, the GER for the lowest MPCE quintile (0–20%) was about 10%, and it progressively increased to 18% for the second quintile, 27% for the third quintile, 41% for the fourth and, finally, 74% for the fifth quintile. Thus, there is a clear negative relationship between the income level and enrolment rate (Figure 5.1). While the all-India average

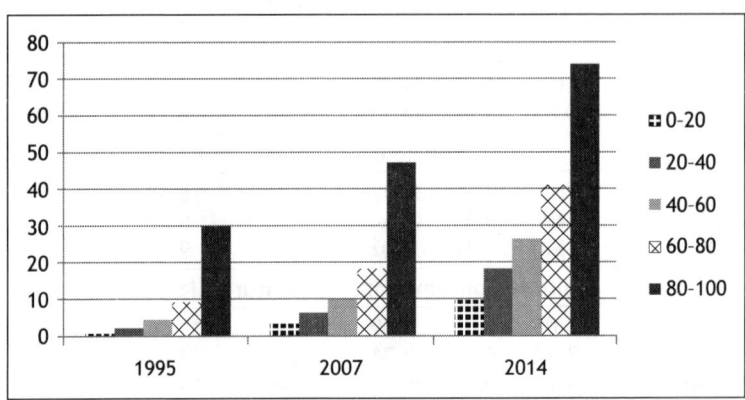

Figure 5.1
GER by Consumption Expenditure

Source: NSSO (1995, 2007, 2014).

was 30%, the GER of lowest MPCE class was seven times less compared to the top quintile. The disparities by MPCE class existed in 1995 and 2007. The GER varied between 1% for the lowest MPCE quintile and 30% for the top quintile in 1995, all-India average being about 10%. In 2007, the GER varied between 4 for the lowest quintile and 47% for the top quintile, the all-India average being 17%.

We now discuss the inter-group inequalities, focusing mainly on gender, caste, ethnic, and religious groups. In 2014, the enrolment for male was 32%, compare to about 28% for female, with a difference of about 4 percentage points (Figure 5.2). In the case of social groups, as against the all India average of 30% GER, it was 17% for ST, 23% for SC, followed by 29% for OBC and 42% for others (Figure 5.3). Thus, GER of ST was 40% of others, of SC about 50% of others, and of OBC about 70% of others. The graded inequalities between the caste and tribal groups are quite evident, as one moves up in caste hierarchy from low caste to upper caste the GER also moves up. Similar pattern is observed in 1995 and 2007.

In the case of religious groups, the GER is the lowest for the Muslim, 16.54%, compared with 42% for other minorities such as Christian, Sikh and Jains, and 32% for Hindus. The GER of Muslim was only 36% of other minorities and about half of the Hindus (Figure 5.4).

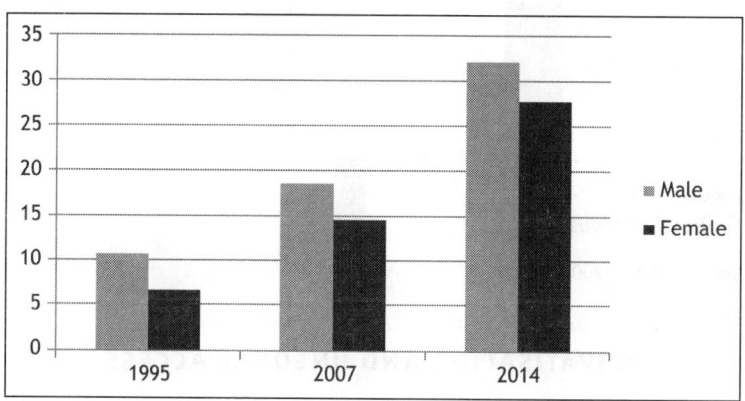

Figure 5.2
GER by Gender

Source: NSSO (1995, 2007, 2014).

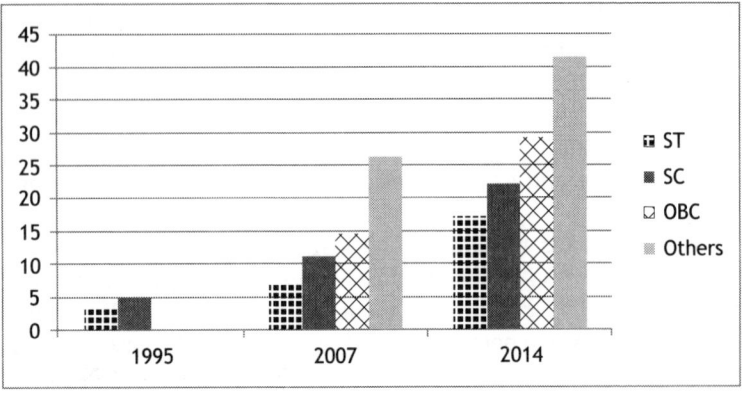

Figure 5.3
GER by Caste and Tribe

Source: NSSO (1995, 2007, 2014).

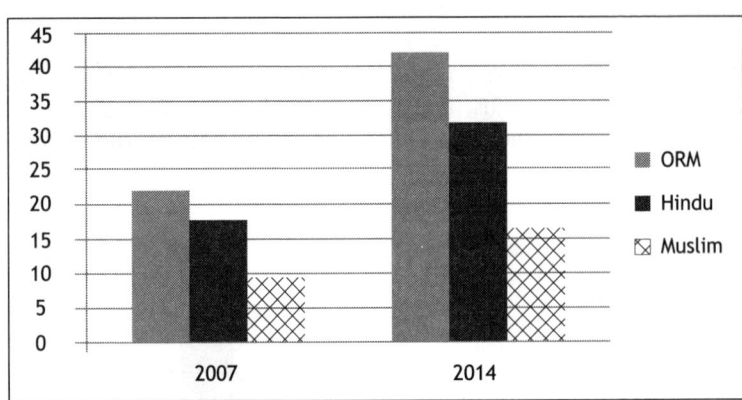

Figure 5.4
GER by Religious Group

Source: NSSO (2007, 2014).

PRIVATISATION AND UNEQUAL ACCESS

The above analysis of 2014 data revealed significant disparities based on income, caste, ethnic, religious and gender identity. It emerged that the GER is the lowest for the relatively poor. It is also low for STs followed by SCs and OBCs. It is also low for Muslims, and their level is almost similar to that of STs. Table 5.5 gives the share

Table 5.4
Share by Types of Institutions Across Consumption Quintile

Quintile	Government	Private Aided	Private Unaided
1995			
0–20	56.65	33.15	10.20
20–40	76.66	20.47	2.87
40–60	66.23	28.52	5.25
60–80	60.18	32.98	6.84
80–100	53.30	38.97	7.73
Total	57.51	35.42	7.07
2007			
0–20	53.86	31.26	12.35
20–40	49.12	28.80	20.41
40–60	54.81	27.47	16.60
60–80	53.10	26.70	18.50
80–100	41.56	30.28	26.87
Total	46.89	29.09	22.57
2014			
0–20	51.15	23.11	25.09
20–40	50.76	24.22	24.07
40–60	49.01	23.12	27.47
60–80	42.44	25.81	31.09
80–100	30.46	27.19	41.99
Total	41.41	25.35	32.70
1995–2007			
0–20	−0.42	−0.49	1.61
20–40	−3.64	2.89	17.76
40–60	−1.56	−0.31	10.07
60–80	−1.04	−1.74	8.64
80–100	−2.05	−2.08	10.94
Total	−1.69	−1.63	10.16
2007–14			
0–20	−0.73	−4.22	10.66
20–40	0.47	−2.44	2.38
40–60	−1.59	−2.43	7.46
60–80	−3.15	−0.48	7.70
80–100	−4.34	−1.53	6.59
Total	−1.76	−1.95	5.44
1995–2014			
0–20	−0.54	−1.88	4.85
20–40	−2.15	0.89	11.84
40–60	−1.57	−1.10	9.10
60–80	−1.82	−1.28	8.30
80–100	−2.90	−1.00	9.32
Total	−1.71	−1.75	8.39

Source: NSSO (1995, 2007, 2014).

Table 5.5
Share by Types of Institution Across Gender

Sex	Government	Private and Aided	Private Unaided
		1995	
Male	58.70	34.32	6.97
Female	55.42	37.37	7.21
Total	57.47	35.47	7.06
		2007	
Male	46.07	29.47	23.15
Female	48.04	28.56	21.75
Total	46.89	29.09	22.57
		2014	
Male	41.59	24.11	33.59
Female	41.19	26.96	31.51
Total	41.42	25.34	32.69
	Growth between 1995 and 2007		
Male	−2.00	−1.26	10.52
Female	−1.18	−2.22	9.64
Total	−1.68	−1.64	10.17
	Growth between 2007 and 2014		
Male	−1.45	−2.83	5.46
Female	−2.17	−0.82	5.44
Total	−1.76	−1.95	5.43
	Growth between 1995 and 2014		
Male	−1.80	−1.84	8.63
Female	−1.55	−1.70	8.07
Total	−1.71	−1.75	8.40

Source: NSSO (1995, 2007, 2014).

of the students by institution type, that is, government, private aided and private self-financing, which helps us to know the role of self-financing institutions in inter-group disparities in enrolment in higher education.

To capture the access of the students to the three types of institutions, namely government, private aided and unaided, we take the percentage of each category of institution in total students for 1995, 2007 and 2014, which gives the access of students to self-financing education institutions vis-à-vis private aided and government.

We discuss GER for income group in term of MPCE quintile, social groups with respect to SC, ST, OBC, others and religious groups, covering Muslims, other minorities and the Hindus.

Access by Income Class

The access to higher education varies by MPCE quintile quite significantly in government, private aided and private unaided institutions. In 2014, of the total students in higher education institutions in the country, the share of private unaided institution was about 33%, 41% by the private aided institutions and remaining 25% by government institutions. However, the share for different income groups in term of MPCE quintile differs. In the case of private unaided institutions, the share for the lowest quintile was 25%, compared to 42% of the top quintile, the all India average being 33%. The share of bottom quintile (0–20) was 59% of the top quintile (80–100), with a difference of 17 percentage points. The share goes up as we move up in MPCE ladder. The unequal access to lower income group in private unaided institutions is quite clear from the recent NSS survey for 2014.

In the case of private aided institutions, the story is somewhat different. As mentioned above, the private aided sector accounts about 25% of total students in the higher education institutions. We find fewer variations in the share across MPCE quintiles. For instance, the share of the bottom quintile is about 23%, compared to 27% of the top quintile, the difference between the bottom and top quintile being only 4 percentage points, as against 17 percentage points in the case of private unaided institutes. In other words, the share of bottom quintile was 85% of the top quintile in private aided institutions, compare to 59% for private unaided institutions, indicating low access to relatively poor persons to private unaided institutions as compared with private aided institutions.

In the case of government institutions, the opposite was true: The share of the bottom quintile was 51%, compared with 30 for the top quintile, all India average being 41%. This indicates that the relatively poor had a higher access to government education institutes. Since the relatively poor classes have less access to the private unaided institutions due to high fee structure, they fall back on the government institution.

ACCESS AND CASTE, TRIBAL
AND RELIGIOUS GROUPS

Similar disparities are observed in the share of ST, SC, OBC, Muslim, and female groups in private unaided educational institutions. In 2014, of the total female students in higher education institutions, about 32% were in private unaided institutions, slightly lower than men (34%) and all India average of 33%. Thus, women have caught up with men in acquiring access to private unaided educational institutions. The share was also on par with men in private aided and government educational institutes.

CASTE AND TRIBAL GROUPS

Unlike female, the disparities emerged quite clearly in access to private unaided education institutions for SC and ST. As can be seen in Table 5.6, as against 33% share of students in private unaided institutions at all-India level, the share of ST was 19%, followed by 28% for SC. The share of these two groups was also lower compared with OBC (37%) and others (31%), the share of OBC being the maximum. Thus, the access of ST and SC to private unaided institutions was less than all India average, and also compared with OBC and others, although the difference was relatively less for SC than ST.

In the case of private aided institutions also, the share of ST and SC was relatively lower, compared to OBC and others, and all India average. Since the ST and SC's access to private aided and unaided was low, they fall back on government institutions in greater magnitude than OBC and others. Of the total students in higher educational institutions, the share of government institutions was 59% for ST, 49% for SC, much more than 37% for OBC and 40% for others, and 41% of all India average.

In the case of religious groups, the share of the Muslims in private unaided was lower than other minorities and the Hindus. In 2014, of the total Muslim students in higher education institutions, about 25% were in private unaided institutions, which was lower than 39% for other minorities and 33% for Hindus. The Muslims share in private aided institute was similar to that of other minorities and the Hindus. The Muslims, however, have relatively high proportion than other minorities and the Hindus in government educational institutes—50% compared with 35% for other minorities, 41% for the Hindus, and 41% of all India average (Table 5.7).

Table 5.6
Share by Type of Institution Across Social Groups

Social Group	Government	Private Aided	Private Unaided
		1995	
ST	75.57	23.46	0.97
SC	62.89	34.34	2.76
Others*	56.09	36.07	7.84
Total	57.44	35.49	7.07
		2007	
ST	59.65	21.10	19.02
SC	52.91	30.68	14.80
OBC	41.75	30.97	25.93
Others	48.19	27.75	22.48
Others*	45.39	29.15	23.99
Total	46.89	29.09	22.57
		2014	
ST	58.80	21.96	19.06
SC	48.56	22.32	28.66
OBC	37.35	25.00	37.07
Others	40.48	27.43	31.49
Others*	38.83	26.15	34.43
Total	41.42	25.34	32.69
	Growth between 1995 and 2007		
ST	−1.95	−0.88	28.15
SC	−1.43	−0.93	15.02
OBC	−	−	−
Others	−	−	−
Others*	−2.98	−3.00	17.32
	Growth between 2007 and 2014		
ST	−0.20	0.57	0.03
SC	−1.22	−4.44	9.90
OBC	−1.58	−3.01	5.24
Others	−2.46	−0.17	4.93
Others*	−2.21	−1.54	5.30
Total	−1.76	−1.95	5.43
	Growth between 1995 and 2014		
ST	−1.31	−0.35	16.97
SC	−1.35	−2.24	13.11
OBC	−	−	−
Others	−1.92	−1.68	8.10
Total	−1.71	−1.76	8.39

Source: NSSO (1995, 2007, 2014).
Note: Others* denotes others including OBC.

Table 5.7
Share by Types of Institution Across Religious Group

Religious Group	Government	Private Aided	Private Unaided
	2007		
Hindu	47.42	29.08	22.00
Muslim	46.55	28.29	24.16
ORM	40.35	30.24	28.04
Total	46.89	29.09	22.57
	2014		
Hindu	41.11	25.40	32.96
Muslim	49.67	24.70	25.11
ORM	34.73	25.45	39.03
Total	41.42	25.34	32.69
	Growth between 2007 and 2014		
Hindu	−2.02	−1.91	5.95
Muslim	0.93	−1.92	0.55
ORM	−2.12	−2.43	4.84
Total	−1.76	−1.95	5.43

Source: NSSO (2007, 2014).

As it emerged, the situation with regard to attainment in higher education in 2014 revealed the following features:

1. In 2014, the private unaided sector accounted about 33% of the total students' population in higher education in the country, followed by 41% government and 25% private aided institution.
2. The access of the relatively economically weaker sections has been much lower, compared with economically better off and, therefore, they depend more on government institution than the economically better off do.
3. The access of girls to private unaided institutions has been nearly on par with the boys, so girls have achieved near parity with boys in access to private unaided institutions.
4. The access of ST and SC to private unaided institutions has been lower than OBC, others and all India average; although, the difference was relatively less for SC than ST. Same is the pattern with respect to their share in private aided institutes. Since the ST and SC's access to private aided and unaided

institutions was low, they depend more on government institutions than OBC and others.

5. The access of the Muslims to private unaided was lower than other minorities and the Hindus. Their share in private aided institutes was similar to that of other minorities and the Hindus. The Muslims, however, have a relatively high proportion than other minorities and the Hindus in government educational institutes.

SHARE IN TOTAL STUDENTS IN SELF-FINANCING PRIVATE INSTITUTIONS

We have so far seen the share of each of the three educational institutions in total students and found that the self-financing institutions account about 33% of the total students in the higher education institutions in the country. We also observed that the share of low-income groups, ST, SC and Muslim in private unaided institutions was relatively low, compared to OBC and others. In this section, we analyse the share of each of the group in the respective total of each institution. To bring out the inequalities, we compare these shares with respect to their share in population in the age group of 18–22 years.

We would first discuss the share for the MPCE class by quintile (Table 5.8). At all India aggregate level in 2014, there is a positive relationship between the MPCE quintile class and share of each quintile in total students in private unaided institutions, which indicates that the share of bottom quintile tend to be lower, compared with the higher quintile. The bottom quintile accounts for only 8% of the total students in private unaided institutes, compared with 34% for the top quintile, almost five times lesser for the bottom quintile, compared with the top quintile. Thus, the relatively poor account much less share in the higher educational institutions.

In the case of private unaided institutions, there is an inverse relationship between percentage share in total students and the quintile class. Of the total students in private unaided educational institutions, the first quintile account for 6%, the second for 10%, the share increased to 16% in the third quintile, 24% in the fourth quintile and 44% in the fifth quintile. Thus, the share of bottom

Table 5.8
Share of Quintiles in Institution Type (2014–15)

Class	Government	Private Aided	Private Unaided	Total
1995				
0–20	2.5	2.4	3.7	2.6
20–40	7.4	3.2	2.2	5.5
40–60	12.8	9.0	8.3	11.1
60–80	21.2	18.8	19.6	20.2
80–100	56.1	66.6	66.2	60.5
Total	100	100	100	100
2007				
0–20	5.5	5.1	2.6	4.8
20–40	9.1	8.6	7.9	8.7
40–60	14.4	11.6	9.1	12.3
60–80	24.1	19.5	17.4	21.3
80–100	46.9	55.1	63.0	52.9
Total	100	100	100	100
2014				
0–20	9.8	7.2	6.1	7.9
20–40	16.7	13.0	10.0	13.6
40–60	22.1	17.1	15.7	18.7
60–80	26.3	26.1	24.4	25.7
80–100	25.1	36.6	43.8	34.1
Total	100	100	100	100

Source: NSSO (1995, 2007, 2014).

quintile was seven times lesser, compared to the top quintile, and three times lesser, compared to the second top quintile. Similarly, the share of the second bottom quintile was four times lesser, compared to top quintile, and two times lesser, compared with second top quintile. Thus, not only the lesser number of lower income classes enter into private unaided educational institutions (25% for the bottom MPCE class versus 43% for the top MPCE class) but they also constitute a relatively small proportion of the total students in private unaided institutions (about 6% for the bottom MPCE 44% for the top quintile).

In the case of gender (Table 5.9), the share of male was higher (58%), compared with female (42%). Similarly, the share of ST and SC was lower, compared with OBC and higher caste (Table 5.10). The share of the Muslim was lower, compared to other religious groups

Table 5.9
Share of Gender in Institution Type (2014–15)

Sex	Government	Private Aided	Private Unaided	Total
		1995		
Male	63.7	60.4	61.6	62.4
Female	36.3	39.6	38.4	37.6
Total	100	100	100	100
		2007		
Male	57.3	59.0	59.8	58.3
Female	42.7	41.0	40.2	41.7
Total	100	100	100	100
		2014		
Male	57.0	54.0	58.3	56.7
Female	43.0	46.0	41.7	43.3
Total	100	100	100	100

Source: NSSO (1995, 2007, 2014).

Table 5.10
Share of Caste and Tribal Group in Institution Type (2014–15 Vertical)

Sex	Government	Private Aided	Private Unaided	Total
		1995		
ST	4.0	2.0	0.4	3.1
SC	12.2	10.8	4.4	11.1
OBC + others	83.8	87.2	95.2	85.8
		2007		
ST	4.3	2.5	2.9	3.4
SC	15.4	14.4	8.9	13.6
OBC	32.2	38.5	41.6	36.2
Others	48.1	44.6	46.6	46.8
OBC + others	80.3	83.2	88.2	83.0
		2014		
ST	8.1	5.0	3.3	5.7
SC	17.4	13.1	13.0	14.8
OBC	37.7	41.2	47.4	41.8
Others	36.8	40.7	36.2	37.6
OBC + others	74.5	82.0	83.7	79.4
Total	100	100	100	100

Source: NSSO (1995, 2007, 2014).

(Table 5.11). Thus, in the cases of women, ST, SC and the Muslim's share was lower than their share in population of age group of 18–22 years (see Table 5.12, Table 5.13 and Table 5.14).

Table 5.11
Share of Religious Group in Institution Type (2014–15 Vertical)

Sex	Government	Private Aided	Private Unaided	Total
2007				
Hindu	86.5	85.5	83.4	85.5
Muslim	8.0	7.8	8.6	8.0
ORM	5.6	6.7	8.0	6.5
2014				
Hindu	84.4	85.2	85.7	85.1
Muslim	10.1	8.2	6.5	8.4
ORM	5.5	6.5	7.8	6.5

Source: NSSO (2007, 2014).

Table 5.12
Share of Gender in 18–22 Population (2014–15)

Gender	1995	2007	2014
Male	51.3	52.3	53.1
Female	48.7	47.7	46.9
Total	100	100	100

Source: NSSO (1995, 2007, 2014).

Table 5.13
Share of Caste and Tribal Group in 18–22 Population (2014–15)

Social Group	1995	2007	2014
ST	7.8	8	10
SC	20.2	20.2	20.0
OBC	NA	41.8	42.8
Others	NA	30.0	27.2
Others*	72.0	71.8	70.0
Total	100	100	100

Source: NSSO (1995, 2007, 2014).
Note: Others* denotes others including OBC.

Table 5.14
Share of Religious Group in 18–22 Population (2014–15)

Religious Group	2007	2014
Hindu	80.6	80.0
Muslim	14.5	15.3
ORM	4.93	4.7
Total	100.0	100.0

Source: NSSO (2007, 2014).

CHANGES IN GER AT AGGREGATE LEVEL

After having seen the present status on access by income, gender, caste, ethnic and religious group lines in higher education, we now take a look at the changes in enrolment ratio in the private unaided and aided and government institutions. We study the changes during 20-year period between 1995 and 2014.

During 1995–2014, the GER in higher education increased at per annum rate of 6.67% (Table 5.3). The annual rate of increase has been much higher among the lower consumption expenditure classes compared to top classes. The per annum rate progressively increase as we move down in consumption class. The relatively higher per annum increase among the bottom quintile is presumably high due to low base in the initial year; nevertheless, the growth at lower end of income strata has been greater than the upper end—later already achieved high level in GER, which allows a limited scope for further increase.

Coming to the changes in groups, the per annum rate in the GER has been higher for female than males, about 8% for females and 6% for males. It is the relatively high expansion of female students that has brought female GER on par with male in GER 2014. The female–male parity in GER, at least at aggregate level, has been one of the success stories of gender affirmative action policy in India.

The per annum rate has been about 8–9% for STs and SCs during 1995 and 2014, which was slightly higher than others, and 6.67% for all India average. However, despite relatively high growth rate, it was not high enough to minimise the difference in GER between the ST/SC and others. Since religion-wise data is not available for 1995, we calculated growth rate between 2007 and 2014. During this period, the per annum rate was more or less similar for the Hindus and the Muslims. The rate, however, was lower compared with other minorities.

CHANGES BY TYPE OF INSTITUTIONS

As seen in Table 5.4, in 1995, of the total students in higher education institutes, the government institutions account 57.5%, private aided 35.5% and private unaided 7.1% (the private aided and unaided together accounted about 42.5%). Between 1995 and 2014, the share of private unaided institutions has increased from 7% to 33%, at the per annum rate of 8.39%. The increase in private unaided institutions was accompanied by simultaneously decline in the share of private aided from 35.5% in 1995 to 25.3%, and in the share of government institutions from 57.5% to 41.4%. The share declined at an identical per annum rate of about 1.8% for private aided and government institutions. Private unaided expanded at accelerated rate between mid-1990s to mid-2000, replacing government and aided sector which occupied important position before 1990s.

We also look at the changes in the share of the students in private unaided institutions disaggregated by income class and social groups. Table 5.15, presents the changes in the share of students in three category of institutions, namely, government, private aided and private unaided during 1995 and 2014 at aggregate level, and for income, caste, and tribe at disaggregate level. The share

Table 5.15
Share by Type of Institution Across Caste and Tribe

Social group	Government	Private Aided	Private Unaided
	1995		
Gender			
Male	58.7	34.32	6.97
Female	55.42	37.37	7.21
Income Group			
0–20	56.65	33.15	10.2
20–40	76.66	20.47	2.87
40–60	66.23	28.52	5.25
60–80	60.18	32.98	6.84
80–100	53.3	38.97	7.73

Social group	Government	Private Aided	Private Unaided
Caste and Tribal Group			
ST	75.57	23.46	0.97
SC	62.89	34.34	2.76
Others*	56.09	36.07	7.84
Total	57.44	35.49	7.07
2014			
Gender			
Male	41.59	24.11	33.59
Female	41.19	26.96	31.51
Income Group			
0–20	51.15	23.11	25.09
20–40	50.76	24.22	24.07
40–60	49.01	23.12	27.47
60–80	42.44	25.81	31.09
80–100	30.46	27.19	41.99
Social Group			
ST	58.8	21.96	19.06
SC	48.56	22.32	28.66
OBC	37.35	25	37.07
Others	40.48	27.43	31.49
Others*	38.83	26.15	34.43
Total	41.42	25.34	32.69
Growth between 1995 and 2014			
Gender			
Male	–1.8	–1.84	8.63
Female	–1.55	–1.7	8.07
Income Group			
0–20	–0.54	–1.88	4.85
20–40	–2.15	0.89	11.84
40–60	–1.57	–1.1	9.1
60–80	–1.82	–1.28	8.3
80–100	–2.9	–1.88	9.32
Caste and Tribe			
ST	–1.31	–0.35	16.97
SC	–1.35	–2.24	13.11
Others + OBC	–1.92	–1.68	8.1
Total	–1.71	–1.76	8.39

Source: NSSO (2014).

of the unaided private institute has increased at relatively low rate for bottom quintile (about 5%), compared with top income quintile, which is about 9% per annum. The share of the female and male in unaided institutions has increased more or less by the same per annum rate of 8% during 1995 and 2015. The corresponding decline also occurred in government and private aided institutions at similar rate. In the case of social groups, the per annum increase in the share of private unaided institutions was higher for SC and ST, compared with OBC and other, mainly due to low share in the base year. In the case of Muslim, the per annum increase during 2007 and 2014 was quite low, compared with the Hindu and other minorities. Thus, during 1995 and 2014, the share of students in bottom quintile has increased at a lower rate. Among the social groups, the Muslim's share increased at a lower rate. But the share of SC and ST increased at relatively higher rate, presumably due to low base in initial year. The share of female and male increased at similar rate.

PRIVATE UNAIDED INSTITUTIONS AND FINANCIAL ASSISTANCE

We have seen that the access to private unaided higher education institution for the students located at the bottom of income ladder has been relatively low. This has been mainly because of high tuition fees in private self-financing institutions, compared with private aided and government institutes. However, if the high fee structure is supported by financial assistance in the form of scholarship, freeship or fee waiver, it could facilitate the access to the students from lower income strata. But the data for 2014 indicate that the private unaided institutions have not come forward to extend financial support to needy students. Table 5.16 gives the percentage of students with scholarship and fee waiver.

SCHOLARSHIPS

Aggregate by Groups

First we see the variation in the percentage of scholarship holders at aggregate level by group, then we discuss by Institutions. In 2014, out of the total students in higher educational institutions in the country, only 17% received scholarship (Table 5.17). This was indeed a low proportion. However, the proportion of scholarship holder differs among the income, gender, caste, ethnic and religious groups.

Table 5.16
Scholarship by Institution Types: Gender and Quintile (2014–15)

Scholarship	Yes	No	Total
Institution		**Total**	
Government	18.50	81.5	100
Aided	16.1	83.9	100
Unaided	15.8	84.2	100
Total	16.92	83.08	100
		Male	
Government	18.8	81.2	100
Aided	14.87	85.13	100
Unaided	16.53	83.47	100
Total	16.98	83.02	100
		Female	
Government	18.11	81.89	100
Aided	17.54	82.46	100
Unaided	14.78	85.22	100
Total	16.85	83.15	100
		Income Class	
		0–20	
Government	29.15	70.85	100
Aided	22.46	77.54	100
Unaided	18.76	81.24	100
Total	24.81	75.19	100
		20–40	
Government	21.69	78.31	100
Aided	22.03	77.97	100
Unaided	18.32	81.68	100
Total	20.76	79.24	100
		40–60	
Government	24.24	75.76	100
Aided	15.82	84.18	100
Unaided	20.3	79.7	100
Total	21.12	78.88	100
		60–80	
Government	15.18	84.82	100
Aided	18.93	81.07	100
Unaided	18.66	81.34	100
Total	17.13	82.87	100
		80–100	
Government	10.71	89.29	100
Aided	10.87	89.13	100
Unaided	11.62	88.38	100
Total	11.13	88.87	100

Source: NSSO (2014).

Table 5.17
Scholarship by Institution Types and by Social Groups

Scholarship	Yes	No	Total
Institution		**Total**	
Government	18.5	81.5	100
Aided	16.1	84.0	100
Unaided	15.8	84.2	100
Total	16.9	83.1	100
		ST	
Government	51.07	48.93	100
Aided	38.17	61.83	100
Unaided	33.2	66.8	100
Total	44.8	55.2	100
		SC	
Government	36.53	63.47	100
Aided	41.35	58.65	100
Unaided	28.35	71.65	100
	35.09	64.91	100
		OBC	
Government	16.64	83.36	100
Aided	16.17	83.83	100
Unaided	18.49	81.51	100
Total	17.11	82.89	100
		Others	
Government	4.7	95.3	100
Aided	5.24	95.0	100
Unaided	6.18	93.82	100
Total	5.31	94.69	100
		Hindu	
Government	18.93	81.07	100
Aided	16.35	83.65	100
Unaided	15.85	84.15	100
Total	17.17	82.83	100
		Muslim	
Government	10.41	89.59	100
Aided	8.1	92.0	100
Unaided	18.6	81.4	100
Total	11.83	88.17	100
		ORM*	
Government	26.86	73.14	100
Aided	22.96	77.04	100
Unaided	12.95	87.05	100
Total	20.27	79.73	100

Source: NSSO (2014).
Note: *ORM stands for Other Religious Minorities.

In the case of income groups, that is, with reference to the MPCE class, the students located at the bottom quintile receive higher scholarship than those at the top quintile. About 25% of the students in the bottom quintile receive scholarship, and ratio reduced to 21% for the next two quintiles (20–40 and 40–60), to 17% for 60–80 quintile and further down to 11% for the top quintile (80–100). Thus, students from relatively weak background receive higher proportion of scholarship compared to better off students, which indicate a progressive character of the scholarship.

In the case of social groups, similar a progressive trend is seen. About 45% of STs receive scholarship, followed by 35% for SCs, 17% for OBCs and 5 for others. It is seen that a higher proportion of ST and SC students received scholarship, compared with OBC and others.

However, similar trend is not observed in the case of religious groups. About 20% of the other minority students received scholarship, followed by 17% for Hindu and 12% for Muslim. Thus, it is seen that lower proportion of the Muslim students have access to scholarship.

Except the Muslim students, the allocation of scholarships was fairly progressive in so far, as a relatively high proportion of students from weaker section, namely, lower income group, female, ST and SC, receive scholarship as compared with high-income group, male, higher caste, etc. It is only in the case of the Muslim that they lag behind the other minorities and the Hindu in scholarship coverage.

Groups by Type of Institutions

Does the coverage of scholarship for income, female, social and religious groups vary across three educational institution categories, namely, private unaided, private aided and government? The ratio of scholarship holders marginally vary between the three institutions. The scholarship coverage was marginally low for unaided private and private aided institutions (16%), compared with government institutions (18.50%). There are, however, significant variations between male–female, income class and caste, ethnic and religious groups.

In the case of income class, we have seen that, at the overall level, relatively poor groups benefited more from the scholarship. In the case of private aided and government institutions also, the proportion of scholarship holders was relatively higher in the bottom MPCE quintile, compared with the top quintile. For instance, 29% of students in the bottom quintile received scholarship, compared to 11% for the top quintile. Same is the pattern for government institutions: the scholarship coverage is about 29% for the bottom quintile, which is much higher than 11% for the top quintile. In the case of both private aided and government, the proportion of scholarship holders reduces as we go up from the first quintile to the fifth quintile. However, this negative relationship between quintile groups and proportion of scholarship holder is not quite systematic for the private unaided institutions. The proportion of scholarship holder is nearly similar from the first quintile to the fourth quintile, as it varies in a narrow range from 18% to 20%. The only clear difference is between the bottom and the top quintile, and bottom quintile—the ratio being 19% for the bottom quintile and 13% for the top quintile.

Thus, clear progressivity in scholarship coverage that we see in the case of private aided and government institution is not that obvious in the case of private unaided institution, as the negative relationship between the quintile group and proportion of scholarship holder is not significant. There seems to be a lack of focus on the weaker section in the allocation of scholarship in private aided institutions.

In the case of gender also, the proportion of girl scholarship holders was marginally lower in private unaided institutions, 15%, compared with 17% for private aided and 18% for government institutes, while all India average was 17%. Similar difference was observed for male, that ratio of scholarship holders for male being 16%, 15% and 19% for private unaided, private aided and government institutions respectively.

In the case of caste and ethnic groups, we find a similar but a lot clearer trend: the lower coverage of SC/ST is quite evident. About 33% of ST students were covered with scholarship by the private unaided institution, which was low compared with 38% in private aided and 51% for government, the all India average being 45%. Similarly, the scholarship coverage in the case of SC was 28% in unaided private institutions, 41% in private aided and 37% in government, all India average being 35%. Thus, the proportion of scholarship holders form ST and SC in private unaided institutions was significantly lower, compared with private aided and government institutions.

However, the opposite was true in the case of OBC and others groups. The ratio of scholarship holders was nearly the same for the three types of institutions as the ratio varies in a narrow range of 17–18%. In the case of others, although the ratio of scholarship holders was low, it was, in fact, high in private unaided (6%), compared with private aided (5%) and government institutions (4%). Thus, the private unaided institutions have not revealed the social policy focus in their financial assistance; in so far, the scholarship coverage by them is significantly lower for SC and ST, as compared to OBC and other. Alternatively, the coverage is more favourable for OBC and others.

Lastly, in the case of Muslims, unlike SC/ST, the proportion of scholarship holders in unaided private institutions was relatively higher, compared with the Hindus and other minorities. But they lag behind in scholarship coverage in private aided and government institutions. The difference was quite significant. The coverage of Muslim in private aided was 8% compared with 16% for Hindu and 23% for other minorities. Similarly, the coverage was 10% in private unaided, compared with 19% in private aided and 27% in government institutions for other minorities. In both private aided and government institutions, the Muslim receive significantly less coverage.

FEE WAIVER

Coming to the fee waiver, at all-India level, the proportion is much lower as only 4% of the total student received fee waiver (Table 5.18). The ratio was 4% in private aided, compared with 3% for private unaided institutions.

Coming to MPCE class, those at the bottom tend to have higher proportion of fee waiver, compared with those who are at the top of MPCE class, but the proportion of fee waivers was meagre to make significant positive impact on access of poorer to self-financing private institutions. The percentage of students with fee waiver was also lower for ST, SC and others in private unaided institutions (Table 5.19). It is only in the case of OBC that the ratio of fee waiver was same for all the three education institutions.

REFORM IN EQUITY POLICIES

The analysis for 2014 revealed significant disparities based on income, caste, ethnic, religious and gender identity. It emerged that the GER is the lowest for the poor. It is also low for ST followed by SC and OBC; it is also low for Muslim, which is fairly close to ST. The analysis related to the relative importance of institution type, namely, government, private aided and private unaided, indicate that the private unaided sector is emerging at a faster rate, gradually replacing the private aided and government sector, particularly the former.

In 2014, private unaided sector accounted for about 33% of the total students' population in higher education in the country, followed by 41% by government and 25% private aided institution. The access of the economically weaker sections to private unaided institutions is much lower, compared with economically better off, and therefore, former depend more on government institutions than the economically better off. Similarly, the access of ST and SC to private unaided institutes has been lower than OBC and others. Since the ST and SC's

Table 5.18
Fee Waived by Institution Types: Gender and Quintile (2014–15)

Fee Waived	Fully	Partly	No	Total
Institution		Total		
Government	1.74	2.80	95.46	100
Aided	1.85	2.78	95.37	100
Unaided	1.62	1.78	96.60	100
Total	1.72	2.42	95.86	100
		Male		
Government	1.88	3.15	94.96	100
Aided	2.03	3.40	94.57	100
Unaided	1.75	1.96	96.28	100
Total	1.86	2.77	95.37	100
		Female		
Government	1.56	2.35	96.10	100
Aided	1.63	2.05	96.32	100
Unaided	1.43	1.52	97.04	100
Total	1.53	1.98	96.49	100
		Income Class		
		0–20		
Government	2.87	5.14	91.99	100
Aided	1.87	4.75	93.38	100
Unaided	0.42	0.02	99.55	100
Total	1.92	3.57	94.51	100
		20–40		
Government	3.21	3.43	93.36	100
Aided	1.05	1.26	97.69	100
Unaided	1.98	0.97	97.06	100
Total	2.29	2.17	95.54	100
		40–60		
Government	0.74	3.70	95.56	100
Aided	4.22	4.96	90.82	100
Unaided	1.70	1.21	97.09	100
Total	1.93	3.23	94.84	100
		60–80		
Government	1.53	2.13	96.34	100
Aided	1.33	1.75	96.92	100
Unaided	1.94	1.83	96.23	100
Total	1.60	1.93	96.47	100
		80–100		
Government	1.43	1.61	96.96	100
Aided	1.38	2.63	95.98	100
Unaided	1.50	2.38	96.11	100
Total	1.44	2.22	96.33	100

Source: NSSO (2014).

Table 5.19
Tuition Fee Waived by Institution Types and Caste, Tribe and Religious Group

Fee Waived	Fully	Partly	No	Total
Institution		**Total**		
Government	1.74	2.8	95.46	100
Aided	1.85	2.78	95.37	100
Unaided	1.62	1.78	96.6	100
Total	1.72	2.42	95.86	100
		ST		
Government	6.27	8.93	84.8	100
Aided	0.64	11.08	88.28	100
Unaided	2.3	0.78	96.92	100
Total	3.99	7.66	88.34	100
		SC		
Government	3.05	5.84	91.1	100
Aided	3.48	3.94	92.58	100
Unaided	2.94	3.62	93.44	100
Total	3.1	4.67	92.22	100
		OBC		
Government	1.44	2.38	96.18	100
Aided	1.55	2.58	95.87	100
Unaided	1.73	1.91	96.36	100
Total	1.58	2.23	96.19	100
		Others		
Government	0.61	0.76	98.63	100
Aided	1.79	1.62	96.59	100
Unaided	0.94	1.04	98.02	100
Total	1.05	1.09	97.86	100
	Religion			
		Hindu		
Government	1.76	2.74	95.49	100
Aided	2.07	2.83	95.1	100
Unaided	1.74	1.7	96.56	100
Total	1.83	2.39	95.79	100
		Muslim		
Government	1.72	1.78	96.5	100
Aided	0.63	2.42	96.95	100
Unaided	1.24	1.27	97.49	100
Total	1.3	1.79	96.9	100
		ORM		
Government	1.4	5.53	93.07	100
Aided	0.41	2.48	97.11	100
Unaided	0.67	3.03	96.3	100
Total	0.83	3.66	95.51	100

Source: NSSO (2014).

access to private unaided was low, they depend more on government institutions than OBC and others. The access of the Muslims to private unaided was lower than other minorities and the Hindus, so they also depend more on government educational institutes. The access of women to private unaided institutions has been nearly on par with the men, so the women have achieved near parity with men in access to private unaided institutions. It also emerged that the financial support by the private unaided institutes is much lesser, particularly to the students from SC and ST communities.

The analysis reveals that, increasingly, the access to higher education has become unequal than before. The growing unequal access to higher education is mainly due to fast expansion of self-financing (students financing) institutions with high and unaffordable fee rate, accompanied by a low financial assistance through scholarship and fee waiver. The low-income group and SC, ST and Muslim are affected more from the high fee structure than better off OBC and higher castes. This rising trend towards unequal access needs to be reversed through changes in policies. What we need is to bring back the policies that we developed before 1970 and, also, go for some new policy initiatives.

After the independence, we used two sets of policies to make higher education affordable. These policies include the expansion of higher education through public education institutions and private aided institutions (our domestic model of public–private partnership) with an affordable fee structure, and subsidised hostels and scholarship and other facilities. Therefore, the first thing that we need to do is to expand the government public institutions and private aided sectors, particularly for professional courses by allocating increased percentage of GDP on their expansion, that is, higher educational institutions under public and private aided sector. Besides, there is a need to strengthen these institutions in terms of infrastructure and faculty. Second, this should be supplemented by expanding the hostel facilities with subsidies rates and financial support to poorer students. In the case of self-financing institutions, their expansion should be kept in reasonable limit. Moreover, to enable the access of poor to the existing private self-financing institutions, the financial support through scholarships and subsidised hostel and books and other facilities should be extended to those who could not afford the high free structure. As a supplementary measure, the liberal loan facilities should be provided. However, the present method of educational loan by commercial banks, with subsidy on interest by the government, will not serve the purpose. Government should set up a body on the pattern of

Canada or Australia with sizable amount of funds to provide interest free loans, returnable after employment in reasonable instalments to all. These measures should help to provide access to poorer sections, particularly to professional and technical education by private unaided education. These changes in policy for equity in higher education are necessary, otherwise rather than making educational system to perform level playing role, it may turn to be a source of economic and social inequalities.

REFERENCES

Becker, Gary S. 1964. *Investment in Human Capital: A Theoretical and Empirical Analysis with Special Reference to Education*. New York: National Bureau of Economic Research.

Dreze, Jean and Sen, Amartya. 1998. *Indian Development: Selected Regional Perspective*. Delhi: Oxford University Press.

Government of India. 2000. 'Report on A Policy Frame Work for Reforms in Education'. Prime Ministers' Council on Trade and Industry, Government of India, New Delhi.

Haq, Mahbubul. 1995. *Reflections on Human Development*. New York: Oxford University Press.

MHRD (Ministry of Human Resource Development). 1992. *National Policy on Education, 1986–Programme of Action 1992*. New Delhi: Government of India.

———. 2015. *All India Survey on Higher Education 2014–15* (Provisional). New Delhi: Government of India.

Mincer, Jacob. 1958. 'Investment in Human Capital and Personal Income Distribution'. *Journal of Political Economy* 66 (4): 281–302.

Ministry of Finance. 2004. *Central Government Subsidies in India: A Report*. New Delhi: Government of India.

Musgrave, Richard A., and Peggy Musgrave. 1989. *Public Finance in Theory and Practice*, 5th edition. New Delhi: McGraw-Hill Book Company.

National Knowledge Commission. 2009. *National Knowledge Commission: Report to the Nation 2006–2009*. New Delhi: National Knowledge Commission.

National Sample Survey Organisation (NSSO). 1995. *India—Participation in Education, 2007–08, 52nd Round*. Ministry of Statistics and Programme Implementation, Government of India. New Delhi.

———. 2007. *India—Participation and Expenditure in Education, 2007–08, 64th Round*. Ministry of Statistics and Programme Implementation, Government of India. New Delhi.

———. 2014. *India: Social Consumption—Education Survey 2014, 71st Round*. Ministry of Statistics and Programme Implementation, Government of India. New Delhi.

Planning Commission. 1985. *The Seventh Five Year Plan 1985–90* (Vol. I and Vol. II). New Delhi: Government of India.

———. 1992. *Eighth Five Year Plan 1992–97: Sectoral Programmes of Development* (Vol. II). New Delhi: Government of India.

———. 2002. *Tenth Five Year Plan 2002–2007: Sectoral Policies and Programmes* (Vol. II). New Delhi: Government of India.

———. 2013. *Twelfth Five Year Plan (2012–2017): Social Sector* (Vol. III). New Delhi: Government of India and SAGE.

Saito, Madoka. 2003. 'Amartya Sen's Capability Approach to Education: A Critical Exploration'. *Journal of Philosophy of Education* 37(1).

Samuelson, Paul A. 1954. 'The Pure Theory of Public Expenditure'. *The Review of Economics and Statistics* 36 (4): 387–89.

Schultz, T.W. 1960. 'Capital Formation by Education'. *The Journal of Political Economy* 68 (6): 571–83.

Stiglitz, Joseph E. 1999. 'Knowledge as a Global Public Good'. In *Global Public Goods: International Cooperation in the 21st Century*, edited by Inge Kaul, Isabelle Grunberg and Marc A. Stern, 308–25. New York: Oxford University Press.

Supreme Court of India. 1992. 'Miss Mohini Jain v. State of Karnataka and Others 1992 AIR 1858'. Government of India, New Delhi. Available at http://www.right-to-education.org/sites/right-to-education.org/files/resource attachments/India%20Supreme%20Court,%20Jain%20v%20Karnataka,%201992.pdf

———. 1993. 'Unni Krishnan, J.P. and Ors. etc. v. State of Andhra Pradesh and Ors'. Government of India, New Delhi. Available at http://indiankanoon.org/doc/1775396/

———. 2003. 'Islamic Academy of Education vs State of Karnataka and Ors'. Government of India, New Delhi. Available at http://indiankanoon.org/doc/1978528/

———. 2005. 'P.A. Inamdar & Ors vs State of Maharashtra & Ors'. Government of India, New Delhi. Available at http://indiankanoon.org/doc/1390531/

Tilak, J.B.G. 2005. 'Higher Education in Trishanku: Hanging Between State and Market'. *Economic and Political Weekly* 40 (37): 4029–32.

———. 2004. 'Public Subsidies in Education in India, Special Articles'. *Economic and Political Weekly* 39 (4): 343–59.

University Grants Commission. 2003. *UGC (Establishment of and Maintenance of Standards in Private Universities) Regulations, 2003*. New Delhi: Government of India.

PART II

REGIONAL AND SOCIAL
INEQUALITIES

6

Regional Disparities in Availability, Access and Equity in Higher Education in India

Sachidanand Sinha

INTRODUCTION

This chapter attempts to present a situational analysis of issues associated with access to higher education in India. It has been argued that in spite of phenomenal expansion of educational institutions and increase in enrolment in higher education during the last one decade or so, the pattern of inter-regional and social disparities have remained unchanged, and may have become further entrenched for some regions, social groups and sectors of higher education. The complex interplay of privatisation in the neoliberal political environment and the consequent growth of private institutions and open-distance learning have brought about significant changes in the supply side scenario, which may present a spurious notion of socio-economic and spatial equity in the availability and utilisation of educational infrastructure. The emergent disparities in higher education sector in India can be best described within the framework of socio-spatial segmentation (Soja 1980), which presents differential opportunities and outcomes for various social groups living in different parts of this vast and populous country of India.

Some authors have argued that India in the second decade of the current century has entered into a stage of massification of higher education (Agarwal 2009; Brennan 2004; Trow 1973; Varghese 2015). This chapter argues that India may appear to have made a transition into the early stages of massification but given social and spatial intersectionalities and developments in the last two decades, the social character of higher education remains largely elitist.

It has been discussed for long both within the school and higher education sectors that quantitative expansion in higher education

has resulted into poor quality of higher education. This shade of argument is at best located within the 'elite' framework of higher education in a highly hierarchical social structure of India. It is argued that
quantity and quality in education, though interrelated, are essentially independent processes, and causal association between the
two denies the claims of the socially, economically and spatially
marginalised populations of their right to equality of opportunity to
access higher education, which for them is the only route to social
and economic mobility.

While addressing the above issues, this chapter presents a highly
disaggregated narrative both socially and regionally in order to
critique the contemporary developments in the higher education
sector in India with a vision towards informing educational policies
and programmes for the future.

DATA SOURCES AND METHOD OF ANALYSIS

The nature of this chapter being largely empirical, it draws upon a
variety of sources of information and statistical data. Different
series of the Census of India (2011) have been used to collate data
on gross enrolment ratio (GER) at the district level. The census
data on currently attending population by age is the only reliable
source for estimating district level GER in higher education. It
should be instructive to inform that enrolment figures reported by
the official statistics (i.e., MHRD, UGC, etc.) are based on statistics
reported by the institutions. The coverage of institutions reporting
regularly has remained a big issue with data management system in
the country. Moreover, institutional enrolment reported by the colleges is relatively poor in comparison with the households as the
source, which is the case with the Census and large-scale sample
surveys of the National Sample Survey Organisation (NSSO).

This is only the second time (Sinha 2007) district level statistics
on enrolment and educational infrastructure is being used to understand some of the aspects of supply side issues and outcomes. So
far, all the academic and policy discussions have remained largely
confined to inter-state and aggregate level statistics, which conceals more than that it reveals. States of India are not monolithic
in terms of various socio-economic dimensions and there are significant intra-state variations, which needs to identified and inform
the state and central government appropriately on policy issues in
the education sector.

The data on educational infrastructure (colleges and institutions) have been obtained from the town and village amenities published as part of the *District Census Hand Books* for all the 640 districts of India. The reference year for this data is 2009 and therefore may not be as current as the data obtainable from the All India Higher Education Surveys. For this study, the data on institutions of higher education have been appropriately updated with the help of district profiles available on the official websites of the districts.

NSSO (2014) report on *Education in India* of the 71st Round has also been used wherever necessary to understand the status of higher education and dynamics therein. Other sources are from UGC and MHRD.

Several indicators and measures have been used in the study. The analysis relies on estimations of gender parity index and Sopher's disparity index (unmodified) to measure the gap between male and female GER. This index is relatively better as it is sensitive to levels of GER. That means that disparity between GER 10 and 20 for females and males respectively is not the same as 20 and 40. Gender parity index in the two examples will be the same that is 0.50, though the level of GER in the later for females is higher.

INSTITUTIONAL STRUCTURE OF HIGHER EDUCATION

Institutional structure of higher education in India has been variegated ever since the formal education system was modelled after the British education system beginning in the early 19th century. These include universities, colleges and other institutions set up by the central, state and private societies. Universities grant degrees and provide affiliation to colleges, where most of undergraduate courses are offered and conducted. Postgraduate departments are with both colleges and university teaching departments. Not all universities are of the affiliating type; some are unitary bodies, having a single campus, some may even have multiple campuses (Agarwal 2009, 2–3). Some institutions are granted the status of 'deemed-to-be' universities, which also have the legislative power to award degrees. Due to legislative provisions, private sector institutions in the last decade-and-a half have come to play a significant role and their numbers have risen phenomenally during this period, more so during the last decade. Table 6.1 presents the number of universities and colleges as on 2013–14 by types. Figures 6.1 and 6.2 provide the growth of such institutions over time. The

Table 6.1
India: Number of Universities and Colleges, 2013–14

Institutions	Type of Institutions	Number
Universities	Central University	42
	State Public University	310
	Deemed University	127
	State Private University	143
	Central Open University	1
	State Open University	13
	Institution of National Importance	68
	Institutions Under State Legislature Act	5
	Others	3
	Total	712
Colleges	Degree Colleges (general, technical & professional)	36,671
Stand Alone	Diploma Level Technical	3,541
Institution	PGDM	392
	Diploma Level Nursing	2,674
	Diploma Level Teacher Training	4,706
	Institute under Ministries	132
	Total	11,445

Source: AISHE Portal (www.aishe.gov.in).

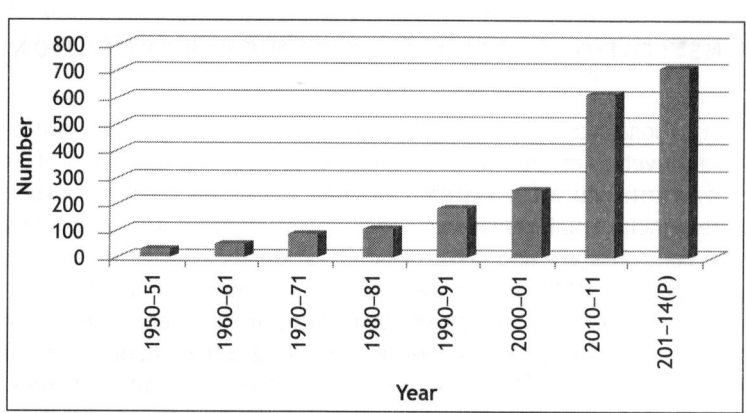

Figure 6.1
Number of Universities
Source: MHRD (2014).

state-wise distribution of institutions of higher education is given in Table 6.2.

In 2007, there were about 380 universities in India. Out of these, 232 were state universities while central universities were about 24,

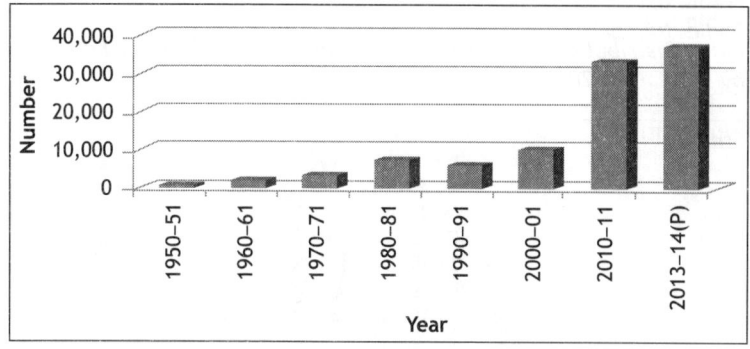

Figure 6.2
Number of all Degree Colleges, 2013–14
Source: MHRD (2014).

some of them recently created and were in their infancy stage of development. There were about 18,000 colleges under different managements. The numbers, since 2007, have swelled to over 35,000 colleges and 700 universities of different denominations, largely due to the phenomenal expansion observed in the private sector. It is also important to note that the universities and colleges vary in size, composition of departments and faculties. A large number among them, until early 2000s, imparted degrees in traditional structure of liberal arts, science and commerce; a very few, both in the government (public) and private sectors, invested in technical and professional courses. Thus, the gap between demand and supply became huge mostly in the technical and professional courses, which allowed for the private initiatives in the public higher education in India.

During the period mentioned above, the character of public-funded universities and colleges have also changed significantly. Due to the declining government funding, most of the public institutions started professional and technical and 'job-oriented' add on in self-financing and distance education modes, thus drastically changing the traditional character of the public-funded institutions. We shall return to this issue later.

ACCESS TO HIGHER EDUCATION: INTER-STATE AND INTER-DISTRICT PATTERNS OF ENROLMENT BY SOCIAL GROUPS

In this section, the study attempts to measure and identify regional and social patterns and narratives of enrolment in higher education

Table 6.2
India: Distribution of Universities and Institutions of Higher Education by States/UTs 2013–14

State	Central University	Central Open University	Institute of National Importance	Others	State Public University	Institute under State Legislature Act	State Open University	State Private University	State Private Open University	Deemed University (Government)	Deemed University (Government Aided)	Deemed University (Private)	Grand Total
1	2	3	4	5	6	7	8	9	10	11	12	13	14
Andhra Pradesh	–	–	–	1	20	1	–	–	–	1	–	4	27
Arunachal Pradesh	1	–	1	–	–	–	–	3	1	1	–	–	7
Assam	2	–	2	–	10	–	1	3	–	–	–	–	18
Bihar	1	–	3	–	14	1	1	–	–	1	–	–	21
Chandigarh	–	–	1	–	1	–	–	–	–	1	–	–	3
Chhattisgarh	1	–	2	–	11	–	1	6	–	–	–	–	21
Delhi	4	1	3	1	6	–	–	–	–	8	2	1	26
Goa	–	–	1	–	1	–	–	–	–	–	–	–	2
Gujarat	1	–	2	–	24	–	1	14	–	–	1	1	44
Haryana	1	–	1	–	11	–	–	13	–	2	–	3	31
Himachal Pradesh	1	–	2	–	4	–	–	16	–	–	–	–	23
Jammu and Kashmir	2	–	1	–	7	1	–	–	–	–	–	–	11
Jharkhand	1	–	1	–	7	–	–	1	–	1	1	–	12
Karnataka	1	–	1	–	25	–	1	2	–	4	–	1	45
Kerala	1	–	3	–	12	–	–	–	–	2	–	–	18
Madhya Pradesh	2	–	4	1	17	–	1	11	–	3	–	–	39
Maharashtra	1	–	3	–	19	–	1	–	–	7	2	1	45
Manipur	2	–	1	–	–	–	–	–	–	–	–	–	3
Meghalaya	1	–	1	–	–	–	–	8	–	–	–	–	10
Mizoram	1	–	1	–	–	–	–	1	–	–	–	–	3
Nagaland	1	–	1	–	–	–	–	2	–	–	–	–	4

State	Central University	Central Open University	Institute of National Importance	Others	State Public University	Institute under State Legislature Act	State Open University	State Private University	State Private Open University	Deemed University (Government)	Deemed University (Government Aided)	Deemed University (Private)	Grand Total
1	2	3	4	5	6	7	8	9	10	11	12	13	14
Odisha	1	–	3	–	12	–	–	3	–	–	–	2	21
Puducherry	1	–	2	–	–	–	–	–	–	–	–	1	4
Punjab	1	–	4	–	8	–	–	7	–	1	–	1	22
Rajasthan	1	–	3	–	19	–	1	31	–	–	–	8	63
Sikkim	1	–	1	–	–	–	–	4	–	–	–	–	6
Tamil Nadu	2	–	6	1	20	–	1	–	–	–	1	2	58
Telangana	3	–	2	–	11	1	1	–	–	–	–	2	20
Tripura	1	–	1	–	–	–	–	1	–	–	–	–	3
Uttar Pradesh	4	–	4	–	22	1	1	20	–	3	3	4	62
Uttarakhand	1	–	3	–	8	–	1	7	–	1	1	2	24
West Bengal	1	–	4	–	20	–	1	–	–	–	–	1	27
All India	4	1	6	4	30	5	1	15	1	3	1	8	72

Source: MHRD (2014).
Note: In UTs of Andaman and Nicobar Islands, Dadra and Nagar Haveli, Daman and Diu, and Lakshadweep, there are no Universities. Some, however, have regional campuses for specific courses such as Pondicherry University has one in Andaman and Nicobar Islands.

through GER for the general and vocational education in India. According to the Census 2011, GER for general education in India stood at 22 for all populations. It was 23.5 for all males and 21.7 for the females, registering almost 10-percentage point increase since the last census (Sinha 2007). NSSO (Table 6.3) 71st Round reports a more conservative figure of 14 and 12 for males and females, respectively. This is due to two reasons: (a) difference in the reference age, which in this study is 18–24 years while it is 18–23 for the NSS;

(b) the difference between enrolment and attendance. Census records whether the person is enrolled or not but makes no effort at ascertaining whether the enrolled person is actually attending classes or not. NSS makes this distinction and therefore the figures from the two sources could be instructive in order to understand that a significantly large proportion of those who are enrolled actually attend classes. Age-specific attendance ratio (AAR), based on the NSS data, reports increase by two-folds. It may be noted that AAR makes no reference of the stage of education. There are two implications of this data. One, that attendance is likely to be higher for students from the economically and socially better-off households. Two, that institutional factors such as the nature of college ensure better attendance as has been reported by women's colleges.

Among the states and UTs, Mizoram and Goa recorded GER above 40, while among the major states, Jammu and Kashmir followed by Kerala, Andhra Pradesh (AP; including Telangana), Maharashtra and Tamil Nadu, reported higher GER than that of the national average. Odisha, Rajasthan, West Bengal, Karnataka, Chhattisgarh and Madhya Pradesh (MP) remained lower, with GER below 15% (see Figure 6.3).

Enrolment in vocational education, which also includes pre-matric and post-senior secondary courses, remains generally low for the country (Table 6.4). Kerala had the highest GER followed by Puducherry, AP and Tamil Nadu. Enrolment in most of the north Indian states in vocational sector remained very low and for the females even lower (Figure 6.8). Kerala story of diversification in the late senior secondary education and undergraduate courses in nursing and medical sciences have had a positive impact on vocational education in the state.

The pattern of GER at the district level presents multiple narratives on the state of higher education (Figures 6.4, 6.5 and 6.6). Southern districts of Kerala, southern Tamil Nadu, north-west AP (now Telangana), non-Konkan western Maharashtra (sugar belt), eastern Uttar Pradesh (UP) and western Bihar, Northeast tribal states and Uttarakhand have reported higher GER than the national average. Punjab, Godavari delta districts, Odisha, Bengal, north-east Bihar and central UP showed medium or values below national level but about 12 GER. A large number of districts of Odisha, Gujarat and Karnataka showed values below GER 12. Table 6.5 supplements the observations made above. For example, 6 districts of AP had medium GER, 18 districts out of the total of 38 in Bihar had GER higher than the national average. None of Chhattisgarh and

Table 6.3
India: Some Aspects of Enrolment in Higher Education

1. Gross Attendance Ratio (GAR)			
Areas	18–23 years	Male	Female
All areas		14	12
Rural		12	9
Urban		18	18
2. Age-specific Attendance Ratio (AAR)			
All areas	18–23 years (irrespective of stage of education)	35	28
Rural		32	24
Urban		40	38
3. GAR for Social Groups			
ST	All areas	8	7
SC	All areas	11	10
OBC	All areas	14	13
Others	All areas	18	18
4. AAR for Social Groups (18–23)			
ST	All areas	26	20
SC	All areas	29	22
OBC	All areas	34	27
Others	All areas	42	38
5. GAR by UMPCE Quintile Class			
UMPCE Quintiles	18–23	Rural	Urban
1	Persons	4	6
2	Persons	5	10
3	Persons	9	16
4	Persons	12	24
5	Persons	21	33
6. AAR by UMPCE Quintiles			
1	Persons	16	17
2	Persons	20	26
3	Persons	25	37
4	Persons	31	50
5	Persons	46	67

Source: NSSO (2014).

Odisha was in the high (20–28) or very high (28 and above) category. The picture for MP is similar. Only 7 out of 27 districts in Gujarat had high GER while 27 out of 35 in Maharashtra, 25 out of 32 in Tamil Nadu and 37 out of 71 in UP had GER between high and very high. The state-level enrolment scenario thus gets underlined by

Table 6.4
GER of 18–24 Age Group All Population by States and UTs (2011)

S. No.	States/UTs	College			Vocational Institute			Gender Disparity	
		Persons	Males	Females	Persons	Males	Females	College	Vocational
1.	Andhra Pradesh	25.99	31.89	20.05	8.34	10.71	5.95	0.27	0.28
2.	Arunachal Pradesh	25.20	29.76	20.60	1.43	1.78	1.07	0.21	0.22
3.	Assam	16.96	19.19	14.80	1.03	1.40	0.67	0.14	0.32
4.	Bihar	19.83	25.87	12.93	1.46	1.92	0.93	0.37	0.32
5.	Chhattisgarh	12.99	14.99	10.98	1.91	2.49	1.32	0.16	0.28
6.	Goa	42.20	39.78	45.04	3.91	4.65	3.05	-0.09	0.19
7.	Gujarat	18.10	20.06	15.90	3.61	4.64	2.45	0.12	0.29
8.	Haryana	23.53	24.77	22.08	6.80	8.57	4.72	0.07	0.28
9.	Himachal Pradesh	22.11	21.19	23.07	7.82	9.53	6.04	-0.05	0.21
10.	Jammu and Kashmir	29.84	32.67	26.78	2.34	2.77	1.87	0.12	0.17
11.	Jharkhand	20.91	25.98	15.58	2.44	3.30	1.54	0.28	0.34
12.	Karnataka	15.16	17.28	12.95	5.74	7.09	4.32	0.15	0.23
13.	Kerala	26.58	26.62	26.54	11.32	12.74	9.93	0.00	0.12
14.	Madhya Pradesh	15.10	17.34	12.57	2.12	2.68	1.49	0.16	0.26
15.	Maharashtra	24.10	27.28	20.52	5.20	6.22	4.05	0.16	0.20
16.	Manipur	31.18	35.44	26.97	1.71	1.90	1.52	0.17	0.10
17.	Meghalaya	17.23	17.18	17.28	1.38	1.35	1.41	0.00	-0.02
18.	Mizoram	47.37	50.64	44.10	2.76	2.68	2.83	0.11	-0.02
19.	Nagaland	21.13	21.60	20.65	1.11	1.05	1.17	0.02	-0.05
20.	Odisha	10.44	12.23	8.67	3.91	5.51	2.33	0.17	0.39
21.	Punjab	19.50	17.72	21.56	3.85	4.12	3.55	-0.11	0.07

22.	Rajasthan	16.68	20.69	12.25	3.09	4.04	2.04	0.27	0.31
23.	Sikkim	17.61	16.99	18.29	1.13	1.13	1.13	-0.04	0.00
24.	Tamil Nadu	24.12	25.84	22.40	6.45	8.64	4.28	0.08	0.33
25.	Tripura	14.01	17.06	11.06	0.92	1.12	0.73	0.22	0.19
26.	Uttar Pradesh	22.45	24.57	19.98	2.51	3.23	1.68	0.12	0.29
27.	Uttarakhand	25.65	25.92	25.37	5.67	7.44	3.84	0.01	0.30
28.	West Bengal	13.73	16.23	11.16	1.00	1.32	0.69	0.19	0.29
29.	Chandigarh	35.29	31.98	39.71	6.15	6.89	5.17	-0.15	0.13
30.	Dadra and Nagar Haveli	12.33	12.26	12.47	2.89	2.78	3.07	-0.01	-0.04
31.	Daman and Diu	7.87	6.42	11.80	1.64	1.52	1.98	-0.29	-0.12
32.	Lakshadweep	17.27	16.96	17.61	2.06	1.93	2.20	-0.02	-0.06
33.	NCT of Delhi	29.03	28.75	29.36	6.77	7.80	5.53	-0.01	0.16
34.	Puducherry	29.00	30.97	27.19	9.48	12.31	6.87	0.08	0.28
35.	Andaman and Nicobar Islands	18.00	16.81	19.32	3.25	3.36	3.14	-0.07	0.03
	INDIA	**22.0**	**23.5**	**20.5**	**3.8**	**4.6**	**3.0**	**0.07**	**0.19**

Source: Census (2011).

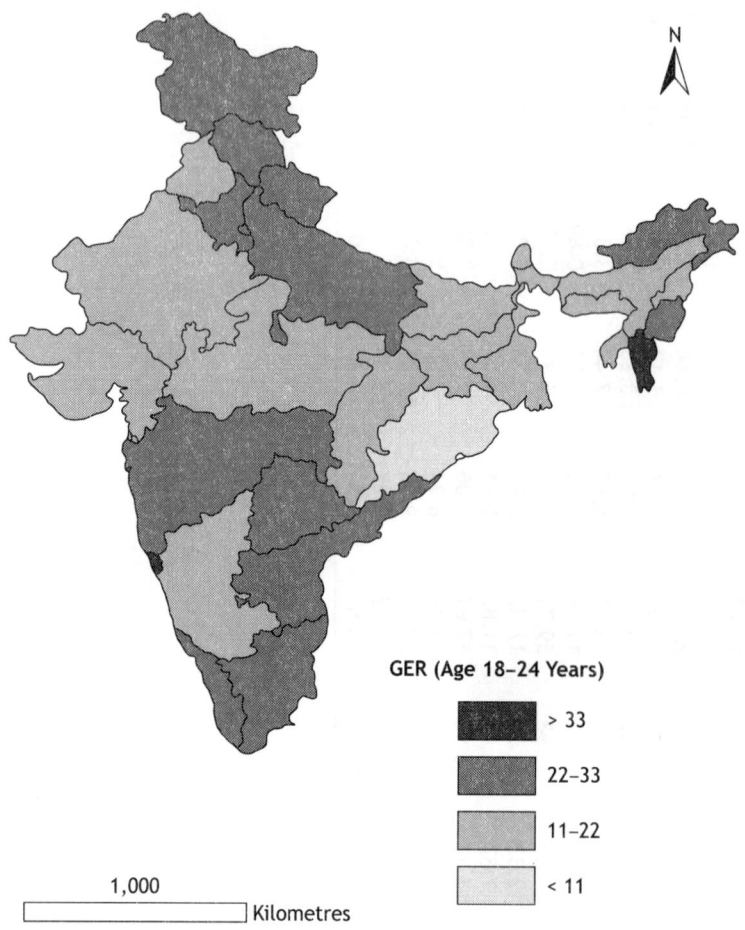

Figure 6.3
GER in Higher Education for all Population (2011)
Source: Census of India (2011b).

pockets of low enrolment in the midst of high to very high enrolment districts.

The emergent narratives are the following:

1. Predominantly tribal districts of India, extending from Gujarat to Odisha through Chhattisgarh, MP and parts of Telangana have low enrolment.
2. Agriculturally better off areas such as Punjab, Western UP, Godavari delta and Bihar have medium to low GER. It seems

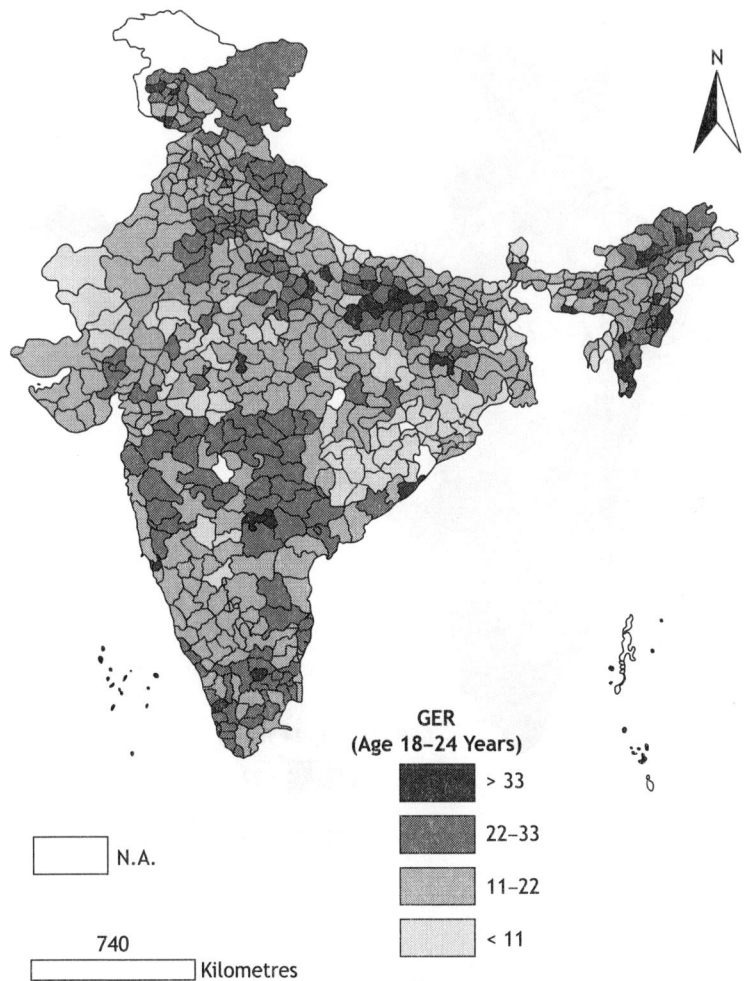

Figure 6.4
District-level GER Total

Source: Census of India (2011a, 2011c, 2011d).

that the prosperous communities of the traditional propertied classes and castes did not take advantage of the educational provisions and hence progress of education among them is less than expected. However, localities having high density of population and higher economic opportunities have higher GER situation. These groups may be able to see the economic and cultural value of education better than others.

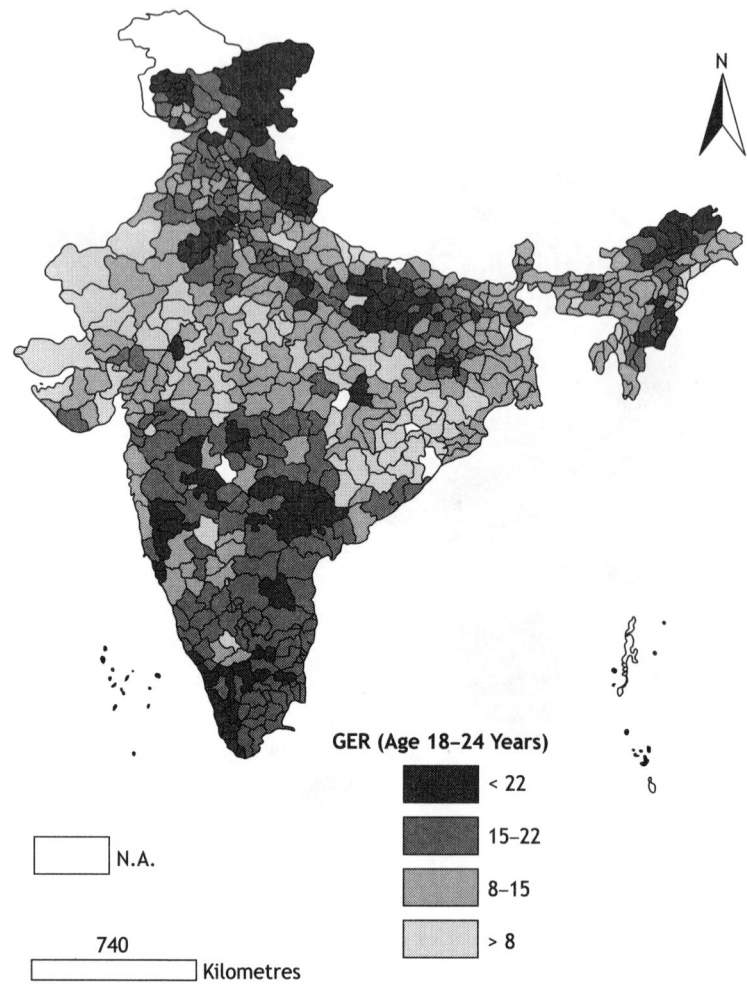

Figure 6.5
District-level GER for Rural Areas
Source: Census of India (2011a, 2011c, 2011d).

3. High urbanisation and states that experienced social reform
    movements have seen a breaking away of economic dominance
    and hegemony of the high castes. For example, the anti-
    Brahminical movement and the rise of the middle castes in
    Maharashtra, Tamil Nadu and parts of UP and Bihar have pro-
    moted enrolment in higher education.

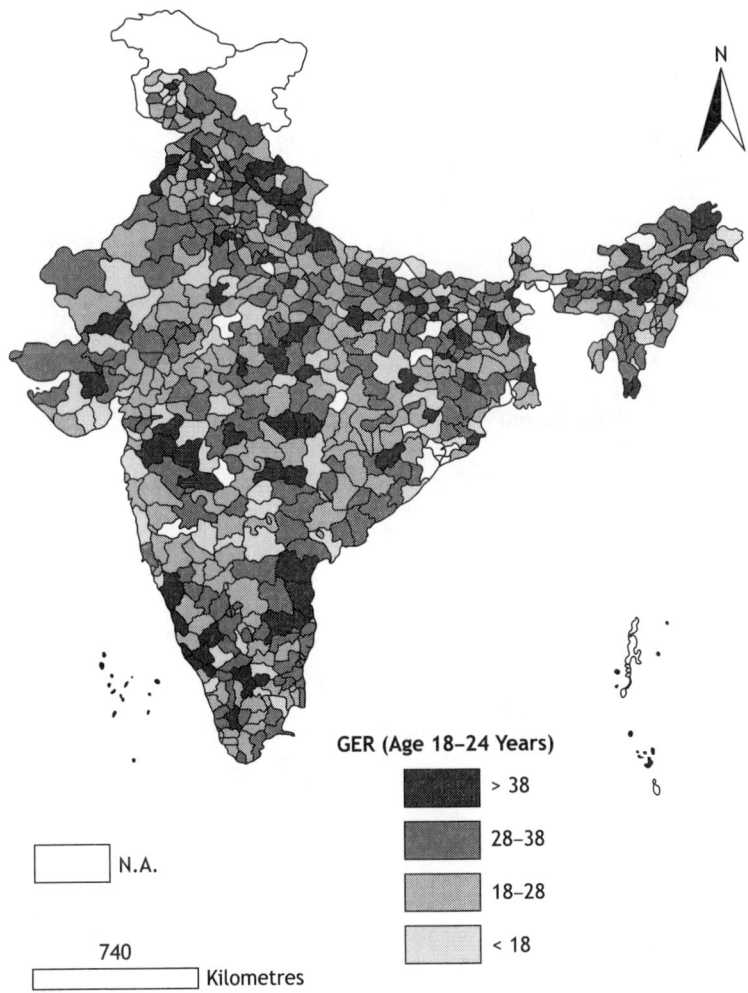

Figure 6.6
District-level GER for Urban Areas
Source: Census of India (2011a, 2011c, 2011d).

This brings into focus the situation with the non-scheduled and scheduled communities in order to see as to whether the principle of equity has in effect translated on the ground in so far as higher education is concern. This will also help understand whether India has made transition into the 'mass' phase of higher education or not.

Table 6.5

GER in Higher Education (Age Group 18–24 Years, 2011)

States/UTs	<12	12–20	20–28	>28	Total Districts
	GER in Degree College (Total)				
	Number of Districts				
Andaman and Nicobar Islands	2	0	1	0	3
Andhra Pradesh	0	6	13	4	23
Arunachal Pradesh	2	6	3	5	16
Assam	4	16	6	1	27
Bihar	4	16	15	3	38
Chandigarh	0	0	0	1	1
Chhattisgarh	9	9	0	0	18
Dadra and Nagar Haveli	0	1	0	0	1
Daman and Diu	1	1	0	0	2
Delhi	0	0	0	1	1
Goa	0	0	0	2	2
Gujarat	4	16	6	1	27
Haryana	1	3	12	5	21
Himachal Pradesh	1	4	5	2	12
Jammu and Kashmir	0	4	10	8	22
Jharkhand	2	14	6	2	24
Karnataka	2	28	0	0	30
Kerala	0	0	9	5	14
Lakshadweep	0	1	0	0	1
Maharashtra	0	9	22	4	35
Manipur	0	1	2	6	9
Meghalaya	2	4	1	0	7
Mizoram	0	2	0	6	8
MP	23	23	3	1	50
Nagaland	3	5	1	2	11
Odisha	24	6	0	0	30
Puducherry	0	1	2	1	4
Punjab	0	12	8	0	20
Rajasthan	12	16	5	0	33
Sikkim	1	2	1	0	4
Tamil Nadu	0	7	20	5	32
Tripura	3	1	0	0	4
Uttar Pradesh	6	28	24	13	71
Uttarakhand	0	1	6	6	13
West Bengal	10	7	1	1	19
Total	116	250	182	85	633

Source: Census (2011).

If one were to take a look at the GER for the SCs and STs (as presented in Tables 6.6 and 6.7), one can observe that in some of the states of India, SCs have done remarkably well. The examples are AP, Kerala, Maharashtra and Tamil Nadu. The combined effects of social reforms and positive discrimination policies have certainly helped the SCs in these states much more than in others. Similarly, barring the Northeast states all tribal districts and tribal populations have low GER. The situation with reference to the non-scheduled population presents a sustained high GER in AP, Bihar, Haryana, Jammu and Kashmir, Kerala, Maharashtra and Punjab (Table 6.8).

The males among the non-scheduled population have high GER in general education. However, the female participation in vocational programmes has not much participation among the non-scheduled females. This may be a reflection of the patriarchal structure of society. The district level picture for the non-scheduled population shows that 270 districts out of 627 have high to very high GER among the non-scheduled population (Table 6.9). The spatial pattern is given on Figures 6.7–6.9. It is instructive to note that even in backward districts the GER of the non-scheduled population is not very different from the other areas, statistically and qualitatively speaking.

One may now turn over to the question of 'massification' and the challenges therein. The massification phase of higher education should be seen in relation to the fact that middle-level courses in skill development and vocational education have remained rather dormant in India. Indian higher education with its dominance of the traditional propertied classes becomes clear as we see that GER for urban monthly per capita expenditure (UMPCE) quintiles and find that those at the bottom have similar values as that of the SCs and STs. One may ask as to who comprised the lowest 40% of the poor? Socio-spatial segmentation hypothesis, therefore, is clearly visible from the above discussion, which brings out marginalisation of the ST preponderant areas. Spaces acquire identity on the basis of social profile and social relations underlying such areas. Here, one can see instances of geographically marginalised communities and property-less classes in the rural areas.

AVAILABILITY OF EDUCATIONAL INFRASTRUCTURE

Provision of educational infrastructure, especially in the context of higher education, has largely been seen from the demand side.

Table 6.6
GER 2011 for Scheduled Castes (2011)

S. No.	State/UTs	College			Vocational Institute			Gender Disparity	
		Persons	Males	Females	Persons	Males	Females	College	Vocational
1	Andhra Pradesh	22.4	27.5	17.2	6.6	8.1	5.2	0.26	0.21
2	Arunachal Pradesh	0	0	0	0	0	0	0	0
3	Assam	13.6	15.3	11.9	0.7	1	0.5	0.13	0.32
4	Bihar	9.3	14	4.4	0.7	0.8	0.5	0.55	0.19
5	Chhattisgarh	12.4	15.1	9.6	1.4	1.9	0.9	0.22	0.33
6	Goa	26.7	28	25.4	2.6	3	2.2	0.06	0.15
7	Gujarat	17.2	20.3	13.8	3.3	4.4	2.1	0.2	0.33
8	Haryana	13.1	14.9	10.9	3.8	5.2	2.2	0.15	0.39
9	Himachal Pradesh	15.2	15.7	14.8	4.7	6.1	3.3	0.03	0.28
10	Jammu and Kashmir	15.4	15.3	15.6	1.6	1.8	1.4	-0.01	0.12
11	Jharkhand	13.1	18.4	7.6	1.3	1.7	0.8	0.44	0.35
12	Karnataka	16.9	20.6	13.1	5.1	6.2	3.9	0.24	0.21
13	Kerala	20.5	18.1	22.8	8.6	8.3	8.9	-0.13	-0.04
14	Madhya Pradesh	10.9	13.1	8.2	1.3	1.7	0.9	0.23	0.26
15	Maharashtra	22.9	26.7	18.8	4.4	5.1	3.5	0.2	0.17
16	Manipur	25.8	28.3	23.4	2	2.4	1.6	0.11	0.19
17	Meghalaya	18.2	19.4	16.9	0.9	1.3	0.5	0.07	0.44
18	Mizoram	28.9	23.8	38	2.5	3.8	0	-0.29	0
19	Nagaland	0	0	0	0	0	0	0	0
20	Odisha	6.7	8.4	5	1.7	2.6	0.9	0.24	0.47

21	Punjab	9.2	8.6	9.8	1.9	2.1	1.7	-0.07	0.1
22	Rajasthan	10.9	14.5	6.8	2	2.7	1.2	0.37	0.36
23	Sikkim	9.7	9.8	9.7	0.6	0.7	0.6	0.01	0.09
24	Tamil Nadu	18.4	20.4	16.4	4.9	6.1	3.7	0.12	0.22
25	Tripura	11.9	14.8	8.9	0.7	0.8	0.5	0.25	0.19
26	Uttar Pradesh	15.1	17.3	12.6	1.4	1.8	0.9	0.16	0.3
27	Uttarakhand	17.6	19	16.1	2.6	3.7	1.5	0.09	0.4
28	West Bengal	9.9	12.5	7.1	0.5	0.7	0.4	0.27	0.28
29	Chandigarh	20.1	18.9	21.5	3.1	3.4	2.7	-0.07	0.11
30	Dadra and Nagar Haveli	23.3	26.2	19.3	7.8	9.5	5.4	0.17	0.27
31	Daman and Diu	34	34.9	32.9	4.4	5.9	2.8	0.04	0.33
32	Lakshadweep	0	0	0	0	0	0	–	–
33	NCT of Delhi	18.9	19.1	18.5	3	3.5	2.4	0.02	0.16
34	Puducherry	23.1	25.7	20.7	7.6	9.8	5.6	0.12	0.26
35	Andaman and Nicobar Islands	0	0	0	0	0	0	–	–
	India	17.1	18.9	15.4	3	3.8	2.2	0.11	0.24

Source: Census (2011).

Table 6.7
GER for Scheduled Tribes (2011)

S. No.	States/UTs	College			Vocational			Gender Disparity	
		Persons	Males	Females	Persons	Males	Females	College	Vocational
1	Andhra Pradesh	18.5	25.6	11.8	4.8	6.6	3.1	0.41	0.35
2	Arunachal Pradesh	28.7	35.4	22.7	1.4	1.8	1.1	0.27	0.22
3	Assam	21.4	25.6	17.6	0.8	1.0	0.5	0.21	0.27
4	Bihar	10.8	15.1	6.2	0.8	0.9	0.7	0.43	0.11
5	Chhattisgarh	7.2	8.7	5.7	0.8	0.9	0.6	0.20	0.20
6	Goa	23.8	24.6	22.9	2.7	3.8	1.6	0.04	0.38
7	Gujarat	9.7	11.1	8.3	2.4	3.0	1.7	0.14	0.25
8	Haryana	0.0	0.0	0.0	0.0	0.0	0.0	–	–
9	Himachal Pradesh	18.7	19.2	18.2	4.8	6.0	3.6	0.03	0.23
10	Jammu and Kashmir	13.3	16.3	10.2	0.9	1.2	0.7	0.23	0.27
11	Jharkhand	14.5	17.2	12.0	1.3	1.5	1.1	0.18	0.14
12	Karnataka	13.7	17.3	10.0	4.4	5.4	3.2	0.28	0.23
13	Kerala	12.3	11.9	12.7	4.5	4.6	4.4	-0.03	0.02
14	Madhya Pradesh	5.3	7.0	3.7	0.6	0.8	0.5	0.29	0.23
15	Maharashtra	11.8	15.1	8.5	2.5	3.0	1.9	0.28	0.21
16	Manipur	34.6	39.3	30.0	1.6	1.7	1.5	0.18	0.05
17	Meghalaya	16.5	16.3	16.8	1.3	1.3	1.4	-0.02	-0.04
18	Mizoram	21.4	23.1	19.8	1.2	1.2	1.3	0.09	-0.01
19	Nagaland	21.9	22.6	21.1	1.1	1.0	1.2	0.04	-0.07
20	Odisha	4.4	5.6	3.3	1.1	1.6	0.6	0.24	0.42
21	Punjab	0.0	0.0	0.0	0.0	0.0	0.0	–	–

22	Rajasthan	12.8	18.4	7.0	2.5	3.6	1.4	0.48	0.43
23	Sikkim	17.4	16.3	18.5	1.1	1.0	1.2	-0.07	-0.08
24	Tamil Nadu	10.7	13.6	8.0	2.6	3.5	1.7	0.26	0.32
25	Tripura	10.4	13.2	7.9	0.6	0.7	0.5	0.25	0.13
26	Uttar Pradesh	13.5	16.1	10.8	1.2	1.7	0.7	0.20	0.39
27	Uttarakhand	29.9	31.9	27.8	3.5	4.9	2.1	0.08	0.38
28	West Bengal	7.6	9.8	5.5	0.4	0.5	0.3	0.27	0.19
29	Chandigarh	0.0	0.0	0.0	0.0	0.0	0.0	–	–
30	Dadra and Nagar Haveli	10.1	13.7	6.6	2.4	2.9	2.0	0.35	0.16
31	Daman and Diu	7.9	8.8	7.1	2.4	2.7	2.1	0.10	0.11
32	Lakshadweep	17.8	18.1	17.6	2.1	2.1	2.2	0.01	-0.02
33	NCT of Delhi	0.0	0.0	0.0	0.0	0.0	0.0	–	–
34	Puducherry	0.0	0.0	0.0	0.0	0.0	0.0	–	–
35	Andaman and Nicobar Islands	14.6	11.6	17.8	1.8	1.2	2.4	-0.22	-0.30
	India	15.4	17.6	13.2	2.0	2.4	1.6	0.15	0.19

Source: Census (2011).

Table 6.8
GER for Non-scheduled Categories (2011)

S. No.	States/UTs	College			Vocational institute			Gender Disparity	
		Persons	Males	Females	Persons	Males	Females	College	Vocational
1	Andhra Pradesh	27.5	33.4	21.5	9.1	11.7	0.06	0.26	2.31
2	Arunachal Pradesh	17.9	20.0	15.2	1.4	1.7	0.01	0.14	2.25
3	Assam	16.6	18.6	14.6	1.1	1.5	0.01	0.13	2.33
4	Bihar	21.8	28.1	14.6	1.6	2.1	0.01	0.36	2.33
5	Chhattisgarh	16.1	18.1	14.1	2.6	3.4	0.02	0.13	2.29
6	Goa	44.6	41.6	48.1	4.1	4.8	0.03	-0.12	2.19
7	Gujarat	19.7	21.5	17.5	3.9	4.9	0.03	0.11	2.30
8	Haryana	26.3	27.4	25.0	7.6	9.5	0.05	0.05	2.29
9	Himachal Pradesh	25.0	23.4	26.7	9.3	11.1	0.07	-0.08	2.23
10	Jammu and Kashmir	33.5	36.5	30.1	2.6	3.1	0.02	0.13	2.18
11	Jharkhand	25.0	30.7	18.7	3.1	4.3	0.02	0.28	2.38
12	Karnataka	15.0	16.7	13.1	5.9	7.3	0.04	0.12	2.25
13	Kerala	27.5	27.8	27.2	11.7	13.3	0.10	0.01	2.18
14	Madhya Pradesh	19.1	21.3	16.5	2.8	3.4	0.02	0.13	2.26
15	Maharashtra	25.7	28.7	22.3	5.6	6.7	0.04	0.15	2.21
16	Manipur	28.4	32.4	24.5	1.8	2.0	0.02	0.17	2.14
17	Meghalaya	21.5	22.4	20.6	1.8	1.9	0.02	0.05	2.04
18	Mizoram	21.7	21.4	22.2	1.5	1.2	0.02	-0.02	1.80
19	Nagaland	16.2	15.9	16.7	1.2	1.2	0.01	-0.03	2.07
20	Odisha	13.7	15.5	11.8	5.5	7.6	0.03	0.14	2.39
21	Punjab	24.6	22.2	27.5	4.8	5.1	0.04	-0.12	2.08

22	Rajasthan	18.9	22.8	14.7	3.5	4.5	0.02	0.23	2.29
23	Sikkim	18.3	17.8	18.9	1.2	1.2	0.01	-0.03	2.03
24	Tamil Nadu	25.9	27.5	24.4	7.0	9.4	0.04	0.07	2.37
25	Tripura	17.3	20.4	14.1	1.2	1.5	0.01	0.19	2.20
26	Uttar Pradesh	24.3	26.5	21.9	2.8	3.6	0.02	0.11	2.30
27	Uttarakhand	27.4	27.4	27.5	6.5	8.4	0.04	0.00	2.31
28	West Bengal	15.6	18.1	13.1	1.2	1.6	0.01	0.17	2.29
29	Chandigarh	38.9	34.9	44.4	6.9	7.7	0.06	-0.17	2.15
30	Dadra and Nagar Haveli	13.6	11.2	20.3	3.1	2.6	0.04	-0.30	1.78
31	Daman and Diu	7.4	6.0	11.5	1.6	1.4	0.02	-0.31	1.87
32	Lakshadweep	8.2	6.5	18.3	0.8	0.5	0.03	-0.51	1.25
33	NCT of Delhi	31.3	30.9	31.9	7.6	8.8	0.06	-0.02	2.19
34	Puducherry	30.3	32.1	28.6	9.9	12.8	0.07	0.07	2.31
35	Andaman and Nicobar Islands	18.3	17.2	19.4	3.4	3.5	0.03	-0.07	2.06
	India	22.4	23.5	21.7	4.2	5.0	0.0	0.05	2.20

Source: Census (2011).

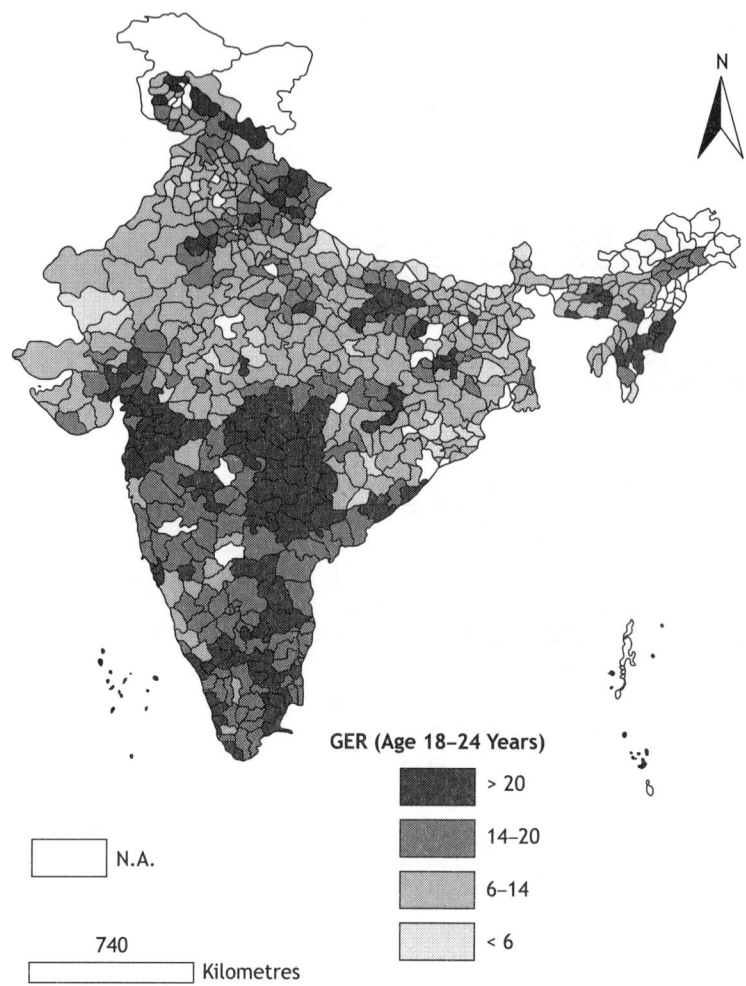

Figure 6.7
GER for Scheduled Castes
Source: Census of India (2011a, 2011c, 2011d).

Demand is subject to the availability of eligible population in the relevant age for entry into the higher education sector. It is argued that availability of facilities in terms of institutions of higher educa-tion is a necessary condition for getting enrolled and progress-ing faster in education. This is not a constraining factor for the well-to-do sections since they can afford to send their wards to faraway places for higher studies. However, lack of infrastructure can be a

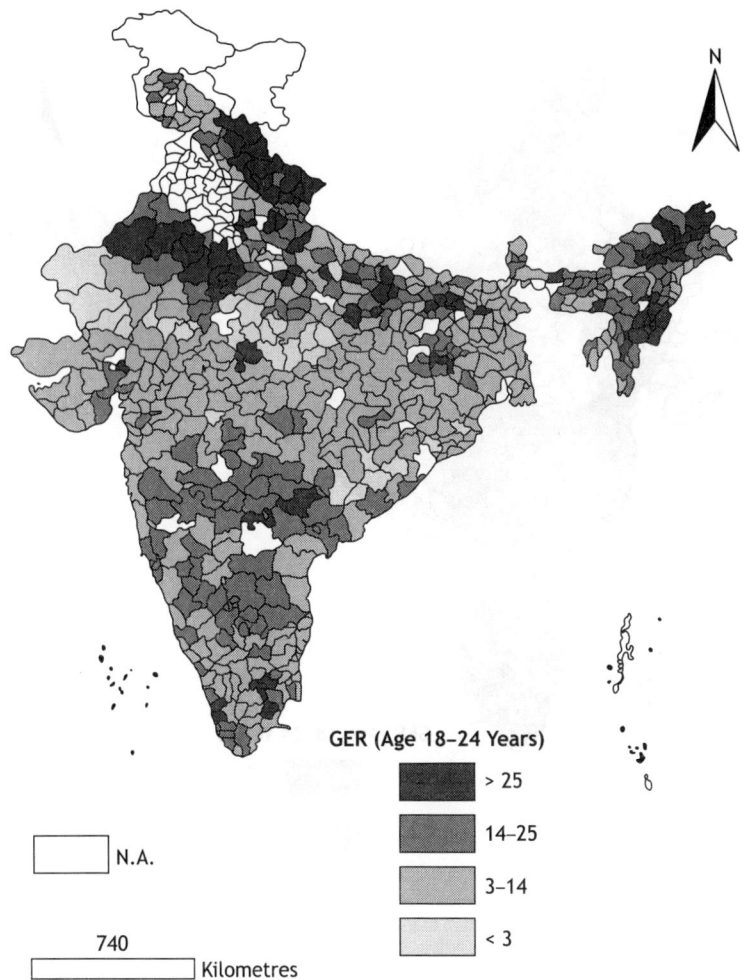

Figure 6.8
GER for Scheduled Tribes

Source: Census of India (2011a, 2011c, 2011d).

serious constraint for realising the educational aspirations of the middle and lower classes. Needless to add, lack of education acts as a barrier to entry into the world, social and economic mobility.

In the next stage of analysis, two indicators of educational supply, namely, the number of colleges per 100,000 population and enrolment per college has been taken into consideration. The value of number of colleges per 100,000 population is not the actual

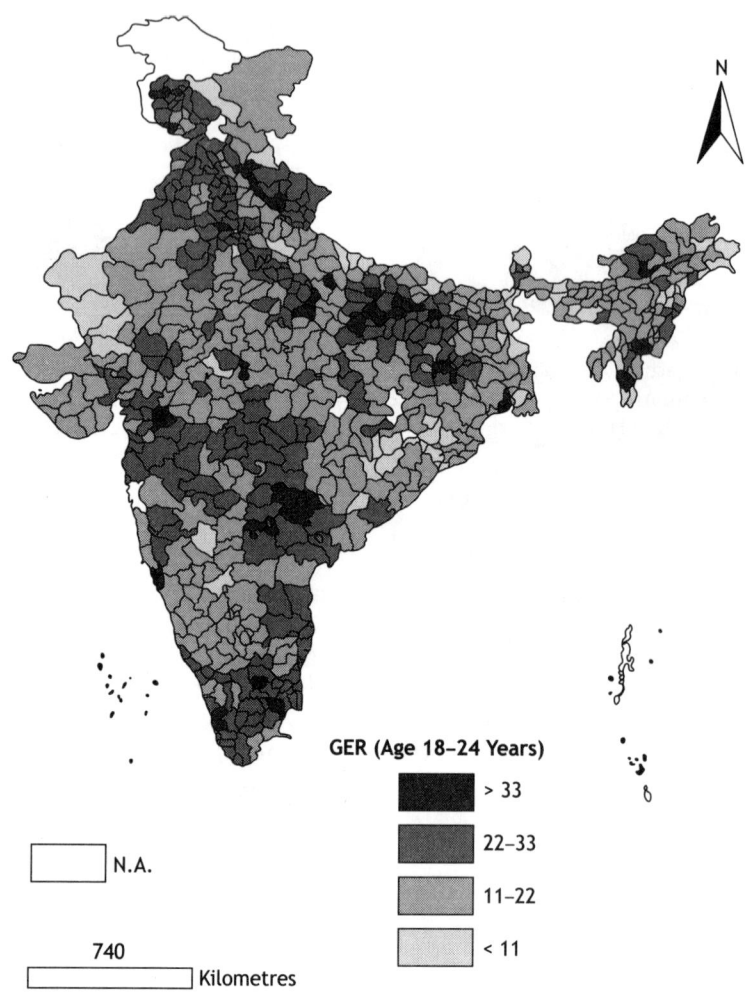

Figure 6.9
GER for the Non-scheduled Categories
Source: Census of India (2011a, 2011c, 2011d).

number available but is only a measure of availability. So areas with low density or size of population may have very high values and on the contrary, areas with large population may have smaller values. Size of enrolment per college shows the level of crowding or lack of it. The maps below present the pattern of distribution of the two measures. Clearly, the patterns are the same as discussed above.

Table 6.9

Distribution of Districts According to Categories of GER Among Non-scheduled Population in Higher Education

States/UTs	Total GER				
	< 11	11–22	22–33	> 33	Subtotal
Andaman and Nicobar Islands	2	0	1	0	3
Andhra Pradesh	0	7	12	4	23
Arunachal Pradesh	3	8	4	1	16
Assam	3	19	4	1	27
Bihar	1	19	17	1	38
Chandigarh	0	0	0	1	1
Chhattisgarh	2	16	0	0	18
Dadra and N Haveli	0	1	0	0	1
Daman and Diu	1	1	0	0	2
Goa	0	0	0	2	2
Gujarat	1	16	9	0	26
Haryana	1	1	16	3	21
Himachal Pradesh	1	5	4	2	12
Jammu and Kashmir	1	4	13	4	22
Jharkhand	1	12	8	3	24
Karnataka	1	29	0	0	30
Kerala	0	2	10	2	14
Lakshadweep	1	0	0	0	1
Madhya Pradesh	1	40	8	1	50
Maharashtra	0	8	26	1	35
Manipur	0	5	2	2	9
Meghalaya	2	4	1	0	7
Mizoram	3	3	1	1	8
Nagaland	6	4	1	0	11
Odisha	11	19	0	0	30
Punjab	0	4	16	0	20
Rajasthan	3	21	9	0	33
Sikkim	1	3	0	0	4
Tamil Nadu	0	9	25	2	36
Tripura	0	4	0	0	4
Uttar Pradesh	4	29	29	9	71
Uttarakhand	0	1	10	2	13
West Bengal	5	12	1	1	19
Total	55	306	227	43	631

Source: Census (2011).

The average number of colleges per 100,000 for general education stood at 18 in 2011 (Tables 6.11, 6.12, and 6.13), this is an appreciable increase since 2001. The number of technical and professional colleges per 100,000 remains one or two, whichever

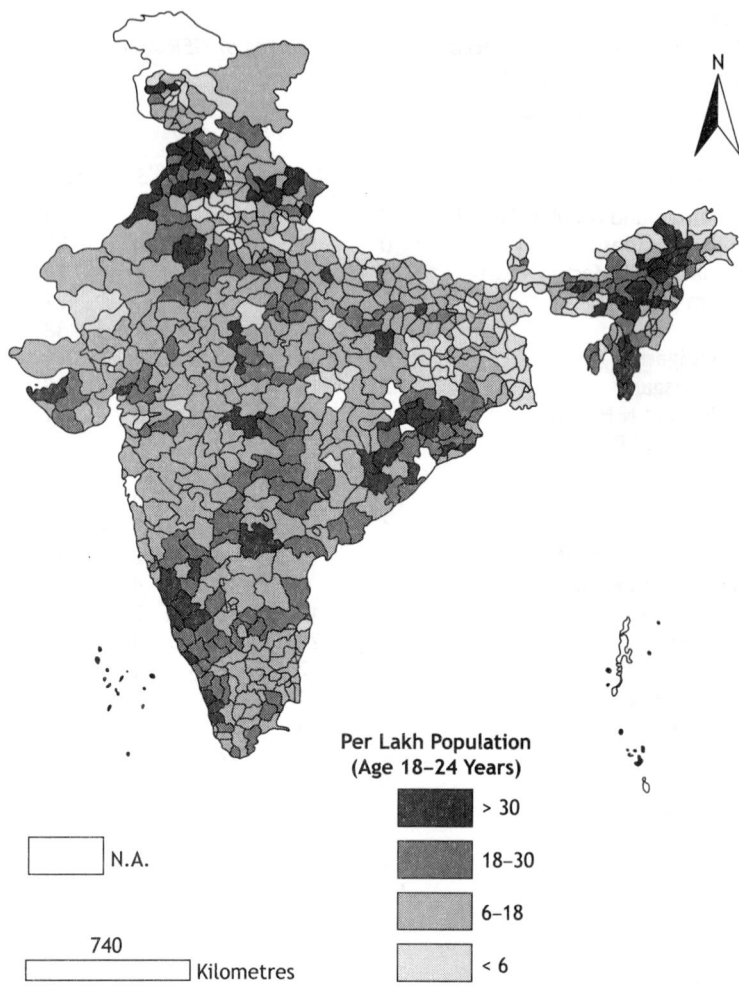

Figure 6.10
Colleges of General Education per 100,000 Population (2011)
Source: Census of India (2011a, 2011c, 2011d).

is far less for India to make any significant gains of demographic dividend. The average size of enrolment works out to be about 2,000 per college, which shows that, in general, Indian colleges are crowded and that the number has to be raised further. There is a little need to describe the inter-state picture as given in Tables 6.10 and 6.11.

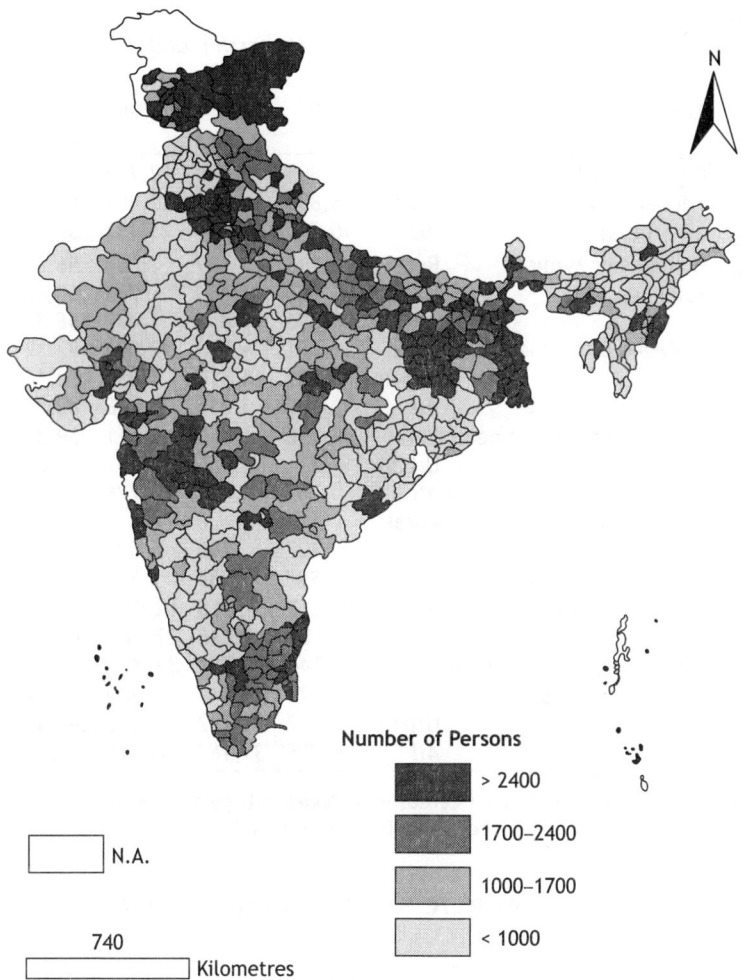

Figure 6.11
Enrolment per College of General Education (2011)
Source: Census of India (2011a, 2011c, 2011d).

Table 6.10 shows that there has been a greater inclination towards the privatisation of higher education. At the aggregate levels, the share of private colleges even in the general education sector has become large although inter-state variation is discernible from the Tables 6.10 and 6.11 and Figures 6.10 and 6.11.

Table 6.10

India: Institutions of Higher Education by Ownership and Areas

S. No.	Type of Institutions	Area	Govt	Pvt	Total	% of Pvt to Total
1.	Colleges of General Education (including all others)	Rural	3,895	3,843	7,736	49.68
		Urban	6,880	10,521	17,401	60.46
		All	10,775	14,364	25,137	57.14
2.	Colleges of Medical Sciences	Rural	295	389	684	56.87
		Urban	300	463	763	60.68
		All	595	852	1,447	58.88
3.	Colleges of Engineering	Rural	371	1,728	2,099	82.32
		Urban	329	1,510	1,839	82.11
		All	700	3,238	3,938	82.22
4.	Colleges of Management	Rural	456	1,055	1,511	69.82
		Urban	311	1,956	2,267	86.28
		All	767	3,011	3,778	79.70
5.	Colleges of Law	Rural	0	0	0	0.00
		Urban	307	286	593	48.23
		All	307	286	593	48.23
6.	**All Degree colleges (1 + 2 + 3+ 4) (Excl. Polytechnic etc.)**	**Rural**	**5,017**	**7,015**	**12,030**	58.31
		Urban	**8,127**	**14,736**	**22,863**	64.45
		All	**13,144**	**21,751**	**34,893**	62.34
7.	Polytechnic/ITIs/ Vocational	Rural	3,279	3,441	6,720	51.21
		Urban	7,017	35,742	42,759	83.59
		All	10,296	39,183	49,479	79.19

Source: Collated from *District Census Hand Books* (Village and Town Amenities), reference year 2009, Census of India (2011).

PRIVATE–PUBLIC SHARE IN ENROLMENT

One notices substantial regional variations in terms of private institutions of higher education between states. The mushrooming of private institutions is the result of insatiate demand for higher education and also because the courses offered by the private institutions are mostly employment-friendly. This is why private sector is demand driven and, therefore, has greater capacity and flexibility to absorb change in economy and society.

Table 6.14 shows that barring a few states and urban areas across the states, private institutions have larger share of total enrolment in higher education. Table 6.14 shows that private aided colleges account for a good share of student enrolment. The question, therefore, is as to how one defines private aided colleges in the structure

Table 6.11
Colleges/Institutions per 100,000 Population in 18–24 Years and Enrolment per Institution (2011)

	No. of Colleges per 100,000 Population in 18–24 Years Age						Enrol/Institution	
States/UTs	All Govt/Pvt Degree Colleges of Gen. Ed.	All Degree Colleges of Law	All (Govt+Pvt) Degree Colleges of Med.	All (Govt+Pvt) Degree Colleges of Engg.	All (Govt+Pvt) Degree Colleges of Mgmt.	All Polytech/ ITIs & Colleges of Voc. Edu.	All Degree Colleges of General Edu.	All Poly/ITIs and Voc.
1	2	3	4	5	6	7	8	9
Andaman and Nicobar	6	0	0	6	0	38	3,031	87
Andhra Pradesh	18	0	0	6	4	32	1,422	257
Arunachal Pradesh	33	0	1	1	2	27	766	53
Assam	30	0	0	0	1	32	571	32
Bihar	11	0	0	1	1	21	1,774	70
Chandigarh	11	1	2	2	2	1	3,121	5,171
Chhattisgarh	12	0	1	1	1	9	1,042	207
Dadra and Nagar Haveli	2	0	0	0	2	2	7,401	1,735
Daman and Diu	2	0	0	0	0	40	4,170	41
Goa	19	1	2	2	2	50	2,179	79
Gujarat	15	1	1	2	2	47	1,214	76
Haryana	5	0	0	4	4	20	4,503	336
Himachal Pradesh	15	1	1	4	4	37	1,473	212
Jammu and Kashmir	15	0	0	0	1	46	1,984	51
Jharkhand	5	0	0	0	0	10	3,995	249
Karnataka	19	1	1	1	3	61	786	95
Kerala	25	0	2	4	4	81	1,067	140

Table 6.11 (continued)

Table 6.11 (continued)

States/UTs	No. of Colleges per 100,000 Population in 18–24 Years Age						Enrol/Institution	
	All Govt/Pvt Degree Colleges of Gen. Ed.	All (Govt+Pvt) Degree Colleges of Law	All (Govt+Pvt) Degree Colleges of Med.	All (Govt+Pvt) Degree Colleges of Engg.	All (Govt+Pvt) Degree Colleges of Mgmt.	All Polytech/ITIs & Colleges of Voc. Edu.	All Degree Colleges of General Edu.	All Poly/ITIs and Voc.
1	2	3	4	5	6	7	8	9
Lakshadweep	37	0	0	0	0	37	461	55
Madhya Pradesh	13	1	1	2	1	9	1,133	238
Maharashtra	14	1	1	2	2	54	1,741	97
Manipur	24	0	1	1	0	105	1,276	16
Meghalaya	24	1	0	0	0	22	712	62
Mizoram	56	1	1	6	3	17	853	162
Nagaland	33	0	0	0	2	13	631	86
NCT of Delhi	4	0	1	3	10	4	7,678	1,665
Odisha	31	0	1	4	3	38	339	102
Puducherry	29	1	7	9	9	153	997	62
Punjab	41	0	0	2	2	20	481	191
Rajasthan	19	1	0	2	2	9	877	331
Sikkim	14	1	1	2	4	15	1,278	76
Tamil Nadu	12	0	1	6	4	80	1,990	81
Tripura	21	0	0	1	0	19	663	50
Uttar Pradesh	13	0	2	2	2	7	1,676	377
Uttarakhand	25	1	3	2	2	30	1,020	192
West Bengal	5	0	1	2	1	14	2,802	73
India	18	0.42	1	2	2	34	1,917	366

Source: Census (2011).

Table 6.12

Colleges of General Education per 100,000 Population (2011)

| | Number of Degree Colleges | | | | |
| | <6 | 6–18 | 18–30 | >30 | Total |
States/UTs	Number of Districts				Districts
Andaman and Nicobar	2	1	0	0	3
Andhra Pradesh	0	12	10	1	23
Arunachal Pradesh	9	2	2	3	16
Assam	0	7	11	9	27
Bihar	6	29	2	1	38
Chhattisgarh	1	17	0	0	18
Daman and Diu	2	0	0	0	2
Goa	0	1	1	0	2
Gujarat	2	17	5	2	26
Haryana	14	7	0	0	21
Himachal Pradesh	0	9	3	0	12
Jammu and Kashmir	7	12	1	2	22
Jharkhand	16	8	0	0	24
Karnataka	0	7	19	4	30
Kerala	0	4	6	4	14
Madhya Pradesh	5	38	5	2	50
Maharashtra	2	24	8	1	35
Manipur	1	4	2	2	9
Meghalaya	4	2	0	1	7
Mizoram	0	0	1	7	8
Nagaland	1	3	3	4	11
Odisha	0	4	13	13	30
Puducherry	0	0	3	1	4
Punjab	0	1	6	13	20
Rajasthan	2	20	8	3	33
Sikkim	3	0	1	0	4
Tamil Nadu	1	27	4	0	32
Tripura	1	0	3	0	4
Uttar Pradesh	12	43	14	2	71
Uttarakhand	0	5	3	5	13
West Bengal	14	4	0	0	18
Total	105	308	134	80	627

Source: Census (2011).

of institutions in India. The private aided colleges are of diverse nature in India. But a majority of them receive substantial share of their funding from the state/central government and also development grants from UGC, if they fulfil the requirements. If public

Table 6.13

Enrolment per College of General Education (2011)

States	Enrolment per Degree College				Total Districts
	<1,000	1,000–1,700	1,700–2,400	>2,400	
	Number of Districts				
Andaman and Nicobar	2	0	0	1	3
Andhra Pradesh	6	9	6	2	23
Arunachal Pradesh	14	0	1	1	16
Assam	23	4	0	0	27
Bihar	3	15	9	11	38
Chhattisgarh	7	10	1	0	18
Daman &Diu	1	0	0	1	2
Goa	0	0	1	1	2
Gujarat	10	8	5	3	26
Haryana	0	0	1	20	21
Himachal Pradesh	1	7	4	0	12
Jammu and Kashmir	1	4	2	15	22
Jharkhand	0	2	1	21	24
Karnataka	26	4	0	0	30
Kerala	5	7	2	0	14
Madhya Pradesh	21	22	3	4	50
Maharashtra	5	13	6	11	35
Manipur	2	2	2	3	9
Meghalaya	1	2	3	1	7
Mizoram	6	2	0	0	8
Nagaland	10	1	0	0	11
Odisha	30	0	0	0	30
Puducherry	2	2	0	0	4
Punjab	19	0	0	1	20
Rajasthan	22	10	1	0	33
Sikkim	3	0	0	1	4
Tamil Nadu	0	6	18	8	32
Tripura	3	0	0	1	4
Uttar Pradesh	6	26	21	18	71
Uttarakhand	5	3	3	2	13
West Bengal	1	1	3	13	18
Total	235	160	93	139	627

Source: Census (2011).

money is spent by a group of private managers, could this lead to such institutions be categorised as private? However, given the situation that such colleges receive public funding and also have government representatives on the governing boards of schools, it would

Table 6.14
Per Cent Distribution of Students Attending Educational Institutions by Type of Management

Level	Graduation and Above					
Areas	Rural			Urban		
Inst. Type	Govt	Pvt Aided	Pvt Unaided	Govt	Pvt Aided	Pvt Unaided
State/UT						
Andhra Pradesh	23.38	14.29	62.34	25.52	12.50	61.98
Arunachal Pradesh	90.38	1.92	7.69	53.03	46.97	0.00
Assam	84.91	13.21	1.89	60.32	22.22	17.46
Bihar	84.78	8.70	6.52	82.61	4.35	13.04
Chhattisgarh	91.11	4.44	4.44	59.32	11.86	28.81
Delhi	73.65	2.70	23.65	80.11	10.80	9.09
Goa	63.86	36.14	0.00	16.47	83.53	0.00
Gujarat	40.98	45.90	13.11	36.22	49.61	14.17
Haryana	58.44	11.69	29.87	25.81	37.90	36.29
Himachal Pradesh	70.90	3.73	25.37	63.40	0.65	35.95
Jammu and Kashmir	85.71	7.14	7.14	87.03	1.08	11.89
Jharkhand	85.11	4.26	10.64	74.51	14.71	10.78
Karnataka	45.33	32.00	22.67	16.26	51.22	32.52
Kerala	22.82	24.83	52.35	28.81	17.51	53.67
Madhya Pradesh	63.04	15.22	21.74	40.28	13.89	45.83
Maharashtra	22.50	65.00	12.50	20.26	62.09	17.65
Manipur	84.07	7.08	8.85	82.10	8.64	9.26
Meghalaya	33.33	58.33	8.33	21.81	58.51	19.68
Mizoram	90.57	0.00	9.43	93.14	2.94	3.92
Nagaland	37.96	13.14	48.91	13.84	41.51	44.65
Odisha	55.81	37.21	6.98	62.22	17.04	20.74
Punjab	37.78	24.44	37.78	28.07	34.21	37.72
Rajasthan	54.65	1.16	44.19	48.70	5.19	46.10
Sikkim	84.62	3.85	11.54	68.57	9.52	21.90
Tamil Nadu	18.10	32.76	49.14	20.33	29.12	50.55
Telangana	29.45	5.48	65.07	9.43	7.55	83.02
Tripura	100.00	0.00	0.00	90.63	5.21	4.17
Uttar Pradesh	35.56	30.00	34.44	36.11	34.03	29.86
Uttarakhand	85.57	4.12	10.31	80.79	6.40	12.81
West Bengal	86.21	5.17	8.62	72.60	17.12	10.27
Andaman and Nicobar Islands	45.10	49.67	5.23	75.00	19.32	5.68
Chandigarh	81.71	17.07	1.22	52.71	44.96	2.33
Dadra and Nagar Haveli	0.00	97.14	2.86	7.02	92.98	0.00
Daman and Diu	68.97	31.03	0.00	32.61	45.65	21.74
Lakshadweep	68.52	29.63	1.85	67.92	0.00	32.08
Puducherry	64.90	15.23	19.87	20.35	3.49	76.16
All India	48.06	22.55	29.39	38.26	28.19	33.56

Source: NSSO (2014).

Table 6.15
Reasons for Attending Private Institution (2014)

Reasons	Rural	Urban
1. Govt inst. not available nearby	29.1	13.4
2. Pvt inst. have better learning environment	29.7	34.7
3. Medium of instruction is English	0.9	2.0
4. Quality of education in govt inst. not satisfactory	9.3	11.1
5. Couldn't get admission in govt inst.	27.5	35.7
6. Can't say	3.5	3.1

Source: NSSO (2014).

be only fair to call such colleges, especially in the general education segment, as public rather than private. In any case, they operate more like public institutions rather than as for-profit private higher education institutions. And if this is accepted then the percentage of enrolment in such colleges and the government would add to a larger share in some disciplines and faculties of education.

Another questions is, why do students choose private institutions? Is it because the public institutions have poor reputation and the courses offered are not according to the market demand. The NSSO 71st Round provides useful insights into this proposition. The rural respondents revealed that about 28% of them went to private institutions because they could not get admission in public institutions. Another 29% said that government colleges were not available in the neighbourhood. That means, among other reasons, nearly 56% went to private colleges not because of their choice but because they did not have any other option. Only one-thirds of respondents made the choice in favour of private institutions (see Table 6.15). The issue however remains to be thoroughly examined further with reliable database.

CONCLUSION

This study attempted to provide some empirical evidence on the issue of regional disparities at the state and district levels, the effect on social groups such as SCs, STs and others. The context to the analysis is the massification phase of higher education where massive expansion has taken place. This expansion is not equally felt in all regions of the country. As evident from the discussions, 'massification' hypothesis needs much deeper analysis especially as such a transition must necessarily transform the educational system towards catering to skill development and vocationalisation. This dimension is very weak in India.

The spatial perspective on social character of space, or what is referred to as socio-spatial segmentation, seems to have been at work and it has been in favour of the elite and propertied classes. The traditionally deprived communities have improved their status and participation largely owing to the policy of positive discrimination. Yet the share of such segments in the total enrolment remains lower than their share in population indicating the distances to be travelled to reach the goal of equity. However, education as a potential means towards social and economic mobility gets further reinforced. One significant conclusion that can be drawn from the study is that equity in access in higher education can be achieved more through the promotion of public institutions than private institutions.

REFERENCES

Agarwal, P. 2009. *Indian Higher Education: Envisioning the Future*, 2–3. New Delhi: SAGE.

Brennan, J. 2004. 'The Social Role of the Contemporary University: Contradictions, Boundaries and Change'. In *Ten Years On: Changing Education in a Changing World*, 22–26. Buckingham: CHERI & The Open University Press.

Census of India. 2011a. *District Census Hand Books* (Village & Town Amenities). New Delhi: Office of the Registrar General and Commissioner of India, Ministry of Home Affairs, GoI. http://www.censusindia.gov.in/2011census/dchb/DCHB.html

———. 2011b. *C–10 Population Attending Educational Institution by Age, Sex and Type of Educational Institution*. New Delhi: Office of the Registrar General and Commissioner of India, Ministry of Home Affairs, GoI. http://www.censusindia.gov.in/2011census/C-series/C10.html

———. 2011c. *C–11 Population Attending Educational Institution by Completed Educational Level, Age and Sex*. New Delhi: Office of the Registrar General and Commissioner of India, Ministry of Home Affairs, GoI. http://www.censusindia.gov.in/2011census/C-series/c_11.html

———. 2011d. *C–14 Population in Five Year Age Group by Residence and Sex*. New Delhi: Office of the Registrar General and Commissioner of India, Ministry of Home Affairs, GoI. http://www.censusindia.gov.in/2011census/C-series/C-14.html

Ministry of Human Resource Development. 2014. *All India Survey of Higher Education 2013–2014*. New Delhi: GoI.

NSSO. 2014. *Education in India: NSSO 71st Round*. New Delhi: Ministry of Statistics and Programme Implementation.

Sinha, S. 2007. 'Redefining Educationally Backward Regions'. In *Higher Education In India: Issues Related to Expansion, Inclusiveness, Quality and Finance*, 56–78. UGC: GoI.

Soja, E.W. 1980. 'The Socio-Spatial Dialectic'. *Annals of the Association of American Geographers* 70 (2): 207–25.

Trow, M. 1973. *Carnegie Commission in Higher Education: Problems in Transition from Elite to Massification*. Berkeley, USA: McGraw Hill Books.

Varghese, N.V. 2015. 'Challenges of Massification of Higher Education in India'. CPRHE Research Papers 1, CPRHE/NUEPA, New Delhi.

7

Higher Education in India: Access, Quality and Structure

Vani K. Borooah

INTRODUCTION

There are several studies of inter-group disparities in school enrol-ment and learning in schools (ASER 2014; Bhalotra and Zamora 2010; Borooah 2012; Borooah and Iyer 2005; Deolalikar 2010). Against this emphasis in the literature on schools, academic interest in the issues pertaining to inequalities in the higher education sector in India has been relatively neglected (Deshpande 2013).[1]

The issue of underrepresentation by certain groups in higher education is important for a number of reasons. First, conventional wisdom has it that education is the handmaiden of prosperity. As Chamarbagwala (2006) notes, those in India with a college educa-tion have gained the most from its economic growth. As a result, in contemporary India, acquiring a tertiary qualification has become the key to gaining entry to the most dynamic segments of employ-ment (Mohanty 2006). Second, if India aspires to be an open and equitable society, then gross imbalances between social groups, in spheres of activities which are important to personal success, such as higher education, make a mockery of such aspirations.

In addition to access, there is a question of inequalities in the *quality* of higher education received by persons from the various social groups. This chapter uses data from the 71st National Sample Survey (NSS) Round (Education Survey: January–June 2014) to exam-ine the quality of higher education received by different social

---

[1] See, however, Basant and Sen (2014) who analysed three Rounds of the NSS—55th (1999–2000), 61st (2004–05) and 66th (2009–10)—to investigate the influence of socio-religious group affiliation on participation in higher education and to examine how this might have changed over time. In a similar vein, Sundaram (2006), using data from the 55th (1999–2000) Round of the NSS, sought to examine the issue of fair access to higher education.

groups in India. It shows how the choice of subject, the medium of instruction (MoI) and the type of higher educational institution (HEI) attended varies systematically by social group. Over half of persons in higher education in India in 2014 studied in Hindi or a regional language as the MoI, and this chapter shows that this greatly limited their subject choice, confining them to humanities and excluding them from engineering, medicine, law and management. The chapter develops an analytical model of the desirability of affirmative action in higher education admissions with more stringent admission standards applied to 'forward class' than to 'backward-class' applicants. This is needed in order to compensate for the differences in family resource endowments of applicants from the two groups. The chapter, however, points to the danger of an overzealous application of affirmative action—by which admission standards for 'backward-class' applicants are set too low—diluting the intellectual quality of admissions from this group.

THE DATA

The data for this study is from the 71st Round of the NSS and pertains to the period January–July 2014. The analysis is supplemented by data from the 64th Round, which pertains to the period July 2007–June 2008. Both the 64th and the 71st and NSS Rounds, unlike the more 'generalist' Rounds, are aimed at providing specific information on education.[2]

The 71st (and the 64th) NSS Round provided information about whether the respondents between the age of 5 and 29 years were currently in attendance at a variety of educational levels from primary school upwards. From these levels, we chose, as our point of focus, those currently attending graduate or postgraduate courses, irrespective of subject, with the aim of acquiring a degree, diploma or certificate through these courses. Persons were said to be in Higher Education Attendance (HEA) if they were currently attending such (graduate or postgraduate) courses and not in HEA if they were not. Table 7.1 shows the distribution of persons in HEA by age: 79%

[2] At the outset of describing the data, it is again important to draw attention to the fact that all the results reported in this study are based upon grossing up the survey data using the observation-specific weights provided by the NSS for each of the surveys.

Table 7.1
*The Distribution of Numbers in Higher Education Attendance in India, by Age**

Age→	16	17	18	19	20	21	22	23	24	25	26	27	28	29	Total
HEA Numbers 71st Round →	498	14,965	48,989	49,269	61,957	37,882	32,154	16,576	10,540	9,447	4,216	2,541	2,487	841	292,364
% of Total →	0.2	5.1	16.8	16.9	21.2	13.0	11.0	5.7	3.6	3.2	1.4	0.9	0.9	0.3	100.0
HEA Numbers 64th Round →	583	7,333	24,050	23,337	31,434	17,623	13,165	7,413	5,007	2,802	1,587	874	912	269	136,387
% of Total →	0.4	5.4	17.6	17.1	23.1	12.9	9.7	5.4	3.7	2.1	1.2	0.6	0.7	0.2	100.0

Source: NSSO (2007, 2014).
Note: *16–29 years of age.

of such persons in the 71st Round and 80% in the 64th Round were between 18 and 22 years of age.[3]

The second item of particular interest to this study was the construction of the social groups with each person in the estimation sample being placed in one, and only one, of these groups. The NSS categorised persons by four social groups (scheduled tribes or STs, scheduled castes or SCs, other backward classes or OBCs and 'others') and simultaneously by eight religion groups (Hinduism, Islam, Christianity, Sikhism, Jainism, Buddhism, Zoroastrianism and 'others'). Since Jains and Zoroastrians comprised less than 0.25% of the sample, they are not separately identified in this study but included in the 'others' category. The fact that Muslims, too, have their 'backward classes' and 'forward' classes, with a conspicuous lack of intermarriage between the two groups, meant that it was sensible to separate Muslims into two groups—OBC Muslims and non-OBC Muslims.[4]

Combining the NSS 'social group' and 'religion' categories, we subdivided households into the following groups that are used as the basis for analysis in this paper:

1. STs. These comprised 13.1% of the 65,923 households in the 71st NSS Round and 9.5% of the grossed up NSS of 2,484,620 households.
2. SCs. These comprised 16% of the 65,923 households in the 71st NSS Round and 18.9% and of the grossed up NSS of 2,484,620 households. Over 90% of households in this category were Hindu.[5]
3. Non-Muslim OBCs (NMOBC). These comprised 32.7% of the 65,923 households in the 71st NSS Round and 36.1% of the grossed up NSS of 2,484,620 households with 96% of these households being Hindu.
4. Muslim OBCs (MOBC). These comprised 6.4% of the 65,923 households in the 71st NSS Round and 6.7% of the grossed up NSS of 2,484,620 households.[6]

---

[3] There may have been persons older than 29 in HEA but these were not recorded by the NSS since it imposed an age ceiling of 29 years in collecting data on HEA.
[4] See Sachar Committee Report (2006).
[5] This category also included some Muslim households. Since Muslims from the SC are not entitled to SC reservation benefits, these Muslim SC households have been moved to the MOBC category.
[6] Including Muslim SC households (see previous footnote).

5. Non-OBC Muslims. They are, hereafter, referred to as Muslim upper classes (MUC) comprised 6.2% of the 65,923 households in the 71st NSS Round and 5.7% of the grossed up NSS of 2,484,620 households.

6. Non-Muslim Upper Classes (NMUC). These comprised 25.7% of the 65,923 households in the 71st NSS Round and 23.1% of the grossed up NSS of 2,484,620 households: over 90% of the households in this category were Hindu.

Table 7.2 shows the gross tertiary attendance ratio (GTAR) values (defined earlier) by social group.[7] This shows that the GTAR increased dramatically in the six years between the 71st and 64th Rounds from, in aggregate, 14.2% to 27.6%, with all groups experiencing a considerable rise in their GTAR. Paralleling this increase of 14 percentage points in the GTAR was an increase in the number of universities in India from 436 in 2009 to 733 in 2015 with the largest growth being in the number of private universities. Of the 733 universities in 2015: 46 were central universities, 336 were state universities, 127 were 'deemed' universities and 224 were private universities.[8]

The MOBC had the lowest GTAR (14.8%) in the 71st Round, followed by a GTAR of 15.2% for the ST, 15.7% for the MUC, 20.4% for the SC, 29.6% for the NMOBC and 46.3% for the NMUC. A striking feature of the GTAR for the ST is that its value is very different depending upon whether one is considering Hindu or Christian ST: the GTAR was 28.4% for the Christian ST but only 13.3% for the Hindu ST.

Between the two Rounds, the GTAR for the MOBC increased from 7.4% to 14.8%, for the MUC from 7.8% to 15.7%, for the ST from 6% to 15.2%, for the SC from 9.5% to 20.4%, for the NMOBC from 13.2% to 29.6% and for the NMUC from 27.4% to 46.3%.

---

[7] Strictly speaking, GTAR should include in the numerator all persons in HEA. The NSS data, however, only provides information about persons up to the age of 29 years in HEA.

[8] See the University Grant Commission's (UGC) list of universities in India (http:// www.ugc.ac.in/oldpdf/alluniversity.pdf). 'Central' and 'state' universities were funded by, respectively, the central government and the state governments; 'deemed' universities were those Institutes which the UGC regarded as the equivalent of universities and which, therefore, were allowed to award degrees; private universities were approved by the UGC but were not allowed to have off-campus colleges.

Table 7.2
Gross Tertiary Attendance Rate in India, by Social Group (71st and 64th Rounds)

71st Round

	Scheduled Tribe	Scheduled Caste (excl. Muslims)	Non-Muslim OBC	Muslim OBC (incl. SC Muslims)	Muslim Upper Class	Non-Muslim Upper Class	Total
Numbers in HEA 16–29 years	16,217	43,009	108,262	13,240	11,134	100,503	292,364
Total aged 18–22	106,062	211,179	365,769	89,299	71,141	216,951	1,060,401
GTAR (%)	15.2	20.4	29.6	14.8	15.7	46.3	27.6

64th Round

	Scheduled Tribe	Scheduled Caste	Non-Muslim OBC	Muslim OBC	Muslim Upper Class	Hindu Upper Caste	Total
Numbers in HEA 16–29 years	4,632	18,231	45,265	4,463	6,082	57,715	136,387
Total aged 18–22	77,006	192,795	343,425	60,025	77,735	210,364	961,350
GTAR (%)	6.0	9.5	13.2	7.4	7.8	27.4	14.2

Source: NSSO (2007, 2014).

THE QUALITY OF HIGHER EDUCATION IN INDIA

The preceding material focused, through the GTAR, on the likelihood of being in HEA. But this begs the question of the *quality* of higher education that students received. Both the 71st NSS and the 64th NSS Rounds provide information on items that could reasonably be considered as *proxies* for 'quality'. One such item is the *total* expenditure on education by persons in HEA who were aged 18–22 years. For example, a clue to differences in the quality of higher education received by women and men is provided by comparing the mean amounts that the two groups spent on such education: the mean total expenditure of women and men in HEA was, respectively, ₹27,613 and ₹32,710. So, while gender disadvantage in terms of attendance might be small, there was clear gender disparity in terms of expenditure on higher education by those in HEA.[9]

Similarly, there was a clear hierarchy of expenditure on higher education by those in HEA from the different social groups. As Figure 7.1 shows, for persons in HEA, those from the NMUC spent the most (mean ₹38,677), followed by the NMOBC (₹29,897) while those from the SC, the ST, MOBC and MUC (respectively, ₹18,335,

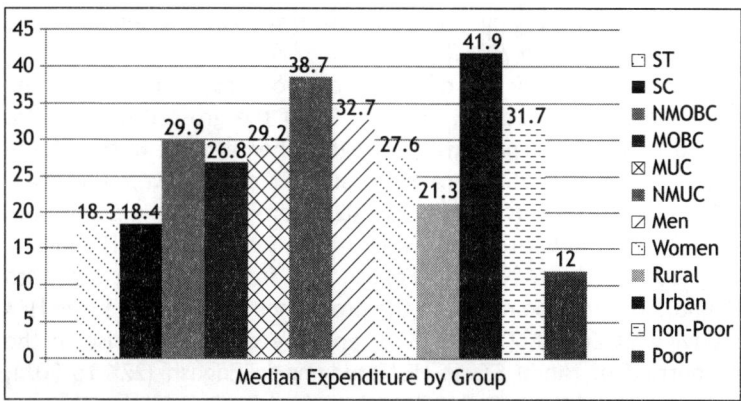

Figure 7.1
Median Expenditure on Higher Education by Those Aged 18–22 Years and in Higher Education Attendance (in thousands)

Source: Own calculations from NSS 71st Round (January–July 2014), after applying sample weights. NSSO (2014).

---

[9] Note that we are comparing all men and women in HEA and, by the constraint of the NSS, the upper limit for this is 29 years.

₹18,406, ₹26,751 and ₹29,164) spent the least. Mean expenditure on higher education by those in the rural sector was considerably lower than that spent by urban residents (₹21,289 versus ₹41,927) and mean expenditure on higher education by those in poor households was considerably lower than that by those in non-poor households (₹12,010 versus ₹32,656).

ENGLISH AS A MEDIUM OF INSTRUCTION

Another proxy of quality is the MoI in higher education. Without prejudice, one could regard higher education courses with English as the MoI (hereafter, 'studying in English') as offering better employment prospects (and, therefore, of higher 'quality') than courses delivered in other languages.[10] Figure 7.2 shows, for the 71st and 64th Rounds, the proportion of persons in the different social groups in HEA, who were studying a course with English as the MoI.

In the 64th Round (2007–08), 47% of all persons in HEA were studying in English; by the 71st Round, this proportion had risen to 49% and this rise in the popularity of studying in English was particularly experienced by persons from the ST: the proportion of ST persons in HEA studying in English rose from 30% in the 64th Round to nearly 41% in the 71st Round.

Persons from the ST divide into two groups: Hindu ST and Christian ST (respectively, 86% and 9% of the grossed up NSS 71st Round 1,091,429 ST persons). However, when it came to the 16,216 ST persons in HEA, 75% were Hindu and 17% persons were Christian. Of the latter group (Christian ST), 82% were studying in English (up from 78% in the 64th Round) while of the former group (Hindu ST), only 30% were studying in English (up from 21.7% in the 64th Round). The four point rise in the proportion of Christian STs in HEA studying in English (78% to 82%) and the eight point rise in the proportion of Hindu STs in HEA studying in English (22% to 30%), between the 64th and the 71st Rounds, largely explains the rise from 30% to 41% in the aggregate proportion of ST persons in HEA studying in English. In addition, between the two Rounds, the proportion of Christians, in the total of ST persons in HEA, increased from 14% to 17% while the proportion of Hindus, in the total of ST persons in HEA, decreased from 82% to 75%.

---

[10] See Krishna (2013) on the importance of English in India.

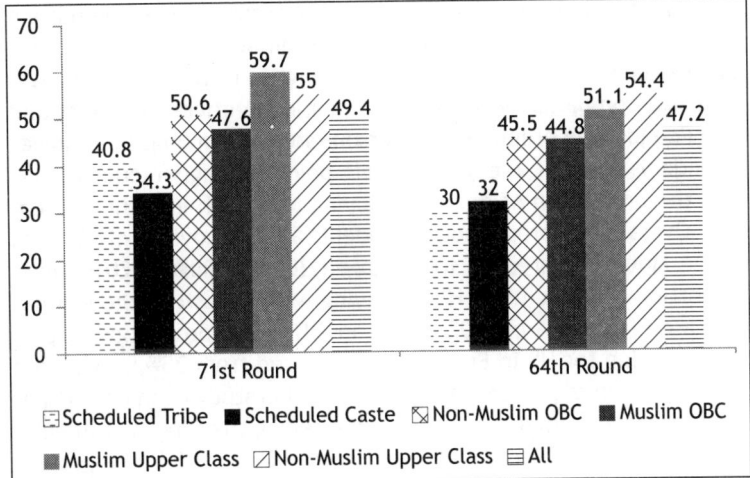

Figure 7.2
Proportion of Persons in HEA Studying in English, by Social Group

Source: Own calculations from the NSS 71st Round (January–July 2014) and 64th Round (2007–08), after applying sample weights. NSSO (2007, 2014).

COPING WITH ENGLISH AS THE MEDIUM OF INSTRUCTION IN HIGHER EDUCATION

The fact that, as Figure 7.2 shows, nearly half of those in HEA in 2014 were taking courses which were delivered in English raises the question of how well they coped with the language since, for many students, higher education provided their first experience of studying in English, their pre-HEA MoI being in another language.

This failure to cope with English was highlighted anecdotally when, in July 2015, the Indian Institute of Technology (IIT) at Roorkee failed 72 students after their first year of studies which, in turn, was supposed to entail their automatic expulsion from the Institute. Of these 72 students, 90% were from the 'reserved' categories (that is, groups for whom a certain proportion of places were reserved under affirmative action policies—STs, SCs and OBCs). Explaining this failure, one of the students said, 'English is our big problem. We are from Hindi-medium schools and then we come to the campus and realise it is all high-level English. We see students speaking English, asking questions in English and we can do none of that. Our confidence drains away' (Vishnu 2015).

These problems are likely to be exacerbated as an increasing proportion of students, who had done their schooling in Hindi or a regional language, choose to do their higher education in English. Table 7.3 compares by social group, for, respectively, the 71st and 64th Rounds, the proportion of persons studying in English at higher secondary (HS)—at the jumping off point for higher education—with the proportion of persons studying in English in higher education. Overall, the proportion of students at HS studying with English as the MoI has increased from 25% in 2008 to 30% in 2014 while proportion of students in HEA studying with English as the MoI has increased from 47% in 2008 to 49% in 2014. The proportion of persons studying for HS in English has increased from 25% to 30%, but the proportion of persons in higher education studying in English has also increased from 47% to 49%. In that sense, the 'English Difficulty Gap', defined as the difference between HEA and HS in the proportions of students with English as the MoI, has declined from 22 points in 2008 to 19 points.

The lowest proportion of students in HEA studying with English as the MoI were from the SC (only one in three SC students in HEA were studying in English in 2014 and this figure was largely unaltered since 2008) and the highest proportion of students in HEA studying with English as the MoI were from the NMOBC and the Muslim and NMUC (over one in two of students from these groups who were in

Table 7.3

Proportion of Persons with English as the Medium of Instruction at Higher Secondary and in Higher Education (71st and 64th Rounds)

	71st Round (January–July 2014)		64th Round (January–July 2004)	
	English MoI in HS	English MoI in HEA	English MoI in HS	English MoI in HEA
Scheduled Tribes	25.8	40.8	20.7	30
Scheduled Castes	18.9	34.3	14.6	32
Non-Muslim OBC	26.7	50.6	18.9	45.5
Muslim OBC	35.1	47.6	35.9	44.8
Muslim Upper Class	38	59.7	38.4	51.1
Non-Muslim Upper Class	40.8	55	33.7	54.4
All	30.2	49.4	24.9	47.2

Source: Own calculations from the NSS 71st and 64th Rounds, after applying sample weights. NSSO (2007, 2014).

HEA were studying in English in 2014). For each of the six groups, however, there was a considerable gap between the proportions of students studying in English at two levels (HS and in HEA), suggesting that the problems of coping with English as a MoI in higher education may not have diminished much between the 64th and the 71st Rounds.

A MULTINOMIAL LOGIT MODEL OF SUBJECT CHOICE IN HIGHER EDUCATION STUDY

The NSS 71st Round also provides information on the broad subject categories in which persons, aged 18–22 years, in HEA are enrolled and also the type of institutions—government, private aided or private unaided—in which they are enrolled. Table 7.3 shows that, in 2014, the largest proportion (39%) of persons in HEA were enrolled on humanities courses (down from 43% in 2008), followed by 17% in commerce, 16% in science, 15% in engineering (up from, respectively, 16%, 12% and 10% in 2008) and 3% in IT courses (down from 9% in 2008). So, in summary, the shift in subject popularity between 2008 and 2014 has been the reduction in the popularity of humanities and IT, paralleled by the increased popularity of science and engineering. The proportion of persons in medicine and in business did not change greatly between 2008 and 2014. As Table 7.3 also shows, the groups most likely to study humanities were the ST and the SC, women, the poor and those living in rural areas while the groups most likely to study engineering were the NMOBC and the NMUC, men, the non-poor and those living in urban areas.

The multinomial logit model has been used to analyse choice outcomes in a variety of situations in which there are more than two possible outcomes (say, choice of subject studied in college, transport mode in commuting, voting for political parties at elections). The basic question that such a model seeks to answer is what is the probability that a person with a particular set of characteristics will choose a particular outcome? If there are J available choices, indexed $j = 1...K$, these answers can be obtained by estimating a multinomial logit equation where the dependent variable $Y_i = j$ if person i chose item j from the K available choices.[11]

---

[11] With J mutually exclusive and collectively exhaustive outcomes, indexed $1...J$, the multinomial logit model is defined by a pair of equations. The first, defines

Table 7.4
Courses of Study in Higher Education by Social Group, Gender, Poverty and Location (NSS 71st Round*)

	Percentage of Students in the Group Studying the Subject							
	Humanities	Science	Commerce	Medicine	Engineering	Management	IT	Others	Total
Scheduled Tribe	49.5	14.1	18.4	1.3	6.8	0.8	2.6	6.5	100
Scheduled Caste	52.7	12.9	14.9	1.5	8.7	1.5	2.2	5.7	100
Non-Muslim OBC	36.5	19.7	14.7	2.4	16.7	2.1	2.7	5.2	100
Muslim OBC	35.7	19.5	16.4	2.0	13.1	3.5	3.2	6.7	100
Muslim Upper Class	47.7	13.3	12.9	4.4	10.8	2.5	1.7	6.7	100
Non-Muslim Upper	38.7	15.9	17.0	2.4	14.5	2.5	3.3	5.8	100
Class									
Men	35.0	15.8	17.2	1.5	19.0	2.5	3.4	5.6	100
Women	43.3	16.0	16.7	3.5	8.9	2.5	3.2	5.9	100
Poor	56.4	16.6	13.1	0.5	5.2	1.2	1.3	5.7	100
Non-poor	37.5	15.9	17.2	2.6	15.1	2.5	3.4	5.8	100
Rural	50.2	17.1	13.3	2.0	8.5	1.3	2.5	5.3	100
Urban	24.3	14.5	21.7	3.0	22.0	3.9	4.4	6.4	100
Total	38.7	15.9	17.0	2.4	14.5	2.5	3.3	5.8	100

Source: Own calculations from the NSS 71st Round (January–July 2014), after applying sample weights. NSSO (2014).
Note: *Aged 18–22 years.

Table 7.5 shows the predicted probabilities (see Long and Freese 2014) of subject choice resulting from estimating a multinomial logit model for 17,235 persons who were in HEA in the 71st NSS. The available subject choices considered in the model were (a) humanities, (b) science, (c) commerce, (d) engineering and (e) 'others' (mainly, medicine, management and IT). The personal characteristics which conditioned the choice of subject area by a person were social group, gender, poverty status, rural/urban location and state of residence.[12] Under each subject heading, the first column shows the predicted probability of a person in HEA from the relevant row category studying that subject, while the second column, under that same subject heading, shows the *marginal probability* which is the difference between the predicated probability for that category and that of the group's reference category (denoted by [R]).

The most noticeable feature of Table 7.5 is the fact that subject choice is severely restricted if English is not the MoI in HEA. The predicted probability of persons in HEA studying humanities is over 60% for those whose MoI (in higher education) was not English compared to 13% for those whose MoI was English. On the other hand, the predicted probability of persons in HEA studying engineering was over 23% for those whose MoI (in higher education) was English compared to just over 1% for those whose MoI was not English. Similarly, the predicted probability of persons in HEA studying subjects like law, management and IT was 27% for those whose MoI (in higher education) was English compared to less than 9% for those whose MoI was not English.

In this context, it is worth pointing out that a major handicap that SC students in HEA suffer from is that (as Figure 7.2 shows) only

---

the *log odds ratio* of a person i choosing outcome j, $j>1$, relative to being in the 'base' status $j = 1$, as a linear function of $X_i = \{X_{ik}, \ k = 1 \ldots K\}$, the vector of values of K explanatory variables ($X_{i1} = 1$) for the person

$$\log\left(\frac{\Pr(Y_i = j)}{\Pr(Y_i = 1)}\right) = \sum_{k=1}^{k} \beta_{jk} X_{ik} = X_i \beta_j$$

where Y_i is an integer variable which takes the value j if, and only if, outcome j occurs for person i, and β_j is the vector of coefficients associated with outcome j, β_{j1} being the coefficient associated with the intercept term. The second equation defines the probability of outcome j ($j=1\ldots J$) occurring for individual i as

$$\Pr(Y_i = j) = \exp(Z_{ij}) / \left[1 + \sum_{r=1}^{J} Z_{ir}\right] = F(X_i \beta_j)$$

[12] A person was defined as 'poor' if his/her household's monthly per capita consumption expenditure (MPCE) was in the bottom 20% of the distribution of MPCE.

Table 7.5

Predicted Probabilities from a Multinomial Logit Model of Subject Choice in Higher Education

	Humanities		Science		Commerce		Engineering		Others	
	Predicted Probability	Marginal Probability	Predicted Probability	Marginal Probability	Predicted Probability	Marginal Probability	Predicted Probability	Marginal Probability	Predicted Probability	Marginal Probability
MoI: W English [R]	0.130		0.215		0.150		0.233		0.272	
MoI: W Hindi	0.601	0.471**	0.120	-0.094**	0.190	0.040**	0.011	-0.222**	0.077	-0.194**
MoI: W Regional	0.603	0.473**	0.108	-0.107**	0.188	0.038**	0.013	-0.221**	0.089	-0.183**
Language										
Scheduled Tribe	0.403	0.047*	0.147	0.014	0.161	-0.034	0.138	-0.007	0.152	-0.021
Scheduled Caste	0.434	0.078**	0.126	-0.006	0.151	-0.044**	0.119	-0.026**	0.169	-0.003
Non-Muslim OBC	0.404	0.048**	0.174	0.041**	0.134	-0.061**	0.139	-0.006	0.149	-0.023**
Muslim OBC	0.367	0.011	0.183	0.050*	0.147	-0.048*	0.119	-0.025*	0.185	0.012
Muslim Upper Class	0.439	0.083**	0.133	0.000	0.145	-0.051**	0.101	-0.043**	0.183	0.011
Non-Muslim Upper	0.356		0.132		0.195		0.145		0.172	
Class [R]										
Men [R]	0.358		0.144		0.163		0.178		0.157	
Women	0.434	0.076**	0.159	0.014	0.154	-0.008	0.083	-0.096**	0.170	0.013*
Non-poor [R]	0.389		0.151		0.159		0.138		0.164	
Poor	0.430	0.041*	0.156	0.006	0.166	0.008	0.096	-0.041**	0.151	-0.013
Rural [R]	0.424		0.172		0.132		0.112		0.160	
Urban	0.343	-0.082**	0.135	-0.037**	0.198	0.066**	0.154	0.042**	0.171	0.011

Source: Own calculations from the NSS 71st Round (January–July 2014), after applying sample weights. NSSO (2014).

Notes: [R] denotes the reference category.

The multinomial logit model was estimated for persons who were in HEA in the 71st NSS

**Significant at 5% level; *Significant at 10% level

about a third, compared to over half of their upper class peers, follow higher education courses with English as the MoI. So, even if SC participation in higher education is increased, a relatively poor command of English either debars them from, or handicaps them in, studying subjects like engineering, medicine, law, IT and management. Perhaps it is for this reason that the well-known Dalit academic, Kancha Ilaiah, argued, 'The Dalit's main agenda is not reservations. My way of equality is English education. My hope is education, not reservation—and I emphasise, English education' (*Times of India* 2013).

According to Table 7.5, the predicted probabilities of SC and NMUC persons in HEA studying humanities were, respectively, 43.4% and 35.6% and, the difference in the two probabilities (the marginal probability) of 7.8 points was significantly different from zero. Similarly, persons in HEA for every other group had a higher predicted probability of studying humanities (and a lower predicted probability of studying engineering and 'others' subjects like law, management and IT) compared to their NMUC counterparts. In terms of gender, the predicted probabilities of women and men in HEA studying engineering were, respectively, 8.3% and 17.8% and, the difference in the two probabilities (the marginal probability) of 9.6 points was significantly different from zero. Poor persons and persons from rural areas, in HEA, were more likely to study humanities (43% and 42.4%, respectively) than their non-poor (38.9%) and urban (34.3%) counterparts.

A MULTINOMIAL LOGIT MODEL OF INSTITUTION CHOICE IN HIGHER EDUCATION STUDY

In addition to providing information on the broad subject categories in which persons in HEA were studying, the NSS 71st Round also provided information on the type of institutions—government, private aided and private unaided—in which they were enrolled. Table 7.6 shows the types of HEIs at which persons, aged 18–22 years, in HEA were enrolled. In 2014, 41% were in government HEI (down from 49% in 2008), 26% were in private aided HEI (down from 32% in 2008), and 33% were in private unaided HEI (up from 19% in 2008). So the biggest change between 2008 and 2014, in the type of HEI attended, has been that while in 2008 only one in five persons, aged 18–22 years, in HEA was enrolled in a private unaided HEI, by 2014 this number had risen to one in three.

Table 7.6

Type of Higher Education Institution Attended, by Social Group, Gender, Poverty and Location (NSS 71st Round)*

	Government	Private Aided	Private Unaided	Total
Scheduled Tribe	59.5	21.3	19.3	100
Scheduled Caste	50.6	21.7	27.7	100
Non-Muslim OBC	35.9	24.9	39.3	100
Muslim OBC	43.6	28.1	28.3	100
Muslim Upper Class	55.7	22.1	22.2	100
Non-Muslim Upper Class	37.7	30.4	31.9	100
Men	42.4	24.0	33.6	100
Women	39.4	28.8	31.9	100
Poor	57.8	23.0	19.2	100
Non-poor	39.9	26.4	33.7	100
Rural	45.7	23.5	30.8	100
Urban	35.2	29.5	35.3	100
Total	41.1	26.2	32.8	100

Source: Own Calculations from the NSS 71st Round (January–July 2014), after applying sample weights. NSSO (2014).

Note: * Aged 18–22 years.

Table 7.6 also shows that government HEI were particularly popular with ST and SC students with nearly 60% of ST students (down from 63% in 2008) and 51% of SC students (down from 54% in 2008), aged 18–22 years and in HEA, enrolled in government HEI. They were also popular with poor students and rural students with 58% of poor students (up from 56% in 2008) and 46% of rural students (down from 50% in 2008), aged 18–22 years and in HEA, enrolled in government HEI.

On the other hand, as Table 7.6 shows, private unaided HEI were particularly popular among NMOBC and NMUC students with 39% of NMOBC students (up from 22% in 2008) and 32% of NMUC students (up from 20% in 2008), aged 18–22 years and in HEA, enrolled in private unaided HEI. They were also popular with non-poor students and urban students with 34% of non-poor students (up from 20% in 2008) and 35% of urban students (down from 22% in 2008), aged 18–22 years and in HEA, enrolled in private unaided HEI.

Table 7.7 shows that, in 2014, 77% of the student body, aged 18–22 years, in private-unaided HEI was drawn from just two groups: 44% from the NMOBC and 33% from the NMUC. In 2008, 82% of the student body, aged 18–22 years, in private-unaided HEI was

Table 7.7

The Social Group Composition of Higher Educational Institutions (71st and 64th Rounds)*

	71st Round (2014)			64th Round (2008)		
	Government	Private Aided	Private Unaided	Government	Private Aided	Private Unaided
Scheduled Tribe	8.0	4.5	3.2	3.9	2.2	2.3
Scheduled Caste	17.9	12.1	12.3	14.8	14.4	7.3
Non-Muslim OBC	32.5	35.3	44.5	29.7	37.1	38.3
Muslim OBC	5.2	5.3	4.2	3.2	3.3	4.9
Muslim Upper Class	5.0	3.1	2.5	4.4	4.4	3.6
Non-Muslim Upper Class	31.5	39.8	33.3	44.0	38.6	43.7
Total	100	100	100	100	100	100

Source: Own Calculations from the NSS 71st Round (January–July 2014), after applying sample weights. NSSO (2014).

Note: *Aged 18–22 years.

drawn from two groups: 38% from the NMOBC and 44% from the NMUC. Private-aided HEI were also largely the preserve of the NMOBC and NMUC: in 2014, 75% of the student body, aged 18–22 years, in private-aided HEI were drawn from the two groups, 35% from the NMOBC and 40% from the NMUC. In 2008, 76% of the student body, aged 18–22 years, in private-unaided HEI was drawn from two groups: 39% from the NMOBC and 37% from the NMUC.

Analogous to the multinomial logit model of subject choice, discussed in the previous section, this section estimates a multinomial model of choice of higher education institution type conditional on the person's choice of subject, and his/her social group, sex, poverty status, rural/urban location and state of residence. These estimates are then used to derive, for persons in HEA from the relevant groups, the predicted probabilities of being in each of the three types of institutions—government, private aided and private unaided.

These probabilities and marginal probabilities, shown in Table 7.8, suggest that, in terms of subject, the likelihood of someone being in a government higher education institution was highest for those studying humanities (53.7%) and lowest for those studying engineering (19.4%). The marginal probabilities associated with government

Table 7.8
Predicted Probabilities from a Multinomial Logit Model of Higher Education Institution Type Chosen by those in HEA

	Government		Private aided		Private Unaided	
	Predicted Probability	*Marginal Probability*	*Predicted Probability*	*Marginal Probability*	*Predicted Probability*	*Marginal Probability*
Humanities [R]	0.537		0.259		0.204	
Science	0.419	-0.118**	0.281	0.022	0.300	0.096**
Commerce	0.457	-0.080**	0.274	0.016	0.269	0.064**
Engineering	0.194	-0.343**	0.238	-0.020	0.568	0.363**
Others	0.308	-0.229**	0.227	-0.031**	0.465	0.261**
Scheduled Tribe	0.502	0.114**	0.248	-0.021	0.250	-0.093**
Scheduled Caste	0.480	0.092**	0.239	-0.030	0.280	-0.062**
Non-Muslim OBC	0.419	0.031*	0.242	-0.027*	0.339	-0.004
Muslim OBC	0.452	0.064*	0.291	0.022	0.257	-0.086**
Muslim Upper Class	0.450	0.062	0.247	-0.022	0.303	-0.040
Non-Muslim Upper Class [R]	0.388		0.269		0.343	
Men [R]	0.436		0.245		0.319	
Women	0.411	-0.025**	0.264	0.019*	0.325	0.006
Non-poor [R]	0.419		0.255		0.326	
Poor	0.510	0.092**	0.240	-0.015	0.250	-0.077**
Rural [R]	0.425		0.245		0.330	
Urban	0.424	-0.001	0.263	0.018	0.313	-0.017

Source: Own calculations from the NSS 71st Round (January–July 2014), after applying sample weights. NSSO (2014).
Notes: [R] denotes the reference category
The multinomial logit model was estimated for 17,130 persons who were in HEA in the 71st NSS.
**Significant at 5% level; *Significant at 10% level

institutions show that the difference between each subject category and reference category of humanities, in their respective predicted probabilities of being studied in a government institution, was significantly different from zero. At the other end of the institutional spectrum, the predicted probability of engineering being studied in a private unaided institution was 56.8% with only a 20.4% chance that it would be studied in a government institution.

In terms of social groups, the lowest likelihood of studying in a government institution (38.8%) and the highest likelihood of studying in a private unaided institution (34.3%) were associated with persons in HEA from the NMUC. Conversely, the highest likelihood of studying in a government institution (50.2%) and the lowest likelihood of studying in a private unaided institution (25%) were associated with persons in HEA from the ST.

AN ECONOMIC ANALYSIS OF RESERVATION POLICY IN HIGHER EDUCATION

Reservation policies in higher education in India reflect the government's (constitutionally mandated) duty to favour persons from the 'reserved' categories (STs, SCs and OBCs), at the expense of persons from the 'non-reserved' or 'general' categories, in admissions to higher education institutions. This duty is formalised through the requirement that a certain proportion of seats in publicly funded educational institutions have to be filled by persons from reserved categories. For example, on information available for 2013, there were a total of 9,885 seats in the 17 IITs of which 4,844 (49%) were in the general category and the rest were reserved: 2,599 for the (non-creamy layer) OBC (25.9%); 1,437 for the SC (14.5%); 721 for the ST (7.3%); 140 for those general category candidates with physical disabilities (0.7%); 75 for OBC candidates with physical disabilities (0.8%); 44 for SC candidates with physical disabilities (0.4%); 25 for ST candidates with physical disabilities (0.2%) (*The Hindu* 2013).

The instrument for filling the places reserved for certain categories of students is to apply different admissions criteria for the 'general category' and 'reserved category' applicants. For example, in 2015, the IITs admitted as the general category students those who had obtained 124 marks (24.5% of a possible 504 marks) in the Joint Entrance Examination (JEE) while simultaneously admitting, under the 'reserved' category (for SC, ST and 'people with disability'), those students who had obtained 62 marks (12.5% of a possible 504 marks) in the JEE. Furthermore, the reserved category students who had obtained 31 marks (6.1% of a possible 504 marks) were admitted to a one-preparatory course with a view to equipping them for admission to the IITs in the following year (see Rao, Shah and Gole 2015).

There may be a correlation between candidates' test scores and their latent intellectual quality, which is the real object of interest but which, by definition, is unobservable. Strictly speaking, however, selection tests such as the JEE are primarily a measure of the ability of candidates to score on that particular test: the phrase often used in India is 'cracking the JEE'. The use of selection tests for college admission is just a particular example of situations in which the outcome of a test—positive or negative—is used to determine whether or not a condition (a prospective pupil is worthy of admission) exists. As such, it is susceptible to a fallacy that is inherent in such situations: confusing the chance that a candidate would pass the test if he/she is a 'good' candidate with the chance that a candidate is a 'good' if he/she passed the test. In legal situations, this is referred to as the *prosecutors' fallacy* (Aitken 1996; Thompson and Schumann 1987); in medical situations, it is termed the *doctors' fallacy* (Mlodinow 2009, 114–16; Zackrisson et al. 2006); and in labour market situations, it is the *employment fallacy* (Borooah 2010).[13] A similar fallacy could arise in situations where people are denied access to higher education on the basis of the outcome of a selection test. This is referred to here as the *selection fallacy*.

Suppose that 1,000 candidates sit the test and the prior belief is that, of these, 280 (28%) are 'good' candidates in the sense of being 'intellectually worthy' of admission. The nature of the test is such that a 'good' candidate will have a 95% chance of passing the test

---

[13] A prosecutor argues that since the probability of observing a particular piece of evidence (say, blood type identical to that found at the scene of the crime), *under the assumed innocence of the defendant*, is very small the probability of the defendant being innocent, *given that his blood type matches that at the crime scene*, must also be very small. A doctor argues that since the probability of a person testing HIV positive, *if he/she was HIV free*, is very small, the probability of a patient being HIV free, *given that he/she tested HIV positive*, must also be very small. A labour market analyst argues that because only a small proportion of persons in regular employment are from a particular group, the probability of a person from that group being in regular employment must also be small.

(and, therefore, a 5% chance of failing the test) and a 'not good' candidate will have an 85% chance of failing the test (and, therefore, a 15% chance of passing the test). In statistical parlance, the probability of a 'true positive' (95%) is referred to as the 'sensitivity' of the test and the probability of a 'false negative' (85%) is referred to as the 'specificity' of the test.[14]

On the basis of prior belief, there are 280 'good' candidates of whom 266 (95% of 280) will pass the test and 14 (5% of 280) will fail. Similarly, the prior belief is there are 720 'not good' candidates of whom 612 (85% of 720) will fail the test and 108 (15% of 720) will pass the test. So, in total, 374 candidates will pass the test, and of these, 266 (71%) will be 'good' and, therefore deserving admission, and 108 (29%) will be 'not good' and, therefore, not deserving admission.

This result arises for two reasons. First, there is the prior belief that, given the rigorous nature of the educational course, only a limited proportion of candidates (28% on our assumption) have the intellectual ability to benefit from it. The second reason is that the probability of a 'false positive'—meaning a 'not good' student passes the test—is pitched at 15%. Why should we expect the probability of a 'false positive' to be so high? As stated earlier, at its most basic, a selection test measures the ability of a candidate to pass the test. With suitable parental encouragement, coaching and burning of midnight oil, it is not unreasonable to assume that 15% of 'not good' pupils can be taught (or can teach themselves) to pass the test and thus generate 'false positives'.

Now suppose that candidates are of two types, 'forward class' and 'backward class', and that of the 1,000 candidates, 800 are forward class and 200 are backward class. The prior belief is that there is no difference in intellectual ability between the two groups so that the expectation is that 56 backward- and 224 forward-class candidates (28% of their respective totals) have the intellectual ability needed to cope with higher education. If the sensitivity of the test is the same for both groups, there is a 95% chance that a 'good' candidate, regardless of group, will pass the test. However, because forward-class candidates have the advantage of greater parental resources, the chances of 'not good' candidates passing the test—the likelihood of a 'false positive'—will be higher for

---

[14] So the probability of a 'true negative' (5%, in the example) is 1-sensitivity, and the probability of a 'false positive' (15%, in the example) is 1-specificity.

forward-class candidates than for backward candidates. Suppose that the probability of a false positive is 5% for backward-class and 17.5% for forward-class candidates then we can make the following calculations:

1. Of the 800 forward-class candidates, the prior belief is that 224 are 'good' and 576 are 'not good'. Of the 224 'good' and the 576 'not good' forward-class candidates, respectively, 213 (95% of 224) and 101 (17.5% of 576) candidates will pass the test. This means that of the 314 forward-class candidates, who pass the test, 68% will be 'good' candidates and 32% will be 'not good' candidates.
2. Of the 200 backward-class candidates, the prior belief is that 56 are 'good' and 144 are 'not good'. Of the 56 'good' and the 144 'not good' backward-class candidates, respectively, 53 (95% of 56) and 7 (5% of 144) candidates will pass the test. This means that of the 60 backward-class candidates, who pass the test, 88% will be 'good' candidates and 12% will be 'not good' candidates.

Because of the difference in parental resources between the forward- and backward-class candidates, the ratio of forward-to-backward class—persons who were admitted but who did not 'deserve' admission—is 2.7:1 (32:12). Furthermore, as a consequence of the difference between the two groups in their capacity to generate false positives, the proportion of backward- and forward-class candidates admitted, respectively, 16% (60/374 pupils) and 84% (314/374 pupils) does not reflect their respective shares of 20% and 80% in the candidate population.

If, say, government invested in backward-class candidates by offering them resources to prepare for the test and thereby lifted their probability of producing a false positive from 5% to 10%, then of the 144 'not good' backward-class candidates, 14 would pass the test. This would raise the proportion of backward-class pupils in higher education from 16% (60/374) to 18% (67/381) and access inequality would be considerably reduced.

The foregoing analysis can be formalised in a *Bayesian* framework. Bayes' Theorem (named after the Reverend Thomas Bayes, an 18th-century Presbyterian minister) says that the probability of a theory being true (event T, i.e., a candidate for the test is a 'good' pupil), given that the data has been observed (passed the selection test [event A]) is

$$P(T \mid A) = \frac{P(A \mid T)}{P(A)} \times P(T) \tag{1}$$

where $P(T)$ represents the *prior* belief that the theory is true, and $P(A \mid T)/P(A)$ is the Bayesian 'updating factor' which translates one's *prior* belief about the theory's validity into a *posterior* belief.[15] The probability of observing a positive outcome on the selection test is the sum of the probabilities of a 'true positive' (the candidate passed the selection test and was a 'good' pupil) and a 'false positive' (the candidate passed the test and was *not* a 'good' pupil):

$$P(A) = \underbrace{P(A \cap T)}_{\text{prob of true positive}} + \underbrace{P(A \cap \tilde{T})}_{\text{prob of false positive}} = P(T) \times P(A \mid T) + P(\tilde{T}) \times P(A \mid \tilde{T}) \tag{2}$$

where $\tilde{T}$ is the event that the pupil was *not* a 'good' pupil. Substituting the expression in (2) into equation (1) yields:

$$P(T \mid A) = \frac{P(T) \times P(A \mid T)}{P(T) \times P(A \mid T) + P(\tilde{T}) \times P(A \mid \tilde{T})} \tag{3}$$

If, as assumed earlier, 95 out of 100 candidates who are 'good' will *pass* the test (that is, their marks on the test will be deemed to be at or above the limit for admission) and that 85 out of 100 pupils who are 'not good' will fail the test (their marks on the test will be deemed to be below the admission limit): $P(A \mid T) = 0.95$ and $P(\tilde{A} \mid \tilde{T}) = 0.85$, where $\tilde{A}$ is the event that a pupil fails the test. The implication of this is that 5% of 'not good' candidates will pass the test and that 15% of 'good' candidates will fail the test. The assumption is that, prior to the selection test being administered, there is a 28% chance that the candidate tested is a 'good' pupil, that is, $P(T) = 0.28$.

Substituting these assumed values into equation (3) yields

$$P(T \mid A) = \frac{0.28 \times 0.95}{0.28 \times 0.95 + 0.72 \times 0.15} = 0.71 \tag{4}$$

or, in other words, there is a 71% chance that a candidate passing the test will be a 'good' pupil worthy of higher education entry. This

---

[15] The updating factor is the ratio of the probability of observing the data when the theory is true, to that of observing the data regardless of whether the theory is true or false:

$$P(A) = P(A \mid T)P(T) + P(A \mid \tilde{T})P(\tilde{T}),$$

$\tilde{T}$ being the event that the theory is false.

suggests that the *selection fallacy*, which arose from confusing $P(A \mid T) [= 0.95]$ with $P(T \mid A) [= 0.71]$, is *not* negligible.

Of course, this conclusion depends critically on the assumed parameter values: $P(T) = 0.28, P(A \mid T) = 0.95$, and $P(A \mid \tilde{T}) = 0.15$. The latter two parameter values make, respectively, reference to the following two facets of reliability embodied in the test:

1. $P(A \mid T)$ refers to the likelihood that a candidate who is 'good' is *correctly* identified.
2. $P(A \mid \tilde{T})$ refers to the likelihood that a candidate who *is* 'not good' is *incorrectly* identified.

In statistics, $P(A \mid T)$ is the *sensitivity* of the test and $P(A \mid \tilde{T})$ is 1- *specificity* of the test. As equation (3) shows, there are three factors that affect the probability that passing the test identifies a 'good' candidate. They are (a) the likelihood of a 'good' candidate passing the test, $P(A \mid T)$; (b) the likelihood of a 'not good' candidate passing the test, $P(A \mid \tilde{T})$, and (c) a *priori* probability that a candidate appearing in the test is, in fact, a 'good' candidate, $P(T)$.[16]

There is, therefore, an important role for affirmative action policies to reduce inter-group inequality in the likelihood of being admitted into higher education that is derived from inter-group inequality in resource endowments. We assume that an applicant has an intellectual ability based on which it will be decided whether he/she is admitted. Suppose that $\theta \in [0, 1]$ is a measure of intellectual ability and θ^* is the threshold level of ability such that the applicant is admitted if and only if $\theta \geq \theta^*$. Unfortunately, θ is unobservable but it can be proxied by an observable signal, ρ (say, test results) where it is assumed that θ and ρ are positively related. More generally, if R represents the resources (tuition classes, study hours, textbooks, etc.) that the applicant invests in the test:

$$\rho = g\,(\overset{+}{\theta}, \overset{+}{R}) \tag{5}$$

---

[16] Consider two extreme cases. First, suppose that institution tossed a coin to determine whether or not a candidate should be admitted. This is equivalent to assuming that $P(A \mid T) = P(A \mid \tilde{T}) = 0.5$. Second, suppose that that a faulty computer recorded everyone tested as having passed the test, $P(A \mid T) = P(A \mid \tilde{T}) = 1$. Under both scenarios, $P(T \mid A) = 0.7$, there is a 70% chance that a pupil admitted, on either of these methods, would be a 'good' candidate—not much different from the 71% chance that a candidate who passed the properly conducted test would be worthy of admission!

where the '+' sign above each variable indicates that the test result improves with increases in θ and in R. Since we cannot observe θ, a proxy criterion is used so that an applicant is admitted if, and only if, his/her test score reaches, or crosses, a threshold score, that is, $\rho \geq \rho^*$. Using equation (5), we can compute the combinations of θ (intellectual ability) and R (resources) that yield the threshold admission score ρ^*.

This is shown in Figure 7.3 by the *iso-signal* curve, IS. The slope of this curve is

$$\frac{d\theta}{dR} = -\frac{\partial g / \partial \theta}{\partial g / \partial R} \tag{6}$$

This is the marginal rate of substitution between intellectual ability and resources. For an additional outlay of ₹100 on the test, the term $\dfrac{d\theta}{dR}$ represents the amount by which intellectual ability can be reduced, keeping the test score unchanged at ρ^* (that is, remaining on the same iso-signal curve).

Suppose that the set of candidates seeking admission is represented by Ω, where this set can be divided into two mutually exclusive subsets—the set of 'forward class' or 'rich' candidates (Ω_F) and the set of 'backward-class' or 'poor' candidates (Ω_B). If R_F and R_B are, respectively, the average resources of forward-class and backward-class candidates ($R_F > R_B$) then the forward-class group can

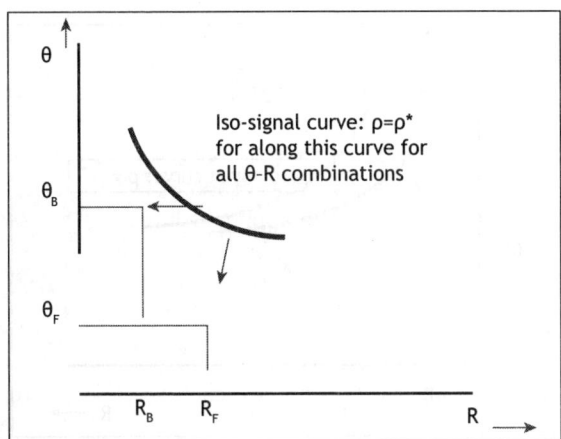

Figure 7.3
The Iso-signal Curve
Source: Prepared by the Author.

secure admission with a lower intellectual ability than the backward-class group since both combinations (θ_F, R_F) and (θ_B, R_B) will produce the threshold score, ρ^*.

If the aim is to admit students of the *equal* intellectual ability, regardless of their class background, then one would have to correct for inter-group inequality in resources by applying *different* threshold scores to students from the two groups. If θ^* is the intellectual ability sought from both groups, whose members have unequal resources $R_B < R_F$, then the appropriate threshold score is $\rho_F^* = g(\theta^*, R_F)$ and $\rho_B^* = g(\theta^*, R_B)$ for the forward- and backward-class groups, respectively, where since $\partial\rho/\partial R > 0$, $\rho_B < \rho_F$. In order to compensate them for their lack of resources, which could generate 'false positives' (discussed earlier), applicants from the backward classes are admitted on the basis of a lower threshold mark (ρ_B^*) than applicants from the forward classes (ρ_F^*) and this disparity in threshold marks ensures that the intellectual ability of those admitted from both groups is the same (θ^*). This is illustrated in Figure 7.4, in which backward- and forward-class students have to meet, respectively, threshold scores of ρ_B^* and ρ_F^* where $\rho_B^* < \rho_F^*$. This difference in admission scores applied to the two groups ensures that students admitted from both groups have the same intellectual ability.

Figure 7.5 plots the relation between θ (intellectual ability) and ρ (test score) for two levels of resources, $R_B < R_F$. The curves slope upwards showing a positive relation between test scores and

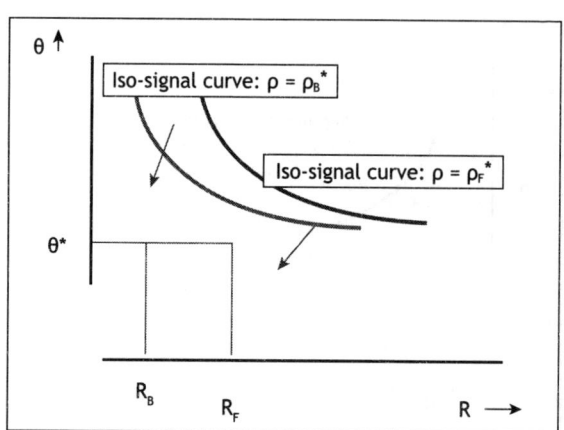

Figure 7.4
Identical Intellectual Ability Resulting from Different Threshold Scores
Source: Prepared by Author.

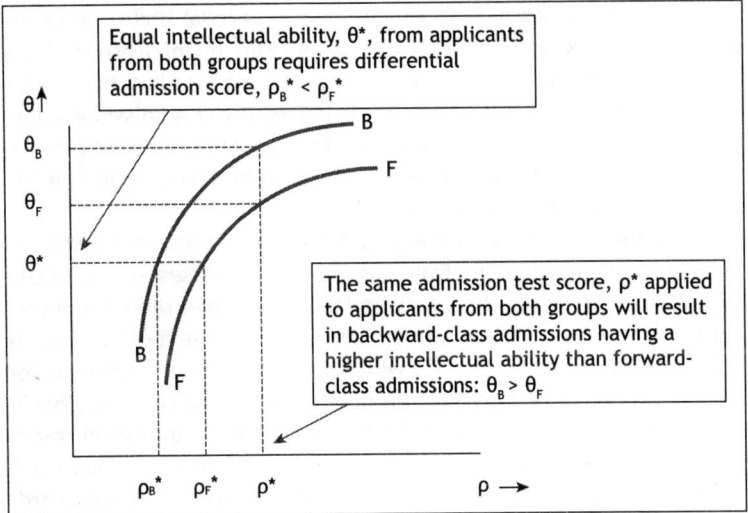

Figure 7.5
Intellectual Ability and Threshold Score
Source: Prepared by Author.

intellectual ability. The curve BB, based on R_B, the (lower) resources of the backward classes, lies above the curve FF which is based on R_F, the (higher) resources of the backward classes. This suggests that with their lower resources—and therefore, their impaired ability to generate false positives—persons from the backward classes will need a higher intellectual ability than persons from the forward classes to achieve the same test score. Conversely, for the same intellectual ability, persons from the forward classes, with their greater ability to generate false positives, will achieve a test score than persons from the backward classes.

If persons from both groups are admitted on the basis of achieving the same test scores, the intellectual ability of backward-class applicants who are admitted will be higher than that of forward-class applicants who are admitted. Equal test scores will discriminate against backward-class applicants by demanding greater intellectual ability from them. On the other hand, if applicants from both groups are to be of the same intellectual ability, θ^*, backward-class applicants must be admitted on the basis of lower test scores than forward-class applicants.

A difficulty arises if the threshold score applied to the 'backward-class' group is lower than ρ_B^*, which, in conjunction with ρ_F^*, forms the threshold pair at which the intellectual ability of those admitted from both groups is the same. This might arise if there were a mandated proportion of available places that had to be filled by persons from the backward classes. If the admissions criterion for this group of $\rho = \rho_B^*$ was too stringent to supply this proportion then some of these 'reserved' places (perhaps a large number of them) would remain unfilled.

When the admission standards are lowered to accommodate the mandate, so that persons from the backward classes are admitted with test scores lower than ρ_B^* (see Figure 7.5) then the intellectual ability of backward-class admissions will also fall below that of forward-class admissions.[17] So, while there is a strong argument for compensating for resource differences between forward- and backward-class applicants by applying a more stringent admission standard to the former than to the latter, one should avoid (as Figure 7.5 shows) the danger of diluting the intellectual abilities of backward-class admissions through excessive laxity in the admission standards applied to them.

CONCLUSION

This chapter began by examining access inequality to higher education in India in terms of the GTAR. There has been a dramatic fall in access inequality between the 64th (2008) and the 71st (2014) NSS Rounds. This fact, combined with a sharp rise in the gross tertiary enrolment rate between the two Rounds, would suggest that in the past seven years, at least with respect to access, there has been significant progress in higher education in India.

To put matters in perspective, Table 7.9 shows the shares of the different social groups in the total of 18–22 year olds and in the total of 18–22 year olds in HEA. So, for example, in the 64th Round (2008) persons from the SC represented 20.1% of all 18–22 year olds and 13.2% of 18–22 year olds in HEA. This underrepresentation by SC youth in HEA had reduced considerably by the 71st Round (2014) when 19.9% of *all* 18–22 year olds and 14.5% of 18–22 year olds in HEA were SC.

---

[17] From the inverse of equation (1):

$$\theta_B = f\ (\rho_B, R_B).$$
So, θ_B falls as ρ_B is reduced.

Table 7.9

Shares of Social Groups in Higher Education Attendance (71st and 64th Rounds)

Social Group	NSS 71st Round		NSS 64th Round	
	Share in HEA of 18–22 year olds	Share in 18–22 year olds	Share in HEA of 18–22 year olds	Share in 18–22 year olds
Scheduled Tribe	5.5	10.0	3.0	8.0
Scheduled Caste	14.5	19.9	13.2	20.1
Non-Muslim OBC	37.2	34.5	33.7	35.7
Muslim OBC	4.9	8.4	3.6	6.2
Muslim Upper Caste	3.6	6.7	4.3	8.1
Non-Muslim Upper Caste	34.3	20.5	42.3	21.9
Total	100	100	100	100
	[230,252]	[1,060,401]	[109,608]	[961,350]

Source: Own calculations from the NSS 71th and 64th Rounds, after applying sample weights. NSSO (2007, 2014).

The values of inequality (defined in Bourguignon 1979), calculated using the shares in Table 7.8, were 12.4 in the 64th Round and 7.8 in the 71st Round. So, in the seven years, between the 64th Round (July 2007–June 2008) and the 71st Round (January–June 2014), access inequality fell by 37% from its 64th Round value. This is, without doubt, an achievement for Indian higher education

The problem that remains is one of ensuring quality in higher education. 'Quality' is an amorphous concept and two proxies for quality were used in this paper: first, total expenditure on education and, second, the proportion of students studying courses with English as the MoI. As regards expenditure, it was shown that there was considerable difference between the social groups in the amounts that their members, who were in HEA, spent on their education: the median expenditure by those from the NMUC who were in HEA was ₹10,000–₹15,000 higher than that incurred by persons from the other groups.

The proportion of those in HEA who were studying in English rose from 47% of persons in HEA in the 64th Round to 49% of persons in HEA in the 71st Round. This might suggest a rise in education quality but for a niggling doubt about the ability of persons studying in English to cope with instruction delivered in English. The basis for this doubt is that while 49% of persons in HEA in 2014 were studying in English, only 30% of persons were studying in English at the HS level. Thus, it is reasonable to suppose that a significant proportion of persons in HEA were, for the first time in their life, encountering instruction delivered in English a fact which would possibly (though not necessarily) adversely affect their learning outcomes.

The chapter developed an analytical model to argue that affirmative action in higher education admissions, by which persons from the backward classes are held to lower standards than those from the forward classes, has much to recommend it because it blunts the ability of forward-class applicants to generate 'false positives' by substituting resources for brains. The model, however, was based on the critical assumption that the distinction between the 'backward' and the 'forward' classes was based *solely* upon resource inequality: persons from the backward classes had fewer economic resources than those from the forward classes.

Reservation in higher education (and in other spheres of activity) in India is, however, based not on *economic* but on *social* backwardness, where this is defined as being born into a 'backward' (as defined on some criteria) caste. When reservation was restricted to the SC and the ST, one could, with some justification, argue that persons from these categories were both socially *and* economically 'backward', while acknowledging sotto voce that there was some residual injustice in reservation policies excluding economically backward persons who were neither SC nor ST.

The overlap between social and economic backwardness, however, became less evident when in 1990, following the Mandal Commission's recommendations, reservation was extended to include the OBC. If the present demands by the prosperous Jats of Haryana and the Patels (Patidars) of Gujarat, to be also accorded the benefits of reservation, are conceded, the link between 'social' and 'economic' backwardness will become tenuous. Reservation policy will cease to be an instrument for uplifting the downtrodden (as it was originally conceived) and take the form of the proverbial goose that laid golden eggs thus benefiting those groups with enough political muscle to stake a claim to reservation's 'golden eggs'.

Even if one puts aside these concerns about lack of commonality between social and economic backwardness, the model developed in this paper points to the danger of reservation policy, operating through positive discrimination, overreaching its purpose by lowering admission standards for backward classes beyond what is needed for neutralising the resource superiority of forward classes. It was noted earlier that, in respect of IIT admissions, SC and ST applicants needed to get just one mark for every two marks obtained by the general category of applicants. As a consequence of such an admissions policy, as Vishnu (2015) reports, in the academic year 2014–15, the IITs admitted 2,029 students from the SC and 856 students from the ST of whom, only 432 and 80, respectively, would have secured admission in open competition based on examination performance. Thus, for every 'reservation-unassisted' SC and ST student admitted to an IIT, 3.7 'reservation-assisted' SC students and 8.5 'reservation-assisted' ST students were also admitted.[18] The latter type of students struggle because in terms of their background and training, they are ill-equipped to cope with academically challenging courses delivered in an unfamiliar language. The fact that they struggle and often fail has repercussions for the quality of education offered: the 72 students, referred to earlier, who should have been expelled from IIT Rorkee, were, in fact, readmitted and given a second chance.

All these considerations call for rethinking the policy of setting aside a certain proportion of seats in higher education for persons from 'reserved categories'. Is a (reservation) unassisted/assisted ratio in the IITs of 1:3.7 for the SC, rising to 1:8.5 for the ST, damaging these institutions by admitting students who are academically unprepared and weak? Would these institutions be strengthened if they had a stronger student base, chosen more on academic merit and less on social background? These points, while applauding the fact of reservation, raise questions about its *strength* and are deserving of serious consideration.

Conversely, if it was thought legitimate, in the cause of correcting historical wrongs, to admit significant numbers from the reserved categories, the majority of whom would not have been admitted on test scores, should educational institutions do more to redress these weaknesses? Many of the IITs have remedial classes and mentoring arrangements but what of other institutions? A serious flaw in India's approach to redressing 'historical wrongs' that it relies solely on outcomes (reservation based quotas) but leaves people to sink or swim after their entry into an institution has been

---

[18] The terms, 'reservation-unassisted' and 'reservation-assisted', are used here only in the context of examination performance.

secured. In the process, some, with great effort (as detailed in Singh 2013), learn to survive but, alongside these survivors, many also drown. An effective and intelligent educational policy can incorporate a more caring and nurturing entry, instead of a 'swim or sink' approach, into the difficult waters of higher education.

REFERENCES

Aitken, C. 1996. 'Lies, Damned Lies, and Expert Witnesses'. *Mathematics Today* 32(5): 76–80.

ASER. 2014. *Annual Status of Education Report (Rural) 2014*. New Delhi: ASER Centre.

Basant, R., and G. Sen. 2014. 'Access to Higher Education in India: An Exploration of Its Antecedents'. *Economic and Political Weekly* 49(51): 38–45.

Bhalotra, S., and B. Zamora. 2010. 'Social Divisions in Education in India'. In *Handbook of Muslims in India: Empirical and Policy Perspectives*, edited by R. Basant and A. Shariff, 165–98. New Delhi: Oxford University Press.

Borooah, V.K. 2010. 'On the Risks of Belonging to Disadvantaged Groups: A Bayesian Analysis of Labour Market Outcomes'. In *Handbook of Muslims in India*, edited by Rakesh Basant and Abusaleh Shariff. New Delhi: Oxford University Press.

———. 2012. 'Social Identity and Educational Attainment: The Role of Caste and Religion in Explaining Differences between Children in India'. *Journal of Development Studies* 48 (7): 887–903.

Borooah, V.K., and S. Iyer. 2005. 'Vidya, Veda, and Varna: The Influence of Religion and Caste on Education in Rural India'. *Journal of Development Studies* 41(8): 1369–404.

Bourguignon, F. 1979. 'Decomposable Income Inequality Measures'. *Econometrica* 47(4): 901–20.

Chamarbagwala, R. 2006. 'Economic Liberalisation and Wage Inequality in India'. *World Development* 34(12): 1997–2015.

Deolalikar, A.B. 2010. 'The Performance of Muslims on Social Indicators: A Comparative Perspective'. In *Handbook of Muslims in India: Empirical and Policy Perspectives*, edited by R. Basant and A. Shariff, 71–91. New Delhi: Oxford University Press.

Deshpande, S. 2013. 'Introduction: Beyond Inclusion'. In *Beyond Inclusion: The Practice of Equal Access in Indian Higher Education*, edited by S. Deshpande and U. Zacharias, 1–12. New Delhi: Routledge.

Krishna, A. 2013. 'Making it in India: Examining Social Mobility in Three Walks of Life'. *Economic and Political Weekly* 48(49): 38–49.

Long, J.S., and J. Freese. 2014. *Regression Models for Categorical Dependent Variables using Stata*. Stata Press: College Station.

Mlodinow, L. 2009. *The Drunkard's Walk*. London: Penguin Books.

Mohanty, M. 2006. 'Social Inequality, Labour Market Dynamics, and Reservation'. *Economic and Political Weekly* 41(35): 3777–89.

National Sample Survey Organisation (NSSO). 2007. *India—Participation and Expenditure in Education, 2007–08, 64th Round*. Ministry of Statistics and Programme Implementation, Government of India, New Delhi.

———. 2014. *India: Social Consumption—Education Survey 2014, 71st Round*. Ministry of Statistics and Programme Implementation, Government of India, New Delhi.

Rao, Y., H.C. Shah, and S.S. Gole. 2015. 'This Year, IITs Will Admit Students with Even 6% in Entrance Examination'. *The Times of India*, 14 July. http://timesofindia.indiatimes.com/home/education/entrance-exams/This-year-IITs-will-admit-students-with-even-6-in-entrance-exam/articleshow/48061694.cms

Sachar Committee Report. 2006. *The Social and Economic Status of the Muslim Community in India*. New Delhi: Government of India (Cabinet Secretariat).

Singh, A.K. 2013. 'Defying the Odds: The Triumphs and Tragedies of Dalit and Adivasi Students in Higher Education in India'. In *Beyond Inclusion: The Practice of Equal Access in Indian Higher Education*, edited by S. Deshpande and U. Zacharias, 174–204. New Delhi: Routledge.

Sundaram, K. 2006. 'On Backwardness and Fair Access to Higher Education: Results from the NSS 55th Round Surveys, 1999–2000'. *Economic and Political Weekly* 43(50): 5173–82.

The Hindu. 2013. '9,885 Seats Available in 17 IITs; Results on June 23'. *The Hindu*, 20 June. http://www.thehindu.com/news/cities/Hyderabad/9885-seats-available-in-17-iits-results-on-june-23/article4834329.ece?css=print

Thompson, W.C., and E.L. Schumann. 1987. 'Interpretation of Statistical Evidence in Criminal Trials: The Prosecutor's Fallacy and the Defense Attorney's Fallacy'. *Law and Human Behavior* 11(3): 167–87.

Times of India. 2013. 'Kancha Ilaiah: Even If 10% Dalit Children Got English Education, India Would Change'. *The Times of India*, 15 February. http://timesofindia.indiatimes.com/interviews/Kancha-Ilaiah-Even-if-10-dalit-children-got-English-education-India-would-change/articleshow/18503625.cms

Vishnu, U. 2015. 'They Get Leg-up at JEE but Hard Landing on Campus'. *The Indian Express*, 6 August.

Zackrisson, S., I. Anderson, L. Janzon, J. Manjer, and J.P. Garne. 2006. 'Rate of Over-Diagnosis of Breast Cancer 15 Years after End of Malmo Mamographic Screening'. *British Medical Journal* 33(13): 689–92.

8

Concerns of Minority Groups in Higher Education Participation: The Plight of Muslim Community

M.M. Ansari

Verily never will God change the condition of a people until they change it themselves with their own souls.

—Quran

THE CONTEXT

Education and training have intense and pervasive impact on almost every parameter of socio-economic development, which is why progress in education has, almost everywhere, preceded economic growth. Empowerment of people through education has moreover significant bearing on the distribution of income and wealth among different social groups. A concerted effort is therefore made by the governments to equalise opportunities for education and skill development of every section of the society, particularly the marginalised communities, including religious minorities.

The outcome of development planning for over six decades presents a picture of light and shade. While there has been commendable progress in almost every sphere of development, socio-economic disparities across the different social and religious groups have perpetuated, which call for a review of policies and programmes that are intended to promote innovative approaches for sharing the benefits of development and for ensuring effective democratic governance.

Specifically, it has been observed that incidence of poverty is the highest among Muslims, which is attributable to abysmally low level of incomes, higher unemployment rates and disproportionally lower participation in public and private sector jobs. An overall low

level of participation in the process of education and skills development activities has adversely affected the prospects of engaging
the Muslim community to participate in the knowledge economy
which is propelled by new technologies and innovative practices.

Of all the religious groups, educational attainments of Muslims
have been one of the lowest, which is evident from both the overall
attainments of literacy rate and the level of participation at different stages of education. For instance, the gross enrolment ratios
(GER) in higher education, in 2009–10, recorded for different religious communities were as follows: Hindus 20%, Muslims 11%,
Christians 31%, Sikhs 23%, Jains 55%, Buddhist 18% and Zoroastrians
64%. Male–female and rural–urban differences were similarly large,
within and across the groups. Obviously, it is the Muslim community,
which is lagging behind, as compared to other religious groups.
Hence, we propose to focus on educational problems of Muslims.

Muslims in India constitute the second largest population of
the country, nearly 14% of the total population, and over 80% of the
total religious minority population. Education and development of
this community has therefore serious implications for maintaining
social cohesion as well as for accelerating economic growth through
empowerment of huge manpower that is traditionally associated
with industrialisation of the country. An objective assessment of
educational problems of Muslim minority group is therefore critical
for initiating appropriate measures for alleviating the suffering of
the community as well as increasing their contributions to national
development.

In this backdrop, the objective of this chapter is twofold: one is
to identify the reasons for educational backwardness of Muslims and
the other is to explore the ways and measures for increasing their
participation in the process of educational development so that this
community may avail the opportunities of accessing rewarding jobs
and business opportunities. The plan of the chapter is as under: second section assesses the levels of educational achievements among
Muslims as compared to other socio-religious groups. The analysis in
this section demonstrates that the Muslim community is lagging far
behind the other social categories. The reasons for educational backwardness are identified in third section, which indicate that the
factors responsible for Muslims' poverty are (a) disproportionally low
political representation in governance, (b) lack of adequate support
to traditional manufacturing activities that engaged the Muslim
artisans and craftsmen for income support, and (c) communal
disturbances, leading to dispossession of economic assets, physical
dislocation and destabilisation of Muslim families. Fourth section

outlines the ways and measures for widening the base of elementary and secondary education, which are prerequisite for increasing GER at higher education level as well as for the wellbeing of the community. A summary of conclusions is provided in the last section.

MUSLIMS' PARTICIPATION IN THE EDUCATIONAL PROCESS

There is consensus among the educational planners and decision-makers that low level of literacy and/or educational attainments are attributable to factors such as availability of essential school infrastructure, including trained teachers and learning resources, economic status of parents to support the child for schooling and school atmosphere, which should be free from all kinds of socio-cultural biases.

The Sachar Committee (Government of India 2006) investigated the reasons for lower level of literacy and education and pointed out that the lack of school facilities in the Muslims dominated areas, abject economic poverty and discrimination by the functionaries of school management were chiefly responsible for undesirably low literacy and enrolment at all levels. Most Muslim children did not attend any school and those who did could not continue their education for the above reasons. Lack of school environment for learning, including teachers' apathy, adverse family circumstances, such as, homelessness and income constraints, are the main reasons for dropouts. Thus, low enrolment and high dropout rates keep literacy rate among Muslims much below the national average. Table 8.1 shows this.

Table 8.1
Literacy Rate of Muslims in India (2001 and 2011)

Category/Year	2001	2011
All India	64.8	74.0
Male	75.3	82.1
Female	53.7	65.5
Muslims	59.1	67.6
Male	67.6	74.9
Female	50.1	50.3

Source: Educational Statistics, Ministry of Human Resource Development, New Delhi.

Participation of Muslim children in higher education depends on the secondary education graduates and the transition rate from secondary to higher education. In this context, the educational statistics compiled by the government shows that the transition rate from secondary to post-secondary education for Muslims is 70%, which is comparable with all other social groups. Therefore, it is the base of secondary education which is comparatively very narrow for Muslims due to heavy dropouts, over 50%. This is the main reason why GER at higher education level is one of the lowest for Muslims. This is borne by the fact that only 50% of children at primary level reach to senior secondary level, of which 70% join various institutions for post-secondary study programmes.

Table 8.2 shows that of the total students' enrolment, the share of Muslim children declined from 14% at primary level to 7% at the higher secondary level, for the reasons stated above.

It is interesting to note that in the recent past, participation as well as retention levels of Muslim Children, particularly girls, have significantly improved, which demonstrates overwhelming response of Muslim parents for educating their children. This may also be attributable to the governments' initiatives to promote 'Education for All'. Table 8.3 shows the relative improvement for boys and girls.

Table 8.2
Muslim Children as Per Cent of Total Children in School Education (2012–13)

Primary	14.20
Upper Primary	12.11
Secondary	9.50
Higher Secondary	7.11

Source: Department of EMIS, NUEPA (2013).

Table 8.3
Trends in Enrolment of Muslim Children in Elementary Education (Grade I–VIII) as Proportion of the Total Children

Enrolment/Year	2006	2012
Total	8.8	12.8
Boys	8.6	12.5
Girls	9.1	13.2

Source: Department of EMIS, NUEPA (2013).

The overall share of Muslim children's participation is much lower than their population in the respective groups. The Sachar Committee (Government of India 2006) noted,

As many as 25 per cent of Muslim children in the 6–14 years age group have either never attended school or have dropped out.

This scenario has not significantly changed as a recent survey conducted at the behest of HRD Ministry across all 640 districts of the country has revealed that at least '60 lakh children between the ages of 6 and 13 are still out of school' and of these 15.57 lakh Muslim children (25%) are out of school' (Kumar 2015). Clearly, out of school children and dropout rates are still very high, which adversely affect the progression rates to subsequent stages of education. In effect, GER at higher education is accordingly low (see Table 8.4).

Table 8.4 shows the GER by religious groups, where the GER among the Muslims is the lowest.

These results show that despite significant expansion and diversification of higher education system during the last six decades, the overall GER is (a) one of the lowest as compared to other developing countries, (b) inequalities in GER across the social and religious groups are very high, and (c) Muslims are lagging far behind all religious groups in educational attainments.

A detailed analysis of growth in enrolments reveals that 'Muslims are still way behind even the OBCs, let alone UCs (upper castes), in terms of higher education' (Kundu 2014, 70).

Table 8.4
Gross Enrolment Ratio at Higher Education by Religious Groups (2009–10)

Religious Group/Category	Total	Rural	Urban
Hindu	20.0	14.7	34.9
Muslim	**11.3**	**6.8**	**19.2**
Christian	31.3	24.3	44.2
Sikh	23.1	18.8	37.3
Jain	54.6	38.5	56.2
Buddhist	17.9	11.7	25.9
Zoroastrian	63.6	NA	NA

Source: NSSO (2009–10) 66th Round.

Obviously, these evidences do not augur well either for economic betterment of the Muslim community or for the entire country that aims at creating an enlightened and prosperous society with social justice. This also shows that the policies and programmes for abridging socio-economic and educational disparities are either misconceived or ineffectively implemented or both. It, therefore, calls for designing of appropriate affirmative action plan as well as effective implementation of the existing policies that have yielded desirable results.

A very perceptive analysis of educational inequalities across the social and religious groups has recently been made is as under:

Inequalities in gross enrolment ratio between various religious groups are much higher. Estimates on gross enrolment ratio are available for Hindus, Muslims, Christians and 'Others'. Enrolment ratio among Muslims was only 14 per cent in 2009–10, while it was 24.2 per cent among Hindus and 37 per cent among Christians. The enrolment ratio among 'Others' that includes Jains, Sikhs, etc., is also high—28 per cent in 2009–10. The enrolment ratio is the highest among the Christians and the least among the Muslims. This is the same situation consistently throughout the period between 1983–84 and 2009–10. While there has been improvement in case of all the four groups between 1983–84 and 2009–10, the inter-group inequalities by religion did not decline much. In fact, the gap seemed to have widened... Despite reasonably high and comparable transition rates, because of low gross enrolment ratio, Muslims do not fare comparably with Hindus or Christians with respect to rate of higher education attainment. In 2009–10, while there were 12.5 percent adult Christians who had higher education, the corresponding figures were 8.6 per cent among Hindus and 3.8 per cent among Muslims. 'Others' also had a high proportion of population—11 per cent with higher education. Further, inequalities seem to have widened between Muslims and Christians and to a lesser extent between Muslims and Hindus. (Tilak 2015)

Consequently, it may be inferred that the Muslim community has heavily suffered in terms of socio-economic opportunities, which, in turn, has also dampened the national morale and wealth generation due to lower contribution of the community to the country's development.

In fact, acquisition of knowledge through formal and informal schooling has always been regarded as a virtuous activity, which every Muslim is required to pursue throughout his/her life. Muslim parents are, therefore, not averse to the idea of getting education from whatsoever source it may be available. And this is evident from the fact that at elementary stage, in 2012, 55% attended government schools, over 21% attended private schools and less than 5% children joined madrasa (school for religious education). Moreover, only 13% children study through English language while 85% study in other regional languages and merely 2% study through Urdu language.

Clearly, Muslim parents have chosen to educate their children without any strong preferences for either the government or private schools or even medium of instruction. This is corroborated by the fact that the share of Muslim children has significantly increased in enrolment (shown in Table 8.3). The issue therefore is as to why Muslims have not been able to cope up with the challenge of improving educational status to effectively function in the emerging knowledge economy. We shall explore this in the following paragraphs.

WHY IS MUSLIM COMMUNITY EDUCATIONALLY BACKWARD?

All the five-year plans have made oft-repeated commitments for reduction in all kind of disparities across the regions and socio-economic groups, mainly through the provisions of adequate infrastructure for all the eligible children as well as positive discrimination for improving education and economic status of deprived groups. In spite of policy stipulations, interpersonal, inter-regional and inter-religious groups' differences have widened, which are attributable to factors like political, economic and social marginalisation of different groups and the lack of effective delivery of educational services.

Since the Muslim community has, by any reckoning, slipped to lower strata of society, serious concerns have been expressed for ameliorating economic conditions of the community. A large body of research and survey studies undertaken by individuals and the institutions has attempted to identify the factors that are responsible for economic deprivation of Muslims. In general, lack of vocational empowerment and physical assets for income generation as well as perceived discrimination in availability of educational and employment opportunities are said to be largely responsible for all kinds of deprivation among Muslims. And, there is ample evidence to prove the point.

First, empirical studies have demonstrated that 'the relationship between literacy and income is reciprocal and that the level of training has positive impact on generation of income". Furthermore, "poverty and illiteracy move together and reinforce each other and thus create a vicious circle, which perpetuates poverty and illiteracy' (Ansari 1987). Clearly, the factors affecting both educational progress and alleviation of poverty have to be simultaneously and comprehensively dealt with through a well-designed policy. Efforts made thus far have however not been commensurate with the requirements of the task of uplifting the poor, including the Muslim minorities.

Second, the *Sachar Committee Report* (Government of India 2006) is entirely devoted to investigate into the problems and issues faced by the Muslim community in respects of educational advancement, economic and employment opportunities. The observations and recommendations of the Committee have been widely appreciated. The outcome of implementation of the relevant suggestions over the last 10 years or so indicates dismal achievements, which is why economic backwardness, social alienation or desolation persists in the community.

In fact, the Committee pointed out that the concerns relating to security, identity, equity and justice have embroiled the community in the process of socio-political engagements that have adversely affected the chances to keep pace with the progress made by the fellow citizens. Perpetual deprivation of educational opportunities over a long period of over six decades or so has led to political, socio-economic and educational marginalisation of the community, as discussed here.

Third, it may be recalled that all the social and religious groups fought together against the British rule. Soon after the Independence, particularly in the wake of partition of the country, Muslims suffered the most in terms of loss of lives and properties as compared to any other religious groups. Ever since, almost every region having larger concentration of Muslim population, suffered from frequent communal violence leading to large-scale dislocation and destabilisation of Muslim families, which has not only resulted in loss of opportunities to maintain a decent standard of life but also promoted ghettoisation of the community in areas that lack in school facilities of reasonable standard.

The feeling of insecurity among Muslims has therefore always been high due to the discriminatory attitude of the police, in which Muslims are least represented. While the ghettoisation is due mainly to insecurity, it has resulted in discrimination in housing, schools and jobs. Moreover, lack of access to good quality schools adversely affected the poor, particularly the female students. Besides this, there are allegations of communalisation of reading material and school atmosphere perpetuate this problem. An eminent educationists, J.S. Rajput, states that

> The factors that result in alienation of Muslim children as they grow beyond 10–11 years of age were identified. These were related to the content in the textbooks, school functions, celebration of festivals, invited talks, photographs and quotes on the walls of the schools, attitude of teachers and the likes. The low priority that education received from the State deprived the Muslim community of educational advancement... One of the most outstanding factors resulting in prolonged backwardness of Muslims in India is the non-availability of "functional schools" in areas inhabited by economically weaker sections of Muslim community. (Rajput 2015)

Muslims have therefore lagged behind all other communities. The widespread discrimination or the lack of opportunities for educational and economic empowerment of Muslims is thus responsible for a widespread feeling of alienation and glaring inequity, discussed above.

Fourth, the economic wellbeing of Muslim families is further aggravated by the lack of opportunities for pursuing rewarding professions for earning higher wages and salaries. The close connection between education and employment is well understood. While low participation in government jobs is due partly to social discrimination, the employment situation in general has deteriorated because of slow progress in professional and technical competence as are required to function in the emerging knowledge economy. Most of the Muslims, particularly the artisans and craftsmen, who have traditionally been engaged in occupations that are adversely affected due to lack of up-gradation of skills and training as well as the latest business and marketing strategies. Unfortunately, the Muslim community, mainly the self-employed workers and entrepreneurs, have not been exposed to the process of modern technology induced industrialisation and business development.

Needless to mention, in the wake of ongoing economic reforms, the pattern and structure of resource allocation by public and private sectors as well as foreign investors have been changing, which in effect is tending, inter alia, to the following:

1. Increase the capital intensity in almost every productive sector, particularly in the areas where private and foreign investments have a dominant role.
2. Displace uneducated and untrained labour force that constitute a significant majority and are unable to function in the knowledge-based and technology-driven economy. This is facilitated by unprecedented increase in the mobility of labour force across the regions.
3. Reduce employment and earning opportunities for the masses that are not adequately trained to work on commercial ventures, which are using knowledge-based economic strategies. This is responsible for increasing income disparity between vocationally trained manpower and the rest of the labour force that is unable to upgrade the skills due to dysfunctional economic and educational systems.

As a result of gradual increase in investments in capital and technology intensive projects, low level of vocational competence of manpower not only deprives them of higher wages paid in the modern sectors but also impedes the efforts to make the economy duly efficient and globally competitive. The purpose of this discussion is to lay emphasis on the point that the lack of quality education, particularly vocational training and skill development, is an important reason for economic deprivation and income inequality across the different social groups, particularly Muslims who have the least exposure to the advances in science and technology, and its uses for improving quality of life through gainful employment.

Fifth, discrimination in the areas of educational provisions, business and various economic activities, coexists with low political participation. The major political parties do not field many candidates in assembly and parliamentary elections. There are alleged unfair delimitation exercises wherein Muslim majority constituencies are reserved for the reserved category candidates. Muslim candidates are neither adequately fielded by the political parties to contest and be elected from Muslim concentrated areas nor they are nominated by the government to ensure a fair representation in decision-making processes.

Such discriminatory practices in the political domain are common in the administrative and quasi-judicial decisions as well. On the basis of research surveys, it has been observed that

> *Even those who are equally qualified, talented and competitive*
> *Muslims have failed to get equal treatment and equal result if*
> *they undergo interviews in different settings. We must not hide*
> *the truth if we have to build India united and strong, Muslims*
> *being the largest minority must have its due share in all the*
> *sectors of powers and influences like others. This is basically*
> *secular demand, which is mainly based on the factor of back-*
> *wardness. (Ali and Khan 2008)*

Finally, it emerges from the foregoing that effectiveness of democratic and participatory governance is lacking in almost every
socio-economic sector, which in effect jeopardises the chances to
redress genuine grievances of the Muslim community and other
deprived groups. Lackadaisical attitude of political administration
and bureaucracy towards the realisation of aspirations of weaker
sections and their fundamental rights is chiefly responsible for this
unfortunate state of affair.

THE WAY FORWARD

The National Policy on Education 1986 stipulated that educationally
deprived groups would be paid greater attention in the interests of
equality and social justice. This policy has however not been effectively implemented in letter and spirit, which is why we have
observed glaring educational inequalities across the socio-economic
and religious groups. Even after six years of implementation of Sarva
Shiksha Abhiyan (SSA) in 2009, which guarantee free elementary
education, over 25% of out of school children in 2015 were Muslims.

Unless the base of elementary and secondary education is widened by ensuring attendance of all the children of school going age
and dropout rates are substantially reduced, GER of Muslims at
higher education cannot be raised to match the level of national
average. Efforts to strengthen the education system by investing in
teachers' training and other support services, commensurate with
requirements for quantitative expansion and qualitative improvement are however lacking, as evident from foregoing analysis and
discussion. Therefore, the measures mentioned here needs to be
initiated.

First, abject poverty among Muslims is chiefly responsible for
lower participation as well as heavy dropout of children from minority community. To overcome this problem, financial assistance and

scholarships to Muslims and other minorities should be extended at par with SCs/STs. Also, the facilities, such as, hostels, fee waiver and reimbursement of other expenses should be assured to all the children from poor families. Such an approach will not only attract the children from poor families but also retain them in the system for a reasonable period of time for imparting critical skills and training that may be required in the world of work. In addition, for improving the retention rates at elementary level, the recommendations made by the Kundu Committee, as under, should be implemented in letter and spirit. For specific recommendations (see Annexure).

The main challenge is how to keep children in primary and middle school.

1. *Implement the Mid-day Meal Scheme in schools in Muslim dominated areas with food items that are in the normal diet of these communities.*
2. *Improve teacher quality to encourage children to attend and for parents to see the advantage in keeping the children in school.*
3. *Improve activities in school to keep the children engaged and interested in attending the classes.*
4. *Raise the scholarship amount available to children in class 1–6, as very small amounts will not serve the purpose to encouraging parents to keep children in school. (Kundu 2014)*

Second, all the schools and teachers should be mandated to identify the eligible children of school going age, who are not attending schools for different reasons. Schools, within the vicinity of one kilometre, must contact out of school children and bring them back to schools. Such children should be provided full support for learning till the mandatory age of 14 years of schooling. Teachers must play the role of inspectors in this regard to ensure 100% literacy and education for all. It is the children of the poorest of the poor who will be made first generation learners. Thus, an important step towards a *sakshar* (literate), *saksham* (capable) and self-reliant India would be taken. Every teacher and school must have this mandate and be held accountable for this responsibility.

Third, the help and support of local NGOs may be taken to attract minority children so that the benefit of the schools functioning under SSA can accrue to the local minority community. There are as many as 90 minority concentrated districts (MCDs) that require special attention for raising the participation of minority children. School infrastructure, including girls' hostels, should be provided at par with SCs/STs children. Moreover, Urdu medium schools may be promoted in government schools of Delhi as Urdu is the mother tongue among Muslims.

Fourth, vocational education and training for skill development must be promoted at senior secondary level to ensure that the children who dropout for different reasons are gainfully employed. A particular attention in this regard should be paid to Muslim girls. Minority institutions and NGOs should be encouraged to promote vocational education. There are best practices and experiences in this regard, of which advantage should be taken. Accordingly, model polytechnics should be established and strengthened in MCDs. It merely requires concerted efforts to extend ongoing schemes for vocational training to the institutions attended by children of poor families.

Fifth, the ongoing schemes for educational advancement of minority communities, particularly the PM's 15-points programme, should be vigorously implemented throughout the country. The mechanisms for monitoring and evaluation of the schemes should be strengthened for improving the effectiveness of delivery systems. Unfortunately, assessment and evaluation reports in this regard are lacking.

Finally, it must be reiterated that

Unequal family incomes translate into unequal access to higher education. A major reason for low participation of low-income groups in higher education is lack of finances to meet household costs of higher education or the need to supplement the household income by work. Literature is also abundant that shows a strong correlation between participation in higher education and students' family background that include socio-economic factors. Hence, it is necessary to address the socio-economic factors. While there are some schemes/subsidies for the socially backward sections and also for women, no such schemes are offered to rural youth, and to economically weaker sections. General public subsidies and specific, targeted subsidies are needed. (Tilak 2015)

In order to overcome the problems of discrimination against deprived communities, it is suggested that

One solution to Dalit and Muslim educational under-achievement lies in creating a social and cultural environment in schools

whereby they cease to be unwelcome and frightening places for children from these groups. This would require teachers to be trained to respect the caste and religious sensitivities of "depressed minorities" in much the same way that teachers in Western countries are trained to be sensitive to racial and religious diversity. (Borooah 2012)

The economic constraints of children from poor families will have to be effectively neutralised to enable their participation in the process of educational development. Equally important is to ensure that social biases, especially by teachers, are eliminated through the secular traditions of the country. Quality school infrastructure in all the minority concentrated areas, if objectively provided, will eventually lead to a higher retention and transition rate at subsequent stages of education.

In general, the State must do much more than what it has done to its poor. The Hon'ble Vice President of India, Shri M. Hamid Ansari has aptly observed that

The default by the State or its agents in terms of deprivation, exclusion and discrimination (including failure to provide security) is to be corrected by the State; this needs to be done at the earliest and appropriate instruments developed for it. Political sagacity, the imperative of social peace, and public opinion play an important role in it. Experience shows that the corrective has to be both at the policy and the implementation levels; the latter, in particular, necessitates mechanisms to ensure active cooperation of the State governments. (Ansari 2015)

CONCLUSION

Of all the religious minorities, Muslim community is the most educationally backward and economically poor. The comparisons of literacy and enrolment ratios at different stages of education demonstrate the low levels of enrolment of Muslim children. At least 25% of out of school children, between 6 and 13 years of age, are Muslims and GER at higher education is as low as 11%, which is even lower than that of SCs (12.2%). The major factors responsible for lower participation of Muslim children are (a) income poverty, because of which most children do not attend any school and those who do so dropout early without completing elementary or secondary level of education,

(b) the lack of quality school infrastructure in the vicinity of Muslims population concentrated areas, which are ghettoised due to large-scale destabilisation and dislocation of Muslim families, particularly in the wake of frequent communal violence in the country, and (c) unfavourable school atmosphere, which results in discrimination against Muslim children by the school functionaries. With a view to increase the level of participation at every stage of education, the minority groups, particularly Muslim children, should be provided financial and other school facilities, including girls' hostel, at the same scale and magnitude as SCs/STs since educational and economic conditions of Muslims are comparable with the groups that are presently given preferential treatment in the matter of education and jobs. An affirmative action in the matters of education and training as well as employment opportunities is urgently called for to pull the community from the morass of poverty and deprivation. Failure to do so will adversely affect the efforts to widen the base of human capital formation through quality education and training, which is critical for improving overall productivity and competitiveness of economy as well as for promoting the Constitutional objectives of equity and justice in the society. A nation cannot progress and promote peace and development without ensuring equity and justice among one-sixth of its population. There are positive signs of the community response, reflected in significant improvement in participation rate of the Muslim boys and girls at all the levels of education, which suggest that Muslim parents are not at all averse to the idea of sending their children for quality schooling. This attitude of poor parents towards acquisition of education for their children ought to be supported through strategic policy intervention and affirmative actions.

ANNEXURE

AMITABH KUNDU COMMITTEE'S OBSERVATIONS AND RECOMMENDATIONS ON MUSLIMS' EDUCATION

Access to Education

The level of literacy among Muslims was lower than Hindus and yet gender disparity was lower among the former. At all levels of education, the outcome indicators for the Muslims were closer to the ST community with the lowest attainment. The enrolment of Muslim children in primary school was fairly high but cane down significantly at higher levels of education. This implies that the Muslim community, irrespective of gender and rural—urban residence, are less likely to attain secondary and higher secondary level of education. The OBC Muslims were the most deprived at all levels of education. The proportionate improvements in educational attainment during 2004–05 and 2011–12 do not alter this pattern. The Muslim community also had far lesser number of graduates and technically educated persons. The Committee thus makes the following recommendations:

1. **Higher Education, Professional Education, Technical Education**

   i. While retaining and improving access to basic education, the focus in the coming decades needs to shift strongly to increasing access for Muslim youth to higher education, technical skills, professional education and access to the English language which is the currency for decent employment.

   ii. In this context, the higher education scholarship for minority students pursuing MPhil and PhD by the Ministry of Environment and Forest (MoEF) at approximately 750 new scholarships per year is negligible. If the overall thrust of the educational vision is to provide basic literacy for the poor among Muslims and simultaneously create skilled professionals and intellectual thought leaders, the approach must change dramatically. Private and public universities must also come forward to recruit and provide scholarships to Muslim minority students to pursue higher learning.

   iii. Vocational training is critical, given the degree of unemployment and the trend towards self-employment among Muslim youth. However, the ITI model has become outmoded in its programmes and finds few takers among the target population. The remodelled ITI programme, as in Gujarat, should be introduced in the Muslim and SC/ST majority areas.

   iv. The new skill development and placement programmes under the National Skill Development Corporation (NSDC) through the private sector should be encouraged and set up in regions with large concentration of Muslim and SC/ST

217

population. Incentives required to allow private sector to do so must also be devised.

2. **Secondary and Higher Secondary Education**

The percentage of enrolment at the secondary school level and above among Muslim population is low compared to Hindus and other socio-religious categories (SRCs), indicating a higher degree of dropout at this level. In order to correct this, efforts must be made to ensure retention, particularly of girl students. At this level of education, immediate employability is a key concern of the families. Also, given that financial constraints are cited as a common reason for such dropout, the Committee recommends the following:

i.   Scholarship amounts for secondary and higher secondary schooling should be raised in order to meet all related costs.

ii. Vocational training courses should be reintroduced in schools where these do not exist.

iii. Students undertaking vocational skill training in school should be given a special stipend to take care of the material requirements of such programmes.

iv. In the globalised and digitalised world, English language has become essential mode of learning. Special classes for students to learn English reading, writing and comprehension skill need to be organised within the schooling system.

3. **Literacy, Primary and Middle School**

Within socio-religious groups, SC/ST among Hindus and OBCs among Muslim have the lowest levels of literacy. The non-OBC Muslim boys aged 6–14 years category in urban areas report the highest percentage figure for persons who never attended a school and also currently not attending schools. It is possible that they are more likely to work to enhance family incomes. It would be important to keep children in school through the following measures:

i.   Rigorously implement and monitor the Mid Day Meal Scheme in schools in Muslim dominated areas with food items that are in the normal diet of these communities.

ii   Improve teacher quality to encourage children to attend and for parents to see and advantage in keeping the children in schools.

iii. Improve activities in schools to keep the children interested in attending the classes.

iv. Raise the scholarship amount available to children in class 1–6.

4. **Education for OBC Muslims**

The Committee has noted the poor outcomes for OBC Muslim boys and girls in all the indicators of educational development. Special attention needs to be paid to this disadvantaged group among the Muslims, including provisioning of scholarships for OBC Muslim boys and girls and vocational training that are inclusive for girls and gender sensitive, going beyond the traditional vocational programmes.

REFERENCES

Ali, Qurban, and Arshi Khan. 2008. 'Status Paper on Muslims'. In *Dalit and Minority Empowerment*, edited by Santosh Bhartiya. New Delhi: Rajkamal Prakashan.

Ansari, M.M. 1987. *Education and Economic Development*. New Delhi: Association of Indian Universities.

Ansari, Mohammed Hamid. 2015. Address by Hon'ble Vice President of India at the *Inauguration of the All India Majlis-E-Mushawarat Golden Jubilee*, New Delhi, 31 August 2015.

Borooah, Vani K. 2012. 'Social Identity and Educational Attainment: The Role of Caste and Religion in Explaining Differences between Children in India'. *Journal of Development Studies* 48 (7): 887–903.

Government of India. 2006. *Social, Economic and Educational Status of Muslim Community of India (Sachar Committee Report)*. New Delhi: Government of India.

Kumar, Chethan. 2015. 49% of Children Out of School are SC/STs, 25% are Muslims: Survey. *The Times of India*, July 27.

Kundu, Amitabh. 2014. *Post Sachar Evaluation Committee: Final Report*. New Delhi: Ministry of Minority Affairs, Government of India.

National University of Educational Planning and Administration (NUEPA). 2013. 'School Education in India: Flash Statistics 2012–13'. New Delhi: Department of Education Management Information System, NUEPA.

National Sample Survey Organisation (NSSO). 2010. 'Employment and Unemployment Survey 2009–10'. 66th Round. New Delhi: Ministry of Statistics and Programme Implementation, Government of India.

Rajput, J.S. (ed.) 2015. *Education of Muslims: Islamic Perspectives of Knowledge and Education: Indian Context.* New Delhi: Noble Education Foundation & Shipra.

Tilak, J.B.G. 2015. 'How Inclusive is Higher Education in India?' *Social Change* 45 (2): 185–23.

9

Higher Education and Gendered Norms: Enabling the 'Use' of Women's Education

Ratna M. Sudarshan

Higher education is a pathway to employment, enabling the acquisition of specialised skills and knowledge, and as the higher education system has grown in India, there has been significantly greater participation of girls, as discussed below. Studies also suggest that the rates of return to higher education are higher for girls than for boys.[1] Despite this, it is a puzzle as to why such a small (and apparently declining) percentage of women with higher education qualifications are to be seen in the workforce.

Historically, few women had the privilege of completing higher education and those who did came from better-off and well-educated families. Privilege, education, political awareness and leadership in changing gendered norms went together in the years before and soon after Independence. Women played a significant part in the struggle for freedom; for example, Devaki Jain (2015) writes about Kamaladevi Chattopadhyay as follows:

> She was born into a privileged family in coastal Karnataka in 1903, and in the custom of the day, was married as a child. Her family included women of exceptional strength and wisdom: both her grandmother and mother were passionate about books and learning, and her mother was a champion of women's education. Both Kamala and her mother were attracted to the Congress Party, whose activities in the Mangalore area matched their own liberal social philosophy, as well as their growing political consciousness. In later years, when Kamala went to jail for her participation in the Congress's civil disobedience movement, her mother went picketing herself.

---

[1] See discussion in Tilak (2015).

In the years just after Independence, in the 1950s and 1960s, the idea that educated citizens, women as well as men, have a duty to contribute to nation building was generally accepted, giving at the same time a public as well as a private purpose to education, especially higher education. Since then, there has been a considerable deepening of educational access, and many more men and women are able to reach institutions of higher education. Expectations from education have become rather more about individual achievement and aspiration. These aspirations touch many aspects of life, yet women's roles and choices show less change than might have been expected 60 years ago. An important indicator of changes in these aspirations is the work-related choices that women make.

This chapter starts by briefly reviewing what is known about women's participation in higher education institutions, and what the data tell us about levels of women's work participation by level of education. Drawing on studies about young women who have been able to complete higher education courses and find suitable work opportunities, the kind of constraints and challenges women face in balancing work and home roles are next reviewed. Based on this, an attempt is made to suggest how better higher education institutions can help to reduce gendered barriers in education to work transitions.

WOMEN IN HIGHER EDUCATION AND IN THE WORKFORCE

The gross enrolment ratio in higher education stood at 21.1 in 2012–13. Women's enrolment in higher education institutions has gone up and almost matches that of men, with 49% of eligible girls enrolling in higher education institutions compared to 56% of eligible boys (Tilak 2015). Free higher education, scholarships, women-only colleges and reservations have all helped to increase women's enrolment in higher education. Tilak (2015) shows that the greatest inequalities are seen by location (rural/urban) and by economic class. Mary John has pointed out that there is near parity between girls and boys from upper castes in higher education, and approximately 30% of both upper-caste urban men and women were in higher education in 2004–05. This was true of 12% of rural upper-caste men and 8% women. Caste and location (rural/urban) when taken jointly create further disadvantage. Less than 4% rural scheduled caste (SC) men and 1.3% rural SC women were in higher education (John 2012). Another axis of difference is seen in subject segmentation by gender, now visible in the enrolments within sub-disciplines rather than disciplines overall; thus, within 'agriculture', women are seen concentrated in agro-chemistry, agro-engineering and technology, and agro-social sciences while being much less present in the sub-fields of animal studies, plant studies and agriculture (Chanana 2013). Thus, the women who have benefited most from higher education are likely to be those living in urban areas (or able to move to urban areas for study) and from the higher income groups, majority of whom would be found in certain courses seen as 'suitable' for women (and matched by occupational segregation in the labour market).

From the data above, it can be seen that the equity challenge facing higher education institutions is a composite of gender, caste, class and location. The focus of this chapter is largely on systemic gender issues that cut across caste, class and location; it is focused on the gender differences that affect the transition from higher education to work and what higher education institutions could do to ease these. The active role of higher education institutions can be expected to make more difference to those from disadvantaged groups, facing intersecting inequalities of gender, class and location, who would have fewer personal/family resources, role models or experience to draw upon. The goal of education may not be to guarantee employment, but as Pappu (2015) points out, especially for low-income groups, expectations of employment are an important motivation for education. She suggests that 'For girls and women too ... a composite of rigorous skill (including life skills) and knowledge training along with provision of career counselling would go a long way in ensuring their participation in the labour force in ways that empower them'.

Higher education is a route of social mobility as much as of occupational mobility. Overall, there is a U-shaped relationship between levels of education and workforce participation rates (WFPRs) as shown in Figure 9.1. This is true for men and women, but men's level of participation is significantly higher; WFPR is high among the illiterate, falls with primary/secondary education and increases again with education above secondary level. The fall could reflect mismatch between jobs sought and jobs available; in the case of women, the possibility of waiting for a suitable job is also socially easier. The decline in work participation levels of women with an increase in their literacy, until this reaches secondary or above, also

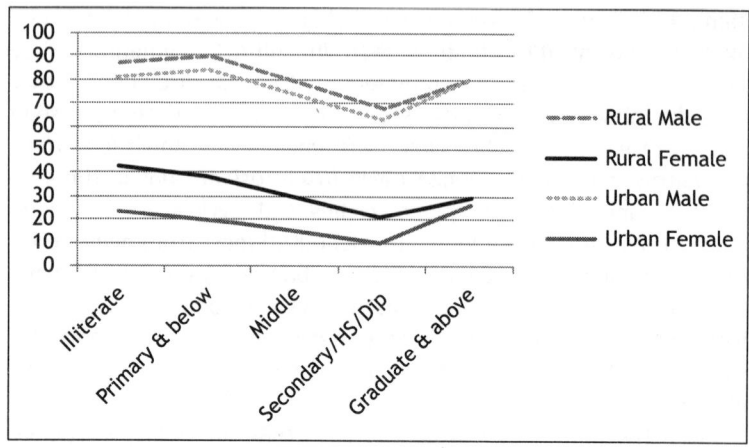

Figure 9.1
Education and Workforce Participation
Source: NSS (2009–10).

reflects attitudes and a 'Sanskritisation' effect of women withdrawing from work as a signal of improved status.[2]

It is generally assumed that higher education will increase the likelihood of women working, both because of the opportunities that become available and because of changes in attitude of educated women. Although many more girls are enrolling in and completing higher education courses and, as the studies discussed below indicate, put in a great deal of effort in order to do so, one of the puzzles that continues to elude an easy answer is why the transition from higher education to work continues to be low for girls, with a large proportion of those who have completed higher education choosing not to join the workforce. The low, even declining, levels of work participation of women have generated much recent research (see, e.g., Chaudhary and Verick 2014; Kapsos, Silberman and Bourmpoula 2014). Why are more girls not 'using' their education in ways that would enhance their own earnings, bargaining power and independence, and also contribute to economic expansion? Of course, among the girls who complete higher education courses, there is a great deal of heterogeneity by social class,

---

[2] Sanskritisation is a term used by Srinivas (1962) to describe the process by which lower-caste groups adopt values and practices of higher-caste groups—here, higher status being associated with women's withdrawal from paid market work.

Table 9.1
Type of Education and Workforce Participation

	Workforce Participation Rates				Ratio of Male to Female WFPR	
	Rural Male	Rural Female	Urban Male	Urban Female	Rural	Urban
No Technical Education	81.3	36.8	73.5	17.5	2.2	4.2
UG-level Diploma/ Certificate	73.2	32.2	78.2	43.5	2.3	1.8
Graduate-level Diploma/Certificate	77.1	27.2	79.1	41.4	2.8	1.9
Technical Graduate	66.8	24.3	86.5	54.2	2.7	1.6
Non-reporting	78.1	11.1	61.3	25.9	7	2.4

Source: NSS (2009–10).

income, type of degree and academic achievement, but the overall picture remains puzzling.

Looking at women's WFPR by the type of higher education suggests that the type of course chosen is an indicator of motivation, intent and likelihood of using the education. As against a WFPR of just 17.5% for urban women without any technical education, the rates are as high as 54.2% for those with technical education (Table 9.1). That these work opportunities are largely located in urban areas is reflected in the fact that women with undergraduate, graduate or technical education in rural areas have lower WFPR than those with no technical education, with the complete opposite being true in urban areas. The lowest ratio of male to female work participation rates is seen among technical graduates in urban areas.

Figure 9.2 shows the age-wise variation in WFPR. While the rates are higher for rural women, these largely result from participation in agricultural work. The work done by younger urban women is most closely linked to their education.

It can also be speculated that the sharper gradient for women in the age group 25–35 years might reflect a cohort effect. It is sometimes suggested that the younger cohorts will make different decisions. A recent study by United Nations Economic and Social Commission for Asia and the Pacific (UNESCAP) and Institute of Social Studies Trust (ISST) throws some light on this question. This survey of youth in the age group 18–24 years collected information from 1,000 boys and girls in Delhi and 1,000 boys and girls in Kolkata. Taking the subset of those who had completed Class 12,

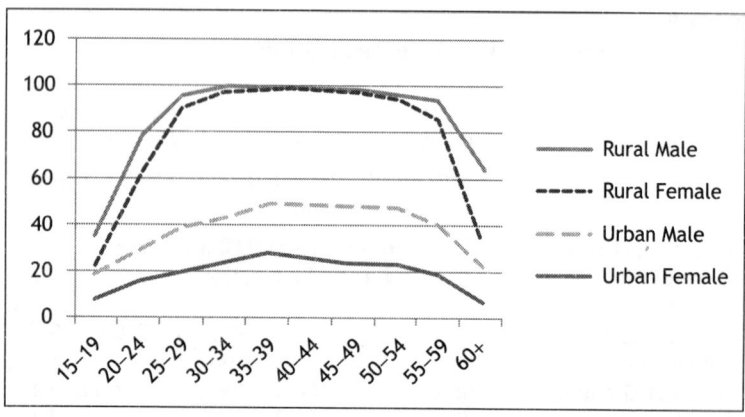

Figure 9.2
Workforce Participation Rates by Age
Source: NSS (2009–10).

the data show that 247 out of 690 boys are currently working (or approximately 36%). For girls, 98 out of 487 are working (or 20%). Out of those who are working, there is not much difference in boys and girls employed full time (67% boys, 65% girls). Those not working are either studying or just not earning. It is of course possible that a greater percentage of girls might be studying, which would also reinforce the understanding that boys are under greater social/family pressures to start earning (ISST 2015).

Work participation rates of graduate women have been declining over the years, standing at 56.7% in 1983 and 32.4% in 2009–10 in rural areas, and 61.1% in 1983 and 26% in 2009–10 in urban areas (Abraham 2013; Pappu 2015). This decline has been explained in different ways: including that women with higher education stay out of the labour force if family income is considered adequate without her earnings, or there is a lack of suitable employment opportunities (see Das and Desai 2003; Mehrotra, Parida, Sinha and Gandhi 2014; Pappu 2015).[3] Whatever the reason, it is notable that higher education has not meant that women will necessarily seek

---

[3] A study in Ghana finds that while more women aged 18–29 have had formal education as compared to those over 50, the impact of this on the ability to get decent work has not been the same. Younger educated women are more likely to be working in private formal or informal sectors, while older educated women are all in secure state employment (Darkwah 2014).

out paid work. No doubt, the orientation of the education system generates aspirations for (scarce) regular formal work and the problem of educated unemployment affects both men and women (Pappu 2015; Sudarshan 2015).[4] The section below discusses the gendered aspects of the transition to work.

IN AND BEYOND HIGHER EDUCATION- GENDERED CHALLENGES

Field observations suggest that girls studying in higher education institutes by and large attend classes and complete compulsory attendance requirements but may be less visible in extra-curricular and optional activities, leaving college premises as soon as classes are over, for example. This behaviour reflects the influence of own or parental concerns regarding safety and constraints on mobility. It is possible that in doing so, girls are limiting the opportunity to develop confidence and non-cognitive skills. Recent studies have used the concept of non-cognitive skills first to argue that success and mobility are influenced by these skills and second to suggest that modifications to curriculum could enable these skills to be taught. Qualities such as locus of control (believing one can control events that affect one's life), self-control and self-esteem, which are counted among non-cognitive skills, are emphasised as skills that may be acquired and would influence the likelihood of success in employment. Others argue that these non-cognitive skills may in fact be class and gender specific and not accessible equally to everyone (see Camfield 2015). One reason behind the lower transition from study to work for women could be because of gendered barriers in achieving the same levels of non-cognitive skills as men. The differences in this aspect between co-educational and single-sex environments in higher education is an area for future study.

For children from middle and upper middle-class households, higher education is a normal and expected progression after completing school. However, many more girls from less well-off backgrounds are also reaching out to higher education today. In an analysis of those enrolled in different tiers of management institutes,

---

[4] Although, as Ajit K. Ghose (2014) points out, 'the rate of unemployment is taken to be an important indicator of labour market conditions when in reality unemployment is a luxury good that only the "rich and educated" can afford.

Krishna and Sarin (2013) find that girls form a higher percentage of those in Tiers-2 and -3 (these are largely private institutions set up recently) than Tier-1 institutes.

> *Just under one-third of all students in these 12 business schools are women, ranging from a low of 16.2 percent in the Tier 1 institution to 36.2 percent in the Tier 3 schools, with this share being 40.2 percent in Tier 2 schools. While low, particularly in the top-tier institution, this percentage is higher than the historic share of women both in higher education and in management positions in India.*

In getting admission into business schools, while economic class and parents education and occupation matter, aspirations, role models, information and guidance also matter. More of those in Tier-1 institutions had moved location, aspired more than their neighbours, had role models from a young age and got information from varied sources. Something more than economic class and other measurable attributes influences patterns of enrolment.

A study of 'champions', girls who have been able to move on from school into undergraduate courses, and who are first-generation learners in higher education, tells a somewhat similar story in that beyond economic and social considerations, there is a level of family support and personal determination that enables the pursuit of higher education (IDS 2015). The study of 'champions' in Rajasthan using a social ecology model finds some interesting differences between champions and non-champions, including that the former have a higher sense of personal agency enabled by the nature of household dynamics. These differences are difficult to quantify and articulate.

These studies suggest that beyond the non-cognitive skills of self-esteem and aspiration, mobility and familial relationships matter. In India, higher education institutes are clustered in urban areas, requiring mobility by rural residents, and accessing higher education institutions is easier for those who had moved location from rural to urban or peri-urban centres earlier. These indicate influence of material factors and social networks that make movement easier.

A recent field study in Kalyanpuri in East Delhi, among girls and boys from low income households, throws some light on the ways in which higher education decisions get influenced by location, income and gender. Talking to young girls who have just completed schooling, and who are looking to study further, some things become clear. One, that being able to apply along with friends adds to individual confidence levels, reassures families that the girls will not be alone and thus makes the decision to study further an easier one. Second, the distance to be travelled every day is a relevant factor, and hence choice of college (to the extent there is a choice) is mainly determined by the location of the college and its distance from home. Third, the choice of subject reflected the additional coaching in this particular subject which they had been able to get from an NGO; thus, the additional inputs coming from outside the school made a difference to their motivation for further study. Fourth, the options of the 'Non-Collegiate Women's Education Board' (NCWEB) of University of Delhi,[5] which allows girls to study for a degree while attending classes only at weekends and over holidays, and of correspondence courses makes a real difference to their ability to study further. While getting into regular courses requires higher marks, it also seems to be difficult for girls to anticipate regular attendance over a period of years. The possibility of obtaining an undergraduate degree without having to attend regularly widens options and encourages greater participation. Some of the girls are also taking on home-based income-generating work already. And all of them help with home duties. Many of their brothers have had to drop out and start working due to family financial difficulties, but the girls get encouragement from their parents and brothers, reinforced by the team at the NGO and by their peer group, to continue their education. The emerging difference with the experience of boys from the same localities is around degrees of mobility, the distance that is possible/acceptable to travel, and the less focused way of studying, that is, girls make time for helping out at home as well.[6]

Another research, based on larger samples, also suggests that in choosing where to study further, location is more important as a criterion for the less well off (e.g., in Krishna and Sarin 2013), particularly for girls. The availability of institutions not too far from home, and with transport facilities enabling girls to return home by

---

[5] NCWEB: In 1943, by a University of Delhi act, NCWEB was established, where in women students were enabled to take some of the examination of the university with special coaching but without attending regular classes. This gave shape to the NCWEB. The board began functioning in September 1944 with three students. At present, the enrolment is more than 13,000. See http://ncweb.du.ac.in/ncweb/

[6] Author's study on 'Gender Equality Outcomes of the SSA' (ongoing).

early evening, makes further education more accessible. Restrictions on girls' mobility is linked to fears about their safety as well as reluctance to see them evolve 'masculine' identities/work roles.

Lower mobility might restrict educational choices but can at times work in women's favour in finding work. Kelkar (2013) found many employers in the IT-enabled sector preferring to hire women as they were willing to stay in 'boring' jobs for domestic reasons. Middle-class women often find themselves recruited into family businesses (see, e.g., De Neve 2011, 87; Sudarshan and Bhattacharya 2009). Sometimes women play what I have elsewhere described as a 'passive economic role'. Munshi (2011: 1071), in his study of the diamond industry and the manner in which three communities occupy this space, points out that 'The marriage institution is key to the maintenance of a strong network'. This 'dense web of marriage ties' facilitates information flows and compliance to verbal contracts. While marriage choices get restricted to within the sub-caste and within the industry, it might not be correct to describe these women as 'not in the labour force' because they are in fact playing an economic role. This type of absorption into the workforce is an acknowledgement of women's ability in the workplace and at the same time an assertion that traditional roles and responsibilities have higher priority and that productive work decisions are familial, not individual decisions.

While significant progress has been made in women's higher education and their eligibility for new types of work opportunities, this goes alongside relatively unchanging views about appropriate gender roles and responsibilities within families. While education and urbanisation are expected to lead to 'modernity' and changing social norms, studies suggest that there is a stubbornness in socio-cultural norms that make women's roles and societal attitudes towards gendered norms of behaviour resistant to change. For example, Mukherjee's analysis of the associations between women's higher education, prosperity and gender bias, based on Census 2001 data for 397 districts in urban India, finds that there may be increasing use of sex-selective abortions by women educated above the middle school and college level, so that it does not appear that higher education is acting to reduce gender bias (Mukherjee 2013; see also John 2012).

Education continues to be an essential requirement for participating in public roles or accessing formal employment. In a poor country where formal and regular employment is very limited, higher education since many decades has been primarily seen as a route to formal employment. Formal employment itself is not very gender-friendly—long hours of work, no time flexibility, virtually no provision for childcare support, and to pursue a progressive career, it very often requires relocation. These attributes do not resonate well with conventional gender roles of women, which place upon them primary responsibility for childcare and family nurture. Expecting women's higher education to lead to higher levels of work participation, sustained over the working ages, rests upon several assumptions, chief among which is that women either forego the married life and its implications or they find partners who are comfortable with a new way of life and different gender roles. The distributional imbalance of men and women's presence in higher education has been largely resolved at an aggregate level, although differences persist when intersecting inequalities of location, class, social group and gender are considered together (Tilak 2015; John 2012). But in the 'use' of education, gender differences remain sharp.

This is not a problem unique to India. As Kreimer (1998) put it,

> The nature of regular employment is such that it can only be carried out by workers free of reproduction duties. In other words, regular employment requires the presence of another worker taking care of reproduction work.... There are clear indications of a new division of labour. Given that the extent of household and family work does not decline and that women have become more employment oriented, traditional strategies of coping with the situation have gained in importance. Instead of a division of labour between genders, there has been a division of labour between women of different generations and/or nationalities and/or classes. Child care and housework are now frequently done by grandmothers, foreigners and lowly qualified women with little perspectives on the labour market.

Work-related choices of women, unlike those of men, continue to seek compatibility with household demands. Whether and where educated women work is a trade-off between expected gains from additional income and the perceived value and status in being at home. Belliappa, in her study of educated women working in the IT sector in Bangalore, describes the attitudes of and towards educated working women as reflecting the emergence of a 'respectable modernity':

> The discourse of 'respectable modernity' ... has several elements of the earlier nationalist discourse on Indian womanhood ... the

new Indian woman continues to carry visible markers of 'Indianness' while she participates in the global economy and culture. She is expected to continue her commitment to home and family relationships, especially to children ... Just as educated women were believed to be a more suitable companion to her husband in the nationalist period, so are 'working women' valued for their intelligence and ability to empathize with men's concerns in the period of globalization. (Belliappa 2013, 66, 153)

Similarly, Vijayakumar speaks of 'flexible aspirations'. Her study of educated women working in the IT sector in a small town near Bangalore found that women value their ability to adapt to circumstances, recognising that marriage alters these, while practical constraints on men's choices did not change with marriage (Vijayakumar 2013). These narratives are indicative of particular pathways of change. Unlike the experience of Southeast Asia, education and work opportunities have not made much impact on marriage rates in India. Ng and Mitter (2005:147) in referring to the high attrition rate of call centre workers note that 'most women leave the job after marriage —and most Indian women marry young'.

Somewhat similar findings have emerged from a study of women in the Indian Administrative Services (IAS). In her analysis conducted around 15–20 years ago, Thakur (n.d.) suggests that there is a gender stereotyping of posts, corresponding with the overall situation of gender disparities within any particular state. Another outcome of implicit norms in society is that while just 25% of women IAS officers in the sample had arranged marriages, 74% of the men had arranged marriages. Women officers could either marry men working in the government services who could understand and cope with similar dual careers, resign after marriage (a consequence of patrilocality, that is, the expectation that a woman should work where the husband is located) or remain unmarried.

Donner's study of educated Bengali women suggests some other reasons why women might choose not to work:

Children's formal education and the need to prepare full Bengali meals are the most often cited reasons for a withdrawal of middle class women from the labour market.... Men and women agreed that a married women could not possibly work full time and provide 'proper' food for her family. (Donner 2011, 58–59)

In the last few years, sustained effort is being made to enhance the availability of skill development courses, beyond the traditional ones offered at Industrial Training Institutes (ITIs). The employability of ITI graduates has been found to be low—for example, in 2010, 30% of 2007 batch was found to be unemployed, in a sample study conducted by National Institute of Labour Economics Research and Development (NILERD; see Mehrotra 2014). Short-term trainings in urban areas offering jobs in the retail sector are attracting both girls and boys, although there is very little evidence available as to whether girls are able to work in a sustained manner in such work, especially after marriage.

GENDERED SOCIAL NORMS AND ROLE OF INSTITUTIONS OF HIGHER EDUCATION

Goldin (2006) suggested that women's work participation rates in the USA and the Organisation for Economic Co-operation and Development (OECD) countries started increasing with a slow and evolutionary change from the 1920s onwards, leading up to a 'revolutionary' change from the mid-1970s and levelling off towards the mid-1990s. Several factors worked to bring about this change, including the rise of part-time work, better household amenities and increased work opportunities, education, as well as intrinsic changes in women's own perspectives. The upswing in women's work participation levels reflects changes in 'horizon', that is, whether women see their labour force involvement as long and continuous or brief and intermittent. With a longer horizon, women would continue into higher education and plan for careers. The second change is in 'identity' or women finding individuality through their work. Both family and recognition at work begin to contribute to personal satisfaction and sense of personhood. Third, 'decision-making': whether labour force decisions are made fully jointly by women who are married or whether women are secondary workers, basing their decisions on those made by their husbands/partners. In a later essay, Goldin draws out the important finding that there can be differences in earnings even when human capital is the same, not because of discrimination but because certain types of jobs display a non-linear relationship with respect to hours worked. For example, a lawyer may work in a large law firm where there is a premium for working long hours; as a general counsel, working fewer hours; or in a small firm that does not penalise shorter or discontinuous work hours. The same formal education could thus lead to different levels of earnings and different degrees of time flexibility depending on where one works (Goldin 2014).

Goldin's assertion is that women need more time flexibility usually because of childcare responsibilities and this reflects in work choice. The more those occupations are able to reduce the non-linearity of pay with respect to hours worked, the lower would be the residual differences observed in earnings by gender.

Although Goldin's analysis is set in a different context, it offers interesting insights to understand the work-related behaviour of women in India. From the examples given earlier, there is some indication that for educated urban women, while there is a perceptible shift in identity, to include both family and work-related achievements as sources of personal satisfaction, marriage seems to be an important limiting factor in 'horizon' because both girls and their parents recognise that career decisions taken after completing education may need to be modified to accommodate to the views and circumstances of the marital family. While there are higher levels of education and higher age at first marriage of women, this goes along with an unyielding work structure that offers no regular part-time work (with some exceptions in the corporate world) and with fairly rigid occupational segregation. Changes are needed both at the level of the individual self and in the structures of the economy and employment opportunities available to enable women to better negotiate a desired pathway managing familial relationships along with career aspirations. It is here that institutions of higher education could play a catalytic role.

Universities and other higher education institutions cannot alter the prior gendered experiences, nor can they directly influence prevalent norms or labour market arrangements. They can enhance, reduce or leave unchanged the ability of women and men to question these. While the education–economy link has always been strong, it is receiving a further push today within the framework of the skills initiative. One of the significant aspects of higher education today is the increasing privatisation reflecting not only in the source of funding but also the types of courses that are available. Given the emphasis on skill development, school leavers now can choose from many more shorter duration vocational courses as well, most oriented towards building skills that are in demand in growing industrial sectors, such as retail. There is among a section of educationists considerable discontent about the increasing 'marketisation' of education (see, e.g., Tilak 2004). The new courses are market-led and might be narrowly framed but offer some opportunities in so far as the training is shorter in duration, and the market link is stronger, it may encourage girls to take on paid work.

Even if girls enter higher education courses with a stronger career orientation than earlier, the question is what kind of support, encouragement and counselling is given to girls to enable them to consciously negotiate the gendered barriers or expectations they might expect to face. One of the effects of higher education is that individual networks can expand beyond the ascriptive, familial and social group networks to include new networks that grow out of personal choice and interpersonal relations, cutting across caste and family boundaries. Srinivas and Beteille (1964: 168) point out that

India has embarked on a course of planned social change and economic development. This involves, among other things, the transmission of certain key ideas, principles and values from the highest to the lowest levels of society. What are the social networks along which such ideas are transmitted? What kind of refraction do they undergo as they pass from one level to another? How is this refraction conditioned by the nature of the social network along which the ideas flow?

Gender equality is a value embedded in the Indian Constitution and sought to be transmitted across society. In so far as education plays a critical role in the creation and expansion of networks through which this value could be transmitted, greater analysis is needed on the role of such networks. The influence of peer group networks developed within educational institutions is probably strongest among the most privileged male students at the best universities. We need more studies to reveal whether girls are able to develop any sustained friendships and networks and whether these play any role in work-related choices.[7]

Moreover, there is value in women's work only if it enhances well-being and empowers them. An innovative study by a team of students and faculty from Lady Shri Ram College, University of Delhi, explored the link between work and well-being of the female workforce in colleges of the University of Delhi. The sample included girls-only colleges and co-ed colleges, distributed over morning and evening

---

[7] The recent efforts at developing an alumni network of students from Lady Shri Ram College, University of Delhi, is an example of encouraging professional networking and mentorships; how successful this might be is still to be seen. As the website says, 'The ELSA Alumni roll call is a powerful and enviable one, comprising a valuable network of women across the world and across professions'. See: http://lsralumna.org/

colleges, and the final sample size was 358. Well-being is understood as made up of material, subjective and relational factors, recognising of course that these dimensions are interconnected (White 2008). The material aspects measure standard of living, relational refers to personal and social relations and subjective measures values and perceptions. Interestingly, the study found social connectedness as a factor that was strongly associated with well-being. The analysis found a higher relational well-being among faculty in girls-only colleges due to higher social interaction and peer group support. This leads to the recommendation that such interactions could be increased and spread across the organisation culture of co-ed and evening colleges with more spaces for faculty members, department rooms, forums, etc., which may lead to regular and productive peer-group interaction and hence higher relational well-being (LSR 2015). Some areas for action are discussed further.

Sensitisation and Training, both for Students and Faculty

To address these issues, special training courses are recommended. Suma Chitnis (1993) has pointed to the variation across regions in attitudes towards women's work. These are a result of different histories and different cultural norms. Broadly speaking, the western and southern parts of the country show more positive attitudes to women's work. Chitnis suggests that many factors could lie behind this, including Dravidian culture; the Kerala tradition of matriarchy; two out of the first three universities established by the British were located in Bombay and Madras; the 19th-century social reform movement had a strong base in Bombay and Madras provinces; Mahatma Phule and Maharshi Karvewho fought for the education of women in the 19th century and launched their mission from Pune, where and in Bombay the SNDT Women's University was set up; the strong base of the Gandhian and nationalist movement in and around Bombay; and the cosmopolitan nature of Bombay. Whatever the exact reason or combination of reasons, there are implications for training that might be organised. One, that there are significant differences in the levels of awareness. Two, there might be greater need to locate training programmes and activities for women managers of higher education in North India. Chitnis suggests further that discussions of such regional differences during trainings are a useful way of illustrating the constraints that women face and how these might be addressed.

Some systematic efforts have already been made to address the need for broad-based training of women managers in higher education. Chanana (2015) has suggested that higher education institutions are not gender-neutral in their organisation and functioning, and even if they were, that would not be enough; the system needs to be pro-women, particularly to enable women to deal with the contradictions between the personal and professional that limit academic participation. Women find it difficult to find space and time for effective networking, especially across gender, and are generally excluded from the networks that do exist in universities. This understanding led to the formulation of a programme to build the capacity of women faculty to enlarge their professional activities and to move up in the system. This is the Capacity Building for Women Managers in Higher Education programme, started in 1997 under the auspices of the University Grants Commission (UGC) in collaboration with the Commonwealth Secretariat, London, and now managed by UGC. The programme has a focus on five dimensions: women's study perspective, governance, academic leadership, personal and professional roles, research—all with focus on women, and it encourages the participants to look inwards to go beyond the stereotypes of the self. Interdisciplinary groups are formed inclusive in terms of caste, tribe, religion, class, rural/urban and tribal locations. There are two level of workshops: Sensitisation, Awareness and Motivation (SAM) and Training of Trainers (ToTs); selected participants from SAM workshops are invited to ToTs and they become SAM trainers. These workshops have reached out to about 4,000 women in the furthest corners of the country. The SAM workshops have brought together many women who have never moved out from their homes and towns and also have had no academic interaction or exposure outside their institutions. According to Chanana, the gains have surpassed expectations.

Training and sensitisation for students and faculty in higher education institutions would help to get a societal acknowledgement of the need to find practical solutions to enable better work-life balance, and involving men in these discussions and solutions is equally necessary if social norms are to shift towards greater gender equality. The intention is to help a shift towards a sense of personal identity that gives greater value to a lifelong career.

Career Counselling

Providing adequate information and counselling to girls enrolled in different courses about possible work opportunities needs further strengthening, and realistically, this needs to be locale-specific information. As pointed out earlier, mobility tends to be more limited for women and it is more likely that they would reach out to new and emerging opportunities that do not require travelling long distances. New technologies offer new opportunities, and call centres and other IT-enabled services in India might have an effect similar to that of the telephone and typewriter in Western countries a century ago, or the garments industry in Bangladesh, in drawing women into work.

Jensen (2012) has tested whether an increase in employment opportunities for women can affect early life-cycle work and family transitions—willingness to take on paid work, delaying age at marriage, working after marriage and so on. In a randomised trial using recruiters for business process outsourcing (BPO) industry, three years of BPO recruiting services were given to women in randomly selected rural villages (approximately 50–150 km from Delhi), designed to increase awareness of and access to BPO jobs. The study finds that women aged 15–21 at the baseline who were exposed to the intervention were 4.6 percentage points more likely to work in a BPO job and 2.4 percentage points more likely to work at all for pay outside the home that the process led to increased investments in further education/training for women, as also to delays in marriage and childbearing. In comparing responses with the control group, the treatment group showed a higher desire to work for pay before marrying (43% against 30%), after marriage but before having children (30% against 19%) and after children had finished school and were married (34% against 23%); however, in both groups, few women expected to work when their children were still young (7.4% against 4.5%).

One can speculate on some of the factors that made this work attractive to women, and their families, in this experimental study. The recruiter offers a tangible link to new and urban networks and thus satisfies an aspiration for progress and fills any gaps there might be in information and ability to access work. Further, these are areas near Delhi, and so while the sample is rural and may not otherwise be aware of the new jobs, distance to the work place is small enough to allow for the possibility if not of daily commuting then of frequent visits to home. The fact that groups of persons are being recruited is also important in providing a sense of security. It is a white-collar job with higher pay than other work in rural areas, and hence with higher social status as well as financial compensation. Responses of women showed that marriage is expected to bring down the percentage of women wanting to work for pay outside the home, and much more strongly, the birth of children. Given that information is not always available, regular career counselling can help shape education and work choices in a more realistic manner.

Curriculum and Non-Cognitive Skills

Developing curricula and learning processes that not only focus on subject knowledge but also distribute opportunities for leadership and presentation of work more widely among students, to encourage a stronger sense of self and enable women to take their work roles and their own educational abilities more seriously as constituents of their identity, is another area that could be strengthened. While such non-cognitive skills do not remove systemic barriers and contextual limitations, their (limited) influence will play its part in pushing outwards what is seen as the 'horizons of possibility' by women themselves and society at large.

Encouraging spaces for informal interaction within higher education institutions, to strengthen social connectedness and help in expansion of social networks, would also contribute to this end.

The Value of the 'Second-best' Option

As discussed, young women have tangibly benefited in their ability to access higher education by the availability of correspondence/part-time courses, shorter duration courses and vocational courses, because these provide greater flexibility to manage other demands on their time, such as assisting in home-management responsibilities. Given that marriage, childbirth and wider familial responsibilities continue to affect the likelihood of women's sustained work participation, the impact of counselling and information encouraging women to seek paid work will be greater if employers also offer flexible hours, part-time work and so on to together encourage a lengthening of the 'horizon'. Correspondence courses and regular part-time work are often viewed as second-best options to be discouraged; however, a pragmatic policy that tries to expand the range of options and opportunities might serve women better.

Several decades ago, the Commission on the Status of Women (GoI 1974) had suggested that attitudes towards women's work were changing, and the real difficulty lay in the fact that not enough attention had been given to providing the necessary infrastructure such as childcare support, which would allow women to compete on more equal terms. Education alone cannot do this. A specific recommendation was that regular part-time employment should be encouraged. This recommendation has not been taken forward. The reality is that just as the availability of correspondence courses has allowed women who are married, or need to work, the opportunity to study, even though this may be a second-best educational process, the possibility of working part time, or with flexible timings, and from home, would allow women to use their education in diverse occupations, even if it is not the most secure or best paid work in the economy. Knowing that 'the best is the enemy of the good', gender equality in our society might be better encouraged by allowing diverse forms of learning and diverse types of work arrangement and giving them all a recognised status.

REFERENCES

Abraham, V. 2013. 'Missing Labour or Consistent De-feminisation?' *Economic and Political Weekly* 48 (31): 99–108.

Belliappa, Jyothsna Latha. 2013. *Gender, Class and Reflexive Modernity in India*. Basingstoke: Palgrave Macmillan.

Camfield, Laura. 2015. 'Character Matters: How Do Measures of Non-cognitive Skills Shape Understanding of Social Mobility in the Global North and South?' *Social Anthropology* 23 (1): 68–79.

Chanana, Karuna. 2013. 'Higher Education in and for a Changing World'. *Journal of Educational Planning and Administration* 27 (2): 141–55.

———. 2015. 'Leadership for Women's Equality and Empowerment in Higher Education'. In *Interrogating Women's Leadership and Empowerment*, edited by Omita Goyal, 81–94. New Delhi: SAGE Publications.

Chaudhary, Ruchika, and Sher Verick. 2014. 'Female Labour Force Participation in India and Beyond'. ILO Working Paper. Available at: http://www.ilo.org/newdelhi/whatwedo/publications/WCMS_324621/lang--en/index.htm

Chitnis, Suma. 1993. 'The Place of Women in the Management of Higher Education in India'. In *Women in Higher Education Management*, edited by E. Dines, 81–103. Paris: UNESCO.

Darkwah, Akosua K. 2014. 'Education: Pathway to Empowerment for Ghanaian Women?' In *Feminisms, Empowerment and Development*, edited by Andrea Cornwall and Jenny Edwards, 87–102. London: Zed Books.

Das, M.B., and S. Desai. 2003. 'Why Are Educated Women Less Likely to Be Employed in India?' Social Protection Discussion Paper series, Paper no. 27868. Washington, DC: The World Bank.

De Neve, Geert. 2011. 'Keeping It in the Family: Work, Education and Gender Hierarchies among Tiruppur's Industrial Capitalists'. In *Being*

Middle-class in India: A Way of Life, edited by Henrike Donner, 73–99. New York, NY: Routledge.

Donner, Henrike. 2011. 'Gendered Bodies, Domestic Work and Perfect Families: New Regimes of Gender and Food in Bengali Middle-class Lifestyles'. In *Being Middle-class in India: A Way of Life*, edited by Henrike Donner, 47–72. New York, NY: Routledge.

Ghose, Ajit K. 2014. 'Employment in a Time of High Growth'. *Business Standard*, 15 February 2014. Available at: http://www.business-standard.com/article/opinion/ajit-k-ghose-employment-in-a-time-of-high-growth-114021501132_1.html

GoI (Government of India). 1974. 'Towards Equality'. Report of the Committee on the Status of Women in India. New Delhi: Government of India.

Goldin, Claudia. 2006. 'The Quiet Revolution That Transformed Women's Employment, Education and Family'. *American Economic Review* 96 (2): 1–21.

———. 2014. 'A Grand Gender Convergence: Its Last Chapter'. *American Economic Review* 104 (4): 1091–19. http://dx.doi.org/10.1257/aer.104.4.1091

IDS (Institute of Development Studies). 2015. *India's Champions: Exploring Determinants of Young Women's Empowerment in Rajasthan*. Jaipur: Institute of Development Studies.

ISST (Institute of Social Studies Trust). 2015. 'Youth Survey in Delhi and Kolkata'. Project Report. Bangkok: UNESCAP.

Jain, Devaki. 2015. 'A Singular Woman'. *The Caravan Magazine*, 1 July 2015. Available at: http://www.caravanmagazine.in/essay/singular-woman-kamaladevi-chattopadhyay#sthash.pAHYVcSW.dpuf

Jensen, Robert. 2012. 'Do Labor Market Opportunities Affect Young Women's Work and Family Decisions? Experimental Evidence from India'. *Quarterly Journal of Economics* 127 (2): 1–40.

John, Mary E. 2012. 'Gender and Higher Education in the Time of Reforms'. *Contemporary Education Dialogue* 9 (2): 197–221.

Kapsos, Steven, Andrea Silberman, and Evangelia Bourmpoula. 2014. 'Why Is Female Labour Force Participation Declining so Sharply in India?' ILO Research Paper No. 10. Available at: http://www.ilo.org/wcmsp5/groups/public/---dgreports/---inst/documents/publication/wcms_250977.pdf

Kelkar, Govind. 2013. 'At the Threshold of Economic Empowerment: Women, Work and Gender Regimes in Asia'. ILO Asia-Pacific Working Paper Series. Available at: http://www.oit.org/wcmsp5/groups/public/---asia/---ro-bangkok/---sro new_delhi/documents/publication/wcms_233096.pdf

Kreimer, Margareta. 1998, June. 'Women's Work and Flexibilization'. Paper presented at the IAFFE Conference, Amsterdam.

Krishna, Anirudh, and Ankur Sarin. 2013. Management Education in India: Avenue for Social Stratification or Social Mobility?' Working Paper, Sanford School of Public Policy, Duke University, Durham, NC.

LSR (Lady Shri Ram College for Women). 2015. 'The "Successful Professional Woman": Work-Life Balance and Well-Being'. Innovation Project. New Delhi: Lady Shri Ram College for Women, University of Delhi.

Mehrotra, S., J. Parida, S. Sinha, and A. Gandhi. 2014. 'Explaining Employment Trends in the Indian Economy'. *Economic and Political Weekly* 49 (32): 49–57.

Mehrotra, Santosh, ed. 2014. *India's Skills Challenge: Reforming Vocational Education and Training to Harness the Demographic Dividend*. New Delhi: Oxford University Press.

Mukherjee, Sucharita Sinha. 2013. 'Women's Empowerment and Gender Bias in the Birth and Survival of Girls in Urban India'. *Feminist Economics* 19 (1): 1–28.

Munshi, Kaivan. 2011. 'Strength in Numbers: Networks as a Solution to Occupational Traps'. *Review of Economic Studies* 78 (3): 1069–1101.

National Sample Survey Organisation (NSSO). 2009–10. *India—Employment and Unemployment 2009–10, 66th Round*. Ministry of Statistics and Programme Implementation, Government of India, New Delhi.

Ng, Cecilia, and Swasti Mitter. 2005. 'Valuing Women's Voices: Call Centre Workers in Malaysia and India'. In *Gender and the Digital Economy: Perspectives from the Developing World*, edited by Cecilia Ng and Swasti Mitter, 132–58. New Delhi: SAGE Publications.

Pappu, Rekha. 2015. 'Towards a Framework for Forging Links: Exploring the Connections Between Women's Education, Empowerment and Employment'. *Indian Journal of Gender Studies* 22 (2): 300–21.

Srinivas, M.N. 1962. *Caste in Modern India and Other Essays*. Bombay: Asia Publishing House.

Srinivas, M.N., and Andre Beteille. 1964. 'Networks in Indian Social Structure'. *Man* 64: 165–68.

Sudarshan, Ratna M. 2015. 'Employment-responsive Education in an Informal Economy: Context and Challenges'. *Journal of Educational Planning and Administration*, 29 (2): 121–35.

Sudarshan, Ratna M., and Shrayana Bhattacharya. 2009. 'Through the Magnifying Glass: Women's Work and Labour Force Participation in Urban Delhi'. *Economic and Political Weekly* 44 (48): 59–66.

Thakur, Sarojini Ganju. n.d. 'Increasing Awareness for Change: A Survey of Gender and the Civil Services'. Mimeo for Department of Administrative Reforms and Public Grievances, Government of India.

Tilak, Jandhyala B.G. 2004. 'Higher Education Between the State and the Market'. Paper presented at UNESCO Forum on Higher Education, Research and Knowledge, 1–3 December 2004, Paris.

———. 2015. 'How Inclusive Is Higher Education in India?' *Social Change* 45 (2): 185–223.

Vijayakumar, Gowri. 2013. 'I'll Be Like Water: Gender, Glass, and Flexible Aspirations at the Edge of India's Knowledge Economy'. *Gender and Society* 27 (6): 777–98.

White, Sarah C. 2008. 'But What Is Well-being? A Framework for Analysis in Social and Development Policy and Practice'. Draft Paper, ESRC Research Group on Well-Being in Developing Countries. Available at: http://people.bath.ac.uk/ecsscw/But_what_is_Well-being.pdf

10

Disability Rights in Higher Education: A Preliminary Investigation of Exclusion and Barriers in Indian Universities

Kalpana Kannabiran and Soumya Vinayan

INTRODUCTION

The era of reforms in India has witnessed the emergence of private players in higher education (HE) and the translation of HE into a private good, raising serious concerns in terms of ensuring equity. In a social context characterised by multiple and intersecting discrimination, social research has foregrounded wide disparities in educational attainment at various levels on grounds of caste, class, region, religion, language and gender. However, there are very few studies that have examined the exclusion, barriers and challenges confronted by persons with disabilities (PWDs) in accessing HE.

With the adoption of United Nations Convention on the Rights of Persons with Disabilities (UNCRPD) in 2006, there has been a marked shift of focus on disability from a welfare concern to a rights framework. Article 24 recognises the rights of PWDs to education. Although there is no explicit mention of HE, the generic focus on education enables an examination of education and learning at all levels—from pre-school learning to HE. While studies have suggested that HE could improve quality of life for PWDs (Wehman 2006), yet it is also true that PWDs have not been able to gain significant access to HE. Attitudinal barriers, resource barriers, structural barriers, policy-related issues, lack of support mechanisms, and skills and knowledge have been found to impede participation of PWDs in HE (Beauchamp-Pryor 2012; Hopkins 2011; Matshedisho 2007; Moswela and Mukhopadhyay 2011). The all-pervasive perception of 'normalcy' (able-normativity) in HE discourse is also a major barrier, which PWDs encounter (Brewster 2014; Holloway 2001;

Madriaga, Hanson, Kay and Walker 2011; Tinklin and Hall 1999). The pervasiveness of non-conducive classroom environments is well researched and documented (Abu-Hamour 2013; Al-Hmouz 2014; Baker, Boland, Nowik and Cedar Crest College. 2012; Cook, Rumrill and Tankersley 2009). Assumptions of able-normativity were also evident in modes of evaluation and assessments (Hanafin, Shevlin, Kenny and McNeela 2007).

Holding the structures and institutional apparatuses that 'contain' education and providing coherence to it is the politics of knowledge production and ideologies of embodiment. It is not merely a question of diversity and inclusion but more importantly questions of power, hegemony and representation that give meaning to the overwhelming presences and significant absences, negations and invisibilities in HE. The question of identity and the specific ways in which thought constructs the human body determine quite directly the structures through which persons with different human/social attributes will be accommodated. HE while available on paper might well be cordoned off through a series of intersecting obstructions (barriers) in knowledge, technology and infrastructure, reproducing and deploying segregations within institutional spaces and reinforcing ableism and other hegemonies even while seeming to 'accommodate' them. On this subject, Nussbaum (2006) argues persuasively that disability is handed as an afterthought in social contract necessitating 'accommodation' and the 'removal of barriers'—the erection of barriers itself is a matter of foundational exclusions of inarticulate premises that structure consciousness and architectural design. How does one get around this problem?

DISABILITY AND HE IN INDIA: FINDINGS OF A SURVEY

Given this context and questions that arise therein, and the paucity of information on these questions, we set out to map the inclusion of PWDs in the realm of HE in India through a survey that attempted to address the gaps and lack of disaggregated data on PWDs in HE in India. The survey, not limited to PWDs, gathered information on understanding disability, disability-related information (if disabled), details of institution of study, period of study, disclosure, evaluation and assessment, and experiences of and encounters with disability, adopting a two-pronged approach. An online version (32) and a field survey were conducted in Central University of

Punjab (4), Central University of Orissa (16), Central University of Gujarat (15), Jawaharlal Nehru University (70), University of Hyderabad (22) and Maulana Azad National Urdu University (MANUU; 10). In addition, the schedule was also canvassed among the participants of a refresher course for university and college teachers from across India with special reference to disability studies (30) in the University of Hyderabad.

PROFILE OF THE RESPONDENTS

A total of 102 PWDs and 97 non-disabled (hereafter ND) participated in the survey. The ND included parent/family or intimate partner of PWD, disability services and rights professional, administrator in HE institution, teacher in special education and other than special education, among others. The PWD respondents included persons with visual impairment (45%), locomotor disability (50%), speech and hearing impairment (3%) and psychosocial and learning disabilities (1% each; Table 10.1).

Out of them, 97% had certification of disability of which 99% were above 40% (benchmark disability which enables PWDs to access affirmative action in education and employment). Nearly all persons with visual impairments had certificates, of which 77% reported total blindness (100% disability). Among persons with locomotor disability, 48% fell in the range of 40–59% disability, while 32% reported 60–79% as per certification (Table 10.2). Respondents could choose whether or not to answer the question relating to causes of disability—a significant proportion of the PWDs (60%) chose to answer this question.

Of the total 199 respondents, 139 (70%) were males and 59 were females (29%) and 1 was transgender. Among PWDs, out of 102

Table 10.1
Persons with Disability (Disability Wise)

Type of Disabilities	No. of Persons
Visual	46 (45.1)
Locomotor	51 (50)
Speech and hearing	3 (2.9)
Psychosocial	1 (1)
Learning	1 (1)
Total	102 (100)

Source: Field Survey.

Table 10.2
Respondents by Disability and Certification

Percentage of Disability as per Certification	Type of Disability					Total
	Visual	Locomotor	Speech and Hearing	Psychosocial	Learning	
Less than 40	—	—	—	1 (100) (100)	—	1 (100) (100)
40–59	5 (15.2) (11.4)	24 (72.7) (48)	3 (9.1) (100)	—	1 (3) (100)	33 (100) (33.3)
60–79	3 (15.8) (6.8)	16 (84.2) (32)	—	—	—	19 (100) (19.2)
80–99	2 (22.2) (4.5)	7 (77.8) (14)	—	—	—	9 (100) (9.1)
100	34 (91.9) (77.3)	3 (8.1) (6)	—	—	—	37 (100) (37.4)
Total	44 (44.4) (100)	50 (50.5) (100)	3 (3) (100)	1 (1) (100)	1 (1) (100)	99 (100) (100)

Source: Field Survey.

respondents, majority were males (77 males and 24 females). Among all the respondents, 56% were in the age group of 20–29 followed by 25% in the age group of 30–39. Among PWDs, 71% were in the age group of 20–29 followed by 15% in the age group of 30–39, whereas the sample was more spread out in the age group of 20–29 (41%), 30–39 (35%) and 40–49 (15%) among ND (Table 10.3). This can be attributed to the fact that most of them were faculty (47%) and hence belonged to the older age group (discussed in detail later).

Out of all respondents, 16% (32) reported no religious affiliation, 62% (124) were Hindus, 11% (22) Muslims, 5% (10) Christians, 4% (8) Buddhist and 2% (3) Sikhs. In terms of social location, 12% were scheduled caste (SC), 5% scheduled tribe (ST), 36% other backward

Table 10.3

Respondents by Gender and Age Group

Socio-economic Indicator	Persons with Disability	Persons without Disability	Total
Gender			
Male	77 (55.4)	62 (44.6)	139 (100)
	(75.5)	(63.9)	(69.8)
Female	24 (40.7)	35 (59.3)	59 (100)
	(23.5)	(36.1)	(29.6)
Transgender	1 (100)	—	1 (100)
	(1)		(0.5)
Total	102 (51.3)	97 (48.7)	199 (100)
	(100)	(100)	(100)
Age Group			
Below 20	9 (60)	6 (40)	15 (100)
	(8.8)	(6.2)	(7.5)
20–29	72 (64.3)	40 (35.7)	112 (100)
	(70.6)	(41.2)	(56.3)
30–39	15 (30.6)	34 (69.4)	49 (100)
	(14.7)	(35.1)	(24.6)
40–49	4 (21.1)	15 (78.9)	19 (100)
	(3.9)	(15.5)	(9.5)
50–59	1 (50)	1 (50)	2 (100)
	(1)	(1)	(1)
Above 70	1 (50)	1 (50)	2 (100)
	(1)	(1)	(1)
Total	102 (51.3)	97 (48.7)	199 (100)
	(100)	(100)	(100)

Source: Field Survey.

Table 10.4
Respondents by Religious Affiliation and Social Location

Socio-economic Indicator	Persons with Disability	Persons without Disability	Total
Religious Affiliation			
No religious affiliation	12 (37.5) −11.8	20 (62.5) −20.6	32 (100) −16.1
Hindu	65 (52.4) −63.7	59 (47.6) −60.8	124 (100) −62.3
Muslim	18 (81.8) −17.6	4 (18.2) −4.1	22 (100) −11.1
Christian	5 (50) −4.9	5 (50) −5.2	10 (100) −5
Sikh	1 (33.3) −1	2 (66.7) −2.1	3 (100) −1.5
Buddhist	1 (12.5) −1	7 (87.5) −7.2	8 (100) −4
Total	102 (51.3) −100	97 (48.7) −100	199 (100) −100
Social Location			
SC	5 (20.8) −4.9	19 (79.2) −19.6	24 (100) −12.1
ST	7 (77.8) −6.9	2 (22.2) −2.1	9 (100) −4.5
OBC	40 (56.3) −39.2	31 (43.7) −32	71 (100) −35.7
Minority	10 (66.7) −9.8	5 (33.3) −5.2	15 (100) −7.5
Others	40 (50) −39.2	40 (50) −41.2	80 (100) −40.2
Total	102 (51.3) −100	97 (48.7) −100	199 (100) −100

Source: Field Survey.

classes (OBC) and rest were others. However, among PWDs, the proportion of SC and ST stood at 5% and 7% respectively (Table 10.4).

In terms of marital status, 37% were currently single (51% for PWDs), 27% were never married (33% for PWDs), 23% were currently married (7% for PWDs and 40% for ND) and 6% were in intimate relationship (5% for PWDs; Table 10.5).

Out of those who reported annual household income, 67% earned an income of up to ₹0.5 million while 24% were in the category of ₹0.5–1 million followed by 7% in the category of above

Table 10.5
Respondents by Marital Status

Marital Status	Persons with Disability	Persons without Disability	Total
Never married	34 (64.2)	19 (35.8)	53 (100)
	–33.3	–19.6	–26.6
Currently married	7 (15.2)	39 (84.8)	46 (100)
	–6.9	–40.2	–23.1
In intimate relationship	5 (41.7)	7 (58.3)	12 (100)
	–4.9	–7.2	–6
Currently single	52 (71.2)	21 (28.8)	73 (100)
	–51	–21.6	–36.7
Married	—	1 (100)	1 (100)
		–1	–0.5
Others	4 (28.6)	10 (71.4)	14 (100)
	–3.9	–10.3	–7
Total	102 (51.3)	97 (48.7)	199 (100)
	–100	–100	–100

Source: Field Survey.

₹1 million. Out of the total respondents, 18% did not report household income. It should be noted in this context that 84% of the PWDs who reported household income belonged to the category of up to ₹0.5 million (Table 10.6).

Information about education of parents was also elicited. Out of the total respondents, 16% reported that their fathers were illiterate, followed by education below graduation (43%), graduation (21%), post-graduation (14%) and above post-graduation (5%). With respect to mother's education, the proportion of illiterate stood at 27% (33% for PWDs and 19% for ND), below graduation at 49%, graduation at 18% (14% for PWDs and 22% for ND), post-graduation at 6% (2% for PWDs and 10% for ND; Table 10.7).

IMAGES OF 'DISABILITY'

'Can change in image trigger change in attitudes? Only extraordinary performance evokes praise. What about real life challenges?' (PWD respondent)

Baglieri and Shapiro (2012) refer to how attitudes towards disability are shaped by one's culture, language, interactions in school, media, literature and curriculum as early in life as nursery

Table 10.6
Respondents by Annual Household Income

Annual Household Income (Million)	Persons with Disability	Persons without Disability	Total
Upto 0.5	74 (67.3) (72.5)	36 (32.7) (37.1)	110 (100) (55.3)
0.501–1	12 (30.8) (11.8)	27 (69.2) (27.8)	39 (100) (19.6)
1.001–2.5	2 (18.2) (2)	9 (81.8) (9.3)	11 (100) (5.5)
2.501–5	—	2 (100) (2.1)	2 (100) (1)
10	—	2 (100) (2.1)	2 (100) (1)
Not mentioned	14 (40) (13.7)	21 (60) (21.6)	35 (100) (17.6)
Total	102 (51.3) (100)	97 (48.7) (100)	199 (100) (100)

Source: Field Survey.

Table 10.7
Educational Qualification of Parents of the Respondents

Educational Qualification of Parents	Persons with Disability	Persons without Disability	Total
Father			
Illiterate	18 (56.3) (17.6)	14 (43.8) (14.4)	32 (100) (16.1)
Below graduation	49 (57) (48)	37 (43) (38.1)	86 (100) (43.2)
Graduation	21 (51.2) (20.6)	20 (48.8) (20.6)	41 (100) (20.6)
Post-graduation	11 (40.7) (10.8)	16 (59.3) (16.5)	27 (100) (13.6)
Above post-graduation	2 (20) (2)	8 (80) (8.2)	10 (100) (5)
BTech (Technical)	1 (33.3) (1)	2 (66.7) (2.1)	3 (100) (1.5)
Total	102 (51.3) (100)	97 (48.7) (100)	199 (100) (100)

Educational Qualification of Parents	Persons with Disability	Persons without Disability	Total
Mother			
Illiterate	34 (65.4)	18 (34.6)	52 (100)
	(33.3)	(19.1)	(26.5)
Below graduation	52 (54.7)	43 (45.3)	95 (100)
	(51)	(45.7)	(48.5)
Graduation	14 (40)	21 (60)	35 (100)
	(13.7)	(22.3)	(17.9)
Post-graduation	2 (18.2)	9 (81.8)	11 (100)
	(2)	(9.6)	(5.6)
Above post-graduation	—	3 (100)	3 (100)
		(3.2)	(1.5)
Total	102 (52)	94 (48)	196 (100)
	(100)	(100)	(100)

Source: Field Survey.

rhymes. The stigma attached to disability in general and psycho-social illnesses are well documented (Ghai 2002; Hans and Patri 2003; Siperstein et al. n.d.). Within disability studies literature, the celebration of achievers such as those of Stephen Hawkins has been highlighted (Wendell 1989).

In this section, we present responses from all the respondents to the question: 'What image first comes to your mind when you hear the word "disability"? (You could draw from your personal experiences, images, third-party accounts, media and so on.)' The responses have been grouped and presented to give an idea of the continuities, divergences, problems and dilemmas in the perception of disability by both PWDs and ND in HE. Since this is a space that sees a shared use of physical spaces and knowledge resources, perceptions and images speak about the source and form that barriers and inclusion might take.

The images evoked by PWDs were of barriers, labelling disrespect, stigma, discrimination, lack of opportunities, the difficulties in rural as distinct from urban settings and a hostile environment. The focus is on 'ability' and difference rather than 'enabling conditions'. This calls to mind a conversation between university researchers and the learning disabled in the UK:

People have negative attitudes because they don't think we are the same as them, they don't think we can keep up with them.... It's about people calling us, we get it when we go on buses, we get it when we go on the streets, in the pubs, cinemas and restaurants, in shops and from work colleagues. (Docherty et al. [1997] 2010, 436)

Recognising the continuities between segregation and isolation in the public domain and barriers in HE is extremely important in order to move towards inclusion and the dismantling of foundational exclusions.

The responses of ND respondents are set apart from those of PWD respondents primarily by the paucity of language and poor comprehension of the problem of disability. The images therefore are stark, individualised and segregatory—from beggars with crutches to movies with disabled protagonists or people in need of

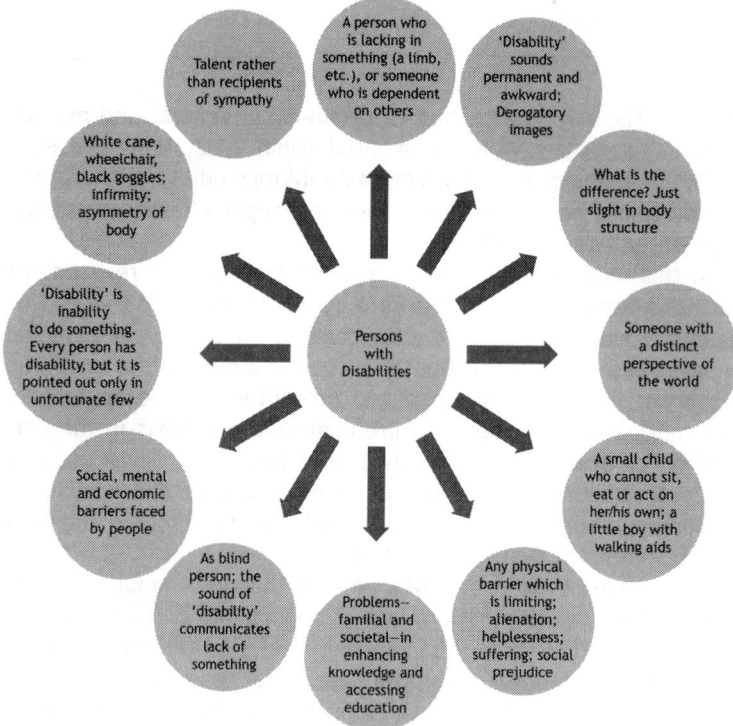

Figure 10.1
Images of Disability (Persons with Disabilities)
Source: Prepared by authors.

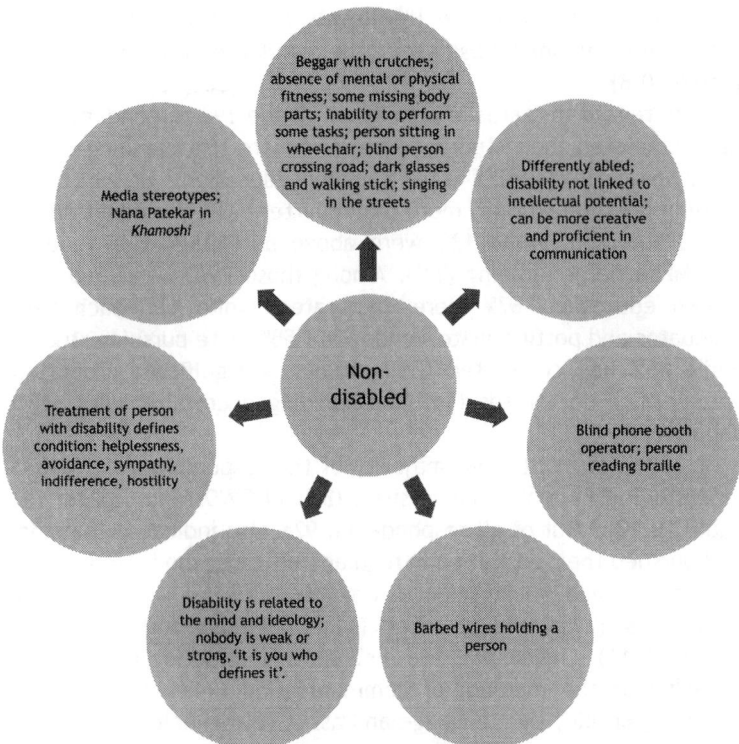

Figure 10.2
Images of Disability (Non-disabled)
Source: Prepared by authors.

help to 'catch up'. This is a grim reminder that 'it's the rest of society that should be educated, we [the disabled] should be educating society' (Docherty et al. [1997] 2010, 436).

INSTITUTION OF STUDY AND NEGOTIATING THE PERIOD OF STUDY

Of the 199 respondents, 66% (131) were students followed by 27% faculty (54) and 4% each (7) were staff/administrators and independent scholars/professionals. In the case of PWDs, 87% (89) were students while 8% (8) were faculty and 3% and 2% were staff/administrators and independent scholars/professionals respectively. This may be suggestive of the low levels of transition from HE to employment among PWDs despite the mandatory affirmative action (Table 10.8).

With regard to status of education, of the 199 respondents, 34% had completed their studies, while 66% were still pursuing education. Among PWDs, 77% were pursuing education,[1] of which 33% were in doctoral studies, more than quarter each in graduation and post-graduation, while 13% were above post-graduation (courses like MPhil before joining PhD). Among those PWDs who had completed education, 67% were doctorates, while 17% each were graduates and postgraduate. Among ND, 55% were pursuing studies, while 45% had completed their studies. A significant proportion were either doctorates (68%) or pursuing doctoral studies (47%; Table 10.9).

In terms of institution, majority of the respondents were studying/studied in central universities (89% of PWDs and 55% for ND; Table 10.10).[2] Out of all respondents, 92% also indicated that they had pursued their education in regular (full-time) mode. In terms of subjects studied, social sciences was a favourite (43%), followed by humanities (29%) and sciences (11%) between both categories (Table 10.11). English was the medium of instruction (91%), while speech was the medium of communication (94%) with only 6% reporting Braille, sign language and assistive technologies.

Choice of the institution, it clearly emerged from the findings of the survey, depended on social network. Majority of the respondents indicated they came to know of the institution of study from family, friends and peers. Teachers also played an important role in referring them to the institution of higher learning. Application forms had been increasingly accessed through the Internet, unlike print media (often newspapers) in earlier days.

In terms of access at the time of entry (with respect to application and entrance), several concerns were raised by both PWDs and ND. It clearly emerged from the responses of the former that physical and attitudinal barriers were cause of anxiety. Some of these were

---

[1] The discrepancy in percentage between current affiliation and status of education is due to the reporting of faculty respondents who have reported continuing education.

[2] Even though the survey was conducted in central universities, the respondents covered included faculty and staff in addition to the students. In addition, the online survey and the survey among the participants of the refresher course were not limited only to central universities. Hence, diverse institutions of study are reported other than central universities.

Table 10.8
Respondents by Age and Current Affiliation

Current Affiliation	Age Group						
	Below 20	20–29	30–39	40–49	50–59	Above 70	Total
Persons with Disability							
Student	9 (10.1) (100)	70 (78.7) (97.2)	9 (10.1) (60)	—	—	1 (1.1) (100)	89 (100) (87.3)
Faculty	—	1 (12.5) (1.4)	4 (50) (26.7)	2 (25) (50)	1 (12.5) (100)	—	8 (100) (7.8)
Staff/administrator	—	1 (33.3) (1.4)	—	2 (66.7) (50)	—	—	3 (100) (2.9)
Independent scholar/professional	—	—	2 (100) (13.3)	—	—	—	2 (100) (2)
Total	9 (8.8) (100)	72 (70.6) (100)	15 (14.7) (100)	4 (3.9) (100)	1 (1) (100)	1 (1) (100)	102 (100) (100)
Persons without Disability							
Student	6 (14.3) (100)	35 (83.3) (87.5)	—	1 (2.4) (6.7)	—	—	42 (100) (43.3)
Faculty	—	3 (6.5) (7.5)	30 (65.2) (88.2)	11 (23.9) (73.3)	1 (2.2) (100)	1 (2.2) (100)	46 (100) (47.4)
Staff/administrator	—	—	2 (50) (5.9)	2 (50) (13.3)	—	—	4 (100) (4.1)
Independent scholar/professional	—	2 (40) (5)	2 (40) (5.9)	1 (20) (6.7)	—	—	5 (100) (5.2)
Total	6 (6.2) (100)	40 (41.2) (100)	34 (35.1) (100)	15 (15.5) (100)	1 (1) (100)	1 (1) (100)	97 (100) (100)

Source: Field Survey.

Table 10.9

Educational Qualification and Status of Education of Respondents

Educational Qualification	Status of Education		Total
	Completed	Studying	
Persons with Disability			
Graduation	4 (15.4)	22 (84.6)	26 (100)
	(16.7)	(28.2)	(25.5)
Post-graduation	4 (16.7)	20 (83.3)	24 (100)
	(16.7)	(25.6)	(23.5)
Above post-graduation	—	10 (100)	10 (100)
		(12.8)	(9.8)
PhD	16 (38.1)	26 (61.9)	42 (100)
	(66.7)	(33.3)	(41.2)
Total	24 (23.5)	78 (76.5)	102 (100)
	(100)	(100)	(100)
Persons without Disability			
Graduation	1 (9.1)	10 (90.9)	11 (100)
	(2.3)	(18.9)	(11.3)
Post-graduation	7 (41.2)	10 (58.8)	17 (100)
	(15.9)	(18.9)	(17.5)
Above post-graduation	6 (42.9)	8 (57.1)	14 (100)
	(13.6)	(15.1)	(14.4)
PhD	30 (54.5)	25 (45.5)	55 (100)
	(68.2)	(47.2)	(56.7)
Total	44 (45.4)	53 (54.6)	97 (100)
	(100)	(100)	(100)

Source: Field Survey.

Table 10.10

Respondents by Type of Institution of Study

Type of Institution of Study	Persons with Disability	Persons without Disability	Total
Central university	91 (63.2)	53 (36.8)	144 (100)
	(89.2)	(54.6)	(72.4)
State university	9 (34.6)	17 (65.4)	26 (100)
	(8.8)	(17.5)	(13.1)
Research institute (ICAR, ICSSR, so on)	—	3 (100)	3 (100)
		(3.1)	(1.5)
Government college (affiliated to Recognised Universities)	—	4 (100)	4 (100)
		(4.1)	(2)

Type of Institution of Study	Persons with Disability	Persons without Disability	Total
Private college (aided affiliated to Recognised Universities	2 (11.8) (2)	15 (88.2) (15.5)	17 (100) (8.5)
Private college (unaided affiliated to Recognised University	—	1 (100) (1)	1 (100) (0.5)
Deemed university	—	1 (100) (1)	1 (100) (0.5)
International university	—	3 (100) (3.1)	3 (100) (1.5)
Total	102 (51.3) (100)	97 (48.7) (100)	199 (100) (100)

Source: Field Survey.

Table 10.11
Respondents by Subjects of Study

Subjects of Study	Person with Disability	Persons without Disability	Total
Humanities	24 (42.1) (23.5)	33 (57.9) (34)	57 (100) (28.6)
Social sciences	43 (50) (42.2)	43 (50) (44.3)	86 (100) (43.2)
Science	14 (63.6) (13.7)	8 (36.4) (8.2)	22 (100) (11.1)
Disability studies	3 (75) (2.9)	1 (25) (1)	4 (100) (2)
Commerce	3 (75) (2.9)	1 (25) (1)	4 (100) (2)
Education	8 (66.7) (7.8)	4 (33.3) (4.1)	12 (100) (6)
Others	2 (66.7) (2)	1 (33.3) (1)	3 (100) (1.5)
Not mentioned	5 (45.5) (4.9)	6 (54.5) (6.2)	11 (100) (5.5)
Total	102 (51.3) (100)	97 (48.7) (100)	199 (100) (100)

Source: Field Survey.

inaccessible applications (by screen reader); compartmentalising PWDs in streams such as arts and language; discriminatory attitudes of the invigilator at the entrance test; lack of clear-cut standing instructions with regard to use of scribes; non-payment of scribes by the authority; poor proficiency of scribes provided (lack of good written skills); unavailability of question paper in Braille or disallowing use of computers during entrance examinations; inaccessible infrastructure at the time of entrance (such as absence of transport facilities to the centre, accessible wash rooms, properly maintained wheelchairs); and so on. On the other hand, the concerns raised by ND focused on preparation for the entrance, availability for accommodation and so on. On the whole, they reported that the process of entry was smooth, while most of them did not notice any special provisions for PWDs though some reported the provision of scribes for the visually impaired and oral examination of PWDs whose responses were audio recorded.

In terms of experience at the time of interview too, PWDs recounted episodes of discrimination, fear of stigma, attitudinal barriers and lack of accommodations with respect to stay and travel. One of the respondents pointed out that he was embarrassed by questions by interviewers on his disability and capability. In the case of ND, the major experiences with respect to interview concerned logistical issues and common problems such as nervousness, levels of confidence and so on.

With respect to admission process, both PWDs and ND mentioned that unlike earlier days, notification on website of the university or email notification along with postal intimation remained the major source of confirmation of admission. Although one-third each of both PWDs and ND felt that the process of admission was easy and comfortable, 19% of PWDs and 16% of ND respectively highlighted that the process of admission was hectic, lengthy and bureaucratic. However, PWDs clearly indicated that they could navigate the admission process due to help from friends, peers, faculty and staff.

The major recommendation, however, was to have a single-window admission facility (already in place in many universities in recent times). It was clearly pointed out that most of the times the campuses are vast and students (who are new to the campus) are made to run around from one location to another and then also made to wait for hostel accommodation, given the limited resources.

In terms of institutional support, in India, after the introduction of the Persons with Disabilities Act 1995, University Grants Commission (UGC), under the 9th Five Year Plan guidelines, introduced several

Table 10.12
Respondents Who Are Aware About Institutional Support Mechanism

Institutional Support	Persons with Disability	Persons without Disability	Total
Student counselling cell	23 (42.6)	31 (57.4)	54 (100)
Equal opportunity cell	47 (59.5)	32 (40.5)	79 (100)
Disability cell	21 (53.8)	18 (46.2)	39 (100)
Committee against sexual harassment	38 (41.8)	53 (58.2)	91 (100)

Source: Field Survey.

initiatives for the PWDs.[3] Despite this, the responses to the institutional support available to PWDs were far from encouraging (Table 10.12). Only 39 out of 199 respondents (38%) were aware about the establishment of a disability cell. Among 102 PWDs, only 21 were apprised of the setting up of a disability cell. Even in the case of the formation of other mandatory committees, the awareness was very low. Among those who were aware of a disability cell, less than 20% were aware about its structure and modalities of functioning.

Disclosure about disability in the case of the PWD respondents did not raise much concern. Of them, 89% reported disclosure to the institution of study with majority (93%) disclosing it at the time of admission. As mentioned earlier, benchmark disabilities (40% or above) are required to access quota in education and employment while the entire process of certification is riddled with problems of 'medicalisation'. The demand by PWDs for the removal of benchmark disabilities in education is located in this context.

CURRICULUM AND ASSESSMENT

Less than a quarter of respondents (24%) indicated that curricula in their courses discussed disability (Table 10.13). This observation is not very encouraging keeping in view the fact that more than 70% of our respondents belonged to humanities and social sciences

[3] These include Teacher Preparation in Special Education (TEPSE), Higher Education for Persons with Special Needs (HEPSN) and visually handicapped teachers (UGC 2008).

Table 10.13
Respondents Who Indicated Disability as Part of Curricula

Disability as a Part of Curricula	Persons with Disability	Persons without Disability	Total
Yes	25 (53.2)	22 (46.8)	47 (100)
	(24.5)	(22.7)	(23.6)
No	77 (50.7)	75 (49.3)	152 (100)
	(75.5)	(77.3)	(76.4)
Total	102 (51.3)	97 (48.7)	199 (100)
	(100)	(100)	(100)

Source: Field Survey.

streams. Most of those who reported inclusion of disability in curricula were engaged in disability studies or as faculty with an interest in the field had included courses on disability. One of the respondents mentioned that exposure was to 'social disability' than 'physical disability', while others mentioned 'social stratification' and 'sociology of marginalised communities'—but no mention of disability as such; disability figured on the other hand in 'barriers to communication' in the course on communication skills in English. Students of psychology also mentioned that 'disability' was part of their curriculum. In classroom discussion, the respondents however indicated that infrastructural accessibility was discussed. One of the engineering students indicated that 'for any kind of project in engineering, first of all they were taught to focus on the sensitive part of the society, that is, children, old and disabled'. Some of the faculty especially from literature stream pointed out that they had used a disability perspective in interpreting literary texts, while special provisions were made for evaluation and assessment of students with disabilities. In general, the perspective was that social science, humanities and psychology curricula partly dealt with disability in their courses. Even then, the focus was very little or limited to electives or exclusively dealt within specialised centres like 'Centre for Disability Studies and Action'.

The traditional approach of assignments (book reviews, term papers), presentations and examinations were the major modes of assessment and evaluation across PWDs and ND. With respect to barriers they encounter in the process of evaluation, the major concern was the availability and proficiency of the scribe. Many of them reported that it was difficult to find a scribe, and sometimes the illegible handwriting and slow pace of writing of the scribe led to low scoring. In addition, PWDs pointed out that undertaking fieldwork was problematic with physical barriers, not to mention the inaccessible places even within the university like hostels with no lifts. Lack of accessible study materials (in Braille or inadequate assistive devices), submission of lengthy term papers and presentations in power point were also the major barriers pointed out. One of the respondents remarked regarding term papers, 'Reading and analysing a whole book within a short period of time is a barrier, while with respect to presentations it was hard to gain attention of audience'. Hostile attitudes of teachers were also reported.

Suggestions for disability-inclusive assessment included inclusive, accessible and democratic classroom; no discrimination based on disability; flexible arrangements of evaluation; use of assistive technologies in examination; extra time during examination; sensitive towards disability concerns and training for teachers to deal with disabled students.

Emphasis on creation of disability committee consisting of disabled students and staff were also focused upon in creating an inclusive curriculum, evaluation and assessment for the disabled in the realm of HE. The variation within the realm of disability was also highlighted by one of the respondents:

The sector of disability in itself is unevenly distributed, disharmonised and disunited. Very few are fortunate to grab opportunities of empowerment and inclusion. The focus therefore can also be to detect how many still need rehabilitation and empowerment in the nooks and corners of the country as a part of research.

ATTITUDINAL BARRIERS

The attitudes of faculty, staff and peers were elicited through the survey. Both disabled and ND pointed out friendly attitudes of faculty, peers and staff, though 'patronising and indifferent attitudes cannot be denied'. The responses pointed out that majority of them were unaware of disability and related issues and 'equated disability with inability and disease' and this 'lack of awareness resulted either in ignorance or in glorification'. Or 'I have heard of a story where a person was asked why that person was using a ladies toilet, given that she did not look like a woman'. Moreover, 'attitude towards people with disability can be a mixture of sympathy, friendliness and patronising'. In other instances, even when faculty, staff and peers were friendly and helpful, a poignant statement by one of the respondents (who had overcome psychosocial disability) pointed to the larger problem of the invisibilisation of psychosocial and intellectual disabilities in HE—a fact that is also reflected in the very low participation of persons from this group in the survey:

> *I practically 'went missing' in the course of my first break-down—and nobody knew, nor paid heed. It did not matter to any that a classmate of theirs was gone ... till date. I was to graduate in 1993; I did a year later, as an ex-student. My college was one of the key reasons for my alienation from life around and it stayed that way forever.*

PHYSICAL BARRIERS

Studies in India (Mehrotra 2013; Rungta 2004) indicate that the existence of physical barriers in India makes buildings and facilities inaccessible or not easily accessible. Access to and barriers encountered in negotiating physical environment were thus explored in the study.

Physical access in terms of availability of several indicators such as lifts, ramps, space mobility, seating and so on (see Table 10.14) was posed and the PWDs were requested to rank the level of convenience of use in a scale of 0 to 10 for each indicator. Low levels of availability can be discerned in the case of availability of manual assistance (15%) as well as assistive devices/services in waiting areas (11%). Only one quarter indicated that they had access to parking lot. In terms of availability of space for mobility in classroom/workspace, accessible toilets at campus residence/hostels as well as access to library and places of residence, majority of them (70% and above) responded in the affirmative. Around 60% also responded that ramps, staircase with railings and accessible toilets near classrooms were available. In addition, approximately 50% also indicated the availability of comfortable access to dining space/canteen (56%), lifts (54%) and public transport (48%). Interestingly, across the indicators of physical access, the mean scores of convenience level (those who replied in the affirmative in a scale of 0 to 10) ranged from 4.7 to 6.2. This clearly indicates that despite the availability of physical access, the convenience of use was not very high.

Table 10.14

Physical Access for Persons with Disabilities: Availability and Level of Convenience

Particulars of Physical Access	% of Respondents Who Reported in the Affirmative	Mean Scores of Convenience Level
Comfortable seating	75.5	6.2
Comfortable access to library and other amenities	74.5	6
Space for mobility in the classroom/office/cabin/ workspace	73.5	6
Availability of accessible toilets at campus residence/ hostels	71.6	6.1
Comfortable access to campus residence and hostels	71.6	5.3
Availability of ramps	65.7	5.2
Availability of accessible toilets near classrooms	60.8	5.9
Availability of staircase with railings	59.8	6
Comfortable access to dining space/canteen	55.9	5.1
Availability of lifts	53.9	5.7
Accessibility to public transport	52	5
Availability of waiting areas of public transport	48	4.9
Accessibility to parking slot	23.5	5.3
Availability of manual assistance such as drivers, interpreters, personal assistance	14.7	4.7
Assistive devices/services in waiting areas	10.8	5.6

Source: Field Survey.

TRANSITION FROM SCHOOL TO HE

Literature clearly indicates that transition from school to HE is crucial—the experiences at school and expectations from college are closely related. The experiences and expectations of students from special schools and general schools might vary. In this context, the navigation and negotiation of communication, and their encounters with disability during school was probed in the survey.

An important factor which facilitates transition from school to HE is the availability of finances. Of the total respondents, 52% had financial support in the form of scholarship or fee waiver to pursue their HE. Interestingly, among PWDs, 61% had financial support to pursue HE, while in the case of ND it stood at 43%. The forms of financial assistance varied from Junior/Senior Research fellowships (UGC-JRF/SRF) to Rajiv Gandhi National Fellowship (RGNF), Merit-cum-Means scholarships, Escort allowances for locomotor disabled (₹2,000 per month), GATE scholarships, Social welfare fellowships, university-level scholarships (₹3,000–5,000 per month) and so on. Fee waiver along with RGNF was also reported by some of the students.

PWDs who had studied in special schools recounted high levels of comfort of sharing space with peers, although there were also anecdotes of discrimination interspersed with narratives of inclusivity. Experiences of discrimination also intersected with other forms of marginalisation:

> I had a very depressing experience both being disabled and being a person from lower caste. I hardly remember people calling me by my name during my school as they used to call me either with the impairment I have or with my caste.

Notions of shame, limitations and sympathy were also expressed by PWDs; lack of proper infrastructure and teacher training at the school level were also highlighted by PWDs—it ranged from the 'unavailability of scribe in school exams' and 'inaccessible study material, curriculum and school environment' to the struggle of parents to get their children admitted in general school rather than special education. One of the respondents clearly pointed out that the transition from blind school (until 12th) to that of regular college was difficult. There were also experiences of inclusivity recounted by students with disabilities who had studied in general schools.

For ND respondents, their encounter with disability in school was very limited. Some of them pointed out that there was segregation of disabled students into separate sections. They were later assimilated with rest of the sections as they progressed into high school. The lack of physical infrastructure figures in the narratives of ND respondents as well. From their early encounters with disability, they gained some understanding of inequality and the difficulties some people go through: 'disability at school is always dealt with indifference or sympathy but no empathy. People will speak kind words but no facilities are provided'. And there are accounts of personal affection.

It is clear from the above discussion that the disabled and ND had varied accounts about their encounter with disability at school. While special education or segregation at school level creates an atmosphere of comfort and special attention, the ND are completely excluded from interacting with the disabled and vice versa. This leads us to acknowledge that assistive technologies, sign language, Braille should be part of general education in order to promote diversity at the school level itself.

CONCLUSION

The discrimination and alienation that PWDs face in access to and negotiation during HE is evident from the discussion above. The most evident exclusion has been the lack of database on disabled and their presence in HE. Disability services in centres of higher learning have been catalyst to navigating access in HE. The status of such services has been found to be severely lacking or inefficient as evident from the study.

Transition from school to HE also depends on strong social networks, which includes support from family, friends and teachers along with availability of financial assistance for HE. Attitudinal barriers—indifference, lack of awareness among peers and faculty to engage with persons with disability, 'othering' language—remain matters of concern along with inaccessible physical environment. The curriculum and evaluation was also not inclusive of disability concerns except in the instances of specialised higher learning such as doctoral studies in the field of disability studies. In the general curricula, despite having a significant number of students and faculty from social science stream, responses show that there was hardly any discussion on disability.

Methods of evaluation and assessment too were conventional without taking into cognisance the inclusive needs of disabled. Lack of assistive technologies coupled with inability of teaching community to effectively engage with and accommodate the needs of disabled without prejudice erects barriers for integration into HE for the disabled. In this context, it is also important to note that nature of disability in itself is diverse and hence inclusive modes also need to be varied in order to bring out constructive outcomes. While special education schools would be better equipped to train PWDs, it is equally important that special education be part of general education to promote inclusivity and recognise diversity.

Moving from the specific observations that emerge from the survey to the general concerns this study flags, we would like to return to our opening observation in this chapter that economic reforms have seen the shrinking of HE to a private good that might or might not have positive externalities for those who are outside the circle of opportunity. This is also a time when there has been a marked withdrawal of programmes in the social sciences, humanities and in general liberal arts in undergraduate institutions accompanied by an onslaught on critical social sciences and humanities within the university system as a whole. This is part of a shift to a techno-cratic, vocational, skill-building mode and to statist discourses that centre on employability rather than on intellectual engagement and knowledge production. Better facilities and teaching translate immediately into information and communication technology (ICT) rather than books and teacher training/continuing education for teachers, and better performance is judged by grades in objective tests rather than the honing of deep learning abilities.

In this larger scenario, we have seen in the survey that PWDs opt in far greater numbers for the social sciences and humanities and are even actively discouraged from opting for careers in science. Central to the problems they face within university systems are problems related to teaching, evaluation and assessments. The impossibility of the time-bound, inflexible examination mode puts students with disabilities at a double disadvantage. They become passive recipients of an adverse judgement of merit in a delegitimised learning space. This, along with attitudinal barriers, inaccessible campus spaces and low transition from education to employment is signpost of cumulative disadvantage that can be tracked quite clearly.

There has not yet been an internalisation of disability-centred perspectives in the decision-making echelons of universities in India. The non-negotiability of questions related to access and inclusion, and the need to look at the ubiquity of barriers rather than the person with disabilities as the problem therefore, remains poorly understood.

The focus by institutional spaces on medical certification as the basis for recognition of disability individualises the problem of disability and restricts it to the medical definition of 'impairment'. Yet, academic spaces offer us immense possibilities of comprehending 'the multiple, overlapping sites in which disability is produced and perpetuated' (Davidson [1997] 2010, 135). Thinking of disability as located in societal barriers rather than in individuals will force a consideration of disability as an issue of social justice for which the remedy will involve a synthesis of recognition, redistribution and reorganisation of material resources. Education, especially HE, holds the key to this synthesis.

ACKNOWLEDGEMENTS

We are grateful to V.J. Jithin (Central University of Punjab), N.K. Renoj (Jawharlal Nehru University, Delhi, and Delhi University), Md Israr Alam (MANUU), Vinod Sen (Central University, Gujarat) and Shree Deepa (University of Hyderabad) for administering the survey for us, and to P. Kumar (Council for Social Development [CSD]) for support with data entry and tabulations.

REFERENCES

Abu-Hamour, Bashir. 2013. 'Faculty Attitudes towards Students with Disabilities in a Public University in Jordan'. *International Education Studies* 6 (12): 74–81.

Al-Hmouz, Hannan. 2014. 'Experience of Students with Disabilities in a Public University in Jordan'. *International Journal of Special Education* 29 (1): 1–8.

Baglieri, Susan, and Arthur Shapiro. 2012. *Disability Studies and the Inclusive Classroom. Critical Practices for Creating Least Restrictive Attitudes.* New York, NY, and London: Routledge.

Baker, Kerrie Q., Kathleen Boland, Christine M. Nowik, and Cedar Crest College. 2012. 'A Campus Survey of Faculty and Student Perceptions of Persons with Disabilities'. *Journal of Postsecondary Education and Disability* 25 (4): 309–29.

Beauchamp-Pryor, Karen. 2012. 'From Absent to Active Voices: Security Disability Equality within Higher Education'. *International Journal of Inclusive Education* 16 (3): 283–95.

Brewster, Stephanie. 2014. 'Disabled Students Perceptions of the Barriers and Enablers to Their Learning within the Institute of

Education'. Available at: http://www.wlv.ac.uk/media/depart
ments/faculty-of-health-education-and-wellbeing/documents/sed-
res-disabledstused-report.pdf

Cook, Lysandra, Philip D. Rumrill, and Melody Tankersley. 2009.
'Priorities and Understanding of Faculty Members Regarding College
Students with Disabilities'. *International Journal of Teaching and
Learning in Higher Education* 21 (1): 84–96.

Davidson, Michael. (1997) 2010. 'Universal Design: The Work of
Disability in an Age of Globalisation'. In *The Disability Studies
Reader*, edited by Lennard J. Davis, 133–46. New York, NY, and
London: Routledge.

Docherty, Daniel, Richard Hughes, and Patricia Philip. [1997] 2010.
'This is What We Think'. In *The Disability Studies Reader*, edited by
Lennard J. Davis, 432–40. New York, NY, and London: Routledge.

Ghai, Anita. 2002. 'Disabled Women: An Excluded Agenda of Indian
Feminism'. *Hypatia*, Feminism and Disability, Part 2 (Summer) 17
(3): 49–66.

Hanafin, Joan, Michael Shevlin, Mairin Kenny, and Eileen McNeela.
2007. 'Including Young People with Disabilities: Assessment
Challenges in Higher Education'. *Higher Education* 54 (3): 435–48.

Hans, Asha, and Annie Patri, eds. 2003. *Women, Disability and Identity*.
New Delhi: SAGE.

Holloway, Sarah. 2001. 'The Experience of Higher Education from the
Perspective of Disabled Students'. *Disability and Society* 16 (4):
597–15.

Hopkins, Laurence. 2011. 'The Path of Least Resistance: A Voice-
relational Analysis of Disabled Students' Experiences of Discrimination
in English Universities'. *International Journal of Inclusive Education*
15 (7): 711–27.

Madriaga, Manuel, Katie Hanson, Helen Kay, and Ann Walker. 2011.
'Marking-out Normalcy and Disability in Higher Education'. *British
Journal of Sociology of Education* 32 (6): 901–20.

Matshedisho, Knowledge R. 2007. 'Access to Higher Education for
Disabled Students in South Africa: A Contradictory Conjuncture of
Benevolence, Rights and the Social Model of Disability'. *Disability
and Society* 22 (7): 685–99.

Mehrotra, Nilika. 2013. 'Disability, Gender and Caste Intersections in
Indian Economy'. In *Disability and Intersecting Statuses*, edited
by Sharon N. Barnartt and Barbara M. Altman. Vol. 7, Research in
Social Science and Disability, 295–394. UK: Emerald Group Publishing
Limited.

Moswela, Emmanual, and Saurav Mukhopadhyay. 2011. 'Asking for Too
Much? The Voice of Students with Disabilities in Botswana'. *Disability
and Society* 26 (3): 307–19.

Nussbaum, Martha. 2006. *Frontiers of Justice: Disability, Nationality,
Species Membership*. New Delhi: Oxford University Press.

Rungta S.K. 2004. 'Training and Employment of People with Disabilities: India 2002.' Geneva: International Labour Office. Available at: http://digitalcommons.ilr.cornell.edu/cgi/viewcontent.cgi?article= 1470&context=gladnetcollect

Siperstein, Gary N., Keerthi Sugumaran, Jennifer Norins Bardon, and Robin C. Parker. n.d. *Attitudes of the Public in India towards People with Intellectual Disabilities*. Boston: University of Massachusetts. Available at: http://media.specialolympics.org/soi/files/healthy-athletes/Research Studies/India_FullReport.pdf

Tinklin, Teresa, and John Hall. 1999. 'Getting Round Obstacles: Disabled Students' Experiences in Higher Education in Scotland'. *Studies in Higher Education* 24 (2): 183–94.

UGC (University Grants Commission). 2008. 'Guidelines for General Development Assistance to Central, Deemed and State Universities during XI Plan'. Available at: http://www.ugc.ac.in/oldpdf/xiplan pdf/universitesdevelopmentassitenceoctober.pdf

Wehman, Paul. 2006. *Life beyond the Classroom: Transition Strategies for Young People with Disabilities*. Baltimore, MD: Paul Brookes.

Wendell, Susan. 1989. 'Towards a Feminist Theory of Disability'. *Hypatia* 4 (2): 104–24.

PART III

EQUITY IN OUTCOMES

11

Equity and Excellence: A Study of Jawahar Navodaya Vidyalaya

Madhusoodanan J., Nidhi S. Sabharwal and C.M. Malish

INTRODUCTION

Education is an important source of opportunities for all while it is the origin and, perhaps, the only source of opportunity for children born and living in disadvantaged circumstances. The opportunity gaps in education in the present translate into disparities in income and social well-being of tomorrow. While opportunities at the entry level are exacerbated by wealth disparities, disparities at the outcome level depend on the individual responsiveness to institutional efforts and initiatives. Public policies and institutional initiatives to promote equity and excellence in education attempt to mitigate disadvantages at birth, sustain the strengths that each child brings in and promote engaging and supportive means for children to achieve levels equal to societal expectations. Providing challenging and rich learning opportunities to children from diverse and disadvantaged background will have a profound positive impact on their lives and on the destiny of nations. The public interventions may imply creating effective schools—competent teachers, effective teaching practices, engaging students in classrooms, supportive leadership and active community involvement. In other words, equity in excellence requires ceaseless efforts to impart education and monitor progress.

The educational policies in India have emphasised equality of opportunities in access to education. The quantitative expansion of the system is a result of this policy. The efforts to expand the system were not always totally supported by programmes to improve quality. The programmes related to school construction, pre-service teacher training and curriculum revision were in a sense directed towards achieving quality in an expanding system. The committees and commissions on higher education seem to have believed in counter-posing quality and quantity. The belief was that an expansion of the system will result in spreading thin the scarce resources and poor quality in provisions and of products.

Common to many countries, the policymakers in India have faced the challenge of achieving excellence along with equity. In general, quality education like any other service depends on available resources; it is, therefore, no surprise that this benefit has been a privilege for the wealthier classes. As J.P. Naik (1979, 56) noted, 'there is a close link between privilege in society and quality in education. It is not easy to break this link and it is even more difficult to break privilege itself'. The National Policy on Education, 1986, recognised the challenge of improving quality (excellence) while expanding access and still being able to achieve equity and social justice.

A close examination of programmes and policies to improve quality and achieve excellence in India shows that India followed a dual policy to address issues related to quality in school and higher education. The programmes stemming from the National Policy on Education, 1986, were comprehensive approach to improve quality system wide. The establishment of DIET (District Institute of Education and Training) to provide in-service and pre-service training, mass training programmes of school teachers, the operation blackboard to ensure quality infrastructural facilities and teaching learning conditions in the classrooms and specifying minimum levels of learning were massive efforts to promote quality across board.

The policy also introduced selective approach to develop excellence in education. The selective approach included creating schools of excellence with flexible admission policies to attract students from rural areas. The Jawahar Navodaya Vidyalayas (JNVs) programme of the Government of India has been one such selective approach to promote equity in excellence. In accordance with the National Policy on Education, 1986, pace-setting schools of excellence known as Navodaya schools were established with the intent to achieve quality education with equity and social justice.

The National Policy on Education, 1986, recommended setting up of the schools for the rural poor in every district of India, modelled similar to the elite private boarding schools. The JNVs were set up as pace-setting residential schools based on the theoretical approach that

[E]qual inputs need not always lead to equal outcomes in education. The idea of providing additional resources to students from

deprived groups is to equalize the conditions for competing and succeeding in the system. In fact, unequal inputs may be needed to achieve equity in educational outcomes' (Varghese 2011, 2–3).

JNVs are centrally funded schools and are considered to be the boldest-ever experiment in the field of secondary and senior secondary education in the country. The equity and social justice principle is achieved by focusing on the children of parents who are poor and children residing in underserved rural areas with reservation of seats for the scheduled castes (SCs), scheduled tribes (STs) and girls.

The JNV model is embedded in the approach that equity and excellence are not at odds. This model attempts to break the relationship between quality of education and privilege in society which is associated with one's location (rural/urban), wealth, caste and gender. The visible impact of excellence with equity in JNVs can be seen with the achievement of a consistently high pass percentage at class X, minimal inter-group differences in pass percentage, high transition rates of students moving on to higher education and a substantial number of students across socio-economic groups securing admissions to premier institutes such as IITs and National Institutes of Technology (NITs). Recent reports indicate that close to 95% of the class XII batch who appeared for the JEE (Main) in 2016 qualified the exam, securing admissions in the NITs. The success rate of qualifying these exams for the JNV students has been consistently high (in 2015, this rate was 89.4%) and far above the national average of 16.7% (Mukul 2016). Thus, the JNV model shows that a concerted public intervention can achieve simultaneous goals of excellence and equity in a systematic manner.

How do the JNVs achieve this difficult task of balancing equity with excellence even when the students background are diverse with majority from rural areas and families with less educated parents and lower income levels? This chapter will delve deeper into the processes institutionalised in JNVs that help students from the rural areas and disadvantaged groups to achieve higher levels of educational outcomes and make a successful transition from school to higher education.

We studied the model of JNVs both at the macro level and at the micro level by selecting one JNV located in a remote rural area of Maharashtra in order to understand how the principles of equity and excellence are achieved simultaneously within this model. At the macro level, we analysed the educational processes and educational outcomes of students of JNVs spread across 29 states in India.

The source of data is the Navodaya Vidyalaya Samiti (NVS) which collates and publishes the JNVs system-level data. Through an in-depth study of one JNV located in a rural area of Maharashtra, we attempted to develop a deeper understanding on how the simultaneous pursuits of equity and excellence are achieved in practice. The data are based on interviews with the principal, teachers and children of JNV, Jalna, Maharashtra. The first author of this chapter is the principal of this school.

The chapter is divided into six sections. In what follows, the authors describe the institutional processes embedded in JNVs to achieve equity and excellence. The second section provides a discussion on the admission policies of JNVs and their role in ensuring equality and equity. The resulting diversity in student composition with respect to their social and economic status, gender and place of residence is discussed in this section. The third section covers the institutionalised processes that enable a student's success and excellence and cover long-term planning; teaching-learning processes; remediation measures and the role of the principal. Academic excellence in terms of high level of performance at classes X and XII and transition rates to higher education across JNVs are discussed in the fourth section. The fifth section includes an in-depth analysis of the academic achievements of JNV, Jalna. The sixth section concludes the chapter.

PROCESSES AT THE SYSTEM LEVEL IN JNVs TO ACHIEVE EQUITY AND EXCELLENCE

As urban–rural educational disparity continued to exist after 40 years of Independence (rural 29.7%, urban 57.4%; Census of India 1981), JNVs were established to provide quality education to rural talents who may not have access to quality schools and lack social, cultural and economic resources to nurture their talents. The plan to set up one such *vidyalaya* (school) in each district was initiated during the 7th Five Year Plan period (1985–90). At present, there are 598 JNVs spread in 28 states except in Tamil Nadu and 7 union territories. JNVs are fully financed and administered by the Government of India through an autonomous organisation called NVS. Navodaya Vidyalayas select high achievers and gifted students and make highest quality of education available to them. The following section will describe the processes that have been institutionalised in JNVs to achieve equity and excellence.

Achievement of Equity

Among the centrally funded schools, JNVs have a unique character. JNVs are the only centrally funded schools which aim to provide focused attention for the education of children from rural areas. Except Ashram schools which aim to provide education mainly to tribal population, all other centrally funded schools are, in general, exclusive institutions. Most of the centrally funded schools cater education to selective clientele, although 25% reservation for economic weaker section is now operational. For instance, centrally funded Kendriya Vidyalas (KVs) and Army Schools, are for children of Central government employees and for children of defence personnel.

In JNVs, at least 75% of the seats in a district are filled by candidates selected from rural areas and remaining seats are filled from urban areas of the district. Reservation of seats in favour of children belonging to SCs and STs is provided in proportion to their population in the concerned district, provided that in no district, such reservation will be less than the national average (15% for SCs and 7.5% for STs) but subject to a maximum of 50% for both the categories taken together. These reservations are interchangeable between SCs and STs and over and above the candidates selected under open merit. One-third (33%) of the total seats are reserved for girls. There is a provision for reservation of 3% seats for disabled children of either sex.

Besides the above, it has to be noted that adequate weightage is given in selecting the candidates from SCs and STs and from girl students. In fact, lower qualifying marks are fixed in order to enable the candidates to qualify from the reserved categories and girls in comparison to the qualifying marks fixed for open categories. Thus, the equity and social justice principle is achieved by focusing on the children of parents who are poor and children residing in underserved rural areas with reservation of seats for the SCs, SCs and girls.

ADMISSION PROCESS

Admissions in JNVs are made through Jawahar Navodaya Vidyalaya Selection Test (JNVST) at class VI which is conducted by Central Board of Secondary Education (CBSE). The admission test encompasses reasoning/mental ability skills, mathematics and proficiency in language. The medium of language to write the exam is chosen by the child depending on the proficiency in the chosen language. The medium of instruction in class V determines the proficiency of the language of the child. Only the candidate from the district where JNV is located is eligible to apply for admission. A candidate who is appearing for the selection test must be studying in class V for the whole of the academic session. No candidate is eligible to appear in the selection test second time under any circumstances.

Thus, the JNVs net is spread very wide. The wide spread of JNV is through its focus on providing educational opportunity to children in class VI, a vulnerable age when there is high incidence of dropout in transition from class V to class VI. JNVs attract the talent at this vulnerable age and nurture this talent to ensure that all its children excel through their education horizon. That is upper primary, secondary and then higher secondary until they graduate from the school.

Every year, every JNV select about 80 most meritorious students. Once a child gets admitted in class VI, he/she gets complete education free of cost including free boarding and lodging, uniforms and textbooks for seven years or up to class XII. Some of the estimates (as given by JNV, Jalna) indicate that on an average, approximately, ₹1,900 per child per month is spent by the government. Even if this is an underestimate, the fact remains that JNVs are perhaps less expensive than some of the elite private schools where post-secondary educational experience of graduates are similar. The non-poor and general-category male students of classes IX–XII are charged ₹200 per month in welfare of vidyalayas called Vidyalaya Vikas Nidhi. No doubt, the expenditure spent on children can very well be justified on the ground that the children are largely pooled from rural masses and are able to shine like glittering stars in the sky in various walks of their life as they get seven years of sound education. The principle of equality among children at JNVs is further fostered by motivating students to imbibe values through providing equal opportunities in the residential system.

INSTITUTIONAL PRACTICES TO ACHIEVE EXCELLENCE

The organisation of academic activities at the institutional level varies substantially from other public institutions imparting instructions at the secondary level of schooling. There is a strong focus on academic and administrative planning, decentralised governance structures for effective management of the schools, parents' voice and participation in school management committees, comprehensive teaching–learning processes, remedial measures for those who are not performing well and an equal emphasis on co-curricular activities for an all-round development of the children. Fully residential and co-educational schools, JNVs are affiliated to CBSE with classes from VI to XII. The academic instructions are imparted using the three-language formula which further strengthens learning outcomes across JNVs. Modern techniques are used to impart high-quality education, while pedagogical strategies are implemented to create a stress-free environment in order to make learning a joyful experience. The insti-tutionalised processes are discussed in detail in this section.

ACADEMIC PLANNING

Perspective academic planning (PAP) is a comprehensive document prepared by NVS for every academic year. It details roles and respon-sibilities of all stakeholders and guidelines for each of the macro and micro activities pertinent to school functioning. It includes academic calendar with details of schedule of class tests, examinations and vacation, conduct of co-curricular activities, functioning of library and smart classrooms and information and communication technol-ogy (ICT) infrastructure to list a few. List of items required for each class and laboratories is given in details. PAP also mentions 14-point safety and security measures to be followed by each school to make sure that every students of JNVs can study in a safe and secured atmosphere. Each of JNVs has to adhere to guidelines provided in PAP, and deputy commissioners of NVS regional offices ensure that all schools follow guidelines.

While NVS and regional offices provide administrative and aca-demic leadership, management mechanism exists at school coordi-nate planning, management and monitoring at school level. At school level, JNVs follow systematic planning, management and monitoring strategies to accomplish their aim to nurture inclusive excellence. Under the guidance of NVS and its regional offices, JNVs follow par-ticipatory school management to achieve equity and excellence. Members of Vidyalaya Management Committee (VMC), principal, parents, teachers and community members work together to realise the goal of inclusive excellence. JNV executes various institutional mechanism and strategies for academic and administrative manage-ment for achieving equity. They are (a) Vidyalaya Management Committee; (b) institutional planning; (c) effective classroom man-agement; (d) remedial teaching and fostering communication skill

(e) continuous and comprehensive evaluation (CCE); (f) school resources and facilities and other activities.

Vidyalaya Management Committees

Various committees and sub-committees are functional for micro and macro school management in JNVs. VMC is the highest management and advisory body at school level. The chairman of the VMC is district collector cum magistrate of Jalna. In the absence of district collector, sub-divisional magistrate, in the capacity of the chairman's nominee, plays a vital role in the VMC. The committee meets regularly and discusses various issues pertinent to school functioning such as lifting water from river to address water shortage, installation of solar water panel and development of plantation in school premises.

Meetings are normally held in school premises itself. Since district collector or his/her nominee is chairing the committee, mobilising resources and sorting out administrative difficulties are easy. This enables the school to find out and resolve challenges pertinent to school functioning. Since it is a fully residential school where students and teachers stay together, JNVs requires continuous support from various state and Central government departments. Hence, effective functioning of VMC enables effective coordination between school and various government bodies. Purchase Advisory Committee (PAC), a sub-committee of VMC, assists and monitors the procedure of purchases made by the vidyalaya. Apart from VMC and PAC, strong presence of Parent Teacher Council (PTC) is the backbone of effective school management. PTC meets regularly and discusses and resolves academic and school development issues.

Decentralised Institutional Planning

JNVs follow decentralised institutional planning. It is a participatory school management process in which various stakeholders of school such as teachers, parents, students and community members are involved. Decentralised planning process starts every year before the commencement of the academic year. Various committees are formed to prepare plans for each areas such as academics, administration, infrastructure development and school–community engagement to list a few. Consolidation of recommendations and suggestions from each committee contribute to the preparation of an annual institutional plan. Keeping in mind broader objectives of the JNV system, the institutional plan makes sound assessment of felt needs, constraints, availability of resources and feedback from the stakeholders and puts forward targets to be achieved in the forthcoming academic year. It is a roadmap for means through which set targets can be achieved and which spells out roles and responsibilities of each stakeholder and evaluation and monitoring mechanisms. Since the institutional plan is prepared with active participation of stakeholders, they own the responsibility to achieve mutually shared and agreed upon objectives.

Effective Classroom Management

JNVs follow effective classroom management as a strategy to meet the academic targets set in the institutional plan. In order to facilitate effective learning, classroom transactions are made with adequate preparation by individual teachers. Campus accommodation provided to teachers helps them to budget adequate time for before-class academic preparation. Classroom sessions are planned according to learning requirements of diverse students so that attention is made to capture and sustain the interest of the students. Along with academic aspects, teachers gives due importance to discipline in the classroom.

Remedial Teaching and Fostering Communication Skill

Despite the effective classroom management, there can be students who are unable to cope with the academic work normally expected of their age groups. Therefore, JNVs provide remedial teaching for lower performers. Students who require additional learning inputs are identified well in advance at the very beginning of the academic year. Remedial teachings are arranged for those students in addition to normal classroom hours. Remedial instruction is arranged in a systematic manner according to the nature of the pupils' difficulties such as distraction and lack of concentration, inability to express ideas and also lack of motivation. Students are given motivational sessions and concerted effort is made to equip them to perform in par with their counterparts. The instructional content is very carefully developed keeping in mind the capacity and requirement of the students.

Given their inability to understand complex contents, sessions are arranged in such a way that complex concepts are taught after making them fully aware about basic concepts. Remedial work is given in small doses and it is so organised as to give a sense of achievement to the students. Since teachers can provide more individual attention during remedial sessions, students slowly develop a sense of self-confidence. Friendly, helpful and sympathetic attitude of teachers towards the students gradually lead to boosting confidence levels of students and hence learning outcome. JNVs recognise pivotal significance of communication skill and proficiency in English language. Therefore, JNVs provides opportunity for all to develop their communication skill. Students are provided training to develop both speaking and listening skills in English. Irrespective of their academic grades score, each student gets an opportunity to develop his/her language competency. This also helps to boost their confidence level.

Continuous and Comprehensive Evaluation

By following guidelines of CBSE on CCE, JNVs make continuous evaluation of students. An academic year is divided into two terms and CCE is done for each sessions. The CCE is intended to provide holistic profile of the learner through evaluation of both scholastic and co-scholastic areas spread over two terms in a year. Students according to their interest take part in various co-scholastic activities. Their participation and performance in each of co-scholastic activities are evaluated as part of CCE. This helps to nurture overall development of students and inculcate values of equity, fraternity and empathy.

Co-curricular and National Integration Activities

In order to make learning a joyful experience and inculcate academic rigour and secular values, JNVs have excellent academic and co-curricular infrastructure. JNVs have libraries with thousands of reference books, subject books, journals, newspapers and magazines. Students are encouraged to make use of them for academic purpose and developing general awareness about social, cultural and political atmosphere of the country. Co-curricular activities receive equal attention in JNVs.

Smart classrooms equipped with advanced technology promote interactive learning. They not only provide avenues to learn and experiment but also give scope for developing innovative and creative ideas. Exposure and experimentation with cutting-edge technology make them capable to face technological challenges they may confront in their future world of learning and earning.

Museum-cum-resource room also provides resources for learning. Recently, English language labs have been established with a purpose to bring definite improvement in the speaking/learning ability of children in English. The vidyalayas impart computer education to all students of classes VI–XII. They are also given e-mail and Internet facilities which in turn enable them to search for any material relevant to their study purpose and help them to do even online registrations for CET, JEE, AIPMT and other such competitive examinations.

JNVs organise sports activities at school, regional and national levels. Vidyalayas annual sports events provide opportunity for students to showcase their sports skills. Apart from regular coaching and sports activities at each JNV, special coaching camps are organised for sports such as football and cricket at school, regional and national levels. Some students also get the opportunity to play at the international level. For example, one of the students of JNV, Jalna, had participated in an international-level fencing competition called 'Thailand Open 2013' held in Bangkok in 2013.

JNVs celebrate both national and local festivals. It provides a flavour of unity in diversity. In order to uphold the tradition and culture of the society and secular values as well as to unfold the latent talents of the children, JNVs open a vista of opportunities where students compete in inter-house competitions. Students are also benefiting by art workshops organised by the schools.

In the wake of increased fractious tendencies and intolerance in several parts of the country, JNVs are committed to promote the communal harmony and strengthening fraternity and national integration. Keeping this marvellous concept in mind, the vidyalayas organise and observe various religious, cultural and community programmes and even visit villages to witness the real sufferings of the humankind. While celebrating diversity in terms of religion, culture and language, students are inculcated basic principles of secularism and respect for people and culture other than themselves.

The JNVs not only aim to provide high-quality education to the talented children, they also aim to materialise exceptional objectives like national integration through students' migration. Every year, 33% of students in class IX are shifted from Hindi-speaking JNVs to non-Hindi-speaking JNVs and vice versa. This helps students to understand and respect other cultures and through the inter-group interactions, they develop competency in a new language. For example, in the year 2015–16 JNV, Jalna, students were sent to JNV, Hamirpur, Himachal Pradesh, and JNV, Hamirpur, sent its students to JNV, Jalna.

Along with inside-school activities, JNVs recognise the role of school–society linkage. JNVs consider education process as a social process and every school has an ethical responsibility to engage with its social surrounding. JNVs thus collaborate with neighbouring schools like Kasturba Gandhi Balika Vidyalaya, Amba, and Zilla Parishad Prashala, Amba. Last but not the least, schools make meticulous effort to ensure students are given balanced and nutritious diet.

The Leadership

The principal, by virtue, as the leader of the institution, has to play the pivotal role by directing and monitoring the efforts of all stakeholders timely and to ensure that the process-driven action, coupled with strong desire to achieve excellence, will take us far ahead of our target. He/she should also develop integrated personality of the students under residential co-educational set-up of the vidyalaya, leading to character building through value orientation and ultimately developing students to be good human beings and an asset to our nation. He/she should also establish a 'brand name' for his/her vidyalaya by virtue of its activities in the field.

The activities where a JNV principal is directly involved can be classified into three types. Activities that monitor students' academic outcomes, activities that monitor students' co-curricular activities and activities that monitor the status of physical infrastructure that students access. The first type of activities which involves monitoring academic outcome includes conducting regular meetings with the class teachers, subject teachers and house masters to monitor students' academic success, observing academic records of subject teachers as per CCE and observing English department activities. Under the second type, the principal is directly involved in planning and overseeing co-curricular activities such as exhibition on maths and science students' projects. The principal is also involved in staff development. As an example, we have a list of activities that a principal of a JNV is engaged in. These activities pertain for two months of an academic session. These are provided in Table A11.1. These activities thus indicate that the principal aims to nurture and promote the talent and creativity of the students by providing the best opportunities and resources to make them more resourceful, innovative, creative, competitive, cooperative, collaborative, adaptive and productive members of ever-changing global society.

Excellence in Educational Outcome

At the time when JNVs were proposed, there was apprehension among academics that the JNV model will widen inequities in education (Nambissan and Batra 1989). We find, however, that socio-economic as well as gender inequity in educational outcomes within the JNV school system is minimal. The effectiveness and efficiency of the institutional processes discussed above are reflected in educational outcomes across JNVs. Moreover, the residential nature of JNV schools is also seen to have the potential to increase academic achievement of the children from the disadvantaged groups by changing their social and educational environment. Empirical studies in the USA (Curto and Fryer 2011) on impact of residential schools on academic achievement of the students from disadvantaged backgrounds show a positive causal relationship between residential schools and academic achievement. Curto and Fryer's study shows that attending such schools increases academic achievement per year of attendance. JNVs provide an education to students equivalent to the best residential school system irrespective of their family's socio-economic condition. We find that across JNVs, consistently (2010–14), close to 100% of the students qualify the class X exams with very small percentage, having to take improvement exams. Similarly, we find that across JNVs, 98% of the students graduate from class XII (Tables 11.1a–11.1d; NVS 2015). CBSE class XII results in 2016 also showed that JNVs are the best

Table 11.1a
CBSE Board Exam 2014: Class X

Region	Regd.	Appeared (Excluding Transfer)	Qual	Qual (%)	EIOP[a]	EIOP (%)	Transfer Case
Bhopal	6,345	6,343	6,334	99.86	9	0.14	1
Chandigarh	2,827	2,821	2,818	99.89	3	0.11	6
Hyderabad	5,388	5,388	5,384	99.93	4	0.07	0
Jaipur	3,893	3,887	3,882	99.87	5	0.13	6
Lucknow	5,195	5,186	5,172	99.73	14	0.27	1
Patna	4,374	4,365	4,356	99.79	9	0.21	1
Pune	3,795	3,795	3,791	99.89	4	0.11	0
Shillong	4,088	4,079	4,071	99.80	8	0.20	0
NVS	35,905	35,864	35,808	99.84	56	0.16	15

Source: NVS (2015).
Note: [a]Eligible for improvement of performance.

Table 11.1b
CBSE Board Exam 2014: Class XII

Region	Regd.	Appeared	Passed	Pass (%)	Compt.	Compt. (%)	Failed	Failed (%)	RW, NE RL, etc.	RW, NE RL, etc.(%)
Bhopal	5,019	4,996	4,911	98.30	74	1.48	11	0.22	0	0.
Chandigarh	2,336	2,323	2,284	98.32	36	1.55	3	0.13	0	0.
Hyderabad	3,255	3,248	3,231	99.48	14	0.43	3	0.09	0	0.
Jaipur	3,318	3,304	3,269	98.94	30	0.91	5	0.15	0	0.
Lucknow	4,746	4,686	4,547	97.03	102	2.18	25	0.53	12	0.26
Patna	2,910	2,885	2,784	96.50	87	3.02	14	0.49	0	0.
Pune	2,174	2,161	2,131	98.61	22	1.02	7	0.32	1	0.05
Shillong	2,953	2,913	2,706	92.89	142	4.87	31	1.06	34	1.17
NVS	**26,711**	**26,516**	**25,863**	**97.54**	**507**	**1.91**	**99**	**0.37**	**47**	**0.18**

Source: NVS (2015).
Note: RW - Result withheld, NE - Not Eligible, RL - Result Later.

Table 11.1c
CBSE Board Exam 2010: Class X

Region	Regd.	Appeared	Qual	Qual (%)	EIOP[a]	EIOP (%)	UFM	NE
Bhopal	5,420	5,388	5,309	98.53	79	1.47	0	0
Chandigarh	2,640	2,617	2,562	97.9	54	2.06	1	0
Hyderabad	5,179	5,169	5,164	99.9	5	0.1	0	0
Jaipur	3,359	3,342	3,297	98.65	45	1.35	0	0
Lucknow	4,680	4,640	4,589	98.9	49	1.06	0	2
Patna	3,819	3,778	3,706	98.09	72	1.91	0	0
Pune	3,296	3,288	3,267	99.36	21	0.64	0	0
Shillong	3,103	3,067	2,940	95.86	127	4.14	0	0
NVS	31,496	31,289	30,834	98.55	452	1.44	1	2

Source: NVS (2015).
Note: [a]Eligible for improvement of performance.
            UFM – Unfair means.

Table 11.1d
CBSE Board Exam 2010: Class XII

Region	Regd.	Appeared	Passed	Pass (%)	Compt.	Compt. (%)	Failed	Failed (%)	NE
Bhopal	3,984	3,956	3,751	94.82	170	4.3	35	0.88	0
Chandigarh	1,979	1,955	1,848	94.53	92	4.71	15	0.77	0
Hyderabad	2,968	2,960	2,927	98.89	31	1.05	2	0.07	0
Jaipur	2,897	2,881	2,768	96.08	98	3.4	15	0.52	0
Lucknow	4,031	3,995	3,744	93.72	203	5.08	47	1.18	2
Patna	2,167	2,133	1,967	92.22	123	5.77	43	2.02	0
Pune	1,694	1,686	1,638	97.15	41	2.43	7	0.42	0
Shillong	2,320	2,297	2,196	95.6	81	3.53	20	0.87	0
NVS	22,040	21,863	20,839	95.32	839	3.84	184	0.84	1

Source: NVS (2015).

among the private and public-managed schools. JNVs reported 97% pass rate which was higher than that of KVs (95%) and the national pass percentage was 83%.[1]

At JNVs, social identity does not predict academic achievement. This is in contrast to the findings of empirical studies which

---

[1] http://www.financialexpress.com/photos/business-gallery/262310/cbse-result-2016-class-12-govt-schools-beat-private-ones-jnv-is-cbse-topper-2016/4/

indicate inter-group differences in achievement gaps in the test scores of school children in India aged 8–11 years (Borooah et al. 2015; Desai, Adams and Dubey 2010). In particular, children belonging to higher income households, literate parents, 'higher' social groups and living in urban areas did significantly better than those from poor households, illiterate parents, 'lower' social groups and children in rural areas (Borooah et al. 2015). The studies highlight that after controlling for the variables not related to caste and religion, children from all social groups compared to Brahmin (representative group) were significantly less likely to attain academic achievements, for example, in reading, writing and arithmetic.

By focusing on excellence in learning outcomes of the children from the disadvantaged groups, the model of JNV aims to achieve equity in excellence and reduce the inter-group achievement gaps within the school system. At the macro level, across JNVs, we find a minimal variation in the CBSE results between social and gender groups both at the class X and class XII (Table 11.2). Students from the SC group had slightly a higher pass percentage (98%) than the average (97.54%). Thus, at JNVs, we find high educational outcomes of those student groups who are likely to be left behind.

CASE STUDY: JNV, JALNA

As discussed earlier, we undertook a case study of JNV, Jalna. As a follow-up of the National Policy on Education, 1986, JNV, Jalna, was set up on 15 December 1987 in a village called Amba which is 6 km away from its taluka place called Partur in Jalna district. JNV, Jalna, like all 597 JNVs, is governed by the rules and regulations of NVS, an autonomous organisation and apex body which looks after JNVs across India. The commissioner is head of the NVS which has eight regional offices located in Bhopal, Chandigarh, Hyderabad Jaipur, Lucknow, Patna, Pune and Shillong. Deputy commissioner of each regional NVS looks after on an average 50–80 JNVs coming under the jurisdiction of each regional office.

JNV, Jalna, is under the jurisdiction of the Pune regional office. It is situated in a remote village which is 65 km away from the seat of the district collector-cum-magistrate and the chairman of the VMS. Since its inception, the vidyalaya imparts good-quality modern education and ensures that the students attain a considerable level of competency.

Table 11.2
Socio-economic Status of Parents (Based on Students' Admission in Class VI)

Income Group (per year)	2010	2011	2012	2013	2014
Below ₹50,000	55	58	60	47	59
Between 50,000 and 100,000	4	2	9	4	9
Above ₹100,000	13	15	5	22	7

Source: JNV, Jalna.

Diversity and Equity in Student Composition

Majority of students in JNV, Jalna, are from rural areas, lower income group background, low educational level of parents and disadvantaged groups. An analysis of JNV, Jalna, in terms of admission of students at entry level, that is, class VI, for the years 2010–2014 depicts the following. The Tables 11.2, 11.3, and 11.4 throws light on the fact that more than 75% of the students hail from rural background, from disadvantaged socio-economic backgrounds and a high proportion of parents of students have up to secondary-level education (Tables 11.2–11.4).

Achieving Equity in Excellence

Table 11.4 shows that at JNV, Jalna, in every category of students and in every year we have data of, the pass percentage at class X

Table 11.3
Socio-economic and Educational Status of the Students

Year	2010	2011	2012	2013	2014
Number of students admitted in Class VI	72	75	74	73	75
Rural	57	60	57	59	60
Urban	15	15	17	14	15
Boys	35	48	45	45	49
Girls	37	27	29	28	26
SC	17	14	19	15	18
ST	5	2	4	2	3
OBC	18	21	26	27	25
General	32	38	25	29	29
Pass % at Class X	100	100	100	100	100

Source: JNV, Jalna.

Table 11.4
Education Status of Parents

Parents Education	2010	2011	2012	2013	2014
Below primary	2	3	3	4	3
Up to secondary	64	45	53	42	52
Above secondary	6	27	18	27	21

Source: JNV, Jalna.

is 100%. For the last few years, the vidyalaya is consecutively pro-ducing 100% quality results in CBSE for classes X and XII (science and humanities). The results of non-board classes are also in par with the board classes. Almost every year, there are a few students from class XII who secure 0.1 Merit Certificate from CBSE at all-India level and some of the students from class X also achieve 10-point combined grade point average (CGPA).

Furthermore, in class XII exams, we find minimal inter-group dif-ferences in mean scores between rural and urban, boys and girls and between social groups. The given Figures 11.1, 11.2, 11.3, 11.4, and 11.5 clearly depict the performance of the class XII stu-dents of the vidyalaya in various subjects of AISSCE, March–April

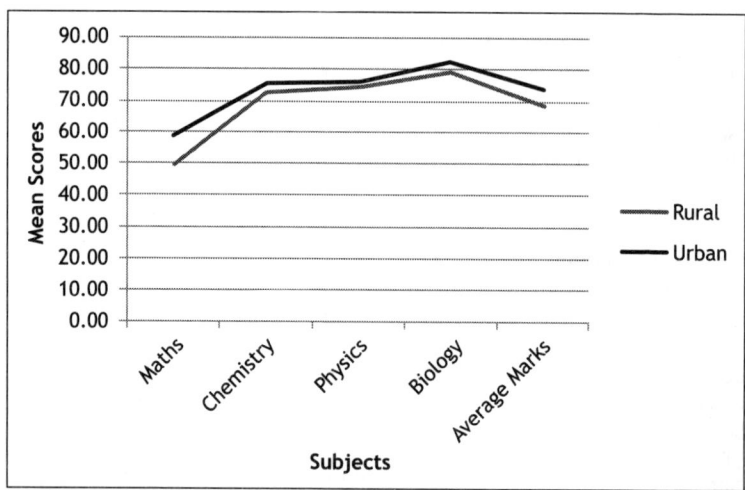

Figure 11.1
Mean Scores of Students in Science by Location (2015–16)
Source: Office records of JNV, Jalna.

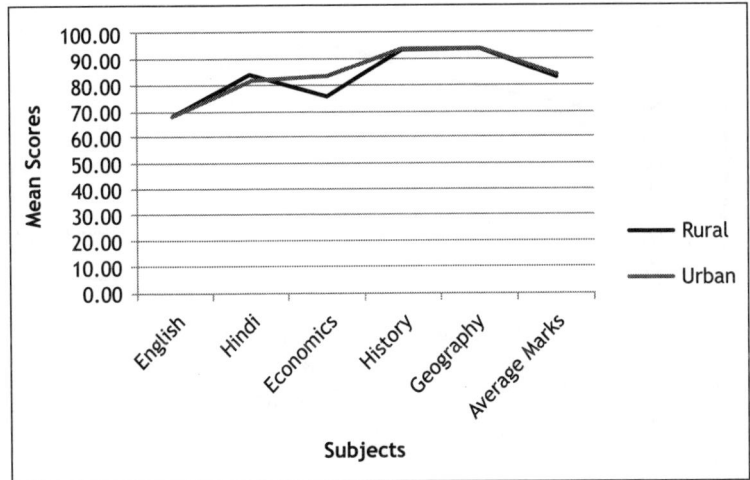

Figure 11.2
Mean Scores of Students in Arts by Location (2015–16)

Source: Office records of JNV, Jalna.

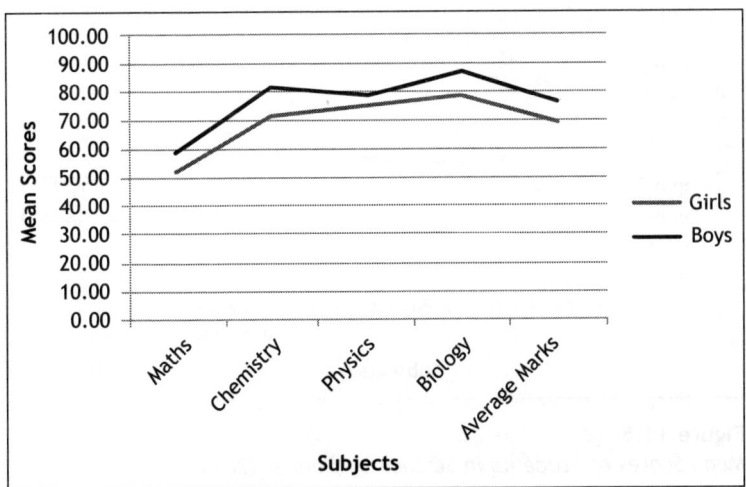

Figure 11.3
Mean Scores of Students in Science by Gender (2015–16)

Source: Office records of JNV, Jalna.

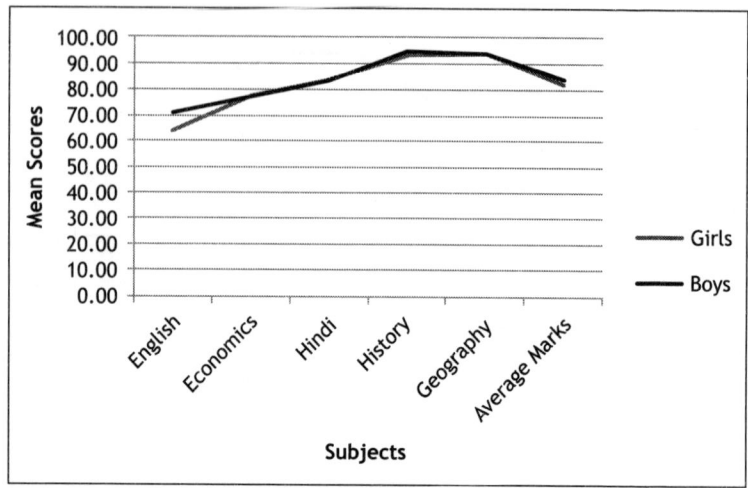

Figure 11.4
Mean Scores of Students in Arts by Gender (2015–16)
Source: Office records of JNV, Jalna.

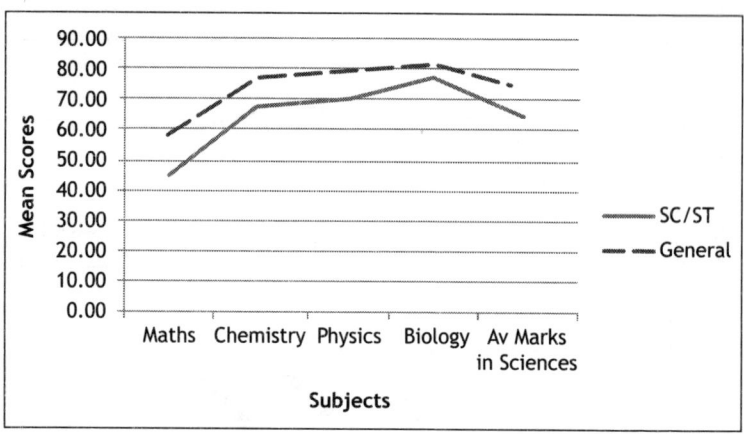

Figure 11.5
Mean Scores of Students in Science by Gender (2015–16)
Source: Office records of JNV, Jalna.

2015 conducted by CBSE. With respect to achievement of rural students as compared to urban, there is minimal inter-group difference in the mean scores in class XII. This also indicates the equalising impact of the residential nature of the school. As discussed

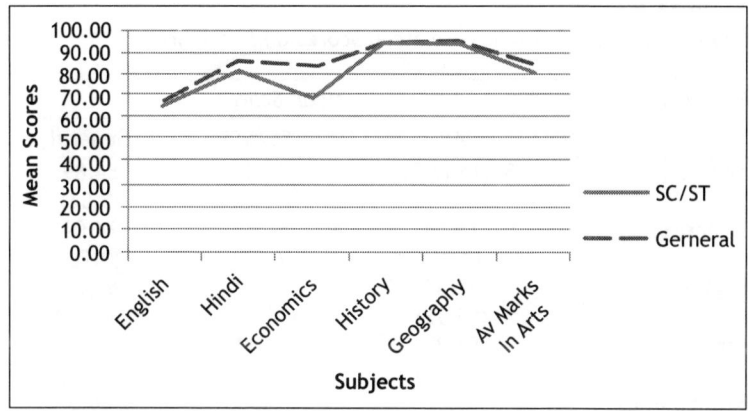

Figure 11.6
Mean Scores of Students in Arts by Gender (2015–16)
Source: Office records of JNV, Jalna.

earlier, the residential nature of JNV schools changes the social and educational environment which has a positive impact on academic achievement of all children irrespective of their family and locational background. This impact is seen across almost all subjects except in mathematics and economics (Figures 11.1 and 11.2).

Additionally, in most subjects in both science and arts, mean scores for boys and girls are similar (Figures 11.3 and 11.4). In fact, in the science stream, girls out-perform the boys, breaking the stereotype (Figure 11.3).

We also find lower variation across the scores in many subjects which means that there is consistency in performance across student groups (Table 11.5). For example, students are doing equally well, irrespective of their social groups, in history and geography as they have highest mean scores and lowest standard deviation in these two subjects. However, in sciences as compared to subjects in arts stream, there is significantly higher variation from the mean scores indicating that there are higher differences in the scores between students.

Students also find economics a tough subject. In economics, the mean score and standard deviations are low. It seems that there is a pattern of those who score low in mathematics score low in economics also. However, like in economics, the mean scores are low in mathematics but unlike in economics, the standard deviations are high. This further reinforces the idea that mathematics seems to be

Table 11.5
Subject and Social Group-wise Mean Scores and Variance

Subjects	Mean Scores		
	All	*SC/ST*	*General*
Arts	82.14 (7.37)	80.8 (9.18)	84.89 (5.54)
Sciences	73.84 (8.86)	65.25 (6.87)	74.03 (9.78)
English	67.57 (15.32)	65.87 (16.27)	68.84 (14.71)
Hindi	83.45 (10.85)	81.11 (12.39)	85.21 (9.41)
Mathematics	53.87 (14)	45 (6)	58.3 (14.94)
Economics	77.56 (18.03)	69.43 (21.8)	82.73 (13.25)
Geography	94.14 (2.37)	93.86 (2.60)	94.32 (2.25)
History	93.50 (3.61)	93.71 (3.71)	93.36 (3.63)
Biology	80.05 (9.28)	77.89 (9.25)	81.67 (9.36)
Physics	75 (10.62)	69.89 (5.71)	78.83 (12)
Chemistry	73.43 (11.76)	68.22 (8.54)	77.33 (12.64)

Source: JNV, Jalna.
Notes: Figures in parenthesis are standard deviation.

a subject that students find tough and it may also be impacting performance in economics. Thus, Figures 11.5 and 11.6 indicate that, in general, the children are performing low in English, mathematics, economics and physics in comparison to the other subjects. Low performance in basic subjects, that is, English and mathematics, affects performance in subjects like economics and physics.

With respects to mean scores of various social groups, we find that the performance of students in history and geography is very high in both general and SC/ST categories students. These results indicate that SC/ST find it easy to learn and write their exams of history and geography. In history and geography, students write their exams in Hindi medium which has some similarity with their mother tongue 'Marathi'. It was shared with us that there is a considerable share of students in class XI who are new admissions or also called 'lateral entries'. They find it easier in expressing their views in Hindi than in English. In fact, their performance in English is not so appreciable, whereas all science subjects have to be written in English. It was explained, 'since the lateral entry students do not have a good command in English, their performance is comparatively low in all subjects irrespective of the social group they belong to'. The students are able to write the exam in their regional language which may explain the level of performance in these two subjects. We do find that the English language remains a stumbling block. We find a low mean score and a high variation in the English scores.

For the general category group, the mathematics score varies substantially, while both the mean scores and variance in mathematics is lower for the SC/ST group than the general students. While the variance of SC/ST scores in biology, physics and chemistry is not dramatically different from that of general category students, and their means scores are also similar, these results suggests that group identity does not significantly impact educational outcomes.

The Navodaya children have also been successful in securing admissions in elite institutions such as IITs and NITs. In the last five years, 10 JNV, Jalna, students have been admitted to IITs and NITs, and many other students (close to 20) are pursuing engineering and medical study programmes in reputed state government colleges. As mentioned above, the transition rate from high school to college is close to 100% at JNV, Jalna.

In order to facilitate the Navodaya children to get into highly reputed professional educational institutes such as IITs and NITs, adequate arrangements are even made with specialised coaching centres such as Dakshana Foundation, TIME and Resonance. They provide an intensive coaching to the interested and selected students of Navodaya free of cost. This augments the scope of Navodaya students doing professional education in par with the students falling from wealthy rich background. Thus, they can also conquer any phase of the world with courage and conviction and with devotion and dedication.

An analysis of diaries written by selected students explicates how academic and social climate created by the JNV system fosters their overall development. Major features of academic and social climate can be elaborated as follows. Students consider 'school as family' where they enjoy care and support from peers, teachers and staff. Given the special feature of JNVs, that is, fully residential school system, feeling that students enjoy their school as a family indicates that social support system exists in JNVs. According to students, it is the highly 'committed teachers' that made their life a 'heaven' in JNV. Not only cognitive but also non-cognitive aspects of their career are nurtured and moulded by their teachers. As one of the students has stated, 'Teachers were helping a lot; they were there for us for 24 hours in morning study, evening study, night study, academic time and also in afternoon. We thought that they had sacrificed their personal life for us'. JNVs also stress on 'nurture human values' and 'personality development' through scholastic and co-scholastic activities. It in turn boosts confidence level of students and instils new vision about social world. As stated by one student, 'Navodaya gave me a lot, without accepting any return gift. Navodaya has developed my personality and made my friends and me capable for society, for our country'.

CONCLUSION

The discussions in the chapter indicate possibilities of achieving equity in excellence through carefully crafted programmes and liberal public funding support. It can be seen from the JNVs experience that strategies and process adopted at the institutional level play an important role in overcoming disadvantages by birth. Therefore, the JNV system is a good example of achieving equity and excellence and equity in excellence in education.

While academic planning provides macro guidelines and direction to specify the role, responsibility and process to be followed in planning, implementing and monitoring of the activities at the national, regional office and institution levels, micro planning at school level is done with active participation of stakeholders. By following the PAP and keeping the spirit of its guidelines, the following institutional mechanisms and strategies are adopted in JNVs. First, regular meetings of VMCs strengthen effective coordination between school and various state and Central government departments which in turn helps to sort out development issues related to the school. Second, participatory school management process facilitates decentralised institutional planning in which various stakeholders of school such as teachers, parents, students and community members are involved. Various sub-committees are formed to prepare plan for each area such as academics, administration, infrastructure development and school–community engagement to list a few. Consolidation of recommendations and suggestions from each committee contribute to the preparation of an annual institutional plan based on which activities are conducted and evaluated. This process instils a sense of ownership and accountability among its stakeholders.

Third, effective classroom management by teachers under the instructional leadership of principal promotes effective learning in classroom. Fourth, students who require additional learning inputs are identified in the early phase of the academic year and systematic remedial teaching is provided. This helps largely to bridge the gaps in learning and outcome. Focus on nurturing communication skill and English language competency further boosts the morale and confidence level of students with diverse learning abilities. Fifth, CCE followed in JNVs provides due significance to scholastic and co-scholastic competencies. This fosters overall development of students and improves aspirational levels of students.

Sixth, it is the presence of the state of art learning infrastructure that facilitates joyful learning experiences and exposure to cutting-edge technologies accessed by all children, irrespective of their family background. The socio-economic status of the child, that is, whether he/she belongs to the family of a peasant or a prince, at entry stage has no relevance in the Navodaya set-up because there is no difference between the 'haves' and 'have-nots' as far as the allocation of infra-structure and other amenities are concerned. Every child is equitably treated in terms of issue of uniforms, bedding items, daily-use toilet items, textbooks, stationeries and in every sort of other facilities provided. No fee or fine is levied for the infrastructure or welfare component. In fact, the cap of poor and rich gets disappeared as the wellness of the child is treated at par irrespective of the class.

The reason behind excellence is timely monitoring of the completion of prescribed syllabus by making use of the normal academic hours. A just and equitable assessment of performance at every stage based on suitable parameters and extra effort is appended from every end to ensure the manifestation of latent talent inherent in every child to assure the all-round personality development. As a result, every child not only gets an opportunity to exhibit his/her talent and what is embodied in him/her but it also becomes a driving force for building up confidence of the child. Based on the NVS experience, it can be reliably stated that an effective school system can promote equity in excellence.

ANNEXURE

Table A11.1
*Activities Conducted/Observed/Monitored and Carried Out by the
Principal, JNV, Jalna*

Sr. No.	Particulars	Involvement of Principal 'Directly'/ 'Indirectly'
1	Organisation of special cleanliness drive Swachh Bharat Abhiyan	Directly
2	House masters and associate house masters meeting	Directly
3	Class teachers and M&R committee meeting conducted	Directly
4	Organisation of subject committee meeting as per NCERT and PAP	Directly
5	Instructions for maintenance of hygiene, cleanliness and maintenance of notice boards, etc.	Indirectly
6	Observance of academic records of subject teachers as per CCE	Directly
7	Conduct of house inspection	Directly
8	Organisation of subject committee meeting, checking of result analysis, etc.	Directly
9	Conduct of house and mess inspection	Directly
10	Conduct of classroom inspection	Directly
11	Notice for nominations of vidyalaya captain, vidyalaya vice-Captain, monitors, house captains, etc.	Directly
12	Conducted farewell function on the superannuation of retirement of Shri N.P. Singh Parihar, PGT—Hindi	Directly
13	Preparation of observation report on HM/AHM/ MOD and mess management, etc.	Directly
14	Conducted an inspection of exhibits of mathematics, science, social studies and ICT	Directly
15	Circular for adherence of duties as per time table	Directly
16	Observance of English Department activities as per NVS annual calendar and records	Indirectly
17	Celebration of Vishwa Jan Sankhya Divas	Directly
18	Organisation of Swachh Bharat Abhiyan	Directly
19	Observance of progress of botanical garden	Indirectly
20	Organisation of robotics workshop	Indirectly

Sr. No.	Particulars	Involvement of Principal 'Directly'/ 'Indirectly'
21	Observance of scout and guide activities, mathematics lab, Hindi Rajbhasha correspondence, English language lab, preparation of steps for Youth Parliament, AEP activities, Capital Nature Club, textbooks availability, maintenance of computer lab, etc.	Directly
22	Observance of arrangements for sports and their escorts and teams	Directly
23	Monitoring on correspondence of Hindi Rajbhasha	Directly
24	Planning for participation in Digital India Contest	Indirectly
25	Organisation and monitoring of Cluster-level Basket Ball Meet and Regional Sports Meet	Directly
26	Arrangement of admission in classes VI, IX and XI LE for the year 2015–16	Indirectly
27	Report on assignment on equity and excellence in Navodaya	Directly
28	Arrangement of re-tendering	Directly
29	Completion and forwarding of service dues i.r.o. Dr N.P.S. Parihar, PGT—Hindi	Directly
30	Compilation of record i.r.o. ex-PGT—Biology for enquiry conducted at JNV, Thane	Directly
31	Inspection of Sinhgad City School, Pune, as per CBSE	Directly
32	Distribution of JNVST-2016 Prospectus-cum-Application Forms and its publicity through BEOs, DEO and with the help of District Information Officer, Jalna	Indirectly
33	Inspection of JNV, Hingoli, and JNV, Nanded	Directly

Note: LE - Lateral Entry; iro - in respect of.

REFERENCES

Borooah, V.K., N.S. Sabharwal, D.G. Diwakar, V.K. Mishra, and A.K. Naik. 2015. *Caste, Discrimination and Exclusion in Modern India.* New Delhi: SAGE Publications.

Curto, V.E., and R.G. Fryer Jr. 2011. 'Estimating the Returns to Urban Boarding Schools: Evidence from Seed'. NBER Working Paper No.16746. Cambridge: National Bureau of Economic Research.

Desai, S., C. Adams, and A. Dubey. 2010. 'Segmented Schooling: Inequalities in Primary Education'. In *Blocked by Caste: Economic Discrimination in Modern India*, edited by S. Thorat and K.S. Newman, 230–52. New Delhi: Oxford University Press.

Mukul, Akshay. 2016. 'Navodaya Kids Record 95% Success Rate in JEE'. 4 May. Available at: http://timesofindia.indiatimes.com/india/Navodaya-kids-record-95-success-rate-in-JEE/articleshow/52101037.cms

Naik, J.P. 1979. 'Equality, Quantity and Quality: The Elusive Triangle in Indian Education'. *International Review of Education* 25 (2/3): 167–85.

Nambissan, G.B., and P. Batra. 1989. 'Equity and Excellence: Issues in Indian Education'. *Social Scientist* 17 (9/10): 56–73.

NVS (Navodaya Vidyalaya Samiti). 2015. *Perspective Academic Planning, 2015–16*. Noida: NVS.

Varghese, N.V. 2011. 'Expanding Higher Education with Equity'. Paper presented at the Global Conclave of Young Scholars, NUEPA, New Delhi, 27–29 January 2011.

12

Disparities in Outcome: Graduate Labour Market in India

S. Madheswaran and Smrutirekha Singhari

INTRODUCTION

Graduate employment in India has fascinated researchers since the 1960s, when they observed that apparently high graduate unemployment had not diminished the social demand for university education. The classic study by Blaug, Layard and Woodhall (1969) showed that despite unemployment of university leavers, the private rates of return remained high primarily because of high unemployment rates among secondary school graduates and low cost of higher education.

India has around 230 million adolescents in the age group of 10–19 years. The youth population (age group of 15–29 years) in India is expected to increase steadily to approximately 350 million by 2022 (World Bank 2006). Education levels of the youth are also expected to improve significantly in the next decade. This chapter seeks to study the access to employment and earnings differentials in the graduate labour market by gender, caste and religion. The analysis in this chapter is largely based on the quinquennial rounds of data from the National Sample Survey Organisation (NSSO) which is available since 1972–73. The NSSO Rounds pertaining to the years 1983, 1993–94, 2004–05 and 2011–12 have been mostly used in this chapter.

HIGHER EDUCATION AND LABOUR MARKET

The human capital theory (Becker 1964) argues that the investment in education and training enhances skills and capacities of individuals, enhances their productivity and higher earnings. Since then, the productivity-enhancing role of education has attracted attention of researchers and policy. The screening hypothesis (Spence 1973), contrary to the human capital, argued that education acts as a signalling device in the job market rather than augmenting productivity of individuals. Employers do not have much information about the potential employee's quality. They use markets to judge quality—a higher education qualification is treated as an indicator of ability. While the former makes a case for higher public investment in higher education, the screening hypothesis does not support higher public investment in higher education.

It is not always possible to create a total fit between the supply of graduates from the higher education system and demand for graduates in the job markets. Despite poor labour market conditions for the educated, the expansion of higher education system continues in many instances. This results in a situation where people with high qualifications accept inferior jobs that do not require the qualifications they possess. Public policy needs to address way to find a fit between supply of skills and the demand for skilled manpower in the labour market.

The aforementioned requires coordination at two levels—between the demand for qualified manpower and places in higher education system on one hand and places in higher education and students demand for higher education on the other. Traditionally, countries adopted manpower planning approach that projected future employment by sectors and expected supply of university graduates. In these uncertain times, creating this fit has been found difficult and of little use. Moreover, a large share of jobs is filled up through job mobility. As a result, the manpower planning approach has been by and large abandoned and replaced by a study of signals from the labour markets (Madheswaran 1996). This requires a dynamic system of providing the job market information on placement, unemployment rates by levels of competence, job offers and employers' estimation of their needs in terms of manpower to the higher education institutions on a continuing basis. These signals from the labour market help the educational institutions to make adjustments in their capacities, adapt curricula to emerging changes in the job market and also assist individuals to make correct choices. Since social demand—aggregate of students' private demand—is often based on aspirations of students, societal expectations and not necessarily on signals from the job markets, there is usually a possibility of mismatch. This often results in over-education leading to unemployment and underemployment of graduates—a phenomenon common throughout the world in varying degrees (Agarwal 2006).

Since the link between fields of study and occupational areas are relatively loose in most countries and the process of transition from higher education to employment has become more complex and protracted, it has its own dynamics of rising and dashing hopes (Gibbons 1998). The fact that the formal higher education does not necessarily equip students with skills required in the job markets creates a problem of unemployment on one hand and skill shortages on the other. Based on the framework above, an enquiry into this paradox is the main purpose of this chapter.

STRUCTURE OF EMPLOYMENT

In the last decade, the growth of economy at an annual rate of around 8% was accompanied by a dismal growth in jobs at below 1%. The proportion of persons in the labour force declined from 43% in 2004–05 to 39.5% in 2011–12, with a sharp drop in the female participation rate from 29% to 22.5% (Table 12.1). Although the overall unemployment rate is at 2.2%, the unemployment rates for youth in the age group of 15–29 years, particularly those possessing secondary level of education and above, are much higher. More than 52% of the workers are engaged in self-employment and a significant proportion of women workers are primarily home based.

Further, only 10% of the labour force has acquired some technical skill, out of which just one-fourth have received formal technical education of the latter; the proportion of the workforce with

Table 12.1

Labour Force Participation Rate and Workforce Participation Rate (UPSS) by Gender (All Ages) from 1983 to 2011–12

	LFPR			WFPR		
	M	F	P	M	F	P
1983	55.1	30.0	42.9	53.9	29.6	42.0
1993–94	55.6	29.0	42.8	54.5	28.6	42.0
2004–05	55.9	29.4	43.0	54.7	28.7	42.0
2011–12	55.6	22.5	39.5	54.4	21.9	38.6

Source: Computed from unit level data of various NSSO Rounds.
Notes: M, Male; F, Female; UPSS, Usual Principal and Subsidiary Status; LFPR: Labour Force Participation Rate; and WFPR, Workforce Participation Rate.

Table 12.2

Distribution of Technically Educated Labour Force* by Levels of Education

Technical Education	Percentage
Technical Degree (Agriculture/Engineering/ Technology/Medicine, etc.)	18.5
Diploma or Certificate (Graduate and above level)	26.8
Certificate (below graduate level)	54.7

Source: NSSO Survey on Employment and Unemployment in India.
Note: *Labour Force with Technical Education constitutes only 2.5% of total labour force (15–59 years) in 2010.

certificate level qualifications is relatively low in comparison to diploma/degree holders, making the skill pyramid top heavy and lacking an adequate base (Table 12.2). Therefore, there is an urgent need to expand the vocational training at certificate level to upgrade and enrich the skill base and productivity levels of the growing non-farm employment sectors such as construction. At the same time, it is also necessary to undertake recognition of prior learning (RPL) for transforming informal skills into formal skills.

CHARACTERISTICS AND STRUCTURE OF GRADUATE LABOUR MARKET

In general, India's labour market is characterised by a low female participation rate, visible in its poor labour sex ratio and also low worker to total population ratio. The overall labour force participation rate (LFPR) stands at around 40%, which for women is 23%. While the male LFPR has been stable at 55–56% during three decades from 1983 to 2011–12, the female LFPR has shown a decline from around 30% in 1983 to 23% in 2011–12.

The more disaggregated information on work participation rate (WPR) for female by educational level is given in Table 12.3. We first note that there is a U-shaped pattern of the association of female education with female labour force participation. At very low levels of female education, activity rates are high. They are much lower at medium education levels, and rise again at higher levels. Over time, this U shape has been muted and shifted to the right: the low point has shifted from middle school education to

Table 12.3

Work Participation Rate (UPSS) by Education Level (Age 15 Years and Above) from 1999–2000 to 2011–12

Level of general education	Rural				Urban			
	55th (1999–2000)	61st (2004–05)	66th (2009–10)	68th (2011–12)	55th (1999–2000)	61st (2004–05)	66th (2009–10)	68th (2011–12)
Male								
Not Literate	89.5	89.2	87.4	88	83.9	83.1	81.6	83.2
Literate & up to primary	88	89.5	90	89.2	83	85.5	84.4	84.7
Middle	76.8	80.2	78.4	77	73.2	76	76	76.5
Secondary	73.7	73.2	69.7	66.8	66.8	67.3	66.7	65.1
Higher secondary	71.3	70.9	63.4	61.8	60.8	60.8	57.6	58.3
Diploma/certificate*	–	82.1	73	74.8	–	79.8	73	69.1
Graduate & above	83.6	85.1	79.3	78.1	80.6	79.5	78.8	79
All	84.1	84.6	81.2	80	75.2	76.3	74	74.1
Female								
Not Literate	51.3	55	43.2	41.8	27.1	30.4	23.1	24
Literate & up to primary	40.3	44.9	38.4	36.1	17.7	23.4	20.6	22.3
Middle	29	37.1	29.4	27.6	12.9	16.1	15.4	15.8
Secondary	25.7	30.5	22.2	22.2	12.4	12.3	9.7	11
Higher secondary	20.6	25.2	18.3	17.6	12.4	12.9	9.4	10.8
Diploma/certificate*	–	52.3	33.9	40.8	–	48.6	39.3	34.4
Graduate & above	31	34.5	29.7	29.7	27.3	29	25.9	27.9
All	45.2	48.5	37.2	35.2	19.7	22.7	18.3	19.5

Source: NSSO 68th Round, Employment and Unemployment Situation in India, Report No 554, 2011–12.

Note: *In NSS 55th Round survey, there was no separate code for 'diploma/certificate' and as such the estimates of persons with general education level 'diploma/certificate' could not be obtained separately, and they were classified in the equivalent level of general education. From the 61st Round survey, persons with general education level 'diploma/certificate', which were equivalent to below graduate level, were identified separately.

secondary education, while the increase at graduate level is now much smaller than it was in 1987–88. In contrast, male participation rates do not differ by education level. This result is consonant with Chaudhary and Verick (2014). They have shown econometrically that a number of factors significantly affect the probability of women's labour market outcomes. Human capital endowments of women, particularly higher secondary and university education play a crucial role. Indeed, as the level of education goes up, the likelihood of being in regular employment also increases. For a graduate and above educated women, there is a 30% more chance of being in regular salaried work in rural areas and 20% higher probability in the case of urban areas. Furthermore, as the level of education rises, the probability of being self-employed and casual labour decreases. The results confirm that poorly educated (illiterate) women are more likely to be in the labour force and working.

Labour supply as well as labour demand effects could account for the stagnation in female participation rates in urban areas. Among the labour supply effects, rising male incomes and education might lead to lower female participation due to the well-known income effect; rising household incomes lead women to reduce their participation as the necessity for them to work in order for the family to survive reduces. In addition, there might be stigma and social restrictions against employment of educated women in certain menial and blue-collar jobs. At the low level of the education distribution, economic distress compels women to work and it enhances LFPR for women. The low female WPRs imply that India is unlikely to reap the demographic dividend associated with its currently favourable demographic constellation of a rising share of the working age population (relative to young and old dependents).

Employment growth in urban India has been concentrated in construction and low-skilled services. These are not the sectors that are employment friendly for women. For example, a female-intensive export-oriented growth strategy increased employment opportunities for women in many East Asian economies as well as in neighbouring Bangladesh. On the supply side, policies explicitly promoting the acceptability of female employment outside the public sector and policies to allow a greater compatibility of female employment with domestic responsibilities and improve the safety of female workers in the private sector could also draw more women into the workforce. Ultimately, however, values and attitudes towards female employment will need to change in order to change this state of affairs.

STRUCTURE OF LABOUR MARKET BY
SOCIO-RELIGIOUS GROUPS

The scheduled caste (SC) and scheduled tribe (ST) groups have a higher worker to population ratio, but that, too, among Muslims is lower. It may, however, not necessarily mean that the better representation of SCs and STs is a result of higher demand for their labour in the market. It seems mostly a result of the greater need for participation in some remunerative activity by the members (including women and children) of their households on account of poverty and low earning per worker (Table 12.4). A lower WPR among Muslims is primarily a result of a very low participation of women. Women constitute 30% among SC and 37% among ST workers, but only 18% among Muslim workers. Among workers from other groups, women make up 27%.

Participation rate is the highest among STs, so that they account for about 10% among workers against only 8% in population. Only 8% of the ST workers are in regular jobs; the same among SC workers is 14%, 15% among Muslims and among 'others', it is 19%. Therefore, in terms of quality of employment (regular employment), it can be said that SCs, STs and Muslims lag behind the 'others' in the society. Employment among all three of them, however, is generally of lower quality than among other groups in so far the regularity of work and income is concerned. How have different social groups fared in terms of growth of employment? Let us look at the growth rate of employment among different groups over the period 1983/1993–94 and 1993–94/2009–10.

Table 12.4
Participation in Workforce by Social Group

	Share in Population (%)	Share in Workforce (%)	
		Total	In Regular jobs
Scheduled Castes	16.2	20.1	13.6
Scheduled Tribes	8.2	9.6	8.1
Muslims	13.4	10.9	14.6
Others	62.2	59.6	19.2

Source: Estimated on the basis of data from Government of India (2011) and NSSO survey on Employment and Unemployment 65th Round (2009–10).

Different groups had, by and large, similar growth of employment over the two periods. It is important to note that during the period 1983/1993–94, all the three disadvantaged groups lagged behind the 'others' in respect of growth of regular jobs, whereas in the post-reform period, all of them have scored over the 'others'; SCs and Muslims have scored at much higher rate than the 'others'. On the whole, SCs and Muslims have experienced gains in both quantity and quality of employment while STs have continued to perform lower than average. The level of LFPR is seen to vary with levels of general education. Among the illiterate in rural areas, LFPR was the highest for ST and lowest for others. Among graduate and above, LFPR is also highest among ST and the lowest for the 'others' (Table 12.5).

If we look at the recent 2011–12 NSS report, the SC workers are in disadvantaged position as far as the quality of employment concerned. In rural areas, among males, the share of self-employment was the highest among the 'others' category (63.8%) and was the lowest among the SC category (35.7%). The proportion of casual labour was the highest among the SC (55.4%) and was the lowest among the 'others' category (22.1%). The share of regular wage/salaried employees was the highest in the 'others' category (14.1%) and was around 9.4% among other backward classes (OBC), 8.9% among SC and was the lowest among ST (5.8%). Among female workers, the share of self-employment was the highest among the 'others' category (73.3%) and the lowest among the SC (44.4%), while the share of casual labour was the highest among SC (50.6%) and the lowest among the 'others' category (18.4%). Among female workers, the share of regular wage/salaried employees was the highest among females in the 'others' category (8.3%) and the lowest among ST (3.3%).

In urban areas, during 2011–12, the proportion of male self-employed was the highest in the 'others' category (45.2%), it was 43.8% among workers in the OBC category, 29.5% among the SC category and 23.7% among the ST category. Among the male workers, proportion of casual labour was the highest among SC (26.2%) and was the lowest among the 'others' category (7.8%). Among male workers, the share of regular wage/salaried employees was the highest in the ST category (52%), it was 47% among the 'others' category, 44.3% among the SC category and was the lowest among the OBC category (38.8%). Among female workers, the share of self-employment was the highest among the OBC category (48.9%) and the lowest among the SC (31.8%), while the share of casual labour

Table 12.5
Labour Force Participation Rate (UPSS) for Persons of Age 15 Years and Above for Different General Educational Levels for Each Social Group for All India (2011–12)

	ST	SC	OBC	Others	All
Rural					
Not literate	73.3	59.5	56.4	49.5	58.2
Literate & up to below primary	74.4	72.2	65.3	54.4	65.2
Primary	72.4	69	64.9	60.5	65.5
Middle	63.5	56.9	59.1	54.6	57.9
Secondary	51.6	50.1	51.6	51.7	51.4
Higher secondary	52.9	46.4	46.6	47.2	47.2
Diploma/certificate	89	73.6	73.1	71.9	73.4
Graduate and above	79.8	73.1	69.7	66	68.9
All	69.5	60.6	58.1	53.8	58.7
Urban					
Not literate	52.2	44.8	44.6	37.8	43.1
Literate & up to below primary	61.3	59.8	56.8	49.4	55.1
Primary	57.7	60.8	56.7	49.1	54.8
Middle	48.9	54.2	52.2	45.7	49.9
Secondary	44.1	47	43.7	39.3	42.2
Higher secondary	43.8	40.9	38	37.5	38.3
Diploma/certificate	67.1	71.2	65.4	58.1	63
Graduate and above	72.1	65.3	65	60.2	62.3
All	53.4	52	50.5	47	49.3

Source: NSSO Surveys on Employment and Unemployment in India, Social Group.

was the highest among ST (30.8%) and the lowest among the 'others' category (7.7%). Among female workers, the share of regular wage/salaried employees was the highest in the 'others' category (50.4%), it was 48.8% among the SC category, 34.9% among the OBC category and 34.6% among the ST category.

The WPR is the lowest among Muslims compared to other religious communities, especially in the secondary and above educational level. A close look at the recent NSSO report, in urban areas, the proportion of workers engaged in self-employment was the highest for Muslims. Among Muslims, about 50% of urban male workers and about 60% of urban female workers were engaged in self-employment. Among Hindus in urban areas, about 44% of male workers and 40% of female workers were engaged in regular wage/ salaried employment, whereas the access to regular employment for Muslims are 29.8 and 21.9%, which is very low compared to other religious communities.

The share of graduates and above among different socio-religious groups and consumer expenditure classes (CECs) is reported in Table 12.6. It is well recognised that education is the principal means of accessing quality jobs, either public or private. Table 12.6 looks at the distribution of graduates (and above) across various CECs for different social groups. Unsurprisingly, the proportion of graduates in richer households is much higher than the proportion of graduates in poorer households, and this is the case across all social groups. Moreover, Upper Hindus (88.7%) and the 'others' (96.4%) have the highest percentage of graduates in the combined rich and richest CECs. In contrast, only 15% ST graduates, 13.6% SC graduates and 9.5% OBCs graduates are in the poor and poorest CECs (these figures are less than 5% for Upper Hindus and 'others').

Clearly, though the reservation of seats for these groups in educational institutions is perhaps allowing greater access to education, this is not necessarily translating into higher incomes in all cases. At the same time, there exists a class bias within these disadvantaged groups, wherein 74–80% (ST/SC/OBC) graduates belong to the richer classes. This suggests that the 'creamy layer' indeed gets better access to education even in disadvantaged social groups, although there are some differences between groups. Educational endowment opens up better opportunities in the labour market, where access to public sector jobs too is facilitated by the reservation policy. This linkage between income and access to education warrants revisiting the reservation policy for disadvantaged groups, especially in the context of the 'creamy layer' argument. This raises some questions regarding affirmative action policies that do not take into account the within-group differences. In the case of India, the relevant question is whether positive discrimination for the more deprived sub-groups within the reserved groups is called for, particularly among the OBCs, wherein a few economically and politically dominant OBCs have appropriated most of the benefits of the reservation policy. There is an additional concern as to whether certain groups of Muslims, who are currently classified as Upper Muslims, should be designated as OBC, keeping in mind the large disparity within that group (Sharma 2002).

Therefore, disparities still persist and further efforts are needed so that the deprived groups share the fruits of economic

Table 12.6
Percentage of Graduates and Above Across Social Group and CEC (2011–12)

Social Groups	Poorest	Poor	Medium	Rich	Richest	Total (Row %)
Scheduled Tribes	6.7 (12.3)	8.3 (7.0)	11.0 (4.9)	23.4 (4.2)	50.6 (2.0)	100
Scheduled Castes	5.8 (19.9)	7.8 (16.7)	13.8 (15.7)	23.5 (13.4)	49.1 (7.0)	100
OBCs	3.7 (50.0)	5.8 (47.1)	10.5 (46.4)	22.2 (42.1)	57.9 (37.5)	100
Upper Hindus	0.9 (14.1)	3.6 (23.7)	6.8 (26.3)	16.3 (33.0)	72.4 (40.6)	100
Upper Muslims	1.6 (3.6)	4.5 (26.3)	12.4 (5.7)	20.9 (5.0)	60.7 (7.7)	100
Others	0.2 (0.2)	0.9 (5.7)	2.5 (1.0)	9.8 (2.3)	86.6 (5.1)	100
Total (Col. %)	2.4 (100)	4.7 (100)	8.8 (100)	19.0 (100)	65.1 (100)	100

Source: ILER (2014), Report on India Labour and Employment (computed from NSSO 68th Round data).
Notes: Figures within brackets are column percentages.
CEC denotes consumption expenditure class.

development. This calls for inclusive growth that provides equal opportunities for all to participate in the growth process, combined with schemes that would either deliver benefits directly or, more importantly, empower these groups to access opportunities offered by the development process, in general.

EDUCATION AND UNEMPLOYMENT

A precondition to turn the 'demographic bulge' into the 'demographic dividend' is education and skill formation. Educational and skill levels of Indian workers are abysmally low (Table 12.7). A total of 31% of workers are illiterate and only 29% have had secondary or higher level of education.

Second, imparting education is not enough; there must also be jobs for the educated. At present, the unemployment rate, as per Usual Principal Status (UPS), increases consistently with the increasing levels of education for both males and females in rural as well as urban areas. It is true that generally the more educated are able to remain unemployed until a suitable offer comes along. Some part of the higher unemployment rate for the more educated reflects this greater waiting period. At the same time, it is undeniably true that males as well as females, more so the latter, with higher secondary and above education, have very high unemployment rates in both urban and rural areas (Table 12.8). Unemployment rates among those

Table 12.7
Percentage Distribution of Employed (UPSS) by Gender and Level of Education (2011–12)

Educational Categories	Person	Male	Female
Illiterate	30.7	23.0	50.8
Literate & Below Primary	10.9	11.3	9.9
Primary	13.3	13.9	11.9
Middle	16.4	18.5	11.1
Secondary	11.8	13.9	6.4
Higher Secondary	6.6	7.8	3.4
Diploma/Certificate	1.4	1.6	0.8
Graduate and above	8.8	10.0	5.7
Total	100	100	100

Source: Calculated from unit level data of NSSO.
Note: Age 5 and above years.

Table 12.8
Unemployment Rate by Education for Age 5 and Above (UPS 2011–12)

Education Level	Rural			Urban			Total		
	Male	Female	Total	Male	Female	Total	Male	Female	Total
Not Literate	0.6	0.7	0.6	0.9	1.0	0.9	0.6	0.8	0.7
Below Primary	1.0	1.4	1.1	2.9	2.1	2.8	1.4	1.6	1.4
Primary	1.6	1.1	1.5	1.9	1.9	1.9	1.7	1.2	1.6
Middle	2.2	4.2	2.5	2.3	4.7	2.6	2.2	4.4	2.5
Secondary	2.6	8.8	3.5	2.3	8.3	2.9	2.5	8.7	3.3
Higher Secondary	4.3	14.2	5.5	4.9	10.7	5.7	4.5	12.7	5.6
Diploma/Certificate	10.0	25.9	12.6	6.1	11.2	7.0	8.0	18.3	9.7
Graduate	8.0	23.7	10.2	5.8	14.8	7.4	6.6	17.5	8.4
PG and above	10.0	23.2	12.6	4.5	12.4	6.5	6.1	14.9	8.2
Total	2.1	2.9	2.3	3.2	6.6	3.8	2.4	3.7	2.7

Source: IHD (2014), Report on India Labour and Employment (computed from NSSO 68th Round data).
Note: Age 5 and above years.

with a diploma or a certificate are also very high. This shows that even the persons with certificates or diploma from technical institutions are also not getting employable training. If we look at the share of unemployed by the level of education, about 30% of the total unemployed in the year 2011–12 were at least graduates or more qualified. Out of these 30%, 22% were graduates and 8% were post-graduates. The share of unemployed, at least graduate, females was higher (36%) as compared to males (28%). If we compare by location, the share was much higher for urban areas (43%) as compared to rural areas (22%). Another important point is that this share has been increasing; it was 21% in 2004–05 as compared to 30% in 2011–12. The educated unemployment rate is also higher for SCs and Muslims in both rural and urban areas, especially females are in disadvantaged position.

EARNINGS DIFFERENTIALS BY EDUCATIONAL LEVEL ACROSS GENDER, SOCIAL AND RELIGIOUS GROUPS

Wages and earning differentials in labour market can be linked to deprivation or impoverishment in a multidimensional and interactional fashion, rather than in a linear way. On the one hand, 'the poor' are likely to be excluded from wider participation in society because of their relative material disadvantage in the terms of income. However, discrimination may also cause deprivation, for example, poor people may be excluded from not only the means of livelihood as lands are commercialised, traditional occupations become redundant with technological advances, etc. but also from capability formation, thereby preventing moving into the 'included' group from the 'excluded' group. In economic terms, discrimination in labour markets may operate along a number of dimensions—gender, religion, caste and age—that effectively reduce the opportunity for such groups to gain access to social services and limit their participation in the labour market.

An important aspect of rising wage inequality has been the sharp rise of wages of skilled workers relative to the unskilled (Mazumdar and Sarkar 2008). This might be due to the skill-biased technological changes or the dismantling of a structure of trade protection that formerly favoured relatively unskilled, labour-intensive sectors. In the absence of any direct measure of skills, the usual approach is to use the educational level as an indicator of skills. In this case, the expectation is that wages will progressively rise with the increasing levels of education (Abraham 2007). This may be

Table 12.9
Wage Differentials Between the Educated Regular Workers and the Illiterate by Level of Education

Level of Schooling	1983	1993–94	2004–05	2011–12
Not Literate	1.0	1.0	1.0	1.0
Up to Primary	1.4	1.3	1.3	1.1
Up to Middle	1.5	1.4	1.3	1.3
Up to Secondary and Higher Secondary	2.3	2.1	2.3	2.1
Tertiary	3.7	3.6	4.6	4.1

Source: Sarkar and Mehta (2010) and computed from unit level data of various NSS Rounds.

more so in the case of regular workers, as education levels play a much smaller role in determining the wages of casual workers.

As the data in Table 12.9 shows, wages indeed do rise with each educational level, but the rise is steeper after the middle level of education, and tertiary education brings a particularly large increase over secondary education. Wage differentials across educational categories for regular workers have been fairly stable. It is only for graduates and above that the differentials with other levels of education have widened during the first decade of the post-liberalisation period but in the most recent year of 2011–12, this differential has shown some decline.

What has happened to wage inequality among workers within the same educational category? Inequality within the educational categories (Table 12.9) showed remarkable stability in the pre-reform period (from 1983 to 1993–94). In the first decade of the post-reform period, for those who had attained secondary schooling and above, the ratio between wages at the 50th percentile and 25th percentile and between the 75th percentile and 25th percentile showed a perceptible increase. The biggest rise occurred for graduates and above. However, this pattern was not observed for lower educational levels. However, in the most recent period of 2011–12, only the ratio of wage between the 75th percentile and 25th percentile showed some increase for graduates and above. For all other ratios, one can discern a clear decline. Looking at it in totality, the increase in wage inequality appears to reflect both increased differentials between educational categories and increased inequality within them, but this is confined to higher educational levels. The findings of this section encourage us to analyse the factors contributing for this inequality of regular wage workers in the ensuing section.

EARNINGS DIFFERENTIALS BY GENDER

As is well known, the wages of female workers are lower than those of men across most employment categories and locations. The range of difference can be seen in Table 12.10, which gives wages of regular and casual male and female workers in rural and urban areas, as recorded in the various Rounds of NSS quinquennial surveys (from 1983 to 2011–12).

The wages of women workers are at least 20%, and at the maximum 50%, lesser than male wages across different categories, locations and years. Male–female differentials in regular wages in rural areas have widened—average female wage was 72% of average male wage in this category in 1983, which fell to 59% in 2004–05 and increased marginally to 63% in 2011–12. Across all other categories, rural casual, urban regular and urban casual, the gap between male and female wages has narrowed in 1983–2011 to a greater or smaller degree, with the maximum improvement visible in urban regular employment wherein the female wage was 80% of the male wage in 2011–12. An improvement of 12 percentage points was seen in the case of urban casual workers as well, though the category exhibits the widest differential at 62%.

Does education reduce the gender gap in wages? It appears that it does in regular employment but not in casual employment. The female to male wage ratio and t-values among regular salaried workers clearly show that there is a significant wage differential between males and females (Table 12.11). In fact, in the casual labour market, it seems to widen the wage gap between men and women. According to the data from NSSO (2011–12), the wage disparity between men and women declined with increasing level of

Table 12.10
Average Daily Wages of Male and Females (from 1983 to 2011–12)

	1983		1993–94		2004–05		2011–12	
	Male	Female	Male	Female	Male	Female	Male	Female
RR	17.6	12.8	58.5	34.9	144.9	85.3	320.2	202.8
RC	7.8	4.9	23.2	15.3	55.1	34.9	150.4	104.6
UR	25.7	19.5	78.1	63.3	203.3	153.2	462.8	368.8
UC	11.1	5.6	32.4	18.5	75.1	43.9	185.0	114.9

Source: Computed from unit level data of various NSS Rounds.
Note: RR = Rural Regular, RC = Rural Casual, UR = Urban Regular, UC = Urban Casual.

Table 12.11

Average Real Daily Wages of Regular Workers by Gender, Location and Levels of Education, and Ratio of Female Wages to Male Wages for 1993–94 and 2011–12 (at Constant 2001 Prices)

Education Levels	1993–94					2011–12				
	Person	Male ($\bar{Y}_m$)	Female ($\bar{Y}_f$)	t-stats of ($\bar{Y}_m - \bar{Y}_f$)	$\bar{Y}_f / \bar{Y}_m$	Person	Male ($\bar{Y}_m$)	Female ($\bar{Y}_f$)	t-stats of ($\bar{Y}_m - \bar{Y}_f$)	$\bar{Y}_f / \bar{Y}_m$
Rural										
Illiterate	41.30	46.89	26.52	14.63	0.57	69.47	85.73	38.74	14.88	0.45
Literate up to Below primary	56.32	60.42	29.92	10.00	0.50	83.81	91.71	55.15	5.53	0.60
Primary	64.29	66.88	32.18	9.15	0.48	81.88	90.87	46.94	10.01	0.52
Middle	77.80	81.01	47.71	8.09	0.59	99.84	107.73	55.36	11.12	0.51
Secondary	104.42	107.45	84.55	4.68	0.79	133.18	140.71	83.38	8.20	0.59
Higher Secondary	115.44	118.49	95.12	3.67	0.80	155.64	169.77	93.64	7.54	0.55
Diploma/Certificate	–	–	–	–	–	211.34	212.67	205.80	0.29	0.97
Graduate & above	148.50	152.34	111.85	5.59	0.73	246.43	263.11	184.73	5.53	0.70
All	84.56	90.10	52.35	20.55	0.58	141.08	152.36	94.85	12.60	0.62
Urban										
Illiterate	71.36	82.90	46.32	17.29	0.56	84.23	100.38	58.09	8.32	0.58
Literate up to Below primary	86.39	90.86	46.68	12.59	0.51	98.05	107.40	67.56	5.45	0.63
Primary	84.36	88.03	47.22	13.77	0.54	101.84	111.99	60.79	9.43	0.54
Middle	98.28	100.84	63.99	8.71	0.63	116.73	124.39	67.89	8.68	0.55
Secondary	135.26	136.63	126.16	2.53	0.92	156.55	159.57	132.10	2.09	0.83
Higher Secondary	143.56	146.91	123.63	5.15	0.84	189.52	192.14	173.30	1.37	0.90
Diploma/Certificate	–	–	–	–	–	242.33	254.67	187.96	4.78	0.74
Graduate & above	213.01	222.29	172.60	11.38	0.78	350.74	369.08	288.49	7.28	0.78
All	132.62	137.05	107.36	14.70	0.78	209.14	218.87	169.27	8.95	0.77

Source: Computed from unit level NSS data.

Note: Individuals belong to 15–65 age groups in 18 major states of India.

education in both rural and urban areas in regular work except for graduate and higher education level in urban areas. The *Gender Pay Gap Report* in the formal sector 2006–13 further shows that there are increasing wage differentials when level of education increases. It is a serious concern for policy.

A woman worker, with no education, received only 53% of a man's wage in a regular job in rural areas, but with a graduate degree she received 70% of the wage as her male counterpart. In urban areas, the gap was lower—a non-literate woman received 62% of male wages, on an average, while secondary level education enabled her to reach 86% of male wages (though with a graduation degree this fell to 76%). In general, education acted as a leveller between men and women as far as regular jobs were concerned. In the casual labour market, however, education seems to put women at a relative disadvantage. Across both rural and urban geographies, women with primary education are seen to be worse off than the non-literate women in terms of female–male wage differentials. It must also be noted that, in general, education has brought little improvement in wages in casual employment for male as well as female workers. In the case of regular employment, however, education led to a significant increase in wages of both men and women. In fact, the wages of female workers rose faster with education than those of male workers, in regular jobs. It, therefore, appears that regular employment is a necessary condition for education to benefit workers in general, and to reduce the gender wage gap in particular.

EARNINGS DIFFERENTIALS BY CASTE AND RELIGION

Caste-based stratification translates into low endowments of human capital and material resources for individuals and households belonging to castes at the bottom end of the social hierarchy. For instance, the literacy rate for SC individuals is 46% compared to 75% among general caste individuals. The differences at lower levels of education—below primary and primary—are less pronounced across social groups, but start to diverge widely by middle school. Only 4% of SC individuals are graduates compared to 17.4% general caste individuals (Table 12.12). There are also concerns about the quality of schooling (either through access to lower quality schools or discrimination within schools) and hence on the learning outcomes received by children from different castes (for an experimental study on the effect of caste on learning achievement, see Hoff and Pandey 2006).

Table 12.12

Percentage Distribution of Employed (UPSS) by Caste and Level of Education (2011–12)

Educational Categories	ST	SC	OBC	Others
Illiterate	46.2	38.8	31.5	17.9
Literate & Below Primary	13.0	12.2	11.3	8.6
Primary	13.3	15.2	13.1	12.3
Middle	14.0	15.7	17.3	16.5
Secondary	5.9	8.9	12.2	15.4
Higher Secondary	3.7	4.4	6.2	9.8
Diploma/Certificate	0.5	0.8	1.5	2.0
Graduate and above	3.2	4.0	6.9	17.4
Total	100	100	100	100

Source: Calculated from unit level data of NSSO.
Note: Age 5 and above years.

We are, however, more concerned about the earning differentials in the society. While equitable employment opportunities are desirable, jobs, per se, are not important unless they ensure a decent living standard. Ensuring jobs are crucial in as much as they ensure certain minimum income for the deprived people, which they can utilise for capacity building and thereby come out of the trap of deprivation and backwardness. However, this requires equality in the arena of earnings as well since any inequality herein against the already excluded would only create further deprivation and widen the disparities. We discuss some salient factors in the context of Regular Wage Salaried (RWS) employees. Wage data on caste are available by broad administrative categories—SCs, STs and OBC groups of castes, tribes and communities—identified as beneficiaries of affirmative action due to accumulated disadvantage and in the case of SCs and STs, added stigmatisation on account of their caste/tribe status. Those who are not eligible form a heterogeneous residual category of 'others' (everyone else), which is a rough proxy for upper castes.

In India, people in the highest earnings deciles are professionals who are relatively few in number, such that everyone belonging to that education cohort enjoys a high return on their education, irrespective of their castes or religious beliefs (Bhaumik and Chakrabarty 2006). People belonging to the lowest earnings deciles, on the other hand, have low educational endowment and compete with each other for jobs that do not necessarily require any skills. Their market determined earnings, therefore, are low and do not vary significantly across castes and religions. However, individuals who lie between these extremes work in formal or quasi-formal enterprises and the education they have are of heterogeneous quality. Hence, it is possible for a graduate of commerce from a reputed university to get a job as a bank official, thereby gaining access to a fairly substantial salary and associated perks, while someone with a degree in humanities from a relatively unknown university may end up working as a clerk at a small private enterprise, earning an income that is barely enough for survival. The implications of this scenario are twofold:

1. Difference in earnings would be low across castes and religions for individuals with very low and very high levels of education and much higher in the intermediate range of education.
2. The relatively high earnings differential around the median level of earnings could be on account of differences in observed factors such as proportion of people belonging to various castes and religions with a certain level of education, and also on account of differences in unobserved factors that yield different rates of return on education for people belonging to different castes and religions.

The mean earnings of people with different educational endowments, and belonging to different castes and religion are reported in Tables 12.13 and 12.14. It can easily be seen that earnings unambiguously increase with the level of education, for all castes and religions, and for both the years. This strong positive correlation between education level and earnings suggests that earnings differentials across castes and religions are likely to be influenced significantly by inter-caste and inter-religion differences in educational endowment.

However, it is not obvious as to whether inter-caste and inter-religion differences in earnings can be explained by differences in the returns to education across castes and religions. As highlighted above, differences in returns to education are most likely to be observed for people with intermediate levels of education. Hence, if these returns are an important determinant of earnings differentials, after controlling for the level of education, then earnings differentials should be the lowest for the illiterate and professionals, and much higher for people with intermediate levels of education. However, it is evident from Table 12.14 that this is not the case. For example, from 1993–94 to 2011–12, there was virtually no difference between the earnings of illiterate other (or 'upper')

Table 12.13
Average Real Daily Wages of Regular Workers by Caste, Location and Levels of Education, and Ratio of SC Wages to Others Wages for 1993–94 and 2011–12 (at Constant 2001 Prices)

Education Levels	1993–94				2011–12			
	Others* ($\bar{Y}_{others}$)	SC ($\bar{Y}_{sc}$)	t-stats of ($\bar{Y}_{others} - \bar{Y}_{sc}$)	$\bar{Y}_{sc} / \bar{Y}_{others}$	Others* ($\bar{Y}_{others}$)	SC ($\bar{Y}_{sc}$)	t-stats of ($\bar{Y}_{others} - \bar{Y}_{sc}$)	$\bar{Y}_{sc} / \bar{Y}_{others}$
Rural								
Illiterate	41.86	39.93	0.99	0.95	69.83	67.27	0.40	0.96
Literate up to Below primary	58.48	48.79	2.22	0.83	88.00	87.60	0.03	1.00
Primary	66.40	57.24	2.18	0.86	80.91	89.72	−0.89	1.11
Middle	78.62	70.86	1.70	0.90	107.76	92.63	1.95	0.86
Secondary	105.23	98.87	1.24	0.94	140.18	139.09	0.07	0.99
Higher Secondary	116.03	108.61	0.98	0.94	170.10	149.83	1.34	0.88
Diploma	–	–	–	–	213.87	200.96	0.42	0.94
Graduate & above	150.34	128.57	2.20	0.86	261.50	241.85	1.11	0.92
All	90.21	65.29	13.20	0.72	166.13	124.44	6.71	0.75
Urban								
Illiterate	68.50	77.10	−3.44	1.13	83.73	83.33	0.05	1.00
Literate up to Below primary	85.01	89.57	−1.36	1.05	93.98	99.29	−0.59	1.06
Primary	83.50	85.42	−0.65	1.02	107.26	101.91	0.58	0.95
Middle	97.10	102.74	−1.50	1.06	121.14	111.89	1.38	0.92
Secondary	137.12	113.27	6.02	0.83	172.74	148.97	2.04	0.86
Higher Secondary	143.26	150.27	−0.86	1.05	205.85	187.80	1.20	0.91
Diploma	–	–	–	–	273.80	221.53	2.33	0.81
Graduate & above	214.09	194.52	2.40	0.91	394.08	283.55	7.17	0.72
All	136.62	105.12	16.70	0.77	253.83	160.50	14.97	0.63

Source: Computed from NSS data.
Note: Individual belongs to 15–65 age groups in 18 major states of India.
*Others include OBCs.

Table 12.14

Average Real Daily Wages of Regular Workers by Religion, Location and Levels of Education, and Ratio of Muslim Wages to Hindu Wages for 1993–94 and 2011–12 (at Constant 2001 Prices)

Education Levels	1993–94				2011–12			
	Hindu $(\bar{Y}_h)$	Muslim $(\bar{Y}_m)$	t-stats of $(\bar{Y}_h - \bar{Y}_m)$	$\bar{Y}_m / \bar{Y}_h$	Hindu $(\bar{Y}_h)$	Muslim $(\bar{Y}_m)$	t-stats of $(\bar{Y}_h - \bar{Y}_m)$	$\bar{Y}_m / \bar{Y}_h$
Rural								
Illiterate	40.60	49.98	-2.52	1.23	68.25	74.12	-0.84	1.09
Literate up to Below primary	55.40	63.14	-1.42	1.14	88.84	65.55	3.10	0.74
Primary	63.81	66.57	-0.46	1.04	83.94	76.61	0.99	0.91
Middle	79.27	63.55	3.14	0.80	99.98	95.34	0.70	0.95
Secondary	104.66	114.89	-1.30	1.10	134.04	139.17	-0.55	1.04
Higher Secondary	116.58	109.23	0.89	0.94	155.00	143.58	0.77	0.93
Diploma/Certificate	—	—	—	—	214.61	199.52	0.45	0.93
Graduate & above	148.82	154.24	-0.55	1.04	245.03	269.81	-1.17	1.10
All	85.19	78.24	2.62	0.92	143.69	125.06	3.44	0.87
Urban								
Illiterate	72.98	62.21	3.96	0.85	85.00	77.63	1.43	0.91
Literate up to Below primary	86.57	85.38	0.30	0.99	99.07	91.70	0.75	0.93
Primary	85.12	78.20	1.90	0.92	105.63	88.97	2.66	0.84
Middle	99.47	82.30	4.84	0.83	117.74	104.07	1.86	0.88
Secondary	136.62	115.36	4.17	0.84	154.83	148.70	0.67	0.96
Higher Secondary	145.20	123.46	3.66	0.85	194.11	169.15	1.55	0.87
Diploma/Certificate	—	—	—	—	242.77	222.92	0.68	0.92
Graduate & above	213.66	190.47	2.82	0.89	354.36	284.54	5.34	0.80
All	135.17	98.89	17.43	0.73	216.40	140.70	15.77	0.65

Source: Computed from NSS data.

Note: Individual belongs to 15–65 age groups in 18 major states of India.

castes and their illiterate SC/ST counterparts, and the corresponding difference between earnings of people belonging to these two
castes with graduate and above is 72% in the urban regular labour
market. The interesting note is that the earnings differentials
between these two castes with graduate level of education are
widening compared to other level of education (91% in 1993–94,
which has come down to 72% in the regular urban labour market).
Between Hindus and Muslims earning differentials had increased
over the same period with graduate education level.

Our analysis thus far suggests that inter-caste differences with
graduate level education was widening between 1993–94 and 2011–
12 while inter-religion differences were also rising. There is once
again evidence to suggest that education is likely to explain, at least
in part, differences in earnings across castes and religions. To reiter-
ate, while differences in levels of educational endowment almost
certainly explain part of differences in earnings, it is not evident as
to whether differences in returns on education play a role as well.
Hence, we require a more formal decomposition of the inter-caste
and inter-religion differences in earnings and these are reported in
the following section. Quite clearly, deprivation and disparities are
on the rise in the post-Structural Adjustment Programme (SAP)
period. This has serious consequences for social equity in India.

DECOMPOSITION ANALYSIS OF EARNINGS INEQUALITY BY GENDER, CASTE AND RELIGION

In the earlier sections, we discussed in detail the earnings differentials among wage earners by gender, caste and religion. We
observed that differential in earnings is contributed by various
factors such as educational level and employment status, etc. We
need to know the contributions of each these characteristics to
earning inequality. Fields (2002) developed a new approach that
considers simultaneously the impact of several characteristic on
earnings and allows distinguishing the contribution of each of these
characteristic. This method has advantage over the earlier inequality measures such as Gini, Variance, etc. The approach is useful as
it helps to factor in the contribution of various factors including
categorical factors that enter as a string of dummy variables.

We present (in Figures 12.1–12.3) decomposition of factors
(excluding residuals) that contribute to the earnings disparity of all
wage earners. The level of education emerged as the most dominant

factor contributing to the level of inequality in the earnings of wage-workers. The age and occupation was the next important factors. The education factor is the combined effect of all the years of schooling. When we differentiated with years of schooling, we observed that the contribution of workers with education level graduate and above in education component is very high irrespective of gender, caste and religion. It shows that even after controlling for several factors, the relative earnings of workers with graduate and above had registered a huge increase in the last two decades of growth. Human capital—as embodied in age and education—is one of the major factors explaining both the level of and change in regular wage inequality.

The decomposition of factors revealed enormous differences in explaining the levels of earning inequality among wage earners. Two major factors, occupation and educational levels, were the most dominant factors contributing to inequality. The former two factors were also the most important factors for explaining the increase in inequality in the post-reform period (Sarkar and Mehta 2010). Within the education factor, the graduates and above sub-component was the highest contributor, accounting for 33% and 55% contribution in 2011–12 among males and females. As a whole, the better-off sections of workers have gained at the cost of the more vulnerable sections. This requires urgent policy attention if the interests of the poor, less educated and semi-skilled workforce

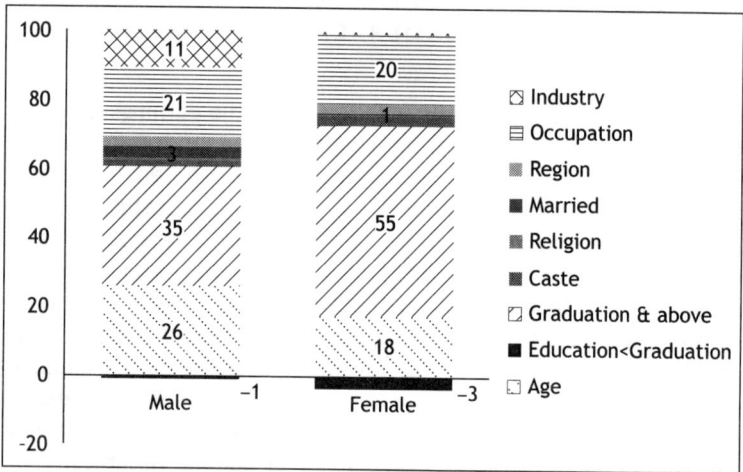

Figure 12.1
Relative Factor Inequality Shares by Gender in Regular Urban Labour Market (LM) (2011–12)

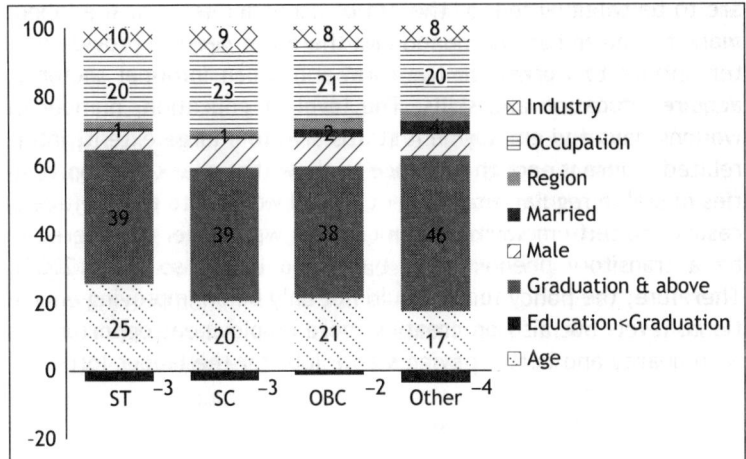

Figure 12.2
Relative Factor Inequality Shares by Caste in Regular Urban LM (2011–12)

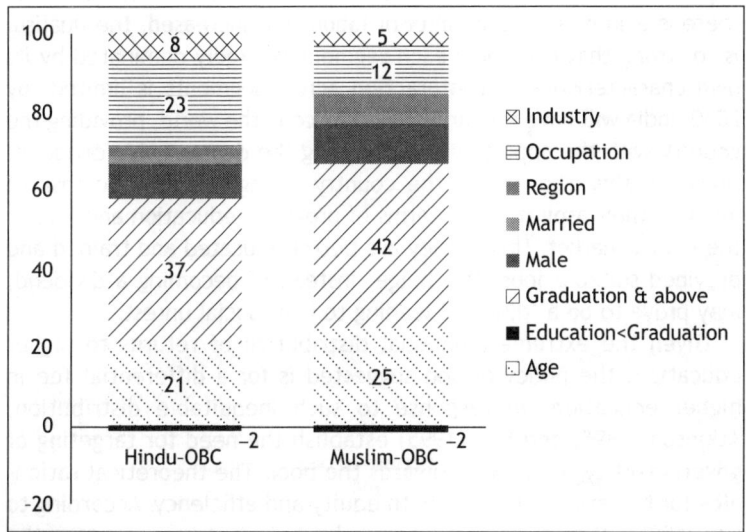

Figure 12.3
Relative Factor Inequality Shares by Religion in Regular Urban LM (2011–12)

are to be safeguarded. In the era of economic reform, the labour market dualism had sharpened and there is a need to provide better options to workers in the rural and urban informal sector to acquire education and skills. The level of education, number of working days and employment status are, to a large extent, inter-related. There is enough evidence to show that a lack of opportunities of stable regular employment forced workers to take refuge in casual and self-employment work, which was earlier considered to be a transitory phenomenon, but is no longer so (Rani 2008). Therefore, the policy focus should not only be on improving educational levels but also on creating more employment opportunities with quality and better paying stable jobs for the labour force.

CONCLUSION

There is considerable segmentation and dualism in the Indian labour market in terms of various categories/sectors (organised versus unorganised/formal versus informal), occupations, locations (rural versus urban), gender, castes, tribes, religion, etc. Contrary to expectations, the labour market dualism has not narrowed. While there is evidence that mobility of labour has increased, the dualism is so strong that even now each segment is largely dominated by its own characteristics and interaction across segments is limited. By 2030, India will have the largest workforce in the world, providing the country with the opportunity for reaping the demographic dividend. However, this also entails the country facing the gigantic task of meeting their aspirations in terms of providing education and jobs in the labour market. Unless they are better educated and trained and provided suitable jobs, this bulge, instead of becoming a dividend, may prove to be a 'disaster' leading to huge social unrest.

Given the extremely unequal distribution of returns to higher education, the policy option suggested is for a differential fee in higher education. In response to such inequitable distribution, Atkinson (1995) and Sen (1995) establish the need for targeting of government expenditures towards the poor. The theoretical rationales for targeting extend to both equity and efficiency. According to Sen (1995), 'the more accurate a subsidy in fact is in reaching the poor, the less the wastage, and less it costs to achieve the desired objective'. However, the political question concerns the actual feasibility and acceptability of aiming public policy toward particular deprived groups. The political economy of targeting has to be concerned not just with the economic problems of selection, information and incentives but also with the political support for, and feasibility of, aiming public policy specifically at removing the deprivation of particular groups (Rani 2014). Now, the Eleventh and Twelfth Five Year Plans emphasise more on inclusive growth, as the economic growth during the reforming period has not resulted in redistribution of income. In this debate, measures to improve equality of educational opportunity deserve special attention. Hence, it is argued for differential treatment of the deprived sections both socially and economically.

Average gender wage differentials are much higher for lower levels of education and are smallest for the university educated. Combined with the fact that, on average, the lower educated are usually at the bottom of the overall wage distribution, and the higher educated at the top, this would fit in with the observation of the sticky floor phenomenon in the regular salaried labour market. Therefore, discrimination is almost entirely responsible for the sticky floor effect, which persists even after controlling for all available personal and job characteristics.

There could be two possible reasons for the sticky floor effect. First, a sticky floor could arise because anti-discriminatory policies are more effective at the top of the distribution. Article 39 of the Indian constitution envisaged equal pay for equal work for both men and women. To this end, legislations, such as the Equal Remunerations Act, 1976, were enacted after the equal remuneration ordinance was introduced in the year 1975. Given the fact that 42% of women in the population under study were below even the National Floor Level Minimum Wage (NFLMW), it is clear that legal obligations set by minimum wage legislations are rarely binding for such jobs. Absence of strong minimum wage legislations means that wage gaps can be larger at the bottom of the distribution. Second, occupational segregation is also a known contributor to wider gaps at the bottom, as men and women only enter into exclusively 'male' and 'female' jobs. Low-skilled jobs for women may pay less than other jobs that require intense physical labour, which men typically do. Our model specification controls for broad industry and occupation groups. This means that within certain low-paying broad industrial categories, men and women could be doing different kinds of jobs and that could be picked up as the discrimination component.

The endowment difference is larger than the discrimination coefficient for caste and religion. It has been argued that unequal labour market outcomes have their roots in discrimination in the past that has caused more harm to deprived backgrounds of the disadvantaged workers. Pre-labour market discrimination affects earnings indirectly by the means of lowering out the school investments, poor quality of education, field of study, accessibility to higher education, poorer nutrition and health status and lower social capital. Therefore, the empirical findings of this chapter provides strong evidence for the extension of affirmative action policy in private sector in India and suggest that the federal government could enact 'Equal Opportunity Law' to provide legal safeguards against discrimination.

In light of empirical results, this chapter suggests the various policy implications. The reason for the demand for reservation in the private sector is that the government provides safeguards to private sector units to promote their business, thereby creating better situations for the encouragement of business and trade. The foreign policy and export–import policy of the government contributes to the betterment of the businesses set up by individuals in the private sector. Foreign investors also invest in the private sector by purchasing shares, which is made possible by the policies of the government. The private sector, in turn, is expected to fulfil its social responsibility. It uses public money via public financial institutions; even then, there is no reservation to SCs, STs, and OBCs in the private sector. The upliftment of the weaker sections is a stated objective of our country, and thus the implementation of reservation in the private sector is part of the social responsibility of both the government as well as the private sector. In fact, it is merely the fulfilment of the constitutional agenda of distributive justice enshrined in various articles and clauses of the Constitution. If, however, the private sector is not fulfilling its social responsibility, the government should make such provisions through legislative measure. Even though the private sector uses public money via public financial institutions, it does not enforce reservation for SCs, STs and OBCs.

While the discursive debate about providing reservation in the private sector is on, there are some concerned citizens who are calling for systematic planning and enforcement of some measures that would contribute both to nation-building and improving the lives of the marginalised communities. It is suggested that an employment opportunity commission be constituted to review and ensure that the weaker sections find their representation at all levels. Further, special provisions should be made for higher education, responsive training and multi-skilling of the Tribals and Dalits so that they are able to compete with the others for jobs. The National Commissions for SCs and STs should be empowered so that they can work as pressure groups, exerting pressure on both the government and the private sector to promote the right to participatory development. Finally, a nationwide debate should be held on these issues and the necessary constitutional amendments should be introduced to enact affirmative action (AA) at all levels in the private sector.

REFERENCES

Abraham, Vinoj. 2007. 'Growth and Inequality of Wages in India: Recent Trends and Patterns'. *Indian Journal of Labour Economics* 50 (4): 927–41.

Agarwal, Pawan. 2006. 'Higher Education in India: The need for Change'. Working Paper No.180, ICRIER, New Delhi.

Atkinson, A. 1995. 'On Targeting Social Security: Theory and Western Experience with Family Benefits'. In *Public Spending and the Poor*, edited by D. Van de Walle and K. Nead, 25–68. Baltimore: Johns Hopkins University Press.

Becker, G.S. 1964. *Human Capital: A Theoretical and Empirical Analysis with Special Reference to Education*. Chicago: University of Chicago Press.

Bhaumik, S.K., and m. Chakrabarty. 2006. 'Earnings Inequality in India: Has the Rise of Caste and Religion Based Politics in India Had an Impact?' Discussion Paper No. 2008, The Institute for the Study of Labor, Germany.

Blaug, M., R. Layard, and M. Woodhall. 1969. *Causes of Graduate Unemployment in India*. London: Allen Lane and Penguin Press.

Chaudhary, R., and S. Verick. 2014. Female Labour Force Participation in India and Beyond. ILO Asia-Pacific Working Paper Series.

Fields, G.S. 2002. 'Accounting for Income Inequality and Its Change'. Unpublished paper, Cornell University, New York.

Gibbons, M. 1998. *Higher Education Relevance in the 21st Century*. Education: The World Bank. http://www.wds.worldbank.org/servlet/WDSContentServer/WDSP/IB/2000/07/19/000094946_991222 0532351/Rendered/PDF/multi_page.pdf

Government of India. 2011. *Census of India 2011*. Office of the Registrar General and Census Commissioner, India. Ministry of Home Affairs, Government of India.

Hoff, K., and P. Pandey. 2006. 'Discrimination, Social Identity and Durable Inequalities'. *American Economic Review* 96 (2): 206–11.

India Labour and Employment Report (ILER). 2014. 'India Labour and Employment Report: Workers in the Era of Globalization'. Academic Foundation, Institute for Human Development: New Delhi.

Institute of Human Development (IHD). 2014. 'India Labour and Employment Report'. New Delhi: IHD.

Madheswaran, S. 1996. 'Econometric Analyses of Labour Market for Scientists in India'. Unpublished PhD Thesis, University of Madras.

Mazumdar, D., and S. Sarkar. 2008. 'Globalization, Labour Markets and Inequality in India'. In *Routledge Studies in the Growth Economies of Asia*, vol. 79. Canada: International Development Research Centre.

National Sample Survey Organisation. 1997. 'Employment and Unemployment in India'. NSS 50th Round, 1993–94, Report No. 409, Department of Statistics, Government of India, New Delhi.

_____. 2012. 'Employment and Unemployment Situation Among Major Religious Groups in India'. NSS 66th Round, 2009–10, Report No. 552, Ministry of Statistics and Programme Implementation, Government of India, New Delhi.

_____. 2014. 'Employment and Unemployment Situation in India'. NSS 68th Round, 2011–12, Report No. 554, Ministry of Statistics and Programme Implementation, Government of India, New Delhi.

Rani, P.G. 2014. 'Disparities in Earnings and Education in India'. *Cogent Economics and Finance* 2: 1. doi:10.1080/23322039.2014.941510.

Rani, Uma. 2008. 'Impact of Changing Work Pattern on Income Inequality'. Discussion Paper 193/2008, International Institute of Labour Studies, Geneva.

Sarkar, Sandip, and Balwant Singh Mehta. 2010. 'Income Inequality in India: Pre- and Post-reform Periods'. *Economic and Political Weekly* 45 (37): 45–55.

Sen, A. 1995. *Inequality Re-examined*. USA: Harvard University Press.

Sharma, Alakh N. 2002. *Access to Employment in India: The Case of Public and Corporate Sector Jobs* (mimeo). New Delhi: Institute for Human Development.

Spence, M.A. 1973. 'Job Market Signalling'. *Quarterly Journal of Economics* 87 (3): 355–74.

_____. 2006. *India's Employment Challenge: Creating Jobs, Helping Workers*. Chennai: Oxford University Press.

13

Disparities in Graduate Employability Skills

Mona Khare

INTRODUCTION

The deliberations on post-2015 Millennium Development Goals (MDGs/ EFAs) on education seem to emphasise two important shifts. They are on improving access to higher and vocational education on the one hand and shifting focus from access to learning outcomes on the other. The Global Thematic Consultation on Education in the post-2015 development agenda proposed 'equitable, quality education and lifelong learning for all' as the overarching goal for education. In fact, in the light of the fact that the United Nations (UN) has made employability as one of its four priorities for national policy action on youth employment, the UN's Youth Employment Network has suggested that all countries need to review, rethink and reorient their education, vocational training and labour market policies to facilitate the school to work transition and to give young people a head start in working life (UN 2001). This chapter discusses the issue of employability of higher education graduates in India focusing on the 'employability skills' possessed by the new recruits and the expectations of the employers from the universities in preparing industry-ready graduates. The study shall also try to explore the challenges the new employees experience in their work place and to what extent they are required to supplement their university education with external trainings of different nature to fill in this gap.

HIGHER EDUCATION AND LABOUR MARKET CONNECT

The discussions on the links between higher education and the economy have a long history. The discourses and debates on this relationship too have evolved with the changing structure of the global economy. The classical economists treated labour as a homogeneous unit and based their wage determination models on the marginal productivity theory. The neoclassical economists brought in the concept of skill differentials across labour (Human Capital Theory) and wage differentials according to varying individual productivity. Attributing variations in skills to levels of education and years of schooling and wage differential according to productivity of the neoclassical tradition established linkages between education and labour market. Any mismatch between the supply of skills (educational) and the demand for those skills may arise due to labour market imperfections. The segmented labour market theory asserts that the relationship between individuals and employment through education is not direct. According to them, education reproduces social class hierarchies existing in the society, which, in turn, are reflected in the labour market structure and job allocations as per social class positions (Carnoy 1987). Those who come from better socio-economic and cultural background and with previous experience, etc. are preferred by employers as they reduce training costs for the employing firm.

The turn of the century, however, saw a rising consensus on the theories of 'education for better livelihood' and shaping education to labour market needs. The early 1990s saw a multi-polar world with emerging economies of the Asian region witnessing high growth rates with widening employment opportunities. A distinct feature of this growth was it being manufacturing led and export based. As rightly pointed by Wood (1994) the 'skill intensity of these exports were high' with increasing regional and international competition. This necessitated an increasing demand for an educated labour force to leverage competitive advantage in exports so as to maintain high rates of growth. This saw expansion of state supported education systems, which, in turn, played an important role in reshaping the growth patterns of these economies. However, the high economic growth of the early 1990s could not be sustained and soon the 'happy state' of economic progress and household prosperity (Varghese 2001) got a jolt with the East Asian Economic crisis of the late 1990s.

The shift in the macroeconomic development framework to a more open and liberalised regime has had its reflections in the higher education sector and in the labour market. The revival of economic growth, centred around knowledge economy by the turn of the century, strengthened the link between education and economic prosperity with increasing demand for not just educated but highly educated and multi-skilled labour force. This was matched by a shift in higher education from an 'elitist' to 'mass' system in many emerging economies with a gradual decline in state financing and increasing private participation in the sector. While the labour market has become more flexible and limited in expansion and job creation (jobless growth), the higher education systems have become more specialised and costly for households, thereby generating greater concerns over the 'value and returns of a university degree' as against the social prestige attached to it traditionally. In fact, a large body of literature points out that the massification of higher education, perpetuating structural inequalities and increasing stratification and differentiation in the society are arising out of 'class-cultural and academic profiles of graduates from different HEIs, along with different rates of graduate return' (Archer, Hutchings, and Ross 2003; Little and Archer 2010; Scott 2005).

At present new questions are being posed on the 'specific role of HE in regulating skilled labour, and the overall matching of the supply of graduates leaving HE to their actual economic demand and utility' (Bowers-Brown and Harvey 2004). Today's universities thus have wider missions and are expected to educate to build expertise, participate in development of knowledge and ensure that both, the knowledge created and the expertise developed, are relevant to the society. Works in recent years have further reinstated this multifaceted role of higher education in shaping the youth for work and society. The *Dearing Report* (Dearing 1997) underlines the important role of higher education in modern globally competitive economy that requires that 'Education and training [should] enable people in an advanced society to compete with the best in the world' (NCIHE 1997). This is consistent with the views of Reich (1991 and 2002) who argues that advanced economies need two sorts of high-level expertise: one emphasising discovery and the other focusing on exploiting the discoveries of others through market-related intelligence and the application of interpersonal skills. He describes such professionals as 'symbolic analysts', who, according to him, are

imaginative and creative, have at their fingertips relevant disciplinary understanding and skills and the 'soft' or generic skills that enable the disciplinary base to be deployed to optimal effect. Higher education's key contribution to national prosperity lies in development of graduates with such achievement at their disposal.

Knowledge and skills both became a matter to cumulative demand by employers as well as the society at large. The new terminology that gained popularity with the world comprised of a set of both cognitive and non-cognitive attributes and skills in a knowledge framework—the 'employability skills'. It is from here that the definition and understanding of the role of education took a new leap.

GRADUATE EMPLOYABILITY AND EMPLOYABILITY SKILLS

Employability is a rather broad term encompassing an individual's preparedness for the world of work. The concept of graduate employability has been explained by the earlier proponents in three ways: one is the 'capability approach' as propagated by Royal Society for the Arts, Manufactures and Commerce (RSA), London, in the late 1980s (RSA 1980 and 1991) and supported by later authors, as the capability or preparedness of the graduates to get employed (Harvey 2001; Heijden 2002) irrespective of the fact whether they actually get a job or not. Harvey (2000) regards employability to be a subset of and fundamentally contingent on transformative lifelong learning. The second may be termed as the 'performance approach' to be understood as the ability of a graduate to get just any job. The third is the 'employers' approach', that is, the propensity of the graduate to exhibit attributes that employers anticipate will be necessary for the future effective functioning of their organisation (Harvey 2001). It is only when a graduate has the capability and ability to be employed and is able to market himself to the employers that he actually gets employed and maintains it. While employment is having a job, employability means 'having the qualities needed to maintain employment and progress in the workplace' (Lees 2012).

According to ILO, employability refers to

> 'the capacity and willingness of workers to remain attractive for the labour market (supply factors), by reacting to and anticipating changes in tasks and work environment (demand factors), facilitated by the human resource development instruments available to them (institutions). It is viewed as 'a set of achievements—skills, understandings and personal attributes—that make graduates more likely to gain employment and be successful in their chosen occupations, which benefits themselves, the workforce, the community and the economy'. (Yorke 2004 and 2006)

In today's dynamic economy and rapidly changing work environment, employability skills do not remain restricted just to the ones required to gain employment but also to constantly improve and upgrade oneself to be able to compete and sustain in the labour market. Employability is the capability to move self-sufficiently within the labour market to realise potential through sustainable employment.

Since technical skills are industry specific, there is a growing acceptance among the international community that for measuring comparative employability, generic employability skills should be given more weight. The employability skills have thus been defined as a mix of knowledge, values and attitude, and it includes communication skills, numeracy, information technology, learning how to learn/personal development planning, problem-solving and team working. It is understood as a function of two basic factors: academic qualification of an individual and the learning environment that helps him build certain generic skills (Khare 2012).

The concept of employability skills is thus highly complex and contextual and can be said to be based on Yorke's (2004) three super ordinate constructs of employability that map somewhat fuzzily on to the listed items:

- Employability as demonstrated by the graduate actually obtaining a job.
- Employability as the students being developed by their experience of higher education (i.e., it is a curricular and perhaps extra-curricular process).
- Employability in terms of the possession of relevant *achievements* (and, implicitly, potential).

It depends on a multitude of factors that can be broadly classified under three heads—knowledge, skills and attitude. Employability, thus, in this chapter, too, has been used in the context of generic skills.

GRADUATE EMPLOYABILITY: EMPLOYERS' PERCEPTIONS

Based on an extensive review of literature and the e-survey[1] by the author, it can be said that a higher education (HE) graduate in labour market is typically expected to

[1] Responses were generated from company executives in India through an e-survey as well as telephonic interviews to a set of pre-defined questions to identify the kind of skills employers are looking for.

- be able to demonstrate understanding of organisations, the external environment in which they operate, how they are managed and the future needs of organisations;
- have skills in critical thinking analysis and synthesis, including being able to identify assumptions, evaluate statements, detect false logic, identify implicit values, define terms adequately and generalise appropriately;
- be effective at problem-solving and decision-making, using appropriate quantitative and qualitative skills and also be able to create, evaluate and assess options, together with being able to apply ideas and knowledge to a range of situations;
- be effective in communication, using information and communication technology (ICT) and a range of media widely used in business;
- have numeracy and quantitative skills, including modelling and data analysis, interpretation and extrapolation;
- self-manage their time, behaviour, motivation, initiative and enterprise;
- have an appetite for reflective, adaptive and collaborative learning;
- be self-aware, sensitive and open to the diversity of people, cultures, business and management issues;
- have leadership, team building, influencing and project management skills; and
- be effective at listening, negotiating and persuasion.

Similar sentiments have been echoed by various other reports in India (sector specific skill gap reports of National Skill Development Corporation or NSDC). As per the *India Skills Report*, 2015, integrity and values top the list (39%) in the skills desired by employers followed by domain expertise (22%), interpersonal skill, learning ability (14%), communication (10%), cultural fitment (8%), numerical and logical ability (4%) and adaptability (3%). Another report by the Asian Development Bank (ADB 2012) points that employers feel that 'graduates are missing key soft skills and English language abilities'. It further adds that today's dynamic economies require high-level talent that is also innovative, risk taking, adaptable and responsive to changing environments. CEO's of various companies also have similar opinion when they say that 'graduates lack soft and workforce skills'. Employers, accordingly, expect their employees to be more attuned to an increasingly competitive external environment, which will require creative thinking, problem-solving and good communication skills.

CLASSIFYING EMPLOYABILITY SKILL GAPS

The skill preferences of the employers' differ from sector to sector, depending on the job profiles and the kind of work each of the sectors entail. It seems that domain knowledge is the most desired in core industries such as engineering, auto, telecom, etc. while communication skill has a premium in hospitality, entertainment and education sectors. In the light of the above, the following identifiable skill gaps were pointed out by our respondents that are generic in nature and cut across all the sectors of work. These can be broadly classified into personal, functional, finance and business process-related skill gaps (see Table 13.1). The personal skill gaps identified are much higher in number than the functional skill gaps.

It can be observed that the personal skill gaps are largely a function of one's attitude that builds over a long period and the seeds of which are sown quite early in life. There is little that can be done

Table 13.1
Personal Skill Gaps

Identifiable	Personal Skill Gaps
Empathy with the customers	Poor listening skills
Orientation towards achieving stretch targets	Mentoring
Adaptability to Change	Inadequate ability to work with and give instructions to workers who are senior in age or experience
People management	Presentable and pleasing personality
Quick decision-making ability	Objection handling and convincing skills
Ability to work under pressure	Ability to understand customer requirements
Lack of coordination and liaisoning	Unable to converse in local languages
Multitasking and time management	Willingness to learn
Ability to motivate the team to achieve set targets	Inadequate organising skills
Poor in conflict management	Inadequate ability to handle complaints
Eye for details	Inadequate soft skills
Leadership and team management skills	Inadequate problem-solving ability

Source: Author's own.

Table 13.2
Functional Skill Gaps

S. No.	Functional Skill Gaps
1.	Customer relationship management
2.	Inadequate interpersonal skills
3.	Inadequate understanding and customer relationship management
4.	Expectations and behaviour
5.	Inadequate negotiation skills
6.	Ability to handle irate customers
7.	Good understanding and knowledge of local language
8.	Inadequate client networking skills
9.	Telephone etiquettes
10.	Understanding consumer behaviour in making purchase decision
11.	Making effective sales pitch Adherence to Processes
12.	Good verbal and non-verbal communication skills presentation skills
13.	Ability to translate marketing knowledge to a retail perspective.

Source: Author's own.

about them at higher levels of learning, except for building ones capabilities, drawing from his basic strengths on personal skills.

It can be seen that most functional skill gaps (Table 13.2) revolve around verbal and non-verbal communication skills. Communication skills, however, are not to be understood in a narrow sense as ability to read, write and speak good English but much beyond that. For an effective and efficient worker, good knowledge of local language, culture and external environment is an additional requirement for good communication both within and outside the organisation. Customer relation, interpersonal relations, negotiation, networking, effecting sales all depend a lot on how well one can convey and convince. Communication skills is an area of concern across all segments, from lower to higher levels of management as well as from small to big towns. It is equally important for a manager to be a good listener. Technological developments of the 21st century have put additional demands on communication methodologies of the managers. They need to be adept in using ICT tools to reach across to the global community and be willing to learn and embrace new technology. Upgrading skills is equally important for other technology-related skills. Technological complexity implies the need for higher

Table 13.3
Financial Skill Gaps

S. No.	Finance-related Skill Gaps
1.	Sound understanding of accounting principles for credit appraisals
2.	Advanced knowledge on project costing and project management tools such as PERT and CPM
3.	Understanding of asset liability
4.	Ability to determine right asset mix of the company
5.	Ineffective utilisation of advertising budgets
6.	In-depth knowledge of tendering process

Source: Author's own.

levels of human knowledge and multi-disciplinary involvement (Boyett and Boyett 2000; Bridges 1996).

Unfortunately, in the middle management levels, willingness to learn appears to be deteriorating and at the senior management level, it is found to be almost stagnant. Two more areas of skill gaps that were emphatically put forth by major employers are finance- and process-related skills. Some of them have been specifically enlisted in Table 13.3.

Among the core departments in any organisation, namely, sales, marketing, finance, and HR, finance has been found to be the weakest spot of the Indian HE graduates. Employers find it most difficult to find skilled and practically ready finance specialists, despite the fact that they might possess formal degrees in the finance-related disciplines. Similarly, some process-related weaknesses identified by the employers' revolve around risk management, compliance, legal and managing intellectual property rights. The employers are of the opinion that greater emphasis should be given in developing additional short-term specialised training courses/internships in different areas of financial management, new terminologies, emerging financial risks and opportunities, hands on experience in software tools, etc.

Marketing research is another area that requires special attention. Market intelligence and awareness of competitor's offering have found to be specially wanting. Knowledge of compliance, regulatory, legal aspects and documentation are also common skill gaps identified across industries. In retail sector, there is the shortage of personnel who are adept at inventory management. Lack of IATA-qualified (International Air Transport Association) personnel is an issue in

Table 13.4
Business Process-related Skill Gaps

S. No.	Business Process-related Skill Gaps
1.	Ability to design processes and process flows
2.	Process management and risk management skills—covering time, cost, quality, delivery
3.	Compliance—ISO/SEI/security processes and the ability to align team processes to meet process compliance requirements
4.	Inventory management
5.	Lack of understanding of information security and privacy issues
6.	Knowledge of legal procedures and processes
7.	Inadequate knowledge of intellectual property management
8.	Inability to upgrade technical knowledge

Source: Author's own.

rapidly expanding tour and travel industry. Interestingly, students from high quality HE institutions are quoted to have a good grasp of functional knowledge but tend to be overly enamoured of intellectual tools and not sensitive enough to the human aspects. Management graduates merely perceive that numbers are numbers and people are people, that numbers are interpreted and acted on by people indifferent ways often escapes them (Barker, Gilbreath, and Stone 1998). Thus, recruiting companies complain that MBA graduates are linear thinkers who lack flexibility (Bickerstaffe 1994). 'Human' aspect of business managers is fast growing in demand, which clearly is reflected in the growing consciousness towards 'corporate social responsibility'. Industry experience is given more preference even in senior management positions.

The employers also opine that Indian executives are lacking more in personal skills as compared to functional skills (Khare 2014). Functional skills are relatively more industry specific and are generally taken care by industries during their probationary trainings. Industries focusing on soft skills and customer orientation-related attributes at the time of recruitment and imparting functional as well as service-oriented trainings on regular intervals to their personnel have workforce that is more adept and has lesser skill gaps. The expectation from the HEIs is thus to focus on imparting personal skills that are more of general nature fitting into the requirements of all industries and the multiple roles that they are required to play. As interestingly put by Longenecker and Ariss (2002), the 'new' managers, we are told, must learn to be coaches, team players, facilitators, process managers, human resource executives, visionary leaders and entrepreneurs. They must also be knowledge-integrating boundary spanners, stimulators of creativity, innovation muses and promoters of learning (Harvey, Novicevic, and Kiessling 2002). They must be more bottom-line driven, more innovative and more focused on the human dynamics of the organisation (Chapman 2001). Innovation and creativity is thus a newfound skill that is high in demand across the globe.

DISPARITIES IN GRADUATE EMPLOYABILITY SKILLS

The social, gender and regional disparities that emerge from the differences in access and participation to higher education get per-petuated further by the quality differentials across boards as well as regional and social context of the learning environment of each individual. There exist regional disparities in employability skills. In a recent study by Purple Leap, it is stated that one-third of gradu-ates from the Tier II, III and IV engineering colleges are not employ-able even after interventional training; the number of readily employable graduates in Tier II, III and IV colleges equal the number of the total talent pool in Tier I engineering colleges (*Times of India* 2012), which (Indian Institutes of Technology IITs and Indian Institutes of Science or IISc) jointly contribute to less than 1% of the engineering graduates in the country. On a scale of 10, the gap between the employability of technical graduates in Tier I and Tier II cities is almost 50% for most of the high growth tech sectors in the country. The situation is far worse in the case of graduates from other streams. Employers find it extremely tough to get good employees, as locals are largely unfit and those who are talented and skilled are from the good institutes in urban centres, unwilling to come to smaller places. The problem may be partly explained by the locational concentration of most of higher education institu-tions in big cities and towns. Migration for education evidently gets translated into migration for employment so that the rural centres continue to remain marginalised. The theory of brain drain becomes operative here, which has serious ramifications in perpetuating the regional disparities in employability skill gaps. English language and computer skills have been quoted to be a major deterrent for small town employability prospects (Khare 2014; National Employability Report 2013).

Also, inter-state disparities in access to college/HE, enrolments and, more importantly, non-general institutions of higher education are acute. As per the *India Skills Report* (2015), based on a survey of more than 55,000 engineers who graduated in 2011, Delhi tops the list of states ranked as per their employable population. However, what is more worrisome is the fact that most talents remains concentrated in big cities. As per the report, the cities that top the list of employable pool of HE graduates are New Delhi, Chennai, Hyderabad, Coimbatore, Pondicherry, Mumbai and Kolkata.

The *National Employability Report 2014* reveals that colleges in Tier I cities are preferred because of the general perception that these cities are likely to offer greater exposure to the students, as most multinational, global companies, government and public–private sectors have their offices here. But, to assume that students from colleges in bigger cities will certainly be more employable is not acceptable. Mostly, it is not so much the location but college ranking that makes a difference in determining a candidates' employability quotient by the employers.

There is a general perception that low tier college graduates have poorer employability skills. The huge differential in the quality of teaching institutions by location further adds to the employability deficit of students coming out of this large majority of the low quality of institutions. A candidate from a Tier III college has 24% lower odds to get a job and a low salary of ₹66,000 per annum, which is much lesser than a student of equal merits from a Tier I college (National Employability Report 2014). Thus, despite equal merit, a Tier III college student is much disadvantaged because of the current entry-level hiring practices, where companies only visit certain high-ranking colleges for their hiring programmes. This is leading to a two-way distortion of the labour market—increasing inequality in the employment market on one hand and preventing companies to access a large set of meritorious students on the other hand.

As per a *Business India* report, a majority of 'employable' graduates in India come from the country's top 30 institutions which are also most likely to be collaborating with industry and are located in big urban centres. The only two Indian institutions that featured in the top 100 Global Employability University Ranking 2013, compiled by French human resources consulting group, Emerging Associates, along with Trendence, a German polling and research institute, are the IIS, Bangalore, ranked 23 and the Indian School of Business (ISB), ranked at 52—both highly renowned institutions in two most dynamic cities of the country. According to the *India Skills Report*

(2014) a large number of engineering colleges are at exceptionally low employability: bottom 45 percentile campuses have less than 1 in 100 candidates employable in an IT product company, while the bottom 20 percentile campuses have none. Thus, the long tail of engineering graduate formed an invisible pool to most of the employers. This is despite the fact that engineering graduates top the employable pool (*India Skills Report* 2014).

It is certainly a matter of great concern that with high enrolment in non-technical, general and social science programmes, the largest pool of graduates is generalists with broad socio-economic knowledge, but without any specific technical skills suited to a particular employment segment.

GENDER DISPARITIES IN GRADUATE EMPLOYABILITY SKILLS

For long, women in India were denied higher education. Today also, the GER for women is lower than the gross enrolment ratio (GER) of men. Further, women in higher education are concentrated traditional arts and social science disciplines or professions such as nursing and teaching. The situation is far worse for women belonging to non-creamy layer and underprivileged groups. Of the total higher education student enrolment, 27.5 million, that is, nearly 56%, are male students and rest 44% are female. The percentage of SC students is only 11.1% of the total, a mere 4.4% for the ST and 27.6% for OBC with the male-to-female ratio being close to the All Category (Government of India 2012–13).

As per the latest All India Survey on Higher Education (AISHE) report, the highest number of students is enrolled in arts/humanities/social sciences courses, where a majority is females (51.1%) and the problem of employability too is the highest among the graduates of this disciplinary group. In engineering and technology, enrols 2.775 million students, where males account for 71.5% of the enrolment. The share of males in commerce stream is 55.89%. Female participation rate in other streams in India, as science, medical and arts, is around 50%, almost equal or in favour of females. Of these, it is only the medical profession that might provide some advantage to women.

Similar inferences can be drawn by looking at the gender and social distribution across various levels of education. While at the

UG/PG levels, the gender gap is lesser (10%), diploma has an unbalanced distribution with 70% males and 30% females. Similarly, PhD and integrated levels both have an unequal distribution with around 60% males and 40% females. PG Diploma students enrolment projects the most lopsided picture with 75% male students and 25% female students. It may be noted here that it is the latter type of courses that are better crafted to prepare the students for the world of work.

Not only that, their number dwindles even after joining the labour market. In an Indian study by Singh (2012) shows that at lower level of management, there are around 27% women engineers which decrease to 14% at middle level and at the upper level, it remains as low as 9%. Similarly, representation of women in research and development, faculty positions in higher education, leadership, management and decision-making positions is critically low (Chanana 2000 and 2012; UNESCO 2010), only 3% of legislative, management and senior official positions are quoted to be held by women (Nandy, Bhaskar, and Ghosh 2014). In another survey by The Associated Chamber of Commerce and Industry of India (*Business Standard* 2012), it was found that only 3.3% women were at the top while 78.9% were at the junior levels (Jha 2008). A study on the Leadership Gender Gap in India Inc. (Figure 13.1), too, points at this discrepancy.

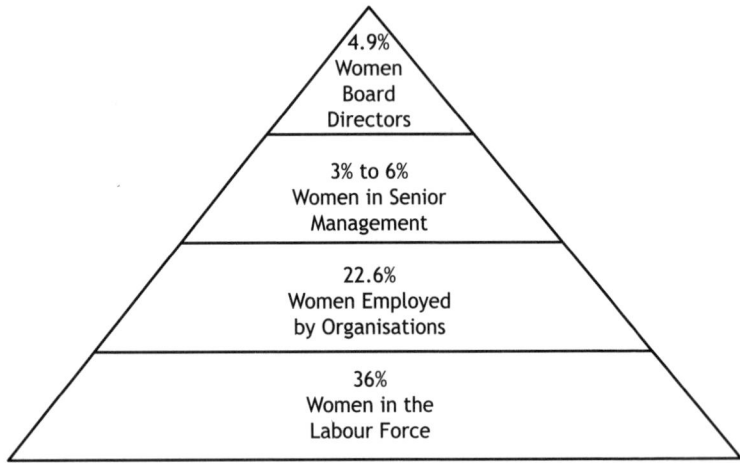

Figure 13.1
Leadership Gender Gap in India Inc.
Sources: Bagti and Carter (2010); World Economic Forum (2009, 2010).

Thus, the better presence of women in higher education has a limited impact on the labour market (UNESCO 2010) and gender remains a strong determinant of many educational inequities (Chanana 2013), thereby, resulting variation in employability skills.

Although there are considerably more males than females in engineering, their employability quotient is equal (see Figure 13.2). The ratio of male-to-female engineers is 1.96, but percentage of employable male and female engineers is similar across sectors, yet the current ratio of females-to-males employed in IT industry is lower than that of the engineering population (*India Skills Report* 2014). This shows that despite being equally talented, there is an inherent social bias against girls pursuing technical education and joining hard-core employment sector. The available literature says that women engineers not only face difficulty in getting jobs as employers are reluctant but they also get less promotion and less salaries as compared to men which eventually lead to less professional recognition. Employers blatantly opine that the hesitation in taking in women is largely because women's personal commitments take priority over their professional commitments. They are less willing to travel and to relocate or shift base (Wij, Rao and Rao 2010; Singh 2012) or stay back late and have less commitment (Chanana 2013).

A silver lining in this darkness is that women are breaking the stereotypical notions of both education and employment and their skills for employability. Most employers perceived women as better multitasked, efficient, flexible and sincere (Shrivastava and Khare

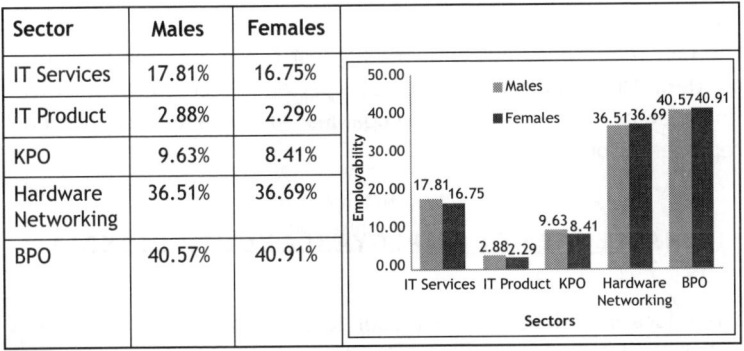

Sector	Males	Females
IT Services	17.81%	16.75%
IT Product	2.88%	2.29%
KPO	9.63%	8.41%
Hardware Networking	36.51%	36.69%
BPO	40.57%	40.91%

Figure 13.2
The Employability of Males Versus Females Engineering Graduates
Source: National Employability Report (2014).

Table 13.5
Percentage in Non-management and Management Roles, by Gender

Title	Men (%)	Women (%)
Percentage in management roles in current position	51.5%	74.1%
Percentage in management roles when first joined the company	20.0%	28.5%
Percentage in non-management roles in current position	41.4%	15.1%
Percentage in non-management roles when first joined the company	52.9%	47.0%

Source: Bagti and Carter (2010).

2012). In fact, the ICT sector has acted as a great enabler for women, as it allows for flexi working timings as well as work from home facility. Even the *India Skills Report* shows that women engineers are no way less employable than the men, with the maximum difference being a single percentage point for IT services and knowledge process outsourcing (KPO).

A similar study on the Leadership Gender Gap in India Inc. (Bagti and Carter 2010) reveals that once women enter the Indian corporate sector, they outnumber men in managerial/leadership positions for their sheer talent and dedication (see Table 13.5).

But, unfortunately, here too, the social biases come in their way as they rise up the managerial ladder. Women represent only 11% of India Inc. chief executive officers (CEOs), more than half of whom are limited to banking/financial services and another 33% to family business enterprises (World Economic Forum 2009). This is despite the fact that companies with the highest representation of women on their top management teams experience, on average, better financial performance than companies with the lowest women's representation.

CHALLENGES OF EMPLOYABLE YOUTH IN INDIA

The educational level of the labour force in India is very low. Only 17% of the labour force has an education level higher than secondary level, about 8% possess higher education degrees and nearly 10% received any vocational training (66th Round of NSS 2009–10) and that too mostly non-formal vocational training. Over the years, the share of workers declined from 57.5% in 1983 to 48.5% in 1993–94 to 44.1% in 1999–2000 and to a further down to 38.8% in 2004–05. There is a corresponding increase in the educated workers.

The percentage of educated job seekers to total job seekers has increased from 70.7% in 2000 to 76.5% in 2009, and only less than 5% of those registered with the employment exchange are getting placement (Figures 13.3 and 13.4).

Among the educated job seekers, the share of higher education graduates witnessed greatest increase in the past few years—from 1.785 million in 2004 to 2.664 million in 2008 (Figure 13.5).

This increase in the share of higher education graduates may be due to the expansion of higher education and the premium enjoyed by them in the employment market. Studies across globe have proved that income elasticity of higher education is much higher than all other levels of education (Varghese 2012; World Bank 2002). Almost 50% are regular workers, closely followed by self-employed. Only a very small percentage (less than 5%) is casual workers (Khare 2014). The arts graduates account for about 40% of the graduate job seekers (Khare 2014), and their share remained the same over the years. However, the share of science, engineering, veterinary and education graduate job seekers declined marginally (Figure 13.6).

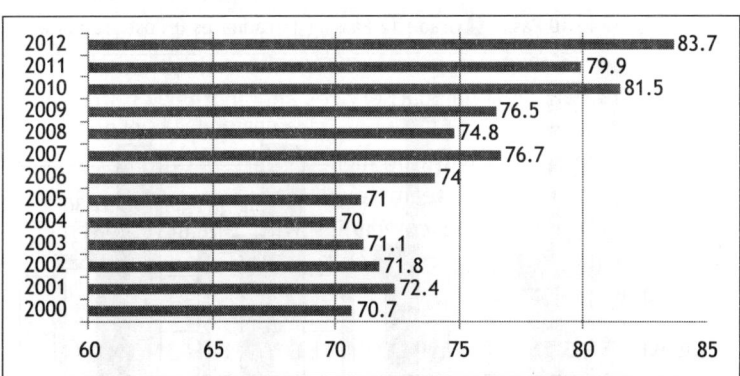

Figure 13.3
Percentage of Educated Live Registered to Total Live Registered in Employment Exchange

Source: Employment exchange statistics, DGET (GOI), various years. www. dget.nic.in

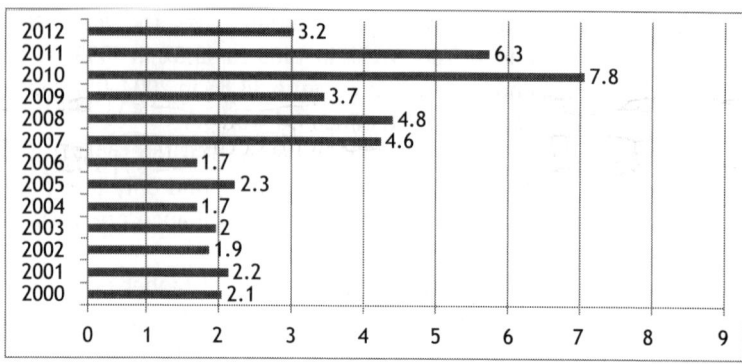

Figure 13.4
*Percentage of Placements to Total Live Registered in Employment
Exchange*

Source: Employment exchange statistics, DGET (GoI), various years (www.dget.
nic.in).

The data clearly reveals the preference of highly educated
and formally trained workers in the fast-growing services sector
(Figure 13.5). This is because of the preference by employers in the
service sector for highly educated employees on one hand and preference of employees to be in the service sector on the other. How

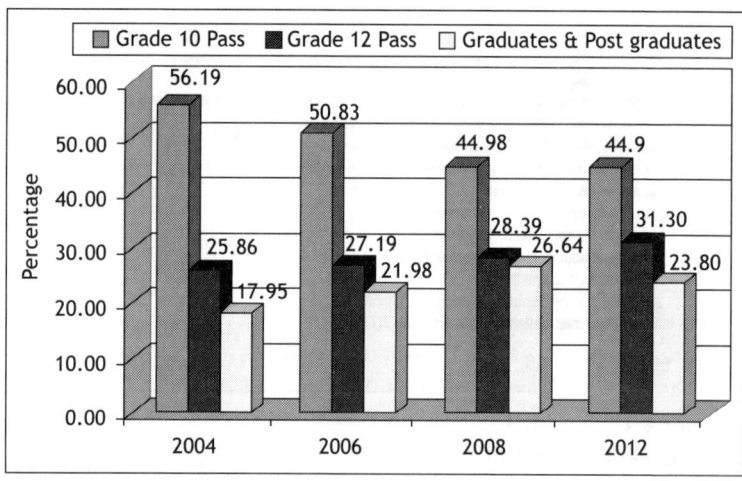

Figure 13.5
Educated Job Seekers by Education Level
Source: Employment exchange statistics, DGET (GoI).

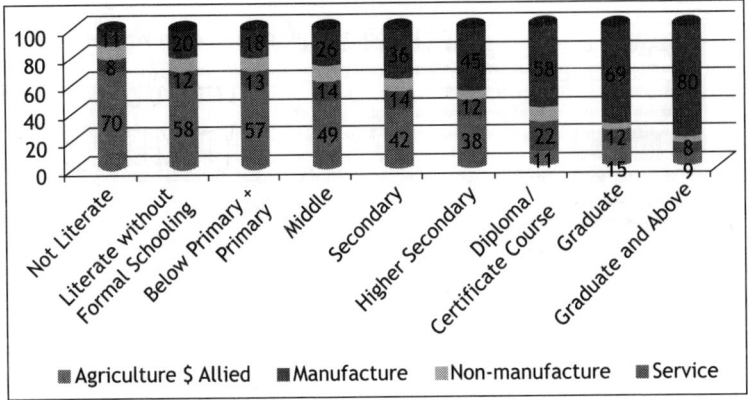

Figure 13.6
Sectoral Share in Labour Force in Age Group 15–59 by Education Level (%)
Source: NSS 66th Round (2009–10).

to make the other sectors attractive for college graduates is an important question.

The Planning Commission has identified 20 high growth sectors expected to provide employment to the burgeoning labour force in the coming years. These are auto and auto component, building and construction materials, building and construction, real estate services, electronics and IT hardware, education and skill development services, food processing, gems and jewellery, healthcare, textiles, leather and leather goods, organised retail, tourism and hospitality, transportation and logistics, media and entertainment, banking, financial services and insurance (BFSI), chemicals and pharmaceuticals, furniture and furnishings, IT and IT enabled services (ITES). Out of these, currently in India, graduate workforce is concentrated in limited sectors. After the IT/ITES, where the percentage of graduate workers is much higher than one half, closely followed by financing services, no other sector is employing a sizeable proportion of graduate workers except for community and personal services, power, trade and hotel. Education sector, having quite a high share of graduate and above employees, has been kept out of this comparison (Figure 13.7).

An industry-wise break up of just the incremental human resource requirement till 2022 in India (IMaCS, NSDC 2008) shows that auto and auto component, building and construction, textiles and clothing, transport and logistics, organised retail, real estate

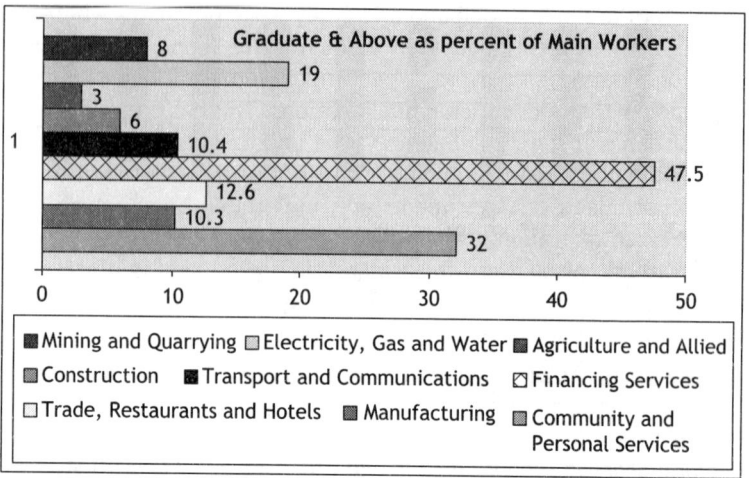

Figure 13.7
Sector Wise Share of Higher Education Graduate Plus Workers
Source: Khare (2012).

and healthcare are going to be on the higher end of the spectrum adding up to a total of 155.9 million additional jobs. Most of these sectors currently employ very low percentage of graduates as main workers. But, as per a recent report on hiring intentions for graduates in India (Lees 2012), though manufacturing, insurance and chemical segments will have strongest hiring intentions but technical and engineering functions will have the greatest headcount increase. The most sought after jobs will be in sales, engineering and research and development functions at the junior-management level. Thus, even if demand in the traditionally robust sectors in India, as per past trends, namely, BFSI, IT and ITES, electronics, is going to be lower, in no way will it undermine the importance of these sectors, for if not locally, additional demand would be generated globally as most developed countries are fearing acute shortage of engineers and professional technicians. Skilled trades positions are currently the most difficult to fill in Europe, the Middle East and Africa (EMEA). While employers in America find engineering posts the hardest to fill, those in Asia Pacific term them to be sales representative (Manpower 2012).

The employers in the industrial sector have been rather disappointed with the kind of graduates emerging from the Indian Higher Education. The small share of graduates from prestigious institutions are in high demand and enjoy wage premiums whereas, a large body of highly educated graduates are found to be falling short of meeting employers expectations and are taking up jobs much below their educational qualifications. This has created a new kind of demand supply imbalance—the double-edged mismatch of over-skilling and under-skilling of the HE graduates. In addition to a university degree, the students are, in parallel, approaching different types of training/educational institutions to augment their employability. Also, there is an increasing awareness and attempt to provide such support on-campus by various public and private higher education universities and colleges.

As per a NASSCOM (2005) report, only one-fourth of India's engineering graduates and only 10% of its other graduates are employable. *The India Skills Report* (2014) prepared by CII, People Strong and Wheebox has stated that two-thirds of our skill pool is not fit to have a job. The essence of other reports by the Federation of Indian Chambers of Commerce and Industry (FICCI) and Ernst & Young, Aspiring Minds, NSDC and Accenture, and CII and KPMG in India is no different. A slide in India's global ranking in the 5th pillar of Global Competitiveness Index, pertaining to Higher Education and training, from 55 in 2007–08 to 85 in 2010–11, is further testimony to the above observations. Of the 500 million to be skilled by 2020 in India, 25% is at the college plus level, which translates to 125 million in figures (IMaCS analysis). Educating and skilling this huge mass in new knowledge and skill domains would be a huge challenge for the Indian higher education sector.

CONCLUSION

There would be two guiding factors of the employability skills—the sectors/industries/professions that are expected to provide greater jobs and the fields of study chosen by an individual. The landscape of training providers in India to supplement the educated employability deficit is complex. Within the broad framework of sustainable employability of HE graduates (Figure 13.8), preparing industry ready graduates and then sustaining them in the industry by constant re-skilling and up-skilling is not an easy task. It is within this framework that all stakeholders of HE system need to reorient themselves.

Sustainable employability has three elements—ability to gain initial employment but of a desired quality and matching with individual's education level (both over valuation and undervaluation of

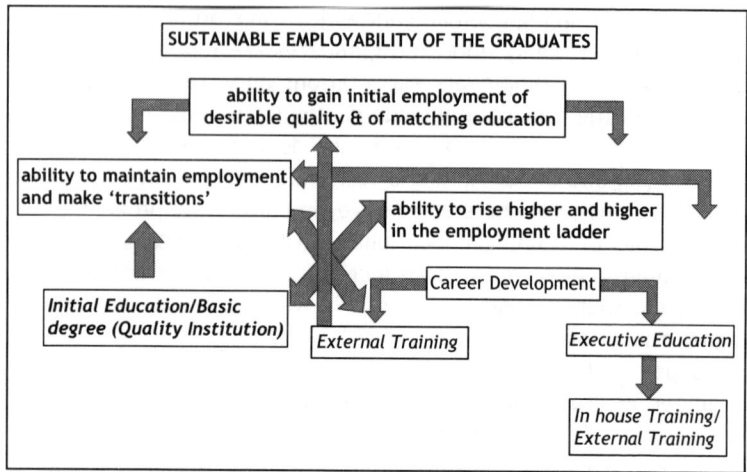

Figure 13.8
Framework for Sustainable Employability of the Graduates
Source: Prepared by the Author.

degrees by the labour market can create problems in the long run and perpetuate imbalances); ability to sustain in today's stressful highly competitive labour market, make transitions within or outside organisations; and ability to rise higher in career. While all three are the functions of an individual's basic degree and the quality of the institution it is earned from, it is the first element that is more dependent on it. It is here that the foundation of one's career path is laid, which then requires further fine tuning and polishing by the ways of training and further education/executive education. The Higher education system is expected to mould itself quickly in the above framework to act as a single window service provider for employability.

In addition, any such attempts at making the transition of the higher education graduates to the future trades easier and smoother would also require to keep macroeconomic employment projections in mind. Of lately, attempts have been made to capture these trends and develop occupational skills classification by the industrial sectors in conjunction with NSDC, but a robust and dynamic employment and employability portal is the need of the hour. On the other hand, for the university and college, systems to gear themselves to this kind of teaching and training may take a longer time for two major reasons—convincing as well as training the teaching faculty for this educational transition.

The inter-group and regional disparities in quality higher education provision and participation along with socio-cultural biases go a long way in explaining the differentials in employability skill gaps across individuals, and it needs special attention by the ways of affirmative action in this direction. Overall, the whole issue of employability skills needs to be understood in the light of skills not just for 'better livelihood' but skills for 'better living'. It is only then liberal arts and other non-professional streams of education will get their due recognition as being important for the society directly and the economy indirectly.

REFERENCES

Archer, L., M. Hutchings, and A. Ross. 2003. *Higher Education and Social Class: Issues of Exclusion and Inclusion*. New York: Routledge.

Asian Development Bank (ADB). 2012. 'Improving Transitions from School to University to Workplace', June 2012.

Bagti, D., and N.M. Carter. 2010. *Leadership Gender Gap in India Inc.: Myths and Realities Report*. http://www.catalyst.org/system/files/Leadership_Gap_in_India_Inc._Myths_and_Realities.pdf

Barker, R.T., G.H. Gilbreath, and W.S. Stone. 1998. 'The Interdisciplinary Needs of Organizations: Are New Employees Adequately Equipped?' *Journal of Management Development* 17 (3): 219–32.

Bickerstaffe, G. 1994. 'Lesson of the Masters'. *International Management* 49 (3): 54–55.

Bowers-Brown, T., and L. Harvey. 2004. 'Are There Too Many Graduates in the UK?' *Industry and Higher Education* 18 (4): 243–54.

Boyett, J.H., and J.T. Boyett. 2000. *The Guru Guide: The Best Ideas of the Top Management Thinkers*. New York: Wiley.

Bridges, W. 1996. *Leading the De-Jobbed Organization*. San Francisco, CA: Jossey-Bass Publishers.

British Council Report. 2014. High University Enrolment, Low Graduate Employment: Analysing the Paradox in Afghanistan, Bangladesh, India, Nepal, Pakistan and Sri Lanka', An Economist Intelligence Unit report for the British Council, January 2014. Available at https://www.britishcouncil.in/sites/default/files/british_council_report_2014_jan.pdf

Business Standard. 2012. 'Financial Services Top Job Generator in Tier II, III Cities'. *Business Standard*, April 21. Available at http://www.businessstandard.com/article/companies/fin-services-top-job-generator-in-tier -ii- iii-cities-112042100037_1.html

Carnoy, M. 1987. 'Higher Education and Graduate Employment in India: A Summary of Three Case Studies'. IIEP Research Report No. 64, International Institute for Educational Planning, Paris.

Chanana, K. 2000. 'Treading the Hallowed Halls: Women in Higher Education in India'. *Economic and Political Weekly* 35 (12): 1012–22.

———. 2012. 'Higher Education and Gender Issues in the Knowledge Economy: Who Studies What, Why and Where?'. In *The Emergent Knowledge Society and the Future of Higher Education: Asian Perspectives*, edited by D. Neubauer, 177–93. Abingdon: Routledge.

Chanana, K. 2013. 'Leadership for Women's Equality and Empowerment in Higher Education'. *India International Centre Quarterly* 39 (3/4): 81–94.

Chapman, J.A. 2001. 'The Work of Managers in New Organizational Contexts'. *Journal of Management Development* 20 (1): 55–68.

Bagti, D. and Carter, N.M. 2010. 'Corporate Women Directors International, Comparative Percentage of Women Directors–Countries, 2007–08'. In *Leadership Gender Gap in India Inc. Myths and Realities Report.* Available at http://www.catalyst.org/system/files/Leadership _Gap_in_India_Inc._Myths_and_Realities.pdf

Dearing, R. 1997. *Higher Education in the Learning Society: Report of the National Committee of Inquiry into Higher Education.* London: HMSO. http://www.educationengland.org.uk/documents/dearing 1997/dearing1997.html.

DGET. Various annual issues. *Employment Exchange Statistics.* Ministry of Labour & Employment, Directorate General of Employment and Training. http://www.dget.nic.in/content/innerpage/employment-exchange-statistics.php.

Government of India. 2012–13. *All India Survey on Higher Education 2014.* New Delhi: Ministry of Human Resource Development.

Harvey, L. 2000. 'New Realities: The Relationship between Higher Education and Employment'. *Tertiary Education and Management* 6 (1): 3–17.

———. 2001. 'Defining and Measuring Employability'. *Quality in Higher Education* 7 (2): 97–109.

Harvey, L., S. Moon, V. Geall, and R. Bower. 1997. *Graduates' Work: Organisation Change and Students' Attributes.* Centre for Research into Quality: University of Birmingham.

Harvey, M., M.M. Novicevic, and T. Kiessling. 2002. 'Development of Multiple IQ Maps for Use in the Selection of Inpatriate Managers: A Practical Theory'. *International Journal of Intercultural Relations* 26 (5): 493–524.

Heijden, Beatrice Van Der. 2002. 'Pre-requisites to Guarantee Life-long Employability'. *Personnel Review* 31 (1): 44–61.

IMaCS. 2008. 'Human Resource and Skill Gap Requirements'. IMaCS [ICRA Management Consulting Services Limited] Skill Gap Studies conducted for the National Skill Development Corporation (NSDC). http://www.nsdcindia.org/knowledgebank/index.aspx

India Skills Report. 2014. *People Strong, CII and Wheebox.* https://wheebox.com/wheebox/resources/IndiaSkillsReport.pdf

India Skills Report. 2015. *People Strong, CII and Wheebox*. https://wheebox.com/wheebox/resources/IndiaSkillsReport.pdf

Jha, S. 2008. 'Women on Top in Exams, Not Promotions'. *The Hindustan Times*, January 2. http://www.hindustantimes.com/india/women-on-top-in-exams-not-promotions/story-ugU91DFTPbnbsVX8lVOcBJ.html

———. 2014. 'Employment, Employability and Higher Education in India: The Missing Links'. *Higher Education for the Future* 1 (1): 39–62.

———. 2016. 'Taking the Skills March Forward In India: Transitioning to the World of Work'. In *India: Preparation for the World of Work*, edited by Matthias Pilz. Springer.

Lees, Dawn. 2012. '*Graduate Employability: Literature Review*'. Graduate Development Service Newsletter: University of Exeter. http://www.qualityresearchinternational. com/esecttools/esectpubs/leeslitreview.pdf

Little, B., and L. Archer. 2010. 'Less Time to Study, Less Well Prepared for Work, Yet Satisfied with Higher Education: A UK Perspective on Links between Higher Education and the Labour Market'. *Journal of Education and Work* 23 (3): 275–96.

Longenecker, C.O., and S.S. Ariss. 2002. 'Creating Competitive Advantage Through Effective Management Education'. *The Journal of Management Development* 21 (9): 640–54.

Manpower Group. 2012. *Talent Shortage Survey: Research Results*. https://candidate.manpower.com/wps/wcm/connect/be31f5804b-6f7c07ada6ff4952b5bce9/2012_Talent_Shortage_Survey_Results_ManpowerGroup.pdf?MOD=AJPERES

Nandy, Sarmistha, Arnab Bhaskar, and Sovonjit Ghosh. 2014. 'Corporate Glass Ceiling: An Impact on Indian Women Employees'. *International Journal of Management and International Business Studies* 4 (2): 135–40.

NASSCOM. 2005. *Extending India's Leadership of the Global IT and BPO Industries*. NASSCOM–Mckinsey Report.

National Employability Report, Engineers. 2014. *Aspiringminds*. www.aspiringminds.in

National Employability Report, Graduates. 2013. *Aspiringminds*. www.aspiringminds.in

NCIHE. 1997. *Higher Education in the Learning Society*. National Committee of Inquiry into Higher Education, The Dearing Report, HMSO, Norwich. http://www.leeds.ac. uk/educol/ncihe/

NSSO. 2009–10. *Employment and Unemployment Survey: NSSO 66th Round (July 2009–June 2010)*. New Delhi: Ministry of Statistics and Programme Implementation.

Reich, R.B. 1991. *The Work of Nations*. London: Simon and Schuster.

———. 2002. *The Future of Success*. London: Vintage Books.

RSA. 1980. *Royal Society for the Arts, Manufactures and Commerce (RSA): Capability Manifesto*. London: RSA.

RSA. 1991. *Royal Society for the Arts, Manufactures and Commerce (RSA): Education for Capability*. London: RSA.

Scott, P. 2005. 'Universities and the Knowledge Economy'. *Minerva* 43 (3): 297–309.

Shrivastava, Aarti, and Mona Khare. 2012. *Skills for Employability: Southeast Asia*. Washington, DC: Results for Development Institute, August.

Singh, Seema. 2012. 'Are Women Engineers Discriminated'. Paper presented at the Regional Conference of the International Network of Women in Science & Engineering, Women in Science and Engineering India, New Delhi, October 12–13.

Tol. 2012. *Times of India*, ASCENT, 31 July 2012.

UNESCO. 1993. 'Women in Higher Education Management'. Paris: UNESCO.

United Nations (UN). 2001. *Recommendations of the High Level Panel of the Youth Employment Network*. New York: United Nations.

Varghese, N.V. 2001. 'Impact of the Economic Crisis on Higher Education in East Asia: An Overview'. In *Impact of the Economic Crisis on Higher Education in East Asia: Country Experiences*, N.V., Varghese. Paris: UNESCO.

———. 2012. *HE Reforms and Revitalization of the Sector, Higher Education Forum, Vol 9*. http://hedbib.iau-aiu.net/pdf/HE_Reforms_and_Revitalization_of_ the_Sector_2012.pdf

Wij, Sangeeta, Rao Nilanjana and Rao Prerna. 2010. *Women in Science and Engineering in India*. http://vulpix.in/new/wp-content/uploads/2012/12/WISE_FINAL_ Compatibility_Mode.pdf

Wood, A. 1994. *North South Trade, Employment and Inequality*. Oxford: Oxford University Press.

World Bank. 2002. *Constructing Knowledge Societies: New Challenges for Tertiary Education*. Washington, D.C.: World Bank.

World Economic Forum. 2009. *The India Gender Gap Review 2009*. World Economic Forum.

———. 2010. 'The Corporate Gender Gap Report 2010'. World Economic Forum, Geneva, Switzerland. Available at http://www3.weforum.org/docs/WEF_GenderGap_CorporateReport_2010.pdf

Yorke, M. [2004] 2006. 'Employability in Higher Education: What It Is – What It Is Not'. In *Learning and Employability Series 1*. York: Higher Education Academy.

PART IV

DIVERSITY AND
DISCRIMINATION

14

Access and Exclusion: Mapping Social Diversity in Education in India

Ashwini Deshpande

INTRODUCTION

Contemporary India offers plenty of examples of how a state of persistent exclusion generates resentment and hostility that manifests itself in violent, secessionist forms. The urgency of increasing diversity in a variety of spheres cannot be overemphasised. The Sachar Committee Report (SCR), accordingly, recommended that concrete steps should be taken to increase diversity in public spaces. Accordingly, the Ministry of Minority Affairs (2008) appointed an expert group to create a diversity index (DI) to measure diversity in public spaces, with a focus on education, employment and housing.[1] India already has a caste-based affirmative action programme in place. However, given the multiplicity of fissures and axes of disadvantage along several social identities, the challenge is to address caste disparity but not at the cost of ignoring other, very pressing, dimensions of group divisions, such as religion, gender and disability.

This chapter discusses the original DI and then proceeds to give some indicative numbers calculated from data on current enrolment in educational institutions at middle and higher education levels for each state across three social dimensions—caste, religion and gender, separately for rural and urban areas—using the National Sample Survey (NSS) Employment–Unemployment Survey (66th Round) data for 2009–10 and the 2007 data (64th Round) on participation and expenditure on education. All the tables that follow are based on author's calculations from the unit-level data of

---

[1] I was privileged to be a member of this group and, thus, was one of the authors of this report that was submitted in 2008.

these two NSS Rounds. The measure used in this chapter is a rough indicator of the DI, as currently the database for calculating the original DI is not in place. The DI is calculated for all-India as well as for all states. The chapter then compares the differential patterns of diversity across the two educational levels: middle and higher, the former with no affirmative action and the latter with caste-based affirmative action in government-run institutions. The aim of the chapter is to see if there is greater caste diversity at the higher education level as compared to the middle education level, as this can illuminate the role of affirmative action in increasing diversity. All the diversity at the higher education level cannot be attributed to affirmative action, as the latter is only applicable to state-run institutions; however, the estimates allow us to discuss the possible contribution of affirmative action in increasing access of marginalised caste groups. The chapter compares caste diversity with religious diversity at comparable levels to further tease out the possible impact of affirmative action, given that there is no affirmative action based on religion. Gender is a cross-cutting category; thus, in addition to examining gender diversity separately, the chapter also looks at gender diversity within the two social categories: caste and religion.

MEASURING DIVERSITY

Why Do We Need an Index?

Concentration or clustering of populations with similar socio-economic, religious and ethnic characteristics in geographical, social, political and institutional spaces has emerged as an area of concern in recent years. It can be argued that such concentration in, say, a housing complex, an educational institution or a production distribution unit reflects the preferences of the concerned decision-makers or administrators for people belonging to certain groups and an implicit or explicit prejudice against certain other groups. While a certain degree of concentration can be attributed to the desire for togetherness of people of different communities, in many spheres this might be due to discrimination and the denial of opportunities to groups that are different, not on grounds of merit but on grounds of their ethnic characteristics or group affiliations. The macro concerns for development as reflected in strategies to accelerate the rate of economic growth in the country, improvement in standard of living for the poor in particular and improvements in educational standards or health care cannot tackle issues of such deprivation and discrimination. In fact, several of the dimensions of discrimination are not even captured by the available information or data. There is no national, regional or micro-level index that could help us gauge the extent of diversity.

The concept of measurement of diversity has its roots in the literature on ecology and biodiversity. In ecology, a DI is a statistic that measures the biodiversity of the ecosystem by measuring the number of species in the ecosystem and their abundance (species richness and species evenness). Some examples of commonly used indices are Simpson's Index or Shannon's Diversity Index. All these indices are statistically robust and thus attractive as analytical tools.

Several of these have been adapted for the measurement of social diversity which is understandably multidimensional. For instance, the USA TODAY Diversity Index was created in 1991 to measure how racially and ethnically diverse a population is. It calculates the probability that two people picked at random will be of a different race and ethnicity. It takes the percentage of each race in the overall population and calculates the chance that any two people are white, black, Asian, American Indian or Native Hawaiian. Then, it calculates the probability of ethnicity—that any two people are Hispanic or non-Hispanic. These racial and ethnic probabilities are multiplied together. Thus, for example, in the year 2000, the DI (thus calculated) was 49. This means that the chance of two randomly chosen US residents being different is 49 out of 100, or almost 1 out of 2. Or, there was nearly one in two chances that two people selected at random would be racially or ethnically different in the year 2000.

A related and commonly used measure is Duncan's Index of Dissimilarity. This index can be used to compare how two mutually exclusive social groups are spread across geographical units (e.g., urban wards in India). Specifically, it calculates what proportion of one group would have to be moved in order to make the distribution of social groups across geographical units even.

The need for measuring the richness of an ecosystem seems intuitively obvious. The exercise for measuring social diversity, while analogous, might not be intuitively apparent and hence has not been used much in policymaking. The case for increasing social diversity in public spaces can be built on the notion of a fair demographic representation. Groups that are subjected to discrimination in society tend to get under-represented (as compared to their proportion in the population) in several public spheres. This leads to inequity and alienation, leading to resentment and frustration. These could assume violent and secessionist expressions, leading to disruption in social and political life, with serious negative consequences for growth, development and social harmony. Thus, while an efficient allocation of resources would dictate that individuals to be distributed in all social and production institutions according to their skill or talent, persistent group disparities suggest the presence of systematic discrimination against certain *groups*. This makes individual characteristics either secondary or completely redundant in determining her/his access to these institutions as group identities overwhelm or dictate the decision-making process.

Notwithstanding serious theoretical and conceptual objections to the exercise amounting to 'simplistic abstraction of a complicated reality', capturing diversity or any other multidimensional concept in terms of a single number has the advantage of easy inter-temporal and inter-regional comparability and being used in policymaking. Given the alarming manifestations and implications of absence of diversity in public spheres and vociferous demands for immediate interventions, numerical representation has become an absolute necessity.

THE DIVERSITY INDEX

The basic idea underlying the DI was to work out the index for each institution with the specific aim of increasing the representation of underrepresented groups by measuring and promoting diversity in different fields. The particular focus was on three fields of employment, education and housing.

It was envisaged that there would be three dimensions along which diversity would be measured:

1. Religious dimension: This will mean dividing the population in the institution into groups such as R_1 to R_k, k being the total number of groups in the country, including the majority group. The Population Census defines seven categories (Hindus, Muslims, Christians, Sikhs, Buddhists, Jains and other religions).

2. Caste dimension: It would be useful to consider fourfold classification for castes as scheduled castes (SCs), scheduled tribes (STs), other backward classes (OBCs) and others (everybody else), which can be indicated as $C_1...C_4$.

3. Gender dimension: This would have two groups—men and women (i.e., G_1 and G_2).

At the time the DI report was released, we had not included disability, but as more data become available on that front, the index should also be enlarged to include disability as an axis of disadvantage. Annexure outlines the formula that was used to calculate the DI by the expert group in 2008. As we can see, it utilises three dimensions—eligible population, total population in the relevant universe and actual share of a group in a given institution.

EXPLANATIONS ABOUT THE VARIABLES USED IN THE INDEX

What Exactly Is the Eligible Population?

The committee recognised that it would be difficult to determine the eligible population with complete accuracy for each job and for each course. In the absence of precise information on that, proxy variables would have to be worked out in a large number of cases. For entry into an educational institution which has a mandate to serve a state or a region, the percentage of the population with the qualifying level of education in the region would constitute Y. The eligible population for employment can be decided in a similar manner. For example, for a lecturer's job, the people meeting the eligibility criteria would be taken as Y. Also, to begin this strategic intervention linked to the DI, it is suggested that it is applied only at entry-level jobs and not for promotions.

Indeed, it would be erroneous to believe that all the people satisfying the eligibility criteria would be aspirants for the position. Indeed, people who are already in employment or are unwilling to move to the institution which is in a different region or those not interested in the job for any other reason may not be included in Y. Also, Y will have to be defined keeping the specific nature of the institution and its catchment area in consideration. It would nonetheless be impossible for any agency to precisely determine the eligible and aspirant population. In this backdrop and also inadequate data availability, the use of proxy indicators seems to be the only way out.

The relevant universe over which Y is defined (whether at state or all-India level) would have to be determined by the specific institution entrusted with the responsibility at sub-national level. So, for instance, when the index is calculated by University Grants Commission (UGC) for central universities, the all-India proportions will be applicable as the catchment area would be the whole country. For a state university, it might be more appropriate to look at the population percentages within the state. The agencies entrusted with the responsibility of constructing DIs at different levels would be expected to regularly improve the database and get better estimation of the eligible population.

RELEVANT UNIVERSE: WHAT IS THE DOMAIN OVER WHICH THE INDEX IS DEFINED?

The DI is defined at micro level for each production company, social institution, housing society, etc. and not for state or local government. Taking Delhi University as an example, one will compute DI separately for four very broad groups: undergraduate students, postgraduate students, lower grade employees and higher grade employees. Three indices articulating religious, caste and gender diversity would be constructed at the first stage. The three will then be combined to obtain a single number reflecting the overall diversity for the university.

ILLUSTRATION FOR HIGHER EDUCATION USING NSS DATA FOR 2009–10 AND 2007

As noted above, the variables used in the index are institution specific, and national datasets do not have data at the institutional level. However, the key innovation of the DI was the introduction of 'eligible population' and including that in the calculation of over- or under-representation. That is, instead of comparing the social composition of an institution to the underlying population distribution, the DI suggested that the social composition of the institution be compared to the distribution of the 'eligible population'.

For the purpose of this chapter, I used the 'currently enrolled' information from the NSS Employment–Unemployment Survey as a rough indicator to understand the relationship between share of a given education level in the population and those eligible to acquire that level of education. I used this data in order to calculate two levels of higher education:

1. The ratio between those currently enrolled in graduate programmes, assuming these to be proxies for 'graduates', and those eligible for enrolling into graduate programmes, assuming roughly that those currently enrolled at higher secondary levels would constitute the pool of those eligible for graduate programmes. I call these 'graduate-eligibles'. Of course, given that NSS data is a cross-section, this overestimates both the graduates (all those enrolled currently in graduate programmes may not eventually graduate) and eligibles (all those currently enrolled in higher secondary programmes may not complete, and among those who do, all might not be interested in pursuing a graduate programme). However, this gives a rough idea of the diversity picture in higher education, particularly graduate programmes. Note also that this ratio is not the same as the original DI, but this can be taken as a rough, easy-to-calculate measure of diversity.

2. Similar figures for those currently enrolled in secondary school ('secondary') and those eligible (in future) for enrolling into secondary school, namely those enrolled in middle school (called secondary-eligibles). Tables 14.1 and 14.2 show these figures for all-India, for all and separately by rural and urban areas. Tables 14.3 and 14.4 show the totals for all-India 2007 using the 64th Round of NSS. Although that was a survey directed towards gauging participation in and expenditure on higher education, it was a 'thin' Round (or a small sample), and, thus, the total numbers are very small and not comparable to the 'thick' or the large sample Round of 2009–10. Since the overall numbers are very small, breaking them up into rural–urban or separate states is not feasible, as the number of observations is insufficient in smaller categories.

The expectation is that to the extent affirmative action increases diversity, it should result in greater caste diversity than religious diversity at the higher educational level, controlling for other factors, such as middle-school-level diversity and other state-specific

Table 14.1

Graduates Compared with Graduate-eligibles, India (2009–10)

	grad/ eligible	grad/ total	elig/ totelig	grad/ eligible	grad/ total	elig/ totelig	grad/ eligible	grad/ total	elig/ totelig
Gender									
Male	0.75	0.60	0.60	0.64	0.65	0.62	0.91	0.55	0.56
Female	0.75	0.40	0.40	0.58	0.35	0.38	0.94	0.45	0.44
Social Group									
ST	0.49	0.04	0.07	0.41	0.05	0.08	0.75	0.03	0.04
SC	0.58	0.13	0.17	0.50	0.16	0.19	0.73	0.11	0.13
OBC	0.75	0.40	0.40	0.66	0.45	0.42	0.88	0.35	0.37
Others	0.88	0.42	0.36	0.69	0.34	0.31	1.04	0.51	0.45
Religion									
Hindu	0.77	0.86	0.83	0.64	0.89	0.85	0.95	0.82	0.80
Muslim	0.59	0.08	0.10	0.38	0.06	0.09	0.82	0.11	0.13
Christian	0.74	0.03	0.03	0.60	0.03	0.03	0.91	0.03	0.03
Sikh	0.64	0.02	0.02	0.58	0.02	0.02	0.73	0.01	0.02
Jain	1.04	0	0	0.77	0	0	0.99	0.01	0.01
Buddhist	0.59	0.01	0.01	0.47	0.01	0.01	0.66	0.01	0.01
Others	0.57	0	0	0.41	0	0	0.75	0	0

Source: Author's calculation based on NSS Data 2009–10.

factors. While examining this rigorously will be part of the future work, we note the following features from Table 14.1: at the graduate level, the ratio of men currently enrolled to graduate-eligibles is the same as that of women (0.75). However, the gender gap arises in the graduate-eligibles and in the share within total graduates (0.6 for men and 0.4 for women). Comparing the ratios across social groups, we find that the ratio of graduates to graduate-eligibles is the lowest for STs (0.49), followed by SCs (0.58), then OBCs (0.75) and finally the others (a rough proxy for upper castes—0.88). The ratios of groups in graduates to total show the same pattern, but the share of STs in total graduates is a miniscule 0.04%. The ratio of eligible to total eligibles also has a similar pattern, but shares of SCs and STs are larger here than they are among the total graduates. This indicates the following: as a proportion of graduate-eligibles, STs and SCs currently enrolled in graduate programmes have the lowest proportions among all social groups. However, these are far higher than their corresponding proportions within all graduates (0.04 and 0.13 respectively). Thus, there is a gap in the eligible population (that can be seen in elig/totalelig column) that needs to be addressed in order to make affirmative action more effective. NSS data allow us to disaggregate the currently enrolled into different streams such as agriculture, engineering/technology, medical and other subjects. The gaps between STs and SCs and 'Others' are the highest for engineering and medicine courses.

The religious distribution shows stark differences among religious groups, with the Hindus being at the top, such that 77% of those who are eligible are in graduate programmes. The corresponding ratios for religious minorities are lower. Comparing graduates to graduate-eligibles ratios across castes and religious groups, we find that SCs have a much larger share than Muslims. It is likely that this is due to the long history of reservations for SCs than for Muslims. However, the ST share is low and is closer to (slightly higher than) the Christian share.

The rural–urban differences show up most unambiguously in the graduates/graduate-eligibles ratios, such that a far greater proportion of those who are eligible end up enrolling in graduate programmes. This could be due to the uneven spread of higher educational institutions in that these are disproportionately located in urban areas.

As mentioned above, the proportions in Table 14.3 are not strictly comparable to those in Table 14.1 due to different sample sizes.[2] Nevertheless, some comparisons are useful. However, these are tentative and should be treated with caution. For gender, we see that representation as measured by graduates/graduate-eligibles of both men and women has increased over the two rounds. Among social groups, representation of SCs, OBCs and others has increased, with the sharpest increase in the representation of OBCs. Given that quotas in higher educational institutions were extended to OBCs in 2006, the increase over the period could possibly reflect greater access for OBCs.

A great deal of differentiation already happens by the time individuals move to graduate school. Thus, it is instructive to compare these numbers to the level of education just preceding this—those in secondary schools, using middle school as the category equivalent to secondary-eligible. We see the all-India figures in Table 14.2.

Comparing Table 14.2 to Table 14.1, we see that the gender gap in secondary/secondary-eligibles is not as sharp as that for other social groups but is sharper than graduates/graduate-eligibles. This suggests that while dropout rates for girls are higher at lower levels, those who manage to cross the threshold end up moving on to graduate levels in similar proportions to boys. Looking at caste/tribe groups, here we find that OBCs have the highest proportion of secondary school-goers. The fact that we see this when they move to the next level (higher secondary—the eligibility for proceeding to graduate school) but not in the graduates/total graduates share suggests that a larger proportion of upper castes from those who are eligible go on to enrolling in graduate programmes, as compared to the OBCs. Overall, the gaps between social groups in the secondary to secondary-eligibles are smaller than those for graduates/graduate-eligibles, suggesting that the transition to graduate programmes adds one more layer of differentiation. Among the religious groups, the ranking for secondary/secondary-eligibles is very different from that for graduates/graduate-eligibles. Hindus do not have the largest share. Several religious minorities surpass the majority. Again, the reversal of this pattern at higher levels of education indicates differential drop out by religious groups. Table 14.4 shows figures for all-India for 2007 and should be compared to Table 14.3.

A comparison of trends in 2007 (Tables 14.3 and 14.4) with those in 2009–10 (Tables 14.1 and 14.2) reveals an improvement over time

---

[2] The comparison with the 64th Round was added at the referee's suggestion on the previous draft.

Table 14.2
Secondary Schoolers Compared to Secondary-eligibles, All India (2009–10)

	All			Rural			Urban		
	sec/ eligible	sec/ total	secelig/ totelig	sec/ eligible	sec/ total	secelig/ totelig	sec/ eligible	sec/ total	secelig/ totelig
Gender									
Male	0.82	0.58	0.55	0.82	0.60	0.54	0.81	0.56	0.55
Female	0.70	0.42	0.45	0.66	0.40	0.46	0.78	0.44	0.45
Social Group									
ST	0.68	0.08	0.09	0.65	0.09	0.11	1.02	0.04	0.03
SC	0.70	0.19	0.21	0.68	0.21	0.23	0.74	0.15	0.16
OBC	0.78	0.43	0.42	0.77	0.44	0.43	0.80	0.40	0.40
Others	0.82	0.30	0.28	0.81	0.26	0.24	0.80	0.41	0.41
Religion									
Hindu	0.77	0.83	0.82	0.75	0.84	0.84	0.81	0.79	0.77
Muslim	0.72	0.12	0.12	0.71	0.11	0.11	0.73	0.15	0.16
Christian	0.89	0.03	0.02	0.84	0.03	0.02	0.96	0.03	0.03
Sikh	0.72	0.01	0.02	0.70	0.02	0.02	0.76	0.01	0.01
Jain	0.58		0	2.03	0	0	0.42	0	0.01
Buddhist	0.94	0.01	0.01	1.17	0.01	0	0.68	0.01	0.01
Others	4.35	0	0.01	0.70	0.01	0.01	1.17	0	0

Source: Author's calculation based on NSS data 2009–10.

Table 14.3

Graduates Compared with Graduate-eligibles, India (2007)

	grad/eligible	grad/total	elig/totelig
Gender			
Male	0.64	0.52	0.43
Female	0.44	0.48	0.57
Social Group			
ST	0.48	0.04	0.05
SC	0.40	0.08	0.11
OBC	0.37	0.33	0.47
Others	0.77	0.54	0.37
Religion			
Hindu	0.49	0.80	0.86
Muslim	0.89	0.13	0.08
Christian	0.27	0.01	0.02
Sikh	1.19	0	0
Jain	0.79	0.05	0.03
Buddhist	0.11	0	0
Others	0	0	0

Source: Author's calculation based on NSS data 2007.

Table 14.4

Secondary Schoolers Compared to Secondary-eligibles, All India (2007)

	All		
	sec/eligible	sec/total	secelig/totelig
Gender			
Male	0.65	0.41	0.43
Female	0.69	0.59	0.57
Social Group			
ST	0.48	0.07	0.10
SC	0.43	0.12	0.18
OBC	0.72	0.44	0.41
Others	0.82	0.37	0.30
Religion			
Hindu	0.70	0.80	0.77
Muslim	0.53	0.14	0.17
Christian	0.66	0.02	0.02
Sikh	0.75	0	0
Jain	0.61	0.03	0.03
Buddhist	1.16	0.01	0
Others	0	0	0

Source: Author's calculation based on NSS data 2007.

in girls' transitioning to higher education. In 2007, 69% of girls eligible for secondary school were enrolled, but at graduate levels, only 44% of eligible girls were enrolled in graduate programmes. This trend changed in 2009–10, with corresponding proportions being 0.7 (secondary/eligibles) to 0.75 (graduate/graduate-eligible). This reveals a significant increase in the educational attainment of girls at the higher education level. We see the same trend for OBCs: 72% secondary/secondary-eligibles to 37% graduate/graduate-eligibles in 2007, changing to 78 and 75% respectively.

GENDER WITHIN SOCIO-RELIGIOUS GROUPS

Table 14.5 shows the gender distribution within socio-religious categories in 2009–10 for graduates versus graduate-eligibles.

This table shows a mixed picture in that the graduate/graduate-eligibles ratio is higher for women than men for some social groups such as STs, others and Sikhs. However, among SCs, OBCs, Muslims, Christians, Jains and Buddhists, this ratio is higher for men.

Table 14.5
Graduates Versus Graduate-eligibles: Gender and Socio-religious Groups (2009–10)

	Male			Female		
	grad/ eligible	*grad/ total*	*elig/ totelig*	*grad/ eligible*	*grad/ total*	*elig/ totelig*
ST	0.46	0.04	0.07	0.55	0.05	0.06
SC	0.62	0.14	0.17	0.52	0.12	0.17
OBC	0.79	0.42	0.40	0.70	0.38	0.41
Others	0.84	0.40	0.36	0.93	0.45	0.36
Hindu	0.77	0.86	0.84	0.78	0.86	0.82
Muslim	0.63	0.09	0.10	0.54	0.07	0.10
Christian	0.86	0.03	0.03	0.61	0.03	0.04
Sikh	0.50	0.01	0.02	0.82	0.02	0.02
Jain	1.24	0	0	0.87	0	0
Buddhist	0.62	0.01	0.01	0.55	0.01	0.01
Others combined	0.65	0	0	0.47	0	0

Source: Author's calculation based on NSS data 2009–10.

STATE-WISE PATTERNS

State-level patterns have been calculated for each of the parameters and the detailed results are available with me upon request. Here, only a few selected indicators are shown. Table 14.6 shows the distribution of states by gender for graduate/eligibles and secondary/eligibles ratios.

We notice a great deal of heterogeneity in that the distribution of states doing well in different categories is not uniform. For the graduate/eligibles ratio, the top five states for women are Puducherry, Chandigarh, Madhya Pradesh, Rajasthan and West Bengal. For secondary/eligibles, the best performing states for women are Mizoram, Assam, Andhra Pradesh, Odisha and Kerala. For SCs, the top five states with the highest graduate/graduate-eligibles ratio are Haryana, Andhra Pradesh, Odisha, Tripura and Sikkim. For Muslims, these are Himachal Pradesh, Meghalaya, Punjab, Goa and Gujarat. Thus, we see that state outcomes on the various indicators are heterogeneous and the ranking of states is not uniform across indicators.

Figure 14.1 indicates the state-wise relationship between budgeted expenditure on education for all departments on revenue account in terms of the gross state domestic product (GSDP) for the available years of various states and union territories for the purpose of comparative study. It is observed from the figure that the percentage of expenditure on education is below the national GDP in respect of the major states such as Delhi, Haryana, Gujarat, Punjab, West Bengal, Goa, Maharashtra, Andhra Pradesh, Odisha, Karnataka, Kerala, Tamil Nadu, Jharkhand, Rajasthan, Madhya Pradesh, Chandigarh, Uttarakhand, Chhattisgarh, Sikkim and Puducherry.

Comparing these patterns to trends in educational expenditures, there is no apparent association between these outcomes and expenditure on education as a proportion of state domestic product. We see that Himachal Pradesh, one of the states with a relatively higher proportion of educational expenditure, performs well on some indicators but not all. On the other end, Odisha performs well on some indicators, but its education spending as a proportion of GDP is on the lower end of the scale. This suggests that while overall education spending might be important for several reasons, it is not sufficient to explain the differential outcomes of social groups, and that we might need to look at other state-specific factors to explain outcomes.

Table 14.6 Gender Eligibility Ratios by State (2009–10)

State	Male grad/eligible	State	Female grad/eligible	State	Male Sec/sec-elig	State	Female sec/sec-elig
Daman and Diu	1.52	Odisha	1.31	Mizoram	1.51	Puducherry	1.20
Delhi	1.34	Karnataka	1.14	Assam	1.11	Chandigarh	1.08
Goa	1.13	Nagaland	1.04	Andhra Pradesh	1.11	Madhya Pradesh	0.99
Tamil Nadu	1.02	Maharashtra	1.02	Odisha	1.09	Rajasthan	0.97
Uttarakhand	0.92	Chhattisgarh	0.98	Kerala	0.96	West Bengal	0.92
Uttar Pradesh	0.90	Kerala	0.98	Chandigarh	0.96	Uttar Pradesh	0.91
Andhra Pradesh	0.90	Jharkhand	0.95	Nagaland	0.95	Andhra Pradesh	0.90
Gujarat	0.88	Jammu and Kashmir	0.94	Goa	0.95	Himachal Pradesh	0.89
Odisha	0.87	Andhra Pradesh	0.92	Lakshadweep	0.95	Punjab	0.86
Chhattisgarh	0.84	Mizoram	0.86	Puducherry	0.90	Haryana	0.85
Rajasthan	0.83	Manipur	0.84	Daman and Diu	0.88	Kerala	0.83
Haryana	0.82	Bihar	0.83	Tripura	0.84	Delhi	0.83
West Bengal	0.82	Assam	0.81	Manipur	0.83	Karnataka	0.81
Manipur	0.82	Lakshadweep	0.81	Jammu and Kashmir	0.83	Gujarat	0.81
Maharashtra	0.79	Andaman and Nicobar	0.79	Andaman and Nicobar	0.82	Odisha	0.79
Meghalaya	0.78	Arunachal Pradesh	0.76	Uttarakhand	0.80	Jammu and Kashmir	0.78
Kerala	0.77	Uttarakhand	0.72	Maharashtra	0.76	Maharashtra	0.76
Puducherry	0.77	Gujarat	0.67	Karnataka	0.75	Sikkim	0.76
Jharkhand	0.77	Uttar Pradesh	0.62	Gujarat	0.75	Bihar	0.74
Madhya Pradesh	0.72	Haryana	0.62	Delhi	0.74	Tamil Nadu	0.72

(Table 14.6 continued)

(Table 14.6 continued)

State	Male grad/eligible	State	Female grad/eligible	State	Male Sec/sec-elig	State	Female sec/sec-elig
Karnataka	0.72	Andaman and Nicobar	0.61	Daman and Diu	0.74	Himachal Pradesh	0.70
Jammu and Kashmir	0.68	Jharkhand	0.60	Meghalaya	0.72	Arunachal Pradesh	0.67
Assam	0.63	Assam	0.58	Sikkim	0.71	Bihar	0.66
Tripura	0.62	Arunachal Pradesh	0.55	Madhya Pradesh	0.71	Tamil Nadu	0.65
Bihar	0.56	Daman and Diu	0.54	Punjab	0.68	Meghalaya	0.64
Arunachal Pradesh	0.56	Manipur	0.54	Tamil Nadu	0.67	Chhattisgarh	0.64
Mizoram	0.54	Tripura	0.53	Himachal Pradesh	0.61	Uttar Pradesh	0.60
Punjab	0.52	Goa	0.53	Delhi	0.61	Madhya Pradesh	0.57
Chandigarh	0.43	Dadra and Nagar Haveli	0.52	Dadra and Nagar Haveli	0.61	Sikkim	0.54
Nagaland	0.40	Nagaland	0.50	Rajasthan	0.58	Punjab	0.54
Himachal Pradesh	0.35	Mizoram	0.49	Tripura	0.57	Jharkhand	0.53
Sikkim	0.33	Meghalaya	0.48	Puducherry	0.55	Haryana	0.52
Andaman and Nicobar	0.30	Chhattisgarh	0.44	West Bengal	0.50	West Bengal	0.50
Dadra and Nagar Haveli	0.15	Uttarakhand	0.29	Chandigarh	0.45	Rajasthan	0.49
Lakshadweep	0	Lakshadweep	0.15	Goa	0.20	Dadra and Nagar Haveli	0.40

Source: Author's calculation based on NSS data 2009–10.

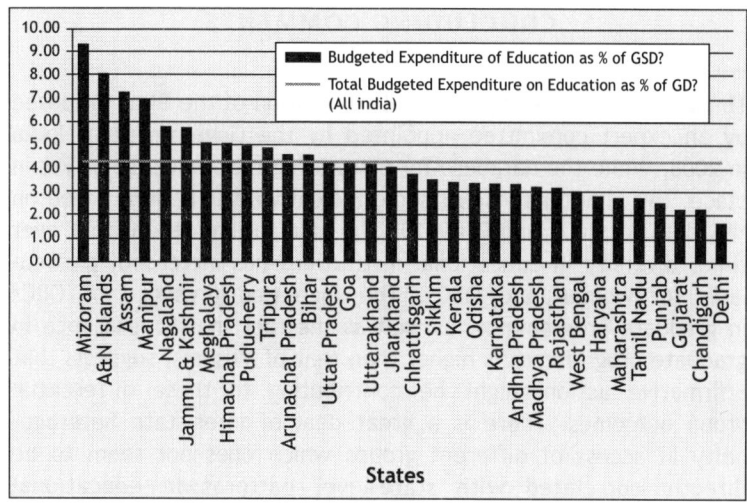

Figure 14.1
Expenditure on Education as Per Cent of GSDP

Source: http://mhrd.gov.in/sites/upload_files/mhrd/files/statistics/ABE_2010–13.pdf (page 12).

HOUSING

The final indicator that the DI considered was housing. While housing remains highly segregated and concentrated, and underscoring the need for diverse communities, the formula suggested by the Diversity Committee (DC) cannot be used for the institutions in housing sector. Also, traditional properties and individual houses cannot be brought under the purview of this discussion, as these are products of historical factors. However, while recognising these limitations, the aim, going forward, should be to increase diversity in new housing societies. Specifically, instances of housing society membership/rental spaces being denied to an individual on account of his/her affiliation to a social group should call for strict penalties against the society in question. Conversely, a housing society that displays religious and caste diversity (specifically, a greater share of religious minorities and SC–ST families) should be adequately rewarded through a system of financial incentives. Diversity in housing should be instituted through these mechanisms. This was discussed in the DI commission but these proportions could not be counted using NSS data.

CONCLUDING COMMENTS

This chapter outlines the original conception of the DI as proposed by an expert committee appointed by the Government of India in 2008. While the database for calculating that index is not yet in place, this chapter presents some indicative calculations based on NSS data for 2007 and 2009–10. The calculations reveal that over time, diversity in educational institutions has increased, particularly for women and OBCs. The increased presence of OBCs in graduate programmes, as well as the fact that SC presence in graduate programmes is higher than that of Muslims, suggests that affirmative action might be contributing to these differential group outcomes. There is a great deal of inter-state heterogeneity in access of different groups which does not seem to be directly correlated with state-level patterns in educational expenditures. Much more rigorous work is needed in order to ascertain factors that might account for differences across groups and states.

ANNEXURE

Let us first consider the two spheres of 'education and employment'. We define 'diversity gap' in two stages, Stage I being time period 2008–09 and Stage II intended for the medium term, say 8–10 years from the above time period.

Stage I

Let x_i be the actual proportion of workers/students in an institution belonging to Group i (say, the proportion of Muslims in the DU faculty/students).

y_i be the proportion of the ith group in the *population eligible to enter the institution*.

At any given point of time, entry to an institution for a job or course would be from the eligible pool of individuals for each social group. The size of this pool for specific groups might reflect discrimination (or its opposite) in the society, but an institution has limited role to play in changing that and hence has to deal with the number of persons belonging to the group within this eligible pool, big or small. To cite an example, passing a BA/BSc/BCom examination is essential for gaining entry into an MA/MSc/MCom course at a university. Understandably, the number of graduates who could be applicants will define the eligible population for admission to the master-level courses. Thus, y_i will be, say, the proportion of graduate Muslims to all graduates in the country who can potentially be considered for admission in a national-level institution, because they qualify the minimum eligibility conditions.

z_i is the proportion of Group i in the total population for the *relevant universe* (say, the proportion of Muslims in the country).

Now, the diversity gap for the ith group, DG_i, can be represented as follows:

$$DG_1 = \frac{(x_i - y_i)}{y_i} \times z_i$$

When $x_i = y_i$, there is perfect diversity and the gap is zero.

When $x = 0$, the group is not represented at all and the value is $-z_i$.

One can see that $x_i - y_i$ would be greater than zero for the over-represented groups and will be less than zero for the under-represented groups for each social category. Since the aim of the index is to capture the extent of under-representation of the groups, the index must capture only the aspect of under-representation adequately. So, for example, if Delhi University has an over representation of Hindu students (defined as x greater than y), then the formula for the index should not reward DU for a high value of the index that might be arising because of this over-representation.

Taking this into account, we redefine the diversity gap as

= $|DG|$ when $x < y$

= 0, when $x > y$

Thus, the DG computed for each group for a given dimension will have a minimum value of zero and a maximum value of z_i. The DG_i should be within each group separately. Thus, we will have seven values of DG for religious dimension, four for caste dimension and two for gender dimension.

The Diversity Index D for mth dimension can be stated as follows:

$$Dm = 1 - \sum_i DG_i$$

Thus, a situation of perfect diversity will mean $D = 1$ and complete exclusion of under-represented groups will mean that the index = 0. Typically, the index will lie between zero and one, higher values implying higher diversity for a given social category.

Aggregating Values of D over the Three Selected Dimensions

It would be desirable to construct DI for an institution by classifying the (a) workers and (b) recipient of services divided into a few broad grades, representing vertical hierarchy. For operational convenience, this can be restricted to two in each, at least in the initial years. The DI should be calculated separately for each of these. To take the example of a university, if we divide all jobs into two broad grades (one consisting of all class-III and -IV employees and the other consisting of all class-I and -II employees). Similarly, the students can be placed into two categories (undergraduates and postgraduates). Now, there will be four DIs, pertaining to each of the three dimensions noted above (religion, caste and gender) for any institution under consideration. We suggest that these four indices be squared and added up for each social dimension. The step can be called 'vertical aggregation'.

The second step can be 'horizontal aggregation'—aggregation across the three social categories. The final composite DI for an institution would have to be worked out by obtaining a weighted average of the three indices, reflecting the three identified dimensions, as suggested above. The question here is whether the weights should be fixed exogenously at national level or should be left to the judgement of the organisation entrusted with this responsibility, at sub-national or state levels. For instance, should an institution assess diversity gaps for each of the social categories and then decide on the weights depending on the relative severity of the gaps? While certain amount of flexibility would be desirable to reflect the socio-political priorities at sub-national level, the veneer of flexibility should not allow institutions to get away from addressing the serious problems due to under-representation of minority groups.

The committee, after considerable deliberation, proposed a mixed system to address these concerns. Taking W_1, W_2 and W_3 to be the weights for the three dimensions, it was decided that each will be allowed to vary within a range. It was proposed that W_1, the weightage for religious dimension, must lie within the range of 0.45 and 0.55. Correspondingly, W_2 for caste dimension should fall between 0.35 and 0.25 and W_3, the gender weightage, can range from 0.15 to 0.25. The suggested range values, in a way, reflect the central concerns of the Sachar Committee, since the idea of increasing religious diversity is one of the key recommendations of the SCR. Also, given the existence of reservation policy applicable with respect to caste categories, the proposal to give a high weightage to religious diversity can be defended. The reason for assigning relatively lower weight to the gender dimension is that the under-represented religious and caste categories would have large incidence of women members and therefore would be counted there.

Ranges for the DI

Now, can we specify a minimum level of diversity that each institution must have to qualify for certain financial allocation of privilege? It would be impossible for any national-level organisation to determine the cut-off points for identification of categories without looking at the actual distribution of the DI for different types of institutions. The committee considers that the responsibility of suggesting meaningful ranges of the DI for identifying the categories must be given to concerned agencies. In the absence of the distribution, and since this is a first-time exercise, the committee proposes three ranges for the DI to facilitate designing of the index-linked interventions. The ranges are given as follows:

If the value of the index lies between zero and one-third, then the institution can be presumed to have 'low' diversity; between one-third and two-thirds to have 'middle' diversity and between two-thirds and one to have 'high' diversity.

15

Equity in Higher Education: What Happens After Entry?[1]

Wandana Sonalkar

INTRODUCTION

Most of the studies in equity in higher education focus on issues related to access to different social groups and their participation. What happens to the students from 'backward' or 'marginalised' sections after they obtain admission in institutions of higher education is a less researched area. At times, we read in newspapers about suicide of students belonging to scheduled caste (SC) or scheduled tribe (ST) social groups in elite educational institutions such as an Indian Institutes of Technology (IITs) or AIIMS. The usual explanation for the suicide is that students who obtained concessions in admission (on the basis of lower qualifying marks), could not keep up

[1] This paper was completed and sent to the editors of the Indian Higher Education Review just a few days before the tragic incidents in Hyderabad Central University (HCU). As discussed in this chapter, suicides by Dalit students have been happening due to harassment at the hands of the authorities. The controversy in HCU, which received solidarity in university campuses all over the country, was soon overshadowed by the events in Jawaharlal Nehru University (JNU). JNU and HCU are premier academic institutions where admissions are based on nation-wide competition tests. JNU strictly follows the legal provisions for reservation of seats for the marginalised groups and also awards extra points in the admission process for such students. Other premier institutions conduct coaching classes for disadvantaged students wishing to compete in the admissions process. Because of these policies, some prime IHEs have seen increasing numbers of students from socially and economically disadvantaged backgrounds gaining entry. These numbers have also been increasing in other premier institutions that take the principle of promoting diversity in the student body seriously. These are also the institutions where sections of marginalised students have been coming together to assert their cultural identity. These assertions, however, go side by side with the experiences of discriminatory treatment by the teaching faculty and the administrations of IHEs. In IHEs where such organised assertions do not take place, students silently suffer discrimination and some of them are driven to suicides, others give up and do not complete their courses.

with the academic rigour of the study programmes in these institutions. The psychological studies analysing reasons for such drastic steps by individual students point to the effect of low 'socio-economic status' on academic performance. They generally emphasise on factors like a family background where education has low priority, low levels of individual motivation, learning difficulties faced by students in the elite institutions etc. A recent article (Sinha and Mishra 2015) points out that it is also important to consider 'subjective' factors, that is, the student's self-perception and ideas of self-worth, which may be influenced by the treatment received from other students, teachers and the administration. These factors may also be influenced by pedagogical practices in the classroom.

This chapter addresses issues related to experiences of students from disadvantaged families, especially belonging to SC and ST, after their entry into institutions of higher education. This is an area that has received less attention in research, although the issues are highlighted in the recent past, mainly from Dalit groups and activists working among Dalits and Adivasis. The policy of reservations in institutes of higher education (IHE) ensures that a fairly large number of students from these disadvantaged groups reach these places of learning. My argument in this chapter is that even when access is facilitated by a reservation policy, the students from disadvantaged groups, such as SC and ST, face considerable discrimination and prejudice.

The plan of the chapter is as follows. The next section will analyse the experiences of prejudice, discrimination and even abuse suffered by such students at the hands of teachers and other students, as evidenced from published work. The second part will present the result of our investigation into this question, by means of inviting students and past students to submit answers to written questions followed by interviews. In the third part, we will discuss possible intervention strategies in terms of administrative policy and pedagogical strategy.

STUDENT SUICIDES AND THE QUESTION OF MERIT: EVIDENCE FROM DIFFERENT INSTITUTIONS

The policy of reserving seats for the categories of SCs and STs finds its justification in Article 15(4) of the Constitution, which provides for protective discrimination in the favour of certain disadvantaged sections of society. According to this, the State can make 'special provision for the advancement of any socially and educationally backward classes of citizens or for the Scheduled Castes and the Scheduled Tribes'. From 1980, we have also had reservation of seats in education institutions for those castes identified as 'other backward classes (OBCs)' by the Mandal Commission. The exact proportions of reserved seats for these categories and the classification of different castes within these categories differ from state to state. There is also a concession of 5–10% in the minimum qualifying marks required for entry by the students from these groups to institutions of higher education.

Thus, the picture we see today is that of a fairly large number of students from the middle castes, as well as Dalits and Adivasis, entering colleges at the undergraduate level and universities and other institutes at the postgraduate level. At present, there is also a situation where there is considerable competition for entry within these categories. In many places, we find that the 'cut-off' marks for the SC category, at least in Maharashtra, are hardly different from those for the open category. The Government of Maharashtra has recently introduced a provision that students from the disadvantaged categories need to specify in their application forms whether or not they need to be considered under the open or reserved quota. This has the effect of excluding competent students from competing in the open category because reserved-category students may find it easier to compete in their categories than in the open quota. In the perception of many of the teachers and administrators who oversee admissions, seats in the open category are reserved for the 'non-category' candidates, and their numbers have in any case been shrunk by the reservations policy. In my own fieldwork experience as a college and university teacher, such views are openly expressed in colleges and universities. This in itself reflects a prejudice against the lower caste and Adivasi students.

Suicide of a Woman Graduate, Chuni Kotal

On August 16, 1992, a student named Chuni Kotal, a girl of 27, from the denotified Lodha tribe, the first graduate woman among the Lodha Savara and Kheria Savara of West Bengal, hanged herself at her husband's one-room residence in Kharagpur, a railway town. Mahasweta Devi, the well-known Bengali writer, who is also an activist working with some tribal and nomadic communities, wrote an essay (Devi 1992) on this incident in which she says, 'Chuni Kotal's suicide has ripped the mask off the face of West Bengal under Left

Front rule: the caste prejudice and persecution and the government's callous indifference'. She says that the reasons leading to
this young woman's suicide were 'palpable ones', and quotes from a
contemporary newspaper report that Chuni Kotal 'became a victim
of sheer injustice and callousness of the university authorities and
the West Bengal government' (as cited in Devi, 1992, 1836).

In what follows, we give a fairly extensive quote from Mahasweta
Devi's article, which was published by the *Economic and Political
Weekly*, as it illustrates in detail the way in which prejudice and
discrimination often operate in IHE's.

*Chuni was appointed a Lodha social worker in 1983 at Jhargram
ITDP office. From childhood she had starved, worked in the
fields, had no money to purchase books, yet doggedly she continued to study.... In 1987, she was appointed suprintendent [sic]
of Rani Shiromani SC and ST girls' hostel at Medinapur.*

She suffered considerable persecution in her job, in which she was
supposed to be on duty 24 hours a day, 7 days a week, and was not
allowed any visitors. Even so, she applied for a master's degree in
anthropology. At the time of her suicide, she was in her husband's
living quarters. Her husband was a high school graduate who had a
job in the railway workshop.

*Chuni felt suffocated in the job. Countless times she had come
to Calcutta to Writer's Building pleading for (a) transfer to her
original job, or (b) better working conditions. The department
remained brutally indifferent.*

*Matters became worse when Chuni enrolled in Vidyasagar
University as an M.A. (Master of Arts) student in Anthropology.*

*Falguni Chakravarty, a male professor, from the very first day
started abusing her as one coming from a criminal tribe, a low-
born, who had no 'right' to study M.A. The university authorities, the head of the department, did nothing about it.*

*This man was allowed to mark her 'absent' though she was
present for days. And Chuni was debarred from sitting for examination for 'irregular attendance'. She lost one year. The district
office made life hell for her for 'leaving the hostel' and going to
study.*

*Thus, the first woman graduate from a very backward tribe
in the state was openly abused because of her low-caste and
birth and nothing was done about it. The second time Chuni sat
for exam. The professor gave her low marks. Thus, she lost two*

*years. In desperation, she complained repeatedly in 1991, the
education minister set up an enquiry commission comprising of
three principals from three district colleges.*

*All through this man (the professor) was allowed to refer to
the criminal nature of her tribe, abuse her. The commission did
not submit any report.*

*On August 13 (just 3 days prior to her suicide), there was a
seminar in the university. By that time Chuni knew where she stood.
She had no hope that the enquiry commission would do justice to
her and punish the 'bhadra log', the babu, who pointed to her low
birth and low-caste relentlessly. She went to the university.*

*Thereafter, she weepingly told a few co-students, "today in
the seminar Falguni babu, quite off the context, referred to the
Lodhas as thieves and robbers. In the corridor, he threatened
me, I'll see that you don't sit for the examination in September.
I am a Lodha. So I shouldn't have dreamt of higher studies. I
complained against the offenders, but they remain untouched.
Unnecessarily I wasted two years, attended classes but was not
allowed to sit for the examination"* (Letter to the editor, Daily
Bartoman, August 25, 1992).

*By August 13, she had made up her mind. Death was the only
way to escape the hunters. On 14th, she went to her husband.
They had married in a court in 1990, but due to her job had not
been able to stay together.*

*Her husband is a Lodha youth who is a high school graduate and
works in the railways workshop. That Chuni was a graduate
and he was not had never created any friction. They had been in
love with each other from 1981. They were to leave for Chuni's
village, Gohaldohi, on the 16th to talk about formal reception, a
community feast after marriage.*

*On 16th August, he left for the workshop at 6.15 am. He
returned at 10.45 am and found Chuni hanging.*

*Chuni's death has revealed brutal caste and class hostility
and persecution suffered by the lower caste students in institutions of higher education. It also shows the inaction by the
government and allowing the district babu to abuse her. The
university authorities also did nothing to throw out the caste-
baiter. Interestingly, the commission appointed by the government submitted its report three days after her death.*

A website run by South Asians resident in North America and
Europe, *Insaf International South Asia Forum*, aiming to work for

secularism, democracy, human rights and social justice in 2011, drew up a list of *recorded* suicides in premier IHEs in the country in the previous four years, which was then posted on several Dalit websites. The list is limited to some leading technical and medical colleges and central universities. Some suicides may have gone unrecorded.

In May 2011, the website Tehelka.com published an article by Yamini Deendayalan, with the somewhat facetious title, 'Icarus goes to Flying School', asking, 'Why are Dalit students in India's best educational institutions committing suicide?' The article gives the social background of the students and the circumstances behind some of the suicides referred to in this list. Mukund Bharti, for example, was an exceptionally bright student who had cleared the IIT entrance examination and ranked eighth. However, he wanted to study medicine and obtained admission to the MBBS course at the AIIMS, Delhi. '*Professors* repeatedly mocked Bharti for being a "category student". While studying at AIIMS, Bharti often that he wished he could change his name to an anodyne "Srijan Kumar". In his final year, the pressure became unbearable and Bharti committed suicide in 2010'. The article goes on to mention that Bharti's younger brother, Gopal, hides his caste; he is studying horticulture at a college in rural Madhya Pradesh.

Following some earlier complaints regarding caste-based discrimination in the AIIMS, the government in September 2006 set up a three-member committee, led by Professor S.K. Thorat, to enquire into the 'Allegation of Differential Treatment of SC/ST Students in all India Institute of Medical Science (sic)'. The enquiry was limited to one IHE, AIIMS, and its report, which came out in 2007, covered a range of forms of classroom-related discrimination (for the undergraduate students specifically), including the absence of remedial English language coaching programs in AIIMS, methods of assessment that gives scope to subjective judgements of individual faculty, discrimination in access to consultation and interaction with teachers and discrimination in practicals and viva voce examinations. Besides this, the students' responses to survey questions mentioned discrimination in the mess, social isolation in hostels and exclusion from participation in sports and cultural events and verbal ragging with caste overtones even though ragging has been banned. The postgraduate students complained that the institution was not following the government-specified reservation policy in the appointment of senior and junior residents.

THE COMMITTEE RECOUNTS THE
CASE OF AJIT KUMAR

Ajay Kumar case has happened during the course of our enquiry. Ajay Kumar Singh hails from UP, his father is not educated, but scored high marks in his entrance examination to be in the general category but was put in the reserved category as he was from the SC community. Despite his background, he passed all his examinations without losing time, reached the final year. During the anti-quota agitation, he came out openly with the pro-reservationists, protested against the behaviour that was meted out to the SC/ST students. His name was on top of the list of 44 students who had written complaint to the Director about some upper caste students who behaved violently with the SC/ST students. It was believed by the SC/ST students that there would be repercussions against them for complaining. Ajay Kumar Singh was failed in three final year subjects. This would do immense harm to his career. During the examination, casteist comments were made against him and references to his role in cooperating with the committee investigating against the crimes against the SC/ST students were made. (Government of India 2006)

The suicide of Mukund Bharati illustrates that matters had not changed in AIIMS even after the submission of the enquiry report.

Even though suicide is an extreme reaction to the experience of discrimination and prejudice, these accounts throw some light on what many students from the SC/ST categories have to suffer. The *Insaf* list of suicides counts many 'premier' IHEs that trumpet the upholding of 'merit' as their only principle in treating students. Discrimination and the open expression of caste bias is no less blatant at state level, as we can see in some of the testimonies of interviewed respondents, and in my own experience as a teacher in a state-level university in a provincial town.

TESTIMONY OF PRESENT AND PAST STUDENTS

The original aim of the researcher was to meet students from different types of IHE's at both undergraduate and postgraduate levels, from arts as well as technical colleges and from rural and urban areas. Certain problems made this impossible, but by interviewing 10–12 students and ex-students, it was still possible to obtain testimonies about different IHE environments. For example, those who had studied in a rural college at undergraduate level and an urban/metropolitan college at graduate level could compare their experiences in two IHEs. The persons interviewed included a woman aged about 40, and a woman and a man of about 35, but most respondents were in their 20s. A set of questions was drawn up, but this informed a semi-structured interview, as the respondents opened up when asked to talk about their experiences. Three respondents gave written answers.

Certain themes recurred in the answers of respondents. First, relations with classmates and other students form a very influential part of the student's subjective experience. The degree of initial comfort felt on joining an IHE as a student depended largely on whether most of the students came from similar backgrounds. This is why the first members of their community to reach a specific level of education undergo the greatest amount of stress. As long as there were such students from similar backgrounds, most respondents said they did not find it difficult to make friends. Friendships usually followed the lines of class, rural/urban origin and language. Caste was not such an important factor in making friends.

Ragging has been banned from all the educational institutions in about the year 2000, and we did not find any students who reported having undergone ragging. However, one respondent from a premier IHE said that in the National Cadet Corps (NCC), seniors made their juniors run errands, sometimes humiliating ones. When asked if there was taunting by the more 'elite' students on caste lines, almost all answered in the negative. Verbal teasing and taunting was more on the basis of language and style of dress. Those SC students who took part in student activism found it much easier to deal with the problems they faced and could interact with those from different, upper class, urban backgrounds. Several respondents said that the behaviour of elite-background students changed (for the better) over the course of time. A graduate of a premier architecture college reported that students groups were initially formed on the basis of income class, language and rural/urban background. The students from well-off, metropolitan families, speaking fluent English formed a tight clan. There was more fluidity between two other groups: one consisting of middle-class students from the metropolis or sizeable cities, and another with those from a rural background. After a time, working together on practical assignments broke down barriers between these two groups. By the third year, academic performance also mattered, though this was not a major criterion for forming friendships.

A woman respondent, who studied in a college run by Christian missionaries in a small town and a central university, said that even among Dalit students at the postgraduate level, there was a gender gap: women students usually came from a second educated generation, while the men were usually first-generation entrants to IHEs. She found that the male students tended to be more sensitive and militant regarding their caste status and treatment by teachers, while the female students were less aggressive.

It was interesting to note that gender was not reported as an important factor. Student groups included both girls and boys, and divisions tended to be more along the lines of class, rural/urban background, and, in one IHE, ideological leanings. Many respondents said that they were excluded from extra-curricular activities organised by students in which the 'elite' groups usually took the lead. It is now common to see associations of 'backward-caste' students who take a militant political stance and organise their own programmes. The participation of other students in these programmes is rare.

When asked about the approachability of teachers, most respondents said that, on the whole, teachers were not approachable, but there were some who were friendlier. We will mention the IHEs that proved different in the next section. In many of the rural colleges, or even those in larger cities, teachers showed favouritism towards some students, and this usually followed caste lines. When teachers from an SC or OBC category were present, they too tended to be partial to students belonging to their own caste. In the premier institutions, where most of the teachers were upper-caste, they sometimes behaved with contempt towards first-generation learners. One respondent spoke about a boy (from Maratha background) who was told by a teacher that he was not fit for university learning, that he should have stayed in his village. This student did gave up his studies, as a result. One SC student reported that a teacher made fun of her on stage when she tried to introduce themes related to Savitribai Phule in a cultural programme.

Asked about classroom practices and student participation, most respondents said that language was a barrier for participation in class discussions. This was more so when students from a rural college moved to an IHE that had English as the medium of instruction. But even in Marathi-medium classes, rural students showed diffidence and a reluctance to speak for the fear that they would be made fun of for their style of speaking. Many respondents felt that remedial language classes would help, and that these should continue throughout the year. Language skills proved to be an important part of academic performance, and there was rarely any instruction in this.

To summarise, students from a rural and/or 'lower-caste' background certainly face difficulties in adapting to the environment of IHEs. In the premier institutions, in the words of one student, 'the class difference is striking'. Most of the 'non-category' students come from an upper-class metropolitan background, while students from the reserved categories belong to lower income groups and come from small towns or villages. Groups tend to follow class lines, though there are friendships across class lines. Participation in practical activity helps in breaking down barriers.

Teachers are more likely to discriminate on the basis of caste. In the premier institutions, most teachers are upper caste, and we often find a blanket dismissal of the abilities of reserved 'category' students. Classroom practices tend to favour those who are more articulate because of their language skills. Only occasionally do teachers make a systematic attempt to overcome this.

TOWARDS A MORE 'INCLUSIVE' PEDAGOGY

We were examining respondents' answers to infer about ways to make a more 'inclusive' pedagogy in the institutions of higher education in India. It seems that the students who got admission through reservation quotas find it difficult, especially in the initial stages, to adapt to the institutional environment and feel the environment unfriendly, alienated and at times even hostile. This is not unexpected since similar experiences were recorded among the deprived groups in the past decades. For example, the autobiographies of Dalits from an earlier era, who have made an impact on society, cite experience of having been made to sit separately in the classroom, forced to use different utensils for drinking water or even denied some facilities because of caste (Pawar [1978] 2016; Pawar and Moon 1989; Rege 2006). Even now, these practices have not completely disappeared. There are occasional news reports of Dalit children being forced to sweep the school premises and clean toilets (Khan 2015). What might be a salutary practice of teaching children to take pride in their school environment and to take care of, it becomes a form of cruel discrimination, reinforcing social divisions. Students who reach higher education have usually faced discrimination on their way, and still face it within the institutions of higher education.

Even in this limited survey, we find prejudice among teachers who consider some students from the reserved category to be 'unfit for learning'. The answers of the respondents echoed the findings of enquiries into suicides of students. Our experience shows that the institutions are compelled by law to admit students from the reserved 'categories' but they face severe obstacles after entry since the attitude of teachers remain unchanged. Sometimes changes in the administration of course can help to neutralise teacher biases. For example, a response from a professional college indicated that discrimination was less when a course was taught by visiting faculty who also assessed the assignments. It seems that a rotation of evaluators may help reduce discrimination in higher education institutions.

In our survey, we found examples of institutions where pedagogical practices are significantly more inclusive. One was a college run by Christian missionaries, where several teachers made efforts to ensure participation of all students in class discussions. The other was a premier state university with a good academic reputation, where the social composition of the student body has changed over time and the majority of students now come from rural/'lower-caste' backgrounds, and have studied in the vernacular medium.

A professor in the Department of Sociology looked on this as an opportunity rather than a disadvantage, and put considerable effort into creating an academic environment that would be comfortable for these students. Some of the methods incorporated by her, which were then reinforced when she shifted to a centre for women's studies, are mentioned here. Bridge materials were produced in the form of translations of important texts. Separate classes were held where the topics covered in the usual class in English were discussed again in the vernacular. When readings were circulated prior to a class, students were designated to lead the discussion on a particular reading. A lot of importance was given to group work, and the groups were deliberately diverse in their composition. This resulted in friction at first; but over time, this led to better understanding among students. Other aspects were seating students in a circle instead of in rows, being invited to address teachers by their first names and use of audiovisual media, especially documentary films with discussion. Further, texts from the anti-caste movement were used for classroom discussion. Study tours also contributed to breaking down barriers among students, as informal interactions became possible.

CONCLUSION

The empirical information generated through our survey and the testimonies from students indicate the type of discriminatory practices prevalent in our higher education institutions. First, there exists prejudices by the teachers and there are real problems. It seems while student body has become diverse, the teaching community and administrators remained to be drawn from higher caste and income groups than those from SC and ST. Therefore, we suggest for more diversity in recruitment of teachers, administrative measures to ensure that teachers from one social group do not have exclusive say in student evaluation will help.

Second, the classroom practices vary and, very often, students from non-reserved categories are more active in the classrooms and teaching—learning process. Therefore, there is a need for conscious efforts to ensure that classroom participation by all students is effective. The teacher may choose different techniques and teaching methods to ensure more participation from the SC and ST students.

Third, teachers need to use diverse cultural symbols in teaching rather than confining to the traditional practices. An extension of such sensitivities and approach in organising extracurricular events or in hostel administration will go a long way in 'legitimising' different cultural practices. Otherwise, culture becomes a subject for student identity politics alone.

Fourth, group work and practical activities bring students together. Therefore, practical group activity based teaching—learning process and study tours help break down barriers among students, and they need to be introduced early in the course rather than at the end of the course. While forming groups for study, teachers should ensure diversity in the composition of groups.

Finally, the higher education establishment needs to recognise and internalise that diversity in higher education institutions is a source of enrichment. The presence of students from different backgrounds not only helps to nurture values of democracy and tolerance, but can also widen the scope of knowledge. This is all the more true in a society like ours where the nexus between knowledge and class and knowledge and power are reinforced by a hierarchical caste tradition that explicitly excludes certain sections of society from learning.

REFERENCES

Deenadayalan, Y. 2011. 'Icarus goes to Flying School'. *Tehelka.com*. Available at: http://www.tehelka.com/2011/05/icarus-goes-to-flying-school/

Devi, Mahasweta. 1992. 'Story of Chuni Kotal'. *Economic and Political Weekly* 27 (35): 1836–37.

Government of India (GoI). 2006. Report of the S.K. Thorat Committee to Inquire into Allegation of Differential Treatment of SC/ST Students In All India Institute of Medical Science. New Delhi: GoI.

Khan, H. 2015. 'Sweep the Floor or We'll Give You a TC: Threat to Dalit Students in Jaipur School'. *The Indian Express*, November 8, 2015. http://indianexpress.com

Manjrekar, Nandini. 2003. 'Contemporary Challenges to Women's Education: Towards an Elusive Goal?' *Economic and Political Weekly* 38 (43): 4577–82.

Pawar, Daya. [1978] 2016. *Baluta*. Translated by Jerry Pinto. Mumbai: Speaking Tiger.

Pawar, Urmila, and Meenaxi Moon. 1989. *Amhihi Itihaas Ghadavala* (Marathi). Pune: Sugawa Prakashan. Translated in English as *We Also Made History* by Wandana Sonalkar in 2008, Zubaan, New Delhi.

Rege, Sharmila. 2006. *Writing Caste, Writing Gender*. New Delhi: Zubaan.

Sinha, C., and A.K. Mishra. 2015. 'Rethinking the Place of Socio-economic Status Identity in Students' Academic Achievement'. *European Journal of Psychological Education Studies* 2 (2): 36–42.

16

Diversity and Discrimination: Role of Higher Education for Civic Learning

Nidhi S. Sabharwal and C.M. Malish

INTRODUCTION

The role of higher education and the mission of institutions imparting higher education is seen as training young people in the values which form the basis of democratic citizenship (UNESCO 1998). It prepares young minds to become effective citizens by enhancing students' knowledge regarding issues pertaining to problems of society like inequality, poverty, discrimination, injustices and, inculcating democratic values of equality, liberty, fraternity and skills needed to participate in effective democratic engagement. Education is seen as defence against the rise of violence, prejudices and intolerance. Higher education also plays an important role in nurturing and sustaining democracy, cooperation among diverse people and instils values of democratic engagement and a sense of social responsibility in citizens. It is a necessary experience in 'cultivation humanity' (Nussbaum 1997).

The need of education for civic learning and democratic engagement for building citizenship is particularly relevant for societies that are characterised by high degree of diversity in its social, ethnic, racial and religious belonging. Although the diverse groups are obliged to respect and practice the common constitutional principles and values, the community determined values, often contradictory to democratic norms and practices influence the behaviour of people from diverse groups. In diverse societies, therefore, the role of education in harmonising the behaviour of people around common values assumes far greater significance, particularly to sensitise the youth to democratic values of equality, liberty and fraternity to cultivate democratic norms of behaviour (Thorat and Sabharwal 2013). In this context, Nussbaum (1997, 295) observed that

It is relatively easy to construct a gentlemen's education for a homogeneous elite. It is far more difficult to prepare people of highly diverse background for citizenship. This enterprise requires learning about, racial, ethnic, religious and gender differences. It requires learning on how to situate one's own tradition within a highly plural and interdependent world.

Thus, challenges of developing positive citizenship are lot more difficult and complex in diverse society compared with a homogeneous society.

In the context of growing student diversity in India in its massified era, this chapter attempts to explore how higher education can be better channelled for civic learning and democratic engagement and how higher education institutions can be re-imagined to uphold the constitutional principles of equality, fraternity and justice.

DIVERSITY AND DEMOCRATIC VALUES IN INDIAN HIGHER EDUCATION

The University Education Commission, 1948–49, under the leadership of Dr S. Radhakrishnan, laid the foundations of democratic values through higher education. The Commission underlined the values of social justice, equality, liberty and fraternity as driving forces to promote democratic values and transform higher education. It stated that higher education must 'cultivate the art of human relationship, the ability to live and work together overcoming the dividing force of the time' (Government of India 1950, 31). However, from the 1960s with the ascendancy of human capital theory, the emphasis shifted to the idea of higher education for development. This change in emphasis was reflected in the title of the first education commission of India—Education for Development—in the 1960s. However, the Indian approach was to link economic development role of higher education with its social role. For example, the Third Five Year Plan (FYP) document (1961–66) described education as 'the most important single factor in achieving rapid economic development and technological progress and in creating a social order founded on the values of freedom, social justice and equal opportunity'.

In India, commissions and education policies upheld the spirit of democracy, equality, fraternity and associative living; yet, there are limited initiatives to cultivate young minds to promote civic learning in higher education. The University Education Commission of post-independent India stated, 'Education is the great instrument of social emancipation by which a democracy establishes, maintains and protects the spirit of equality among its members' (Government of India 1950, 43). The National Policy on Education (NPE) 1968 while stressing the need for equalising educational opportunity envisaged common school system to promote social cohesion and national integration (Ministry of Education 1968). The NPE 1986 stated,

> *To promote equality, it will be necessary to provide for equal opportunity to all not only in access, but also in the conditions for success. Besides, awareness of the inherent equality of all will be created through the core curriculum. The purpose is to remove prejudices and complexes transmitted through the social environment and the accident of birth. (Ministry of Education 1968, 4)*

The Programme of Action 1992, based on the NPE 1986, does talk about the inequality in access to high education on the line of caste, ethnic group, gender and religion and suggested measures. It also emphasised the need to upgrade the curriculum. But the Programme of Action avoids reference to the need for civic learning for citizenship education through changes in the curriculum.

In a similar vein, National Curricular Framework 2005 (National Council of Educational Research and Training or NCERT 2005, 10–11) stresses educational system's commitments to

> *Democracy and the values of equality, justice, freedom, concern for others' well-being, secularism, respect for human dignity and rights.... The curriculum, therefore, should provide adequate experience and space for dialogue and discourse in the school to build such a commitment in children.*

A committee set up in 2011 to 'Strengthen Community Engagement of Higher Education Institutions' suggested that enhanced community engagement would foster values of citizenship and social responsibility. The committee made several significant recommendations, including organisational structure of bodies coordinating citizenship education activities at various levels, curricula flexibility, crediting community engagement in higher education institution.

It can be argued that educational policies in India always favoured and upheld the values of democracy, citizenry, national integration and associative learning and have been incorporated as goals and objectives of education. However, when the country moved from the 'textual mode' to 'action mode' of policy (Olssen and Neil 2004), instrumentality and mechanism for implementation, these ideas became vague and difficult to implement.

Since the Independence, many of the government initiatives at higher education implicitly and explicitly addressed the issues of diversity. We would like to discuss two types of such initiatives. The first is at the institutional level but broadly coordinated by common guideline schemes/programmes to inculcate values. The second is incorporation of approach towards diversity and discrimination in academic programme and launching of specialised centres for teaching and research. While launching of initiatives such as National Service Scheme (NSS), Centre for Value Education and National Cadet Corps (NCC) envisage inculcating values through social engagement and sensitisation training, the establishment of Women's Study Centres (WSCs) and Centre for Studies of Social Exclusion and Inclusive Policies (CSSEIP) represents second type.

NSS, launched in 1969, promotes learning through social services. NSS programme officer, a faculty member-in-charge of NSS, coordinates activities. Under the guidance of programme officer, students are involved in a wide variety of services such as blood donation camps, construction of roads for rural community, conducting of health survey and health awareness programme, campus cleaning initiatives and so on. All the activities are arranged without affecting curricular activities of the students. Although it is implemented in all colleges, the reach of this programme among the entire student community is limited. Moreover, there is no linkage between participation in NSS and curricular activities of student.

NCC aims to groom youngsters into disciplined and patriotic citizens. 'Unity and Discipline' has been the motto of NCC. NCC's (n.d.) core values include 'respect for diversities, national unity and social cohesion, commitment to Indian Constitution, participation in community development, living healthy lifestyles, sensitivity to poor and socially disadvantaged and commitment to values of honesty, truthfulness, self-sacrifice, perseverance and hard work'. NCC imparts a sense of patriotic commitment and motivates students to take up a career in the armed forces of the country. They are involved in social service activities, both inside and outside the campus.

National Resource Centre for Valued Education in Engineering (NRCVEE) at IIT Delhi is another initiative to foster value education. NRCVEE has been set up in IIT Delhi in 2001 with the active involvement of MHRD. It was set up as a national centre for imparting value-education in engineering colleges. Complementarily of technical skills and human values, professional ethics have been the central focus of learning. The Centre independently and in association with other departments offers courses on value education. Apart from courses, the Centre also liaises with organisations to conduct programmes/events such as seminars, workshops, lecture series, etc. both for engineering students and faculty.

Compulsory Social Service (CSS), launched by the University of Calicut in south India, is a distinct programme. The university introduced this initiative in the academic year 1998–99. CSS made 30 days of social service mandatory for all UG students registered with the university. Successful completion of CSS is mandatory for the award of degree. Unlike other initiative so far discusses, CSS covers all UG students irrespective of discipline/branch arts/science/ engineering and type of registration such as private, direct and distant education mode.

The second set of initiatives focused more on establishing academic structures based on an inter-disciplinary approach to foster wider societal implications. Two of the institutional responses to the issue of discrimination and inequalities were setting up of WSCs and CSSEIP. Setting up of academic centres at universities, focusing on issues of discrimination, exclusion and inclusion based on gender, caste, ethnicity and religion, could be seen as a broader social and political response to diversity and associated issues of discrimination in and outside educational systems. Inter-disciplinary approaches in theory and methods and collaborations with a variety of social actors and institutions have been the hallmark of these two centres. Although its coverage is limited, setting up of these centres had been an important milestone in the history of education in India for realising values of secularism, equity and democracy.

In 1974, the report of the National Committee on the Status of Women in India, titled 'Towards Equality', detailed the situation of women in India and suggested urgent interventions in many spheres, including education, health and employment. NPE 1986 placed more emphasis on women's education and the need for incorporating women's studies in the national system of education. Since 1987, University Grants Commission (UGC) began to set up women's study centre in universities. Currently, there are 67 WSCs under UGC. Nearly half of them were set up during the 11th FYP. Women's studies was conceptualised as more than an academic discipline. It has been an institutional strategy to address the issues of discrimination against women. Many women's study research institutes were set up outside the university system through the active funding and support of Indian Council of Social Science Research (ICSSR).

The conviction that higher education is the space, where the impact of social divisions could be studied and transcended, led UGC to propose establishing of the CSSEIP in universities. It was during the 11th plan period that CSSEIP was launched. CSSEIP is also conceived as an institutional strategy to address the issues of exclusion and inclusion and as a mechanism to evolve socially inclusive practices in higher education and broader society. The research carried out by the centre could bring forth fresh insights into the magnitude of exclusion in diverse social, economic and political contexts.

GROWING DIVERSITY AND PREVAILING DISCRIMINATION

Inequality and exclusion in accessing education and knowledge have been a peculiar characteristic of Indian society. Caste and patriarchy system existed in India systemically denied access to resources and educational opportunities for the larger section of society and women. Castes and communities located in lower social strata such as scheduled castes (SCs), schedules tribes (STs) and other backward classes (OBCs) were the major victims of such exclusionary social system. Although reservation policies and various state interventions in education sector made significant contribution to educational growth of disadvantaged social groups, educational disparity along with development disparity continue to exists in India with significant state level variations. However, recent decades have experienced an unprecedented expansion in Indian higher education. India is in its early stages of massification (Varghese 2015) with an enrolment of 33 million students in 2014–15 (MHRD 2015). The expansion implied that more number of non-elite and non-traditional social and income group students are entering into higher education system. Today, students belonging to different religions and lower castes, from poor families, from rural areas and speaking minority languages co-exist with students from high caste, urban and rich parents. For example, in 2008, of the total students in higher education in the country, about 45% were from rural areas and the rest from urban areas, with 42% being women and 58% men. Social composition comprised 4% STs, 13.5% SCs, 35% OBC and 48% the rest. Hindus accounted for about 85%, followed by Muslims 8%, Christians 3% and others (Thorat and Sabharwal 2013).

As per the latest estimates (MHRD 2015), GER stands at 23.6 with significant levels of state, regional, sex and social group wise variation. Although much more to be done, there is commendable improvements in GER of disadvantaged social groups such as SC, ST and OBC. Affirmative action policies in terms of reservation of seats and support and incentive schemes have greatly contributed to growth of GER among the under-represented. It is a positive development. But provision for equality in opportunity in terms of access did not extend to equality in learning outcome and graduate completion rates. Similarly, participation of disadvantaged in professional and technical streams is further low. It has severe implications. Lower enrolment in streams and disciplines that has higher employment prospects is an important concern. Since exit grades and marks determine ones career trajectory, higher dropout rates and significantly lower graduation rates among the disadvantaged also raise serious concerns about social mobility, impacting intra-generational and inter-generational inequity.

Emerging empirical evidences indicate that there is a social divide in higher education spaces as well as among students based on caste, religion, ethnic and regional identities (Malish 2013; Ovichegan 2014; Rao 2013; Sukumar 2008; Thorat and Sabharwal 2014; Thornton et al. 2012). These studies report formation of social and peer groups around 'identities' for activities inside and outside classroom, on campus and in halls of residence, development of fissures in social relations on caste, ethnic, class, linguistic, regional and religious lines and exclusionary behaviours from the students from the dominant group which bring discrimination, psychological and physical violence for minority students and low castes, tribal and women.

Ovichegan (2014, 374) observed that 'this university is yet another arena in which the practice of caste division continues to exist. The university environment reinforces and maintains a divide between Dalits and non-Dalits. Dalit students do, indeed, experience overt and covert discrimination based on caste at this premier university'. Demoralisation and de-motivation of Dalit students by the teachers can manifest in low grades, poor lab facilities, poor marks in practical examinations, sarcastic remarks and, in general, not being meted equal treatment (Singh 2013). The non-transparency of the department and confusion in allotting supervisors resulted in the dropping out of students and fear among SC/ST students in India's premier institutions of higher learning.

Rao (2013) also cites many instances of how SC/ST students were discriminated by the teachers in IITs. He also describes the selection of teachers and pairing of students by teachers. Students also exclude disadvantaged groups, which affects their academic performance. He is of the view that would not be appropriate to attribute the academic under-performance of these groups to social adjustment, pre-schooling, financial constraints, inferiority complex, but it would be of utmost importance and relevance to understand the process of exclusion, the contestants, situations and rituals which spawns helplessness, inferiority complex, segregation, self-exclusion and a feeling of humiliation among the SC and ST students.

In premier institutes, Dalit students have to carry SC/ST tag throughout their academic career, which results in open hostility towards students of the general category. Social interaction with non-Dalit students is limited and issues of poverty, attire and English language make Dalit life difficult (Sukumar 2008). It is further elaborated that the lack of general 'etiquette' puts the Dalit students in difficult situations as they are unable to interact with the opposite sex.

Preliminary findings of the large scale national level study[1] carried out by authors in six states in India, namely, Bihar, New Delhi, Karnataka, Kerala, Maharashtra and Uttar Pradesh, bring forth fresh empirical evidences of diversity-related discrimination in higher education. Insights are based on the preliminary analysis of 3,000-student questionnaire, interviews with faculty members, academic administrators and faculty in-charge of cells and committees and focus group discussion with students belonging to various social groups and women. In resonance with national estimates of student participation, we find that social group diversity of higher education institutions has been significantly changed. Now larger proportion of students is from socially and economically disadvantaged background

---

[1] Research project entitled 'Higher Education for Civic Learning and Democratic Engagement: A Study of Diversity and Discrimination in Higher Education Institutions' is a collaborative project by CPRHE-NUEPA and ICSSR. Core objective of the project is to understand changing nature of student diversity, structures and mechanism to deals with diversity and how student diversity can be better channelled for civic learning in the context of massification of higher education India.

and first generation higher education learner. It seems that increasing student diversity is not conceived as positive development by faculty members and academic administrators. With minor variations in perceptions among the states studied, many consider increasing diversity as the root cause of declining quality in higher education. 'Low grasping power', 'lack of motivation', 'poor English language competency', 'irregular in class', introvert behaviour' and 'shyness to come forward' are few of the major learning problems identified by the faculty members among the disadvantaged students. Caste and gender based jokes are often made in classrooms by the faculty members. Mismatch between aspirational levels of new generation students and expectation levels of teachers rooted in tradition influence general approach of faculty members towards students. Consequently, vulnerability of disadvantaged students is higher as they are not treated as ideal students. Prejudice based on identity is prevalent across all states under study with it being severe in some case study institutions. Consequently, the forms of that prejudice are reflected in engagement of teachers with students. Teacher–student engagement inside and outside classrooms mainly take place with 'good' and 'interested' students, a group in which disadvantaged students are negligible. It leads to unfair (grading) practices wherever semester system is followed.

Identity based peer group formation is dominant in all campuses. Even the seating preference of students is determined by their social group identity. Identity-based peer group formation is a consequence of the fear of discrimination among the disadvantaged groups. The upper castes enjoy a situation of maintaining their social privilege. These perceptions separate and isolate student community into different groups based on their identities. Student elections are the sites where the identity-based separation is more evident than in other spheres.

Along with financial problems, the lack of knowledge and inaccessibility to information about incentives and support system such as stipend, remedial classes and scholarships, to list a few, add further to the challenges faced by the students from the disadvantaged group. The lack of safety and security in campus was highlighted as major concern for women. In some case-study institutions, women students were even afraid to stay back in campus after class hours. It was highlighted that it was mostly male co-students and often 'locals' from outside created this unsafe conditions for women students. This has a consequence on their experiencing co-curricular activities on the campus as women students have to rush back home once their classroom hours are over. Girls from the SC group experience heightened vulnerability to harassment because of their gender and caste.

Strikingly, institutional leaders and faculty in-charge of cells and committees for student welfare consider 'business as usual'. Changing nature of student diversity and challenges of addressing learning requirements of diverse student population were not approached systematically. Most of the cells and committees, such as equal opportunity cell and women cell, are dysfunctional. Administrative necessity rather than sound assessment of situation leads formation of such cells. They are mostly in redressal mode and remain inactive unless and until there is a complaint. Proactive initiatives to promote welfare and academic success of target population are largely missing in all campuses. Sheer lack of institution level planning and coordination between various cells meant for the welfare of students, further stands as a major obstacle.

Diversity associated discrimination in higher educational institutions not only goes against the constitutional ideal of equality but also very idea of higher educational institutions as a secular social institution. Unlike western universities that took centuries to become inclusive social space, Indian colleges and universities, in principle, in its very beginning were open and secular institutions (Betteille 2010). With all its limitations, universities 'served as exemplar and model of a new kind of social existence' (Betteille 2010, 13) where boundaries of caste and class, in principle, became irrelevant in public domain first time. It was expected that this transformation would take place naturally and no systemic approach was adopted to realise this. The empirical evidences on discrimination in higher education institutions remind us that along with existing laws and regulations to address discrimination in higher education institutions, much more need to be done to make our institutions of higher learning secular and democratic spaces.

Legal methods have been recently implemented in higher education spaces to safeguard students of the discriminated groups, such as women, SC and ST, from possible discrimination (UGC 2012). The fact that the government felt the need of such regulation is indicative of the fact of the widespread prevalence of discrimination and exclusion on educational campus. However, legal methods can certainly act as deterrents but alone they may not be sufficient to achieve the desired democratic behaviour.

The educationists believe that education has a great potential to cultivate democratic norms of behaviour and positive citizenship.

Education is a social route or channel through which most of the children pass through schools. A sizable proportion of them also go through higher education institutions. Higher education spaces in India have a great potential to cultivate democratic norms of behaviour, as its social milieu is diverse and different from students' home and community background. Higher education period is also a crucial time of individual's transformation from late adolescence to early adulthood. During this age period, that is, 17–22, the sense of personal and social identity is formed. Colleges can be the space that supports young adults through this identity development stage. Colleges can help students to acquire knowledge, abilities, skills and habits of mind to cultivate multicultural competence and ability to work, interact with people who represent diverse cultures and perspectives and civic skills to participate in citizen action that bridges the gap between ideals in the Constitution and lived realities. It is in this background, we discuss the experiment in civic learning and democratic engagement implemented in the United States of America.

CIVIC LEARNING INITIATIVES IN THE UNITED STATES OF AMERICA

Following the passing of Civil Rights Act and affirmative action policies, presence of racial minorities began to increase drastically (Smith, Altbach and Lomotey 2002). One of the implications was that campuses became more heterogeneous in terms of socio-economic, race and gender background of students. However, increasing diversity was accompanied by violent racial tensions across the campuses. Starting from volatile racial violence in 1960s to symbolic attack against minorities through new media in 1990s, racial relations in higher education campuses continue to remain as racial crisis (Altbach, Lomotey and Rivers 2002). The United States of America developed education policy in 1992 to deal with diversity, improve race-relations and increase civic responsibilities by bringing about reforms in curriculum and pedagogy for civic learning and democratic engagement in colleges and universities. Overtime, hundreds of colleges, universities and community colleges started working together to bring diverse narratives of communities into the curriculum, make campus life constructively inter-cultural and engage in partnerships with the wider community.

Scholars and educators located the problem of inter-group tensions in stereotypes and misinformation about groups, particularly minority groups, and identified approaches to address the issue. Three major approaches were identified: *enlightenment programmes* that provided knowledge about other groups to increase inter-group understanding; *contact programmes* that provided opportunities for members of different groups to interact with each other in controlled settings and *skill programmes* to manage differences in a peaceful manner and collectively solve public problems. Diversity in the student composition in this approach was viewed as a resource for new excellence and means to strengthen democracy.

A large number of educational programmes (diversity courses, social justice education, civic education, etc.) were created to improve race-relations on college campuses and to enhance the civic capital among the youth for enhanced citizenship. The reform also included changes in the orientation of teachers and their sensitisation for the new education reforms. The new reforms also refer to the necessary change in the organisational aspects of the educational institutions that would facilitate the teaching for civil learning and demographic engagement. These reforms were introduced in the early 2000 in many universities. About 10 years later, in 2011, a review of reforms was done (National Taskforce on Civic Learning and Democratic Engagement 2012).

The review indicated that the new civic learning and democratic engagement not only contributed to improvement in civic understanding about diversity and disparities among the students who undertook the diversity courses but also improved the academic performance of students. Longitudinal studies found that prejudice was lower in students who completed diversity courses, specifically addressing race and gender issues, and were also effective in improving students' inter-group tolerance (Bowman 2010; Bowman and Brandenberger 2012). Similarly, Denson and Chang (2009) undertook a quantitative meta-analysis on the influence of curricular and co-curricular diversity activities on racial bias. The findings of this meta-analysis, based on 27 studies from books, journals, thesis and conference papers, demonstrated that diversity initiatives did indeed reduce bias in college students and that the effectiveness of this result depends on the characteristics of the program as well as the students. The variation in effects of curricular and co-curricular diversity activities on racial bias is determined by the presence of diverse students and pedagogy that facilitates learning in a diverse environment.

Another study (Hogan and Mallot 2005) used the Modern Racism Scale to assess the impact of education and personality variables on 315 college students' prejudicial attitudes toward African Americans. This research demonstrated that while completion of a course in race and gender issues increased students' awareness about racism, it had only a transient effect on reducing antipathy toward government programs designed to help Afro-Americans achieve social and economic equity and no effect on their feelings of resentment over those achievements. The results underscored the importance of implementing teaching practices in diversity courses while also indicating that along with completion of diversity course, pedagogical methods were also important. Studies on the impact of pedagogies such as inter-group dialogues, informal interactions with diverse peers and mixed-peer groups had a positive effect on learning and democratic outcomes. King, Magolda and Marcia (2005) and Chang, Denson and Misa (2006), using single- and multi-institutional data from the University of Michigan, the Cooperative Institutional Research Program, National Survey of Student Engagement (NSSE), which collects data from 305 institutes, examined the effects of classroom diversity and informal interaction among African American, Asian American, Latino/American, and white students on learning and democracy outcomes. Racial, ethnic, gender, social class and religious diversity on students' learning were found positive with diverse outcomes. The results indicated that diversity experiences are associated with increases in civic attitudes, behavioural intentions and behaviours, and the magnitude of this effect is greater for interpersonal interactions with racial diversity than for curricular and co-curricular diversity experiences.

Thus, civic education was seen as a *medium* to enhance campus climate for racial/ethnic diversity. While, social diversity in the demographic composition of students, faculty and staff representation in the physical presence of previously under-represented groups on the higher education campus, created *conditions* of inter-group interactions and learning about diverse peers. College campuses were viewed as the laboratory and structural (numerical) diversity was regarded as a resource for fostering positive campus climate, inter-group relations, learning outcomes and democracy outcomes (Allport 1954; Antonio 2001; Chang 2002; Hurtado et al. 1999; Kurlaender and Orfield 2006; Milem and Hakuta 2000; Orfield 2001; Smith 1997; Tropp and Pettigrew 2005).

A FRAMEWORK FOR CIVIC LEARNING

As we have elaborated in earlier section, covert and overt forms of discrimination are distinctive feature of higher education campuses in India. The fact that large number of non-traditional social groups with varying pre-college credential is now attending higher education did not result any institutionalised approach towards managing diversity. Essentially, it leads no room for students to learn basic capacities and skills to live and work in diverse society. Therefore, there is a strong need for inculcating student's values of democracy, equality, fraternity, tolerance and social justice making them capable of associative living. Introducing value education, as many people tend to propagate, may not be the right option for this purpose. Values can be derived from international treaties (for instance UN declaration), constitution and religious texts. There is danger of misinterpretation of values and it may lead to reinforcing of longstanding social prejudices exists in India. It can be overcome by relying on constitutional values that upholds spirit of equity, democracy, secularism and social justice. It is important in the wake of growing intolerance and inequities in society at large and education sector in particular. Therefore, we propose a framework for civic learning comprising of values, knowledge and skill require for the associative living and which ensures diversity oriented campus culture.

When citizens unify around a set of democratic values such as equality, human rights and justice, only then the liberties of social, ethnic and religious groups can be secured to experience freedom, justice and peace. Diverse societies require citizens to embrace and commit to a set of shared values, ideals and goals and to believe and practice these values to make democracy a practicing institution. Citizens who understand this concept of unity in diversity and act accordingly do not materialise from thin air; they are educated for it (Banks 2007). Education for civic learning needs to be informed by deep engagement with these transformative values.

Banks, an Afro-American academician, talks about the meaning and essence of education for civic learning and democratic engagement. Banks observed 'the role of education in the 21st century is to prepare students 'to know, to care, and to act in ways that will develop and foster a democratic and just society' and to 'develop a commitment to personal, social, and civic action, as well as the knowledge and skill needed' (Banks 2007, 23). This, in fact, sum up the core of the civil learning necessary for enriching democracy. That is, students need to know (acquire knowledge) how to act and behave (develop skills), and, types of acts (actions of democratic behaviour) for a democratic commitment. Therefore, this definition has three main components namely knowledge, skills and action.

Taking the knowledge component of civic learning first, the reform in knowledge includes designing curriculum that makes student aware about the positive Constitutional principle and values which form the basis of good citizenship, content which make students aware about the problems of society and sensitise them to the problems. Knowledge that conveys that citizenship is a broad concept along with its minimal and maximal interpretations. While minimal interpretation of citizenship deals with law-abiding citizens and constitutional rights and duties, maximal interpretation discusses 'consciousness of the self as a member of shared democratic culture' (Essomba et al. 2008, 2). The new curriculum thus includes themes that deal with diversity, inequalities, poverty, discrimination associated with caste, ethnicity, gender, race and colour and also the use of examples to incorporate the experiences and perspectives of wide range of groups from a variety of cultures and groups within a pluralistic society. This knowledge could be imparted through special courses to all students irrespective of their discipline, science or social sciences or humanities and also by incorporating a relevant portion in each of the courses. Building the knowledge base of the students in higher education institution is the first important component of the civic learning.

The second component is to develop individual capabilities and skills among the students to deal with diversities and disparities. Curricular content on civic education, of course, plays an important role in imparting knowledge about citizenship. But it may not lead to develop a consciousness for engaging in democratic culture. Developing such a consciousness requires an exposure to everyday practices rooted in constitutional ideals of equality, equity and respect to diverse social sects. Therefore, to prepare democratic citizens, higher education institutions must help students to be able to develop skills to engage in critical thinking and make reflective choices for democratic actions. Such skills are expected to help oneself interrupt prejudicial thoughts about likely discriminatory behaviour against stigmatised groups, induce fraternity and desire for care, develop commitment to personal, social and civic action and develop multi-cultural competences/skill.

New pedagogical methods include inter-group dialogue and mixed-peer groups for various activities, where students from diverse groups come together to learn discussion skills and interact with diverse peers to respect differences. Such practices aim to refine skills of inviting and analysing multiple viewpoints without vilifying the speaker; promoting multi-cultural friendship; inter-group communication and embrace social justice. The dialogue programmes may include the following topics for discussion:

- Critical thinking exercises which may include conversations in which students explore intersections of identity and privilege, value positions are critically articulated, critically appraised, debates and activities where choices are provided and options are available.
- Discussions on democratic principles, activities involving voting and determining the consequences of action for groups of individuals.
- Discussions on power and authority, about power struggles and tensions among opposing viewpoints, on oppressions due to unequal power relations, dynamics of privileges and disadvantages rooted in group identities such as caste, gender, ethnicity, race, religion and other group-identity.
- Discussion on sustainable development, global issues, civil and human rights, environmental issues, moral dilemma situations based on universal principles as distinct from personal gain or good, and development of a sense of the consequences of one's action through role play and discussion.

The third component is to motivate the students for civic action and democratic engagement beyond the campus with a broader public. Elements of knowledge, value of care and skills of critical thinking is expected to inform students' actions and induce students for community engagement activities. In addition to pedagogic interventions that mainly engages with citizenship values and critical thinking, promotion of 'equity campus culture' (Museus and Jayakumar 2012), which enact and espouse values of diversity and equity, has been crucial. It requires changes in belief, values, assumption and actions of the major stakeholders of higher education institutions and the ways in which these institutions are governed and managed. Both academic and non-academic spheres of social existence of students have to be democratic. University—community partnerships can take the form of project assignments that require students to engage with deprived groups, for example, volunteering their time at the local *anganwadi* centres and mentoring students in neighbourhood government schools who are preparing for college. Initiatives such as college—community part-nership aim to create the abilities of student population to engage with diverse social world. It is the whole rationale behind the diver-sity and non-discrimination as well as institution-based reforms for civic learning and democratic engagement.

Taking elements of new civic learning together, namely, new knowledge, which makes students firmly believe in positive values, sensitise them to the problems of society, imbibe the value of care, respect and civility, improve skill and competency to exercise infor-med action to address public problems with diverse partners and induce motivation to engage with communities for civic action (all of these in combination), in fact, has a great potential for positive transformation and social change (Figure 16.1). The new civic learning is a lifelong process and has in itself a potential of being transformative in the sense that it motivates students for action to bring changes from a situation of inequality, poverty, discrimination

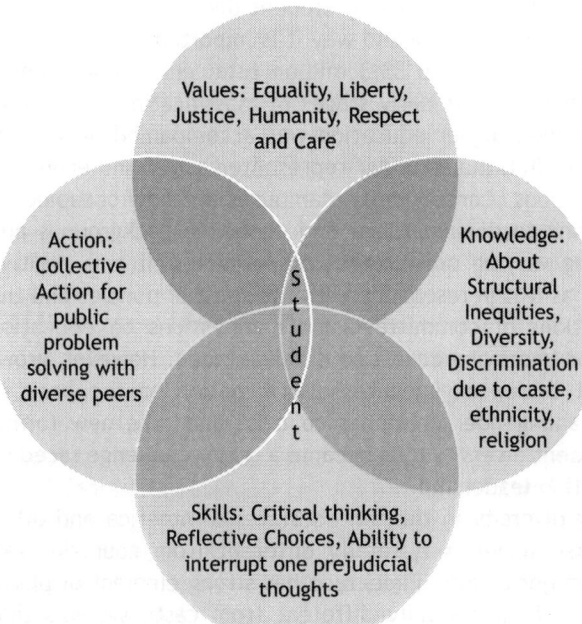

Figure 16.1
Model for Education for Civic Learning and Social Change
Source: Prepared by the authors.

and similar issues into more equality, non-discriminatory behaviour and just society. It is in a sense that the educationists believe that new education for civic learning and democratic engagement can be transformative involving positive social change. The enhanced civic capital through civic learning and democratic action is expected to generate potential for transformative social change for more democratic, egalitarian and just society.

CONCLUSION

Globally, the role of higher education in preparing young minds for the values of equality, social justice, equity and associative learning is gaining wider currency. In India, social purpose of higher education and social transformative potential of education are well conceived in policy documents on education. However, means and methods thorough which these goals could be achieved are vague. In the light of growing student diversity in higher education, we have attempted to show that how student diversity can be better channelled for civic learning and why it is important.

With a GER of 23.6 and 33.3 million total enrolments, Indian higher education is in its early stages of massification. Shift from elitist to massified higher education was accompanied by greater participation from hitherto under-represented social and economic groups and regions. Consequently, campuses are now occupied by students belong to diverse social and economic backgrounds and regions having varying pre-college competencies. It is a positive development as it is in resonance with the spirit of policies and the recommendations of committees and commissions on education that argue for improving access to disadvantaged. However, growing empirical evidences indicates discrimination on the basis of caste, class and gender continues to exist and take new forms. Managing student diversity thus became a major challenge faced by higher education leadership.

Addressing diversity in the United States of America and other racially diverse societies is totally different from countries like India in two major counts. First, race has strong element of physicality which is fundamentally different from caste systems that exists in India. Notion of pure and polluted body in caste system is different from the racial ideology of dominating and subordinated body. Hence, diversity concerns in immigrant countries are to some extent non-comparable with countries like India. Second, long history of civil rights movements and its political energy was one of the driving forces of higher education reforms in the United States of America. Without the aggressive role played by National Association for Advancement of Coloured People (NAACP), racial concerns in the US higher education would not have been adequately addressed and successful.

It is a crucial moment for India for a national dialogue on viewing of higher education strategically for civic learning and promotion of democratic culture. It is crucial because first there is the evidence of undemocratic behaviour on our college campuses in the form of group-divide based on identity and exclusion. Second, being the largest democracy, India should necessarily take steps to educate citizens for democracy—only thoughtful and tolerant people can maintain and develop a democratic society. Ambedkar (1956) emphasised that education is an instrument that cultivates democracy in the society by providing skills for associated living and strengthens the roots of democracy to bring about social transformation. Third, India is now a globally situated economy with a modern and globally diverse workforce. Higher education in India will require to understand that the workforce it prepares does not only acquire technical skills that prepares them for a career but also democratic skills that prepares them to respect differences and be able to engage in a point of view different to their own. Skills for democratic engagement will be an essential component of learning that will enhance employability in a diverse global workplace of the 21st century. Workforce training and civic learning need to be complementary visions of higher education. Thus, to actualise the ideals in the Constitution and to contribute to democratisation of society, higher education institution in India must help students acquire and internalise knowledge, values and skills of democracy.

REFERENCES

Allport, G. 1954. *The Nature of Prejudice*. MA: Addison Wesley.
Altbach, P.G., K. Lomotey, and Rivers. 2002. 'Race in Higher Education: The Continuing Crisis'. In *The Racial Crisis in American Higher Education: Continuing Challenges for the Twenty-first Century*, Revised edition, edited by W.A. Smith, P.G. Altbach, and K. Lomotey, 23–41. New York: State University of New York Press.
Ambedkar, B.R. 1956. 'Prospects of Democracy in India'. In *Dr Babasaheb Ambedkar Writings and Speeches: Dr B.R. Ambedkar*

and his Egalitarian Revolution, Part 3, Vol. 17, edited by Vasant Moon, 519–23. Mumbai: Government of Maharashtra.

Antonio, A.L. 2001. 'Diversity and the Influence of Friendship Groups in College'. *The Review of Higher Education* 25 (1): 63–89.

———. 2007. *Educating Citizens in a Multicultural Society*. New York: Teachers College Press.

Betteille, A. 2010. *Universities at the Crossroads*. New Delhi: Oxford University Press.

Bowman, N.A., and J.W. Brandenberger. 2010. 'Experiencing the Unexpected: Toward a Model of College Diversity Experience and Attitude Change'. *The Review of Higher Education* 35 (2): 179–205.

Bowman, N.A. 2010. 'Disequilibrium and Resolution: The Nonlinear Effects of Diversity Courses on Well-being and Orientations Toward Diversity'. *The Review of Higher Education* 33 (4): 543–68.

Chang, M.J., C.N. Denson, V. Saenz, and K. Misa. 2006. 'The Educational Benefits of Sustaining Cross Racial Interaction Among Undergraduates'. *Journal of Higher Education* 77 (3): 430–55.

Chang, M.J. 2002. 'The Impact of an Undergraduate Diversity Course Requirement on Students' Racial Views and Attitudes'. *The Journal of General Education* 51 (1): 21–42.

Denson, N., and M.J. Chang. 2009. 'Racial Diversity Matters: The Impact of Diversity-related Student Engagement and Institutional Context'. *American Educational Journal* 46 (2): 322–53.

Essomba, M.A., E. Karatzia-Stavlioti, H. Maitles, and I. Zalieskiene. 2008. *Developing the Conditions for Education for Citizenship in Higher Education* (No. 26236). CiCe Thematic Network Project. http://www.londonmet.ac.uk/fms/MRSite/Research/cice/pubs/hec/hec-design-07.p

Government of India. 1950. *The Report of the University Education Commission*. New Delhi: Ministry of Human Resource Development.

Hogan, D.E., and M. Mallot. 2005. 'Changing Racial Prejudices Through Diversity Education'. *Journal of College Student Development* 46 (2): 115–25.

Hurtado, S., J. Milem, Clayton-Pederson, and W. Allen. 1999. *Enacting Diverse Learning Environments: Improving the Climate for Racial/Ethnic Diversity in Higher Education*. San Francisco: Jossey-Bass.

King, P.M., and M.B.B. Magolda. 2005. 'A Developmental Model of Intercultural Maturity'. *Journal of College Student Development* 46 (6): 571–92.

Kurlaender, M., and G. Orfield. 2006. 'In Defence of Diversity: New Research and Evidence from the University of Michigan'. *Equity & Excellence in Education* 32 (2): 31–35.

Malish, C.M. 2013. 'Negotiating Cultural Capital in the Knowledge Economy of India: An Empirical Study of Scheduled Caste Engineering Students in Kerala'. Unpublished PhD Thesis, Indian Institute of Technology, Delhi.

Milem, J.F., and K. Hakuta. 2000. 'The Benefits of Racial and Ethnic Diversity in Higher Education'. In *Minorities in Higher Education, 1999–2000, Seventeenth Higher Education Status Report*, edited by D. J. Wilds, 39–67. Washington DC: American Council on Education.

Ministry of Education. 1968. *National Policy on Education 1968*. New Delhi: Government of India.

Ministry of Human Resource Development (MHRD). 2015. *All India Survey of Higher Education 2014–15*. New Delhi: Government of India.

Museus, S.D., and U.M. Jayakumar, eds. 2012. *Creating Campus Cultures: Fostering Success Among the Racially Diverse Student Populations*. New York: Routledge.

National Taskforce on Civic Learning and Democratic Engagement. 2012. *A Crucible Moment: College Learning & Democracy's Future*. Washington DC: Association of American Colleges and Universities.

National Cadet Corps (NCC). n.d. Available at http://nccindia.nic.in/en

NCERT. 2005. *National Curriculum Framework*. New Delhi: National Council of Education Research and Training.

Nussbaum, M.C. 1997. *Cultivating Humanity: A Classical Defence of Reforms in Liberal Education*. Cambridge, Massachusetts and London: Harvard University Press

Olssen, M., J. Codd, and A. O'Neill. 2004. *Education Policy: Globalisation, Citizenship and Democracy*. London: SAGE.

Orfield, G., ed. 2001. *Diversity Challenges. Evidence on the impact of Affirmative Action*. MA: Harvard Education Publishing Group.

Ovichegan, S. 2014. 'Social Exclusion, Social Inclusion and Passing: The Experience of Dalit Students at one Elite Indian University'. *International Journal of Inclusive Education* 18 (4): 359–78.

Rao, S.S. 2013. 'Structural Exclusion in Everyday Institutional Life: Labelling of Stigmatised Groups in an IIT'. In *Sociology of Education in India: Changing Contours and Emerging Concerns*, edited by G. Nambisan, and S.S. Rao, 119–223. New Delhi: Oxford University Press.

Singh, A.K. 2013. 'Defying the Odds: The Triumphs and Tragedies of Dalit and Adivasi Students in Higher Education'. In *Beyond Inclusion: The Practice of Equal Access in Indian Higher Education*, edited by Satish Deshpande and U Zacharia. New Delhi: Oxford University Press.

Smith, D.G. 1997. *Diversity Works: The Emerging Picture of How Students Benefit*. Washington DC: Association of American Colleges and Universities.

Smith, W.A., P.G. Altbach, and K. Lomotey, eds. 2002. *The Racial Crisis in American Higher Education: Continuing Challenges for the Twenty-first Century* (Revised edition). New York: State University of New York Press.

Sukumar, N. 2008. 'Living a Concept: Semiotics of Everyday Exclusion'. *Economic and Political Weekly* 43 (46): 14–17.

Thorat, S.K., and N. Sabharwal. 2013. 'Need for Policy Reforms in Higher Education: Education for Civic Learning, Democratic

Engagement and Social Change'. Policy Brief No. 14, Indian Institute of Dalit Studies, New Delhi.

Thorat, S.K., and N. Sabharwal. 2014. 'Diversity, Academic Performance, and Discrimination: A Case Study of a Higher Educational Institution'. Working Paper no. 8(4), Indian Institute of Dalit Studies, New Delhi.

Thornton, M., P. Bricheno, P. Iyer, I. Reid, and G. Wankhede. 2012. *Widening Participation and Social Cohesion Amongst Diverse, Disadvantaged and Minority Groups in Higher Education.* Mumbai: Tata Institute of Social Sciences.

Tropp, L.R., and T.F. Pettigrew. 2005. 'Relationships Between Intergroup Contact and Prejudice Among Minority and Majority Status Groups'. *Psychological Science* 16 (12): 951–67.

UGC. 2012. *UGC (Promotion of Equity in Higher Education Institutions) Regulations.* New Delhi: UGC.

United Nations Educational, Scientific and Cultural Organization (UNESCO). 1998. *World Declaration on Higher Education for the Twenty-First Century: Vision and Action.* Paris: UNESCO.

Varghese, N.V. 2015. 'Challenges of Massification of Higher Education in India'. CPRHE Research Papers 1, National University of Educational Planning and Administration, New Delhi.

About the Editors and Contributors

EDITORS

Professor N.V. Varghese is currently the Director of the Centre for Policy Research in Higher Education, National University of Educational Planning and Administration, New Delhi. Earlier, he was the Head of Governance and Management in Education at the International Institute for Educational Planning (IIEP/UNESCO), Paris. He was responsible for managing the Asian Network of Training and Research Institutions in Educational Planning (ANTRIEP) and was also the Secretary General of the International Working Group on Education (IWGE), which is a network of funding agencies in education.

Nidhi S. Sabharwal is currently an Associate Professor at the Centre for Policy Research in Higher Education, National University of Educational Planning and Administration (NUEPA), New Delhi. Dr Sabharwal has previously served as the Director of the Indian Institute of Dalit Studies, New Delhi.

C.M. Malish is an Assistant Professor at Centre for Policy Research in Higher Education, National University of Educational Planning and Administration, New Delhi. He has published articles in reputed international journals.

CONTRIBUTORS

M.M. Ansari is a Member of University Grants Commission (UGC), New Delhi; an interlocutor for Jammu and Kashmir, Government of India; and former Information Commissioner of the Central Information Commission, Government of India.

Vani K. Borooah is Professor Emeritus at the Department of Applied Economics, University of Ulster, Ireland. He joined as a Research Officer in the Department of Applied Economics at the University of Cambridge and was concurrently Fellow of Queens' College, Cambridge.

In 1987, he was appointed to the Chair in Applied Economics at the University of Ulster. Professor Borooah was the President of the European Public Choice Society; and the Irish Economic Association, and is currently the Honorary Professor of economics at the University of Queensland.

Ashwini Deshpande is Professor of economics at the Delhi School of Economics, University of Delhi, India. She has published extensively in leading scholarly journals as well as edited several volumes. She received the EXIM Bank award for outstanding dissertation (now called the IERA Award) in 1994, and the 2007 VKRV Rao Award for Indian economists under 45.

Rajan Gurukkal is Visiting Professor at the Indian Institute of Science, Bangalore and former Vice Chancellor of Mahatma Gandhi University, Kottayam, India. He received the Oravakkal Mathen Memorial Best Academician Award in 1986.

Kalpana Kannabiran is Professor and Regional Director at Council for Social Development (CSD), Hyderabad. She was a founding faculty of NALSAR University of Law, and a Member of the Expert Group on the Equal Opportunity Commission, Government of India, and the General Secretary of the Indian Association for Women's Studies.

Khalid Khan is a doctoral scholar at the Centre for Study of Regional Development, Jawaharlal Nehru University, New Delhi.

Mona Khare is Professor at the Department of Educational Finance, CPRHE, National University of Educational Planning and Administration (NUEPA), New Delhi. Previously, she was a Professor at Barkatullah University, Bhopal, Madhya Pradesh.

Amitabh Kundu is a Visiting Professor at the Institute of Human Development, New Delhi. He was the Chairperson of the Post Sachar Evaluation Committee set up by the Ministry of Minority Affairs and a Member of National Statistical Commission. He was the Dean of the School of Social Sciences at Jawaharlal Nehru University, New Delhi.

S. Madheswaran is a Professor at the Centre for Economic Studies and Policy, Institute for Social and Economic Change, Bangalore. Previously, he was a Lecturer in economics at Gokhale Institute of

Politics and Economics, Pune, and in the Department of Management Studies, Kongu Engineering College, and also at Mohamedad Sathak College, Madras.

J. Madhusoodanan is Principal at the Jawahar Navodaya Vidyalaya, Jalna, Maharashtra.

Sachidanand Sinha is Professor at the Centre for the Study of Regional Development, School of Social Sciences, Jawaharlal Nehru University, New Delhi. He was a member of the UGC working group for the 11th plan and development of model colleges in educationally backward districts of India. He served as the chief advisor on Development of School Text-books for Social Sciences, Government of Rajasthan.

Smrutirekha Singhari is a Research Scholar at the Institute for Social and Economic Change, Nagarbhavi, Bangalore.

Wandana Sonalkar is a Professor and Chairperson at the Advanced Centre for Women's Studies, School of Development Studies, Tata Institute of Social Sciences, Mumbai. Previously, she was teaching economics at Dr Babasaheb Ambedkar Marathwada University, Aurangabad, and is a founding member of Aalochana Centre for Documentation and Research on Women.

Ratna M. Sudarshan is a National Fellow, NUEPA, New Delhi, and a trustee of the Institute of Social Studies Trust, New Delhi.

Sukhadeo Thorat is Professor Emeritus at the Centre for Study of Regional Development, Jawaharlal Nehru University and Chairman, Indian Council of Social Science Research (ICSSR), New Delhi. He is the former Chairman of University Grants Commission. He has been awarded Padamshree by the Government of India in 2008.

Padma Velaskar is a Professor at the Centre for Studies in Sociology of Education, School of Social Science, Tata Institute of Social Sciences, Mumbai, India.

Soumya Vinayan is Assistant Professor at the Council for Social Development (CSD), Hyderabad, and holds a doctoral degree in economics from the University of Hyderabad. She has been Visiting Scholar at the German Development Institute, Bonn, Germany.

Index